Learning Python Networking
Second Edition

A complete guide to build and deploy strong networking
capabilities using Python 3.7 and Ansible

José Manuel Ortega
Dr. M O Faruque Sarker
Sam Washington

BIRMINGHAM - MUMBAI

Learning Python Networking
Second Edition

Commissioning Editor: Vijin Boricha
Acquisition Editor: Akshay Jethani
Content Development Editor: Drashti Panchal
Technical Editor: Rutuja Patade
Copy Editor: Safis Editing
Project Coordinator: Nusaiba Ansari
Proofreader: Safis Editing
Indexer: Manju Arasan
Graphics: Tom Scaria
Production Coordinator: Tom Scaria

First published: June 2015
Second edition: March 2019

Production reference: 1280319

Published by Packt Publishing Ltd.
Livery Place
35 Livery Street
Birmingham
B3 2PB, UK.

ISBN 978-1-78995-809-6

www.packtpub.com

`mapt.io`

Mapt is an online digital library that gives you full access to over 5,000 books and videos, as well as industry leading tools to help you plan your personal development and advance your career. For more information, please visit our website.

Why subscribe?

- Spend less time learning and more time coding with practical eBooks and Videos from over 4,000 industry professionals

- Improve your learning with Skill Plans built especially for you

- Get a free eBook or video every month

- Mapt is fully searchable

- Copy and paste, print, and bookmark content

Packt.com

Did you know that Packt offers eBook versions of every book published, with PDF and ePub files available? You can upgrade to the eBook version at `www.packt.com` and as a print book customer, you are entitled to a discount on the eBook copy. Get in touch with us at `customercare@packtpub.com` for more details.

At `www.packt.com`, you can also read a collection of free technical articles, sign up for a range of free newsletters, and receive exclusive discounts and offers on Packt books and eBooks.

Contributors

About the authors

José Manuel Ortega is a software engineer, focusing on new technologies, open source, security, and testing. His career goal has been to specialize in Python and security testing projects. In recent years, he has developed an interest in security development, especially in pentesting with Python. Currently, he is working as a security tester engineer and his functions in the role involves the analysis and testing of the security of applications in both web and mobile environments. He has taught at university level and collaborated with the official school of computer engineers. He has also been a speaker at various conferences. He is eager to learn about new technologies and loves to share his knowledge with the community.

I would like to thank my friends and family for their help in both the professional and personal fields of my life. I would specially like to thank Akshay Jethani (acquisition editor at Packt Publishing) and Drashti Panchal (content development editor at Packt Publishing) for supporting me during the course of completing this book.

Dr. M. O. Faruque Sarker is a software architect based in London; he has shaped various Linux and open source software solutions mainly on cloud computing platforms for various institutions. Over the past 10 years, he has led numerous Python software development and cloud infrastructure automation projects. In 2009, he started using Python and shepherded a fleet of miniature E-puck robots at the University of South Wales, Newport, UK. Later, he was invited to work on the Google Summer of Code (2009/2010) programs to contribute to the BlueZ and Tahoe-LAFS open source projects. He is the author of Python Network Programming Cookbook, Packt Publishing and received his PhD in multirobot systems at the University of South Wales.

Sam Washington currently works at University College London as a systems administrator in the platform integration team of the central IT department, supporting a variety of web hosting and network services. He enjoys the daily challenges of managing the demands of full-stack enterprise web applications and looking for ways to employ new technologies to improve services and workflows. He has been using Python for professional and personal projects for over 10 years.

About the reviewers

Bassem Aly is an experienced SDN/NFV senior solution consultant at Juniper Networks and has been working in the telco industry for the last decade. He focuses on designing and implementing next-generation networks by leveraging SDN, NFV, and different automation and DevOps frameworks. Also, he has extensive experience in architecting and deploying telco applications on the cloud. He's the author of book *Hands-On Enterprise Automation with Python*, available from Packt Publishing.

> *I dedicate this work to my nephews, Yasmina, Yara, Aly, Mohamed, and Jody, for the happiness and joy that they bring to our family. You are my small world!*

Yakov Goldberg is a Masters-trained, InfoSec professional focusing on digital forensics, incident response (DFIR), and Advanced Persistent Threats. He has experience in advising, deploying customized security controls to Fortune Global 500 companies. He is also an expert in Python, Django framework, AngularJS, ELK stack, reversing malware, and conducting threat Intelligence research. In 2008, Yakov developed his first Python web recon tool named Uberharvest, which was featured in the famous Backtrack (now known as Kali). Over the years, he has worked at Mandiant, the International Monetary Fund and TrapX, focusing on DFIR Today, Yakov is a Digital Forensics and Threat Intelligence Director at enSilo and has CISSP, GIAC GCFA, and CompTIA Sec+ certs.

Packt is searching for authors like you

If you're interested in becoming an author for Packt, please visit `authors.packtpub.com` and apply today. We have worked with thousands of developers and tech professionals, just like you, to help them share their insight with the global tech community. You can make a general application, apply for a specific hot topic that we are recruiting an author for, or submit your own idea.

Table of Contents

Section 4: Sockets and Server Programming

Preface

Network programming has always been a demanding task. With full-featured and well-documented libraries all the way up the stack, Python makes network programming the enjoyable experience it should be.

Starting with a walk-through of today's major networking protocols, throughout this book, you'll learn how to employ Python for network programming, how to request and retrieve web resources, and how to extract data in major formats over the web. You'll utilize Python for emailing, using a variety of protocols, and you'll interact with remote systems and IP and DNS networking. The connection of network devices and configuration using Python 3.7 will also be covered.

As the book progresses, socket programming will be covered, followed by how to design servers and the pros and cons of multithreaded and event-driven architectures. You'll develop practical client-side applications, including web API clients, email clients, SSH, and FTP. These applications will also be implemented through existing web application frameworks.

Who this book is for

This book is ideal for Python developers or system administrators with Python experience who are looking to take their first steps in network programming. Python developers who are interested in going deeper into packages related to asynchronous programming would also benefit from this book. A basic knowledge of Python programming is recommended.

What this book covers

Chapter 1, *Network Programming with Python,* provides a review of basic network elements and principles. It discusses how Python supports network programming and gives an overview of key libraries. It also provides an introduction to Wireshark as a protocol exploration and network programming diagnostic tool. Furthermore, we will review how we can interact with Wireshark from Python with the pyshark module.

Chapter 2, *Programming for the Web with HTTP*, covers the HTTP protocol and the main Python modules, such as the `urllib` standard library and the `requests` package for connecting with the REST API. It also covers HTTP authentication mechanisms and how we can manage them by means of the `requests` module.

Chapter 3, *Application Programming Interface in Action*, covers how to use Python to extract data from the major data formats found on the web: HTML, XML, and JSON. An example of interacting with REST APIs, such as Twitter and Amazon S3, will be used to guide the reader through the essentials of working with XML and JSON.

Chapter 4, *Web Scraping with BeautifulSoup and Scrapy*, covers how to extract the content of a web page by automating the information extraction process using scraping techniques to recover data from the web automatically. This chapter also covers some of the most powerful tools we can find in Python 3.7, with a focus on BeautifulSoup and Scrapy.

Chapter 5, *Engaging with Email*, explores the Python modules that facilitate communication with email servers using SMTP, POP3, and IMAP protocols. Practical code examples in Python 3.7 will illustrate the majority of concepts.

Chapter 6, *Interacting with Remote Systems*, explains the different modules that allow us to interact with FTP, SSH, SNMP, and LDAP servers. You will learn about several network protocols and Python libraries that are used for interacting with remote systems through the Python modules, including `ftplib`, `paramiko`, `pysnmp`, and `python-ldap`.

Chapter 7, *Working with IP and DNS*, explores how to work with IPs, DNS networking, and geolocation in Python. You will learn about acquiring information for DNS servers using the DNSPython module and extracting information relating to geolocation IP addresses.

Chapter 8, *Implementing IPv6 and Address Manipulation*, explains how to work with IPv6 and address manipulation with Python. You will learn by means of practical tasks, such as determining the IP address of your own computer and looking up other computers in the local network.

Chapter 9, *Performing Network Automation with Python and Ansible*, covers the principles of Ansible and how we can interact with Python. We will review how to write a Python script with a view to executing a networking automation task with Ansible and how to write an Ansible module with Python.

Chapter 10, *Programming with Sockets*, introduces the basics of sockets and the principles of UDP and TCP through examples involving the socket module with the IPv4 and IPv6 protocols. We will also cover non-blocking and asynchronous programming and HTTPS and TLS for secure data transport.

Chapter 11, *Designing Servers and Asynchronous Programming,* covers the principles of socket-based server design and how to build small servers based on multiprocessing approaches. We review `asyncio` and `aiohttp` for asynchronous operations and other solutions, such as Tornado, Twisted, and Celery, for building asynchronous network applications.

Chapter 12, *Designing Applications on the Web,* introduces the Django and Flask micro frameworks, which are designed to facilitate the development of web applications under the **Model View Controller** (**MVC**) pattern. Finally, we review how to work with HTTP requests in Flask and interact with databases through SQLAlchemy.

To get the most out of this book

You will need to install a Python distribution on your local machine, which should have at least 4 GB of memory. For Chapter 9, *Performing Network Automation with Python and Ansible,* you will also need to install Ansible and have a local network configured or local virtual machines with Python installed for executing Ansible scripts. For Chapter 11, *Designing Servers and Asynchronous Programming,* examples involving Celery also need to be executed on a localhost Redis server.

In this book, all examples are available for execution in Python version 3.7 and are compatible with the Windows and Unix operating systems.

Download the example code files

You can download the example code files for this book from your account at www.packt.com. If you purchased this book elsewhere, you can visit www.packt.com/support and register to have the files emailed directly to you.

You can download the code files by following these steps:

1. Log in or register at www.packt.com.
2. Select the **SUPPORT** tab.
3. Click on **Code Downloads & Errata**.
4. Enter the name of the book in the **Search** box and follow the onscreen instructions.

Once the file is downloaded, please make sure that you unzip or extract the folder using the latest version of:

- WinRAR/7-Zip for Windows
- Zipeg/iZip/UnRarX for Mac
- 7-Zip/PeaZip for Linux

The code bundle for the book is also hosted on GitHub at `https://github.com/PacktPublishing/Learning-Python-Networking-Second-Edition`. In case there's an update to the code, it will be updated on the existing GitHub repository.

We also have other code bundles from our rich catalog of books and videos available at `https://github.com/PacktPublishing/`. Check them out!

Download the color images

We also provide a PDF file that has color images of the screenshots/diagrams used in this book. You can download it here: `https://www.packtpub.com/sites/default/files/downloads/9781789958096_ColorImages.pdf`.

Conventions used

There are a number of text conventions used throughout this book.

`CodeInText`: Indicates code words in text, database table names, folder names, filenames, file extensions, pathnames, dummy URLs, user input, and Twitter handles. Here is an example: "You can find the following code in the `urllib_exceptions.py` file."

A block of code is set as follows:

```
# setup crawler
from scrapy.crawler import CrawlerProcess
crawler = CrawlerProcess(settings)
# define the spider for the crawler
crawler.crawl(MySpider())
# start scrapy
print("STARTING ENGINE")
crawler.start()
```

When we wish to draw your attention to a particular part of a code block, the relevant lines or items are set in bold:

```
# setup crawler
from scrapy.crawler import CrawlerProcess
crawler = CrawlerProcess(settings)
# define the spider for the crawler
crawler.crawl(MySpider())
# start scrapy
print("STARTING ENGINE")
crawler.start()
```

Any command-line input or output is written as follows:

```
pip install lxml
```

Bold: Indicates a new term, an important word, or words that you see on screen. For example, words in menus or dialog boxes appear in the text like this. Here is an example: "Among the available plugins for Firefox, we can highlight the **HTTP Header Live** add-ons."

Warnings or important notes appear like this.

Tips and tricks appear like this.

Get in touch

Feedback from our readers is always welcome.

General feedback: If you have questions about any aspect of this book, mention the book title in the subject of your message and email us at customercare@packtpub.com.

Errata: Although we have taken every care to ensure the accuracy of our content, mistakes do happen. If you have found a mistake in this book, we would be grateful if you would report this to us. Please visit www.packt.com/submit-errata, selecting your book, clicking on the Errata Submission Form link, and entering the details.

Piracy: If you come across any illegal copies of our works in any form on the internet, we would be grateful if you would provide us with the location address or website name. Please contact us at copyright@packt.com with a link to the material.

If you are interested in becoming an author: If there is a topic that you have expertise in, and you are interested in either writing or contributing to a book, please visit authors.packtpub.com.

Reviews

Please leave a review. Once you have read and used this book, why not leave a review on the site that you purchased it from? Potential readers can then see and use your unbiased opinion to make purchase decisions, we at Packt can understand what you think about our products, and our authors can see your feedback on their book. Thank you!

For more information about Packt, please visit packt.com.

Section 1: Introduction to Network and HTTP Programming

In this section, you will learn about the basics of Python network programming, networking protocols, and the main modules for interacting with HTTP servers.

This section contains the following chapters:

- Chapter 1, *Network Programming with Python*
- Chapter 2, *Programming for the Web with HTTP*

Network Programming with Python

1

This book will focus on writing programs for networks that use the **Internet Protocol (IP)** suite. Why have we chosen to do this? Well, out of the sets of protocols that are supported by the Python standard library, the **Transmission Control Protocol (TCP)**/IP protocol is by far the most widely employable. It contains the principal protocols that are used by the internet. By learning to program for TCP/IP, you'll be learning how to potentially communicate with just about every device that is connected to this great tangle of network cables and electromagnetic waves.

The following topics will be covered in this chapter:

- An introduction to TCP/IP networking
- Protocol concepts and the problems that protocols solve
- Addressing
- Creating RESTful web applications and working with flask and HTTP requests
- Interacting flask with the SQLAlchemy database

In this chapter, we will be looking at some concepts and methods related to networks and network programming in Python, which we'll be using throughout this book.

This chapter has two sections. The first section, *An introduction to TCP/IP networking*, offers an introduction to essential networking concepts, with a strong focus on the TCP/IP stack. We'll be looking at what comprises a network, how the IP allows data transfer across and between networks, and how TCP/IP provides us with services that help us to develop network applications. This section is intended to provide a grounding in these essential areas and to act as a point of reference for them. If you're already comfortable with concepts such as IP addresses, routing, TCP and **User Datagram Protocol (UDP)**, and protocol stack layers, then you may wish to skip to the second section, *Python network programming through libraries*.

In the second part, we'll look at the way in which network programming is approached with Python. This chapter provides a review of basic network elements and principles, as well as a discussion of how Python supports network programming with an overview of key libraries. Finally, we will introduce you to Wireshark, a protocol exploration and network programming diagnostic tool. We will also look at how we can interact with Wireshark from Python with the `pyshark` module.

Technical requirements

Before you start reading this book, you should already know the basics of Python programming, such as the basic syntax, variable types, data type tuple, list dictionary, functions, strings, and methods. At the moment of writing this book, versions 3.7.2 and 2.7.15 are available at `python.org/downloads`. In this book, we will work with version 3.7 for code examples and installing packages.

The examples and source code for this chapter are available in this book's GitHub repository in the `Chapter01` folder: `https://github.com/PacktPublishing/Learning-Python-Networking-Second-Edition`.

An introduction to TCP/IP networking

This first section offers an introduction to essential networking concepts, with a strong focus on the TCP/IP stack.

The following discussion is based on **Internet Protocol version 4 (IPv4)**. Since the internet has run out of IPv4 addresses, a new version, IPv6, has been developed, which is intended to resolve this situation. However, although IPv6 is being used in a few areas, its deployment is progressing slowly and the majority of the internet will likely be using IPv4 for a while longer. We'll focus on IPv4 in this section, and then we will discuss the relevant changes in the *IPv6* section of this chapter.

Introduction to TCP/IP

TCP/IP is a set of protocols that were designed to work together to provide an end-to-end transmission of messages across interconnected networks. TCP provides transparent data transfers between end systems using the services of the lower network layer to move the packets between the two communicating systems. TCP is a protocol that works at the transport layer, while IP works at the network layer.

TCP is responsible for creating connections through a data flow. This process guarantees that the data is delivered to the destination without errors and in the same order in which they came out. It is also used to distinguish different applications in the same device.

IP is responsible for sending and receiving data in blocks. The shipment always does this to find the best route, but without guaranteeing that it reaches the destination.

Both protocols are used to solve the transmission of data that is generated in a network, either internally or externally. The union of these protocols is done to ensure that the information always arrives on the best route and in the correct way to the destination.

The protocol stack, layer by layer

A protocol stack is organized in such a way that the highest level of communication resides in the top layer. Each layer in the stack is built on the services of the immediate lower layer.

The TCP/IP protocol stack has four layers, as follows:

- **Application layer**: This layer manages the high-level protocols, including representation, coding, and dialogue control issues. It handles everything related to applications, and the data is packed appropriately for the next layer. It is a user process that cooperates with other processes on the same host or a different one. Examples of protocols at this layer are TELNET, **File Transfer Protocol (FTP)**, and **Simple Mail Transfer Protocol (SMTP)**.
- **Transport layer**: This layer handles quality of service, reliability, flow control, and error correction. One of its protocols is the TCP, which provides reliable network communications that are oriented to the connection, unlike UDP, which is not connection oriented. It also provides data transfer. Example protocols include TCP (connection oriented) and UDP (non-connection oriented).
- **Network layer**: The purpose of the internet layer is to send packets from the source of any network and make them reach their destination, regardless of the route they take to get there.
- **Network access layer**: This is also called a host-to-host network layer. It includes the LAN and WAN protocols, and the details in the physical and data link layers of the OSI model. Also known as the link layer or data link layer, the network interface layer is the interface to the current network hardware.

The following diagram represents the TCP/IP protocol stack:

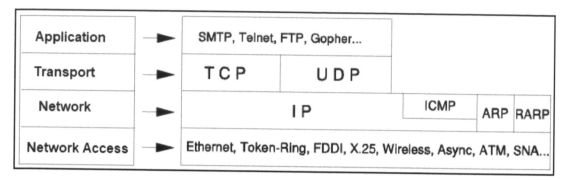

The IP is the most important protocol of the network layer. It is a non-connection oriented protocol that does not assume reliability of the lower layers. IP does not provide reliability, flow control, or error recovery. These functions must be provided by the upper level, in the transport layer with TCP as the transport protocol, or in the application layer if UDP is being used as the transport protocol. The message unit in an IP network is called an IP datagram. This is the basic unit of information that is transmitted from one side of the TCP/IP network to the other.

The application layer is where all of the user interaction with the computer and services occurs. As an example of this, any browser can work, even without the TCP/IP stack installed. Usually, we use browsers such as Google Chrome, Mozilla, Firefox, Internet Explorer, and Opera for communicating with this layer.

When initiating a query for a remote document, the HTTP protocol is used. Each time we request a communication of this type, the browser interacts with the application layer, which, in turn, serves as an interface between the user's applications and the protocol stack, which will provide communication with the help of the lower layers.

The responsibilities of the application layer are to identify and establish the communication availability of the target destination, as well as to determine the resources for that communication to exist. Some of the protocols of the application layer are as follows:

- FTP
- HTTP
- **Post Office Protocol version 3 (POP3)**
- **Internet Message Access Protocol (IMAP)**
- SMTP
- **Simple Network Management Protocol (SNMP)**
- TELNET—TCP/IP Terminal Emulation Protocol

UDP

UDP is a non-connection oriented protocol. That is, when *machine A* sends packets to *machine B*, the flow is unidirectional. The data transfer is made without warning the recipient of *machine B*, and the recipient receives the data without sending a confirmation to the sender of *machine A*.

This is because the data that's sent by the UDP protocol does not allow you to transmit information related to the sender. Therefore, the recipient will not know about the sender's data, except their IP address. Let's have a look at some properties of the UDP protocols:

- **Unreliable**: In UDP, there is no concept of packet retransmission. Therefore, when a UDP packet is sent, it is not possible to know whether the packet has reached its destination since there are no errors in the correction mechanism.
- **Not ordered**: The order in which packages are sent and received cannot be determined.
- **Datagrams**: The integrity of packet delivery is done individually and can only be checked to ensure that the packages arrived correctly.
- **Lightweight and speed**: The UDP protocol does not provide error recovery services, so it offers a direct way to send and receive datagrams through an IP network. It is used when speed is an important factor in the transmission of information, for example, when streaming audio or video.

TCP

The TCP protocol, unlike the UDP protocol, is connection oriented. When *machine A* sends data to *machine B*, *machine B* is informed of the arrival of this data and confirms its good reception.

Here, the CRC control of data intervenes, which is based on a mathematical equation that allows you to verify the integrity of the transmitted data. In this way, if the received data is corrupted, the TCP protocol allows the recipients to request the sender to send them again.

This protocol is one of the main protocols of the transport layer of the TCP/IP model, since, at the application level, it makes it possible to manage data coming from the lowest level of the model.

So, when data is provided to the IP protocol, it binds it in IP datagrams, fixing the field protocol with 6, so that you know in advance that the protocol is TCP. This protocol is connection oriented, so it allows two machines that are communicated to control the status of the transmission.

Several programs within a data network that are composed of computers can use TCP to create connections between them, by means of which they can send a data flow. Thus, the protocol guarantees that the data will be delivered to its destination. The most important thing to take into account is that it has no errors and maintains the order in which they are transmitted.

On the basis of the preceding example, we can devise the properties of TCP:

- **Reliable**: The TCP protocol has the ability to manage the attempts that can be made to send a message if a packet is lost, and can resend those fragments that were not sent on the first attempt.
- **Ordered**: The messages are delivered in a particular order.
- **Heavyweight**: TCP has the ability to verify that the connection can be established through a socket before any packet can be sent, for which it uses three sending confirmation packets, called SYN, SYN-ACK, and ACK.

Protocol concepts and the problems that protocols solve

This section explains concepts regarding IP addresses and ports, network interfaces in a local machine, and other concepts related to protocols, such as **Dynamic Host Configuration Protocol (DHCP)** and DNS.

IP addresses and ports

IP addresses are addresses that help to uniquely identify a device over the internet. A port is an endpoint for communication in an operating system.

When you connect to the internet, your device is assigned a public IP address, and each website you visit also has a public IP address. So far, we have used IPv4 as an addressing system. The main problem with this is that the internet is running out of IPv4 public address space and so it is necessary to introduce IPv6, which provides a larger address space.

The following are the addresses for total IPv4 and IPv6 space:

- **Total IPv4 space**: 4, 294, 967, 296 addresses
- **Total IPv6 space**: 340, 282, 366, 920, 938, 463, 463, 374, 607, 431, 768, 211, 456 addresses

The ports are numerical values (between 0 and 65,535) that are used to identify the processes that are being communicated. At each end, each process that intervenes in the communication process uses a single port to send and receive data.

In conjunction with this, two pairs of ports and IP addresses, you can identify two processes in a TCP/IP network. A system might be running thousands of services, but to uniquely identify a service on a system, the application requires a port number.

Port numbers are sometimes seen on the web or other URLs as well. By default, HTTP uses port 80, and HTTPS uses port 443, but a URL like `http://www.domain.com:8080/path/` specifies that the web browser, instead of using default port 80, is connecting to port 8080 of the HTTP server.

Some common ports are as follows:

- 22: **Secure Shell (SSH)**
- 23: Telnet remote login service
- 25: SMTP
- 53: **Domain Name System (DNS)** service
- 80: HTTP

Regarding IP addresses, we can differentiate two types, depending on whether they are for a public or private rank for the internal network of an organization:

- **Private IP address**: Ranges from 192.168.0.0 to 192.168.255.255, 172.16.0.0 to 172.31.255.255, or 10.0.0.0 to 10.255.255.255
- **Public IP address:** A public IP address is an IP address that your home or business router receives from your **Internet Service Provider (ISP)**

Network interfaces

You can find out what IP addresses have been assigned to your computer by running `ip addr` or `ipconfig` all on Windows systems, or on a Terminal.

If we run one of these commands, we will see that the IP addresses are assigned to our device's network interfaces. On Linux, these will have names, such as `eth0`; on Windows, these will have phrases, such as Ethernet adapter Local Area Connection.

You will get the following output when you run the `ip addr` command on Linux:

```
$ ip
BusyBox v1.28.4 (2018-07-17 15:21:40 UTC) multi-call binary.

Usage: ip [OPTIONS] address|route|link|tunnel|neigh|rule [COMMAND]

OPTIONS := -f[amily] inet|inet6|link | -o[neline]
COMMAND :=
ip addr add|del IFADDR dev IFACE | show|flush [dev IFACE] [to PREFI
X]
ip route list|flush|add|del|change|append|replace|test ROUTE
ip link set IFACE [up|down] [arp on|off] | show [IFACE]
ip tunnel add|change|del|show [NAME]
         [mode ipip|gre|sit]
         [remote ADDR] [local ADDR] [ttl TTL]
ip neigh show|flush [to PREFIX] [dev DEV] [nud STATE]
ip rule [list] | add|del SELECTOR ACTION
```

You will get the following options when you run the `ipconfig` command on Windows:

```
USAGE:
    ipconfig [/allcompartments] [/? | /all |
                                 /renew [adapter] | /release [adapter] |
                                 /renew6 [adapter] | /release6 [adapter] |
                                 /flushdns | /displaydns | /registerdns |
                                 /showclassid adapter |
                                 /setclassid adapter [classid] |
                                 /showclassid6 adapter |
                                 /setclassid6 adapter [classid] ]

where
    adapter             Connection name
                        (wildcard characters * and ? allowed, see examples)

    Options:
       /?               Display this help message
       /all             Display full configuration information.
       /release         Release the IPv4 address for the specified adapter.
       /release6        Release the IPv6 address for the specified adapter.
       /renew           Renew the IPv4 address for the specified adapter.
       /renew6          Renew the IPv6 address for the specified adapter.
       /flushdns        Purges the DNS Resolver cache.
       /registerdns     Refreshes all DHCP leases and re-registers DNS names
       /displaydns      Display the contents of the DNS Resolver Cache.
       /showclassid     Displays all the dhcp class IDs allowed for adapter.
       /setclassid      Modifies the dhcp class id.
       /showclassid6    Displays all the IPv6 DHCP class IDs allowed for adapter.
       /setclassid6     Modifies the IPv6 DHCP class id.
```

You will get IP addresses for the interfaces in your local machine when you run the `ip addr` command:

```
$ ip addr
1: lo: <LOOPBACK,UP,LOWER_UP> mtu 65536 qdisc noqueue state UNKNOWN qlen 1
    link/loopback 00:00:00:00:00:00 brd 00:00:00:00:00:00
    inet 127.0.0.1/8 scope host lo
       valid_lft forever preferred_lft forever
2: docker0: <NO-CARRIER,BROADCAST,MULTICAST,UP> mtu 1500 qdisc noqueue state DOWN
    link/ether 02:42:1d:95:df:04 brd ff:ff:ff:ff:ff:ff
    inet 172.17.0.1/16 brd 172.17.255.255 scope global docker0
       valid_lft forever preferred_lft forever
24: eth0@if25: <BROADCAST,MULTICAST,UP,LOWER_UP,M-DOWN> mtu 1500 qdisc noqueue state UP
    link/ether 66:a7:8e:25:c4:46 brd ff:ff:ff:ff:ff:ff
    inet 192.168.0.8/23 scope global eth0
       valid_lft forever preferred_lft forever
28: eth1@if29: <BROADCAST,MULTICAST,UP,LOWER_UP,M-DOWN> mtu 1500 qdisc noqueue state UP
    link/ether 02:42:ac:12:00:06 brd ff:ff:ff:ff:ff:ff
    inet 172.18.0.6/16 scope global eth1
       valid_lft forever preferred_lft forever
```

Every device has a virtual interface called the loopback interface, which you can see in the preceding listing as interface 1. This interface doesn't actually connect to anything outside the device, and only the device itself can communicate with it. While this may sound a little redundant, it's actually very useful when it comes to local network application testing, and it can also be used as a means of inter-process communication. The loopback interface is often referred to as localhost, and it is almost always assigned the IP address 127.0.0.1.

UDP versus TCP

The main difference between TCP and UDP is that TCP is oriented to connections, where once the connection is established, the data can be transmitted in both directions, while UDP is a simpler internet protocol, without the need for connections.

Now, we have to analyze the differences according to certain features:

- **Differences in data transfer**: TCP ensures the orderly and reliable delivery of a series of data from the user to the server and vice versa. UDP is not dedicated to point-to-point connections and does not verify the availability of whoever receives the data.

- **Reliability**: TCP is more reliable because it manages to recognize that the message was received and retransmits the packets that have been lost. UDP does not verify what the communication has produced because it does not have the ability to check the connection and retransmit the packets.
- **Connection**: TCP is a protocol that's oriented toward the congestion control of the network and the reliability of the frames, while UDP is a non-connection oriented protocol that's designed to establish a rapid exchange of packets without the need to know whether the packets are arriving correctly.
- **Transfer method**: TCP reads data as a sequence and the message is transmitted in defined segments. UDP messages are data packets that are sent individually and their integrity is verified upon arrival.
- **How TCP and UDP work**: A TCP connection is established through the process of starting and verifying a connection. Once the connection has been established, it is possible to start the data transfer, and once the transfer is complete, the connection is completed by closing the established virtual circuits. UDP provides an unreliable service and the data may arrive unordered, duplicated, or incomplete, and it doesn't notify either the sender or receiver. UDP assumes that corrections and error checking are not necessary, avoiding the use of resources in the network interface.
- **TCP and UDP applications**: TCP is used mainly when you need to use error correction mechanisms in the network interface, while UDP is mainly used in applications based on small requests from a large number of clients, for example, DNS and **Voice Over IP (VoIP)**.

DHCP

IP addresses can be assigned to a device by a network administrator in one of two ways: statically, where the device's operating system is manually configured with the IP address, or dynamically, where the device's operating system is configured by using the DHCP.

When using DHCP, as soon as the device first connects to a network, it is automatically allocated an address by a DHCP server from a predefined pool. Some network devices, such as home broadband routers, provide a DHCP server service out of the box; otherwise, a DHCP server must be set up by a network administrator. DHCP is widely deployed, and it is particularly useful for networks where different devices may frequently connect and disconnect, such as public Wi-Fi hotspots or mobile networks.

DHCP environments require a DHCP server that's been configured with the appropriate parameters for the proposed network. The main DHCP parameters include the range or pool of available IP addresses, the correct subnet masks, and the gateway and server name addresses.

A DHCP server dynamically allocates IP addresses instead of having to depend on the static IP address and is responsible for assigning, leasing, reallocating, and renewing IP addresses. The protocol will assign an address that is available in a subnet or pool. This means that a new device can be added to a network without you having to manually assign it a unique IP address. DHCP can also combine static and dynamic IPs, and also determines how long an IP address is assigned to a device.

When a computer in a network wants to obtain a valid network configuration, usually when starting up the machine, it issues a DHCP Discover request. When this request—which is made through a UDP broadcast packet—reaches a DHCP server, a negotiation is established whereby the server grants the use of an IP, and other network parameters, to the client for a certain time.

It is important to take note of the following:

- The client does not need to have the network interface configured to issue a DHCP Discover request.
- The DHCP server can be on the same or a different subnet as the client will be on. If the client does not have network configuration, it cannot reach other subnets.
- When the DHCP server receives the DHCP request, Discover obtains the Mac address of the client, which may affect the IP address assigned to the client.
- The DHCP server grants network configuration to the client for a certain time. Before reaching the deadline, the client may try to renew the concession. If a concession occurs, the client must stop using the network configuration.

To make a DHCP request, you can use a client such as `dhclient` (native GNU/Linux) or the `ipconfig/renew` command (in the case of Windows). When a network configuration is obtained, the client uses it:

```
$ dhclient --help
Usage: dhclient [-4|-6] [-SNTPRI1dvrxi] [-nw] [-p <port>] [-D LL|LLT]
                [--dad-wait-time <seconds>] [--prefix-len-hint <length>]
                [--decline-wait-time <seconds>]
                [--address-prefix-len <length>]
                [-s server-addr] [-cf config-file]
                [-df duid-file] [-lf lease-file]
                [-pf pid-file] [--no-pid] [-e VAR=val]
                [-sf script-file] [interface]*
        dhclient {--version|--help|-h}
```

DNS

DNS allows for the association of domain names with IP addresses, which greatly facilitates access to the machines on the network. Without DNS, referring to a machine implies remembering your IP address. Working directly with IP addresses is not comfortable, because they are difficult to remember and because the IP address of a station can vary for different reasons. Whoever uses the domain name does not need to worry about these changes (although the DNS server must know the real IP in each case).

The domain name system is a distributed and hierarchical database, and although its main function is to associate domain names with IP addresses, it can also store other information. The DNS service is one of the pillars of the network, so its availability must be absolute. To achieve this, redundant servers are used and extensive caching is used to improve their performance.

The `nslookup` tool comes with most Linux and Windows systems and lets us query DNS on the command line, as follows:

```
$ nslookup

Usage: nslookup [HOST] [SERVER]

Query the nameserver for the IP address of the given HOST
optionally using a specified DNS server
```

We can use this command to request the IP address for the `packtpub.com` domain:

```
$ nslookup packtpub.com

Name:          packtpub.com
Address 1: 83.166.169.231
```

With this command, we determined that the `packtpub.com` host has the IP address `83.166.169.231`. DNS distributes the work of looking up hostnames by using a hierarchical system of caching servers. Internet DNS services are a set of databases that are scattered on servers around the world. These databases indicate the IP that is associated with a name of a website. When we enter an address in the search engine, for example, `packtpub.com`, the computer asks the DNS servers of the internet provider to find the IP address associated with `packtpub.com`. If the servers do not have that information, a search is made with other servers that may have it.

When we run our preferred browser and write a web address in its address bar to access the content that's hosted on the site, the DNS service will translate these names into elements that can be understood and used for the equipment and systems that make up the internet.

On Windows computers, this system is configured by default to automatically use the DNS server of our internet service provider. At this point, we may have different DNS providers such as OpenDNS, UltraDNS, or Google DNS as an alternative, but we must always keep in mind that these providers offer us minimum security conditions to navigate. More information about configuration using Google DNS can be found at the following URL: `https://developers.google.com/speed/public-dns/`.

Addressing

This section explains concepts regarding the **Network Address Translation** (**NAT**) protocol and introduces the differences between the IPv4 and IPv6 formats.

NAT

This mechanism makes the traffic from the private network appear to be coming from a single valid public internet address, which effectively hides the private addresses from the internet. If you inspect the output of `ip addr` or `ipconfig/all` commands, then you will find that your devices are using private range addresses, which would have been assigned to them by your DHCP server or by your router through DHCP address dynamic assignment.

The private address ranges that are usually assigned are as follows:

- `10.0.0.0` to `10.255.255.255`
- `172.16.0.0` to `172.31.255.255`
- `192.168.0.0` to `192.168.255.255`

The idea is simple: make computer networks use a range of private IP addresses and connect to the internet using a single public IP address. Thanks to this patch, large companies will only be able to use one public IP address instead of as many public addresses as the number of machines there are in that company. It is also used to connect home networks to the internet.

There are two types of operations with NAT:

- **Static**: A private IP address is always translated into the same public IP address. This mode of operation would allow a host within the network to be visible from the internet.
- **Dynamic**: The router is assigned several public IP addresses so that each private IP address is mapped using one of the public IP addresses that the router has assigned. This is done so that each private IP address corresponds to at least one public IP address.

Each time a host requires an internet connection, the router will assign a public IP address that is not being used. This time, security is increased because it makes it difficult for an external host to enter the network since public IP addresses are constantly changing.

IPv4

IPv4 is the technology that allows computers to connect to the internet, whatever device we use. Each of these devices, in the instance that it connects to the internet, gets a unique code so that we can send and receive data with other connections.

As we already know, the IPv4 protocol transfers addresses that are 32 bits in length. With this type of architecture, it can manage approximately 4.3 billion IPs around the world, but the explosion of internet users in recent years has meant that the system is at its maximum capacity in regards to supporting more IP addresses.

The IPv4 address space is limited to 4.3 billion addresses. To obtain this number, we could decompose an IPv4 address as a 32-bit number consisting of four groups of 8 bits. In this way, we would have 256 different combinations to represent one IP address. This means that the possible values of an octet in an IP address would be in the range of 0 to 255.

To obtain the total number of IPv4 addresses, it would be enough to multiply *256 * 256 * 256 * 256*, since an IPv4 address is composed of four sections with 256 possibilities in each section. In total, we would have 4, 294, 967, 296 addresses. In IPv4, the universe of addresses is divided into ranges or classes, as follows:

- **CLASS A**: 1.0.0.0-126.255.255.255
- **CLASS B**: 128.0.0.0-191.255.255.255
- **CLASS C**: 192.0.0.0-223.255.255.255
- **CLASS D**: 224.0.0.0-239.255.255.255 (Multicast)
- **CLASS E**: 240.0.0.0-254.255.255.255 (Experimental)

By definition, multicast and experimental addresses cannot be used as source addresses, so the previous number must be subtracted from 520, 093, 696. Within the different classes, we have network 0.0.0.0 (the identifier of all IPv4 networks), network 127.0.0.0 (used to identify physical loopbacks in network equipment), and network 255.0.0.0 (which includes the broadcast addresses of all networks). With these restrictions, 116, 777, 216 addresses must be removed from the total.

Due to this, the need to find a replacement was palpable, and it fell to the IPv6 protocol, the sixth revision of IP and the natural successor of IPv4, to create more addresses.

IPv6

IPv6 addresses have a length of 128 bits, and so the total number of addresses will be raised to 128, where each IPv6 address consists of eight groups of 16 bits, separated by colons :, and expressed in hexadecimal notation.

Unlike IPv4, in which addresses consist of four-thirds of decimal digits ranging from 0 to 255, IPv6 addresses contain eight groups of four hexadecimal digits. fe80::e53f: e43b: ad07: 9cab is an example of an IPv6 address.

With the ifconfig command on a Windows machine, we can see an example configuration:

```
Ethernet adapter VirtualBox Host-Only Network:

   Connection-specific DNS Suffix  . :
   Link-local IPv6 Address . . . . . : fe80::e53f:e43b:ad07:9cab%5
   IPv4 Address. . . . . . . . . . . : 192.168.56.1
   Subnet Mask . . . . . . . . . . . : 255.255.255.0
   Default Gateway . . . . . . . . . :
```

Python network programming through libraries

In this section, we're going to look at a general approach to network programming in Python. We'll be introducing the main standard library modules and look at some examples to see how they relate to the TCP/IP stack.

An introduction to the PyPI Python repository

The Python Package Index, or PyPI, which can be found at `https://pypi.python.org`, is the official software repository for third-party applications in the Python programming language. Python developers want it to be a comprehensive catalog of all Python packages written in open source code.

To download packages from the PyPI repository, you can use several tools, but in this section, we will explain how to use the `pip` command to do so. `pip` is the official package installer that comes already installed when you install Python on your local machine.

You can find all of the Python networking libraries in the Python PyPI repository, such as requests (`https://pypi.org/project/requests`) and urllib (`https://pypi.org/project/urllib3`).

Installing a package using `pip` is very simple—just execute `pip install <package_name>`; for example, `pip install requests`. We can also install pip using the package manager of a Linux distribution. For example, in a Debian or Ubuntu distribution, we can use the `apt-get` command:

```
$ sudo apt-get install python-pip
```

Alternatives to pip for installing packages

We can use alternatives such as conda and Pipenv for the installation of packages in Python. Other components, such as virtualenv, also exist for this reason.

Conda

Conda is another way in which you can install Python packages, though its development and maintenance is provided by another Anaconda company. An advantage of the Anaconda distribution is that it comes with over 100 very popular Python packages, so you can start elbowing in Python straight away. You can download conda from the following link: `https://www.anaconda.com/download/`.

Installing packages with conda is just as easy as with `pip`—just run `conda install <package_name>`; for example, `conda install requests`.

The conda repository is independent of the official Python repository and does not find all of the Python packages that are in PyPI, but you will find all of the Python networking libraries such as `requests` (`https://anaconda.org/anaconda/requests`), `urllib`, and `socket`.

Virtualenv

`virtualenv` is a Python tool for creating virtual environments. To install it, you just have to run `pip install virtualenv`. With this, you can start creating virtual environments, for example, `virtualenv ENV`. Here, `ENV` is a directory that will be installed in a virtual environment that includes a separate Python installation. For more information, see the complete guide, which includes information on how to activate the environments: `https://virtualenv.pypa.io`.

Pipenv

Pipenv is a relatively new tool that modernizes the way Python manages dependencies, and includes a complete dependency resolver in the same way conda does for handling virtual environments, locking files, and more. Pipenv is an official Python program, so you just have to run `pip install pipenv` to install it. You can find an excellent guide for Pipenv in English here: `https://realpython.com/pipenv-guide`.

An introduction to libraries for network programming with Python

Python provides modules for interfacing with protocols at different levels in the network stack, and modules that support higher-layer protocols follow the aforementioned principle by using the interfaces that are supplied by the lower-level protocols.

Introduction to sockets

The socket module is Python's standard interface for the transport layer, and it provides functions for interacting with TCP and UDP, as well as for looking up hostnames through DNS. In this section, we will introduce you to this module. We'll learn much more about this in `Chapter 10`, *Programming with Sockets*.

A socket is defined by the IP address of the machine, the port on which it listens, and the protocol it uses. The types and functions that are needed to work with sockets are in Python in the socket module.

Sockets are classified into stream sockets, socket.SOCK_STREAM, or datagram sockets, socket.SOCK_DGRAM, depending on whether the service uses TCP, which is connection oriented and reliable, or UDP, respectively.

The sockets can also be classified according to their family. We have Unix sockets, such as socket.AF_UNIX, that were created before the conception of the networks and are based on socket.AF_INET file, which are based on network connections and sockets related to connections with IPv6, such as socket.AF_INET6.

Socket module in Python

To create a socket, the socket.socket() constructor is used, which can take the family, type, and protocol as optional parameters. By default, the AF_INET family and the SOCK_STREAM type are used.

The general syntax is socket.socket(socket_family, socket_type, protocol=0), where the parameters are as follows:

- socket_family: This is either AF_UNIX or AF_INET
- socket_type: This is either SOCK_STREAM or SOCK_DGRAM
- protocol: This is usually left out, defaulting to 0

Client socket methods

To connect to a remote socket in one direction, we can use the connect() method by using the connect (host, port) format:

```
import socket

# a socket object is created for communication
client_socket = socket.socket(socket.AF_INET, socket.SOCK_STREAM)
# now connect to the web server on port 80
client_socket.connect(("www.packtpub.com", 80))
```

Server socket methods

The following are some server socket methods, which are also shown in the following code:

- `bind()`: With this method, we can define in which port our server will be listening to connections
- `listen(backlog)`: This method makes the socket accept connections and accept to start listening to connections
- `accept()`: This method is used for accepting the following connection:

```
import socket

serversocket = socket.socket(socket.AF_INET, socket.SOCK_STREAM)
#bind the socket to localhost on port 80
serversocket.bind(('localhost', 80))
#become a server socket and listen a maximum of 10 connections
serversocket.listen(10)
```

Working with RFC

The **Request for Comments**, better known by its acronym, **RFC,** are a series of publications of the internet engineering working group that describe various aspects of the operation of the internet and other computer networks, such as protocols and procedures.

Each RFC defines a monograph or memorandum that engineers or experts in the field have sent to the **Internet Engineering Task Force** (**IETF**) organization, the most important technical collaboration consortium on the internet, so that it can be valued by the rest of the community.

RFCs cover a wide range of standards, and TCP/IP is just one of these. They are freely available on the IETF's website, which can be found at www.ietf.org/rfc.html. Each RFC has a number; IPv4 is documented by RFC 791, and other relevant RFCs will be mentioned as we progress throughout this book.

The most important IPs are defined by RFC, such as the IP protocol that's detailed in RFC 791, FTP in RFC 959, or HTTP in RFC 2616.

You can use this service to search by RFC number or keyword. This can be found here: https://www.rfc-editor.org/search/rfc_search.php.

In the following screenshot, we can see the result of searching for RFC number 2616 for the HTTP protocol:

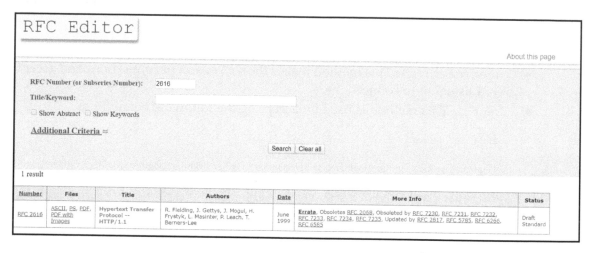

Extracting RFC information

The IETF landing page for RFCs is http://www.rfc-editor.org/rfc/, and reading through it tells us exactly what we want to know. We can access a text version of an RFC using a URL of the form http://www.rfc-editor.org/rfc/rfc741.txt. The RFC number in this case is 741. Therefore, we can get the text format of RFCs using HTTP.

At this point, we can build a Python script for downloading an RCF document from IETF, and then display the information that's returned by the service. We'll make it a Python script that just accepts an RFC number, downloads the RFC in text format, and then prints it to stdout.

The main modules that we can find in Python to make HTTP requests are urllib and requests, which work at a high level. We can also use the socket module if we want to work at a low level.

Downloading an RFC with urllib

Now, we are going to write our Python script using the `urllib` module. For this, create a text file called `RFC_download_urllib.py`:

```python
#!/usr/bin/env python3

import sys, urllib.request
try:
    rfc_number = int(sys.argv[1])
except (IndexError, ValueError):
    print('Must supply an RFC number as first argument')
    sys.exit(2)
template = 'http://www.rfc-editor.org/rfc/rfc{}.txt'
url = template.format(rfc_number)
rfc_raw = urllib.request.urlopen(url).read()
rfc = rfc_raw.decode()
print(rfc)
```

We can run the preceding code by using the following command:

```
$ python RFC_download_urllib.py 2324
```

This is the output of the previous script, where we can see the RFC description document:

```
Network Working Group                                     L. Masinter
Request for Comments: 2324                              1 April 1998
Category: Informational


              Hyper Text Coffee Pot Control Protocol (HTCPCP/1.0)

Status of this Memo

    This memo provides information for the Internet community.  It does
    not specify an Internet standard of any kind.  Distribution of this
    memo is unlimited.

Copyright Notice

    Copyright (C) The Internet Society (1998).  All Rights Reserved.

Abstract

    This document describes HTCPCP, a protocol for controlling,
    monitoring, and diagnosing coffee pots.
```

First, we import our modules and check whether an RFC number has been supplied on the command line. Then, we construct our URL by substituting the supplied RFC number. Next, the main activity, the `urlopen()` call, will construct an HTTP request for our URL, and then it will connect to the IETF web server and download the RFC text. Next, we decode the text to Unicode, and finally we print it out to the screen.

Downloading an RFC with requests

Now, are going to create the same script but, instead of using `urllib`, we are going to use the requests module. For this, create a text file called `RFC_download_requests.py`:

```python
#!/usr/bin/env python3

import sys, requests
try:
    rfc_number = int(sys.argv[1])
except (IndexError, ValueError):
    print('Must supply an RFC number as first argument')
    sys.exit(2)
template = 'http://www.rfc-editor.org/rfc/rfc{}.txt'
url = template.format(rfc_number)
rfc = requests.get(url).text
print(rfc)
```

We can simplify the previous script using the requests module. The main difference with the requests module is that we use the `get` method for the request and access the text property to get information about the specific RFC.

Downloading an RFC with the socket module

Now, we are going to create the same script but, instead of using `urllib` or requests, we are going to use the socket module for working at a low level. For this, create a text file called `RFC_download_socket.py`:

```python
#!/usr/bin/env python3

import sys, socket
try:
    rfc_number = int(sys.argv[1])
except (IndexError, ValueError):
    print('Must supply an RFC number as first argument')
    sys.exit(2)

host = 'www.rfc-editor.org'
port = 80
sock = socket.create_connection((host, port))

req = ('GET /rfc/rfc{rfcnum}.txt HTTP/1.1\r\n'
'Host: {host}:{port}\r\n'
'User-Agent: Python {version}\r\n'
'Connection: close\r\n'
'\r\n'
```

```
)
req =
req.format(rfcnum=rfc_number,host=host,port=port,version=sys.version_info[0
])
sock.sendall(req.encode('ascii'))
rfc_bytes = bytearray()

while True:
 buf = sock.recv(4096)
 if not len(buf):
     break
 rfc_bytes += buf
rfc = rfc_bytes.decode('utf-8')
print(rfc)
```

The main difference here is that we are using a socket module instead of `urllib` or `requests`. Socket is Python's interface for the operating system's TCP and UDP implementation. We have to tell socket which transport layer protocol we want to use. We do this by using the `socket.create_connection()` convenience function. This function will always create a TCP connection. For establishing the connection, we are using port 80, which is the standard port number for web services over HTTP.

Next, we deal with the network communication over the TCP connection. We send the entire request string to the server by using the `sendall()` call. The data that's sent through TCP must be in raw bytes, so we have to encode the request text as ASCII before sending it.

Then, we piece together the server's response as it arrives in the `while` loop. Bytes that are sent to us through a TCP socket are presented to our application in a continuous stream. So, like any stream of unknown length, we have to read it iteratively. The `recv()` call will return the empty string after the server sends all of its data and closes the connection. Finally, we can use this as a condition for breaking out and printing the response.

Interacting with Wireshark with pyshark

This section will help you update the basics of Wireshark to capture packets, filter them, and inspect them. You can use Wireshark to analyze the network traffic of a suspicious program, analyze the traffic flow in your network, or solve network problems. We will also review the `pyshark` module for capturing packets in Python.

Introduction to Wireshark

Wireshark is a network packet analysis tool that captures packets in real time and displays them in a graphic interface. Wireshark includes filters, color coding, and other features that allow you to analyze network traffic and inspect packets individually.

Wireshark implements a wide range of filters that facilitate the definition of search criteria for the more than 1,000 protocols it currently supports. All of this happens through a simple and intuitive interface that allows each of the captured packages to be broken down into layers.

Thanks to Wireshark understanding the structure of these protocols, we can visualize the fields of each of the headers and layers that make up the packages, providing a wide range of possibilities to the network administrator when it comes to performing tasks in the analysis of traffic.

One of the advantages that Wireshark has is that at any given moment, we can leave capturing data in a network for as long as we want and then store them so that we can perform the analysis later. It works on several platforms, such as Windows, OS X, Linux, and Unix.

Wireshark is also considered a protocol analyzer or packet sniffer, thus allowing us to observe the messages that are exchanged between applications. For example, if we capture an HTTP message, the packet analyzer must know that this message is encapsulated in a TCP segment, which, in turn, is encapsulated in an IP packet, and which, in turn, is encapsulated in an Ethernet frame.

 A protocol analyzer is a passive element, since it only observes messages that are transmitted and received from to an element of the network, but never sends messages themselves. Instead, a protocol analyzer receives a copy of the messages that are being received or sent to the Terminal where it is running.

Wireshark is composed mainly of two elements: a packet capture library, which receives a copy of each data link frame that is either sent or received, and a packet analyzer, which shows the fields corresponding to each of the captured packets. To do this, the packet analyzer must know about the protocols that it is analyzing so that the information that's shown is consistent.

Wireshark installation

You can download the Wireshark tool from the official page: `http://www.wireshark.org/download.html`.

On Windows systems, we can install the following wizard in the Windows installer. On a Linux distribution based on the Debian operating system, such as Ubuntu, this is as easy as executing the `apt-get` command:

```
sudo apt-get install wireshark
```

One of the advantages of Wireshark is the filtering we can make regarding the captured data. We can filter protocols, source, or destination IP, for a range of IP addresses, ports, or uni-cast traffic, among a long list of options. We can manually enter the filters in a box or select these filters from a default list.

Capturing packets with Wireshark

To start capturing packets, you can click on the name of an interface from the list of interfaces. For example, if you want to capture traffic on your Ethernet network, double-click on the **Ethernet** connection interface:

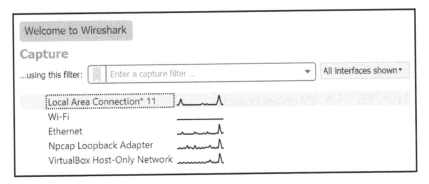

As soon as you click on the name of the interface, you will see that the packages start to appear in real time. Wireshark captures every packet that's sent to or from your network traffic. You will see random flooding of data in the Wireshark dashboard. There are many ways to filter traffic:

- To filter traffic from any specific IP address, type `ip.addr ==
  'xxx.xx.xx.xx'` in the **Apply a display filter** field
- To filter traffic for a specific protocol, say, TCP, UDP, SMTP, ARP, and DNS requests, just type the protocol name into the **Apply a display filter** field

We can use the **Apply a display filter** box to filter traffic from any IP address or protocol:

The graphical interface of Wireshark is mainly divided into the following sections:

- The toolbar, where you have all the options that you can perform on the pre and post capture
- The main toolbar, where you have the most frequently used options in Wireshark
- The filter bar, where you can apply filters to the current capture quickly
- The list of packages, which shows a summary of each package that is captured by Wireshark
- The panel of details of packages that, once you have selected a package in the list of packages, shows detailed information of the same
- The packet byte panel, which shows the bytes of the selected packet, and highlights the bytes corresponding to the field that's selected in the packet details panel
- The status bar, which shows some information about the current state of Wireshark and the capture

Network traffic in Wireshark

Network traffic or network data is the amount of packets that are moving across a network at any given point of time. The following is a classical formula for obtaining the traffic volume of a network: *Traffic volume = Traffic Intensity or rate * Time*

In the following screenshot, we can see what the network traffic looks like in Wireshark:

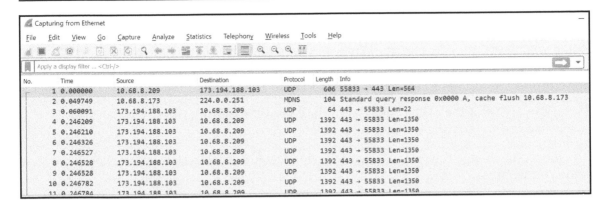

In the previous screenshot, we can see all the information that is sent over, along with the data packets on a network. It includes several pieces of information, including the following:

- **Time**: The time at which packets are captured
- **Source**: The source from which the packet originated
- **Destination**: The sink where packets reach their final destination
- **Protocol**: Type of IP (or set of rules) the packet followed during its journey, such as TCP, UDP, SMTP, and ARP
- **Info**: The information that the packet contains

The Wireshark website contains samples for capture files that you can import into Wireshark. You can also inspect the packets that they contain: `https://wiki.wireshark.org/SampleCaptures`.

For example, we can find an HTTP section for downloading files that contains examples of HTTP requests and responses:

HyperText Transport Protocol (HTTP)

http.cap A simple HTTP request and response.

http_gzip.cap A simple HTTP request with a one packet gzip Content-Encoded response.

http-chunked-gzip.pcap A single HTTP request and response for www.wireshark.org (proxied using socat to remove SSL encryption). Response is gzipped and used chunked encoding. Added in January 2016.

http_with_jpegs.cap.gz A simple capture containing a few JPEG pictures one can reassemble and save to a file.

tcp-ethereal-file1.trace (libpcap) A large POST request, taking many TCP segments.

tcp-ecn-sample.pcap A sample TCP/HTTP of a file transfer using ECN (Explicit Congestion Notification) feature per RFC3168. Frame 48 experienced Congestion Encountered.

http_redirects.pcapng A sample TCP/HTTP with many 302 redirects per RFC 3986 (https://tools.ietf.org/html/rfc3986#section-5.4).

For captures using SSL/TLS, see #SSL_with_decryption_keys.

Color coding in Wireshark

When you start capturing packets, Wireshark uses colors to identify the types of traffic that can occur, among which we can highlight green for TCP traffic, blue for DNS traffic, and black for traffic that has errors at the packet level.

To see exactly what the color codes mean, click **View | Coloring rules**. You can also customize and modify the coloring rules in this screen.

If you need to change the color of one of the options, just double-click it and choose the color you want:

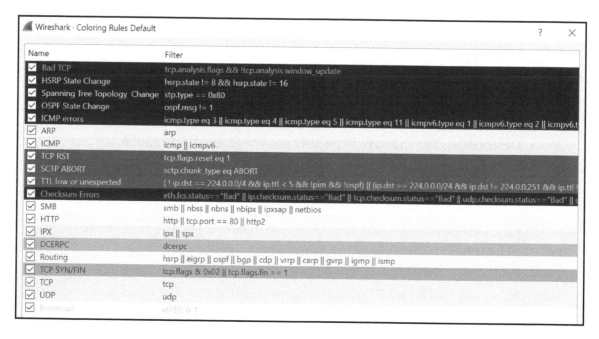

Working with filters in Wireshark

When we have a very high data collection, the filters allow us to show only those packages that fit our search criteria. We can distinguish between capture filters and display filters depending on the syntax with which each of them is governed.

The capture filters are supported directly on `libpcap` libraries such as tcpdump or Snort, so they depend directly on them to define the filters. For this reason, we can use Wireshark to open files that are generated by tcpdump or by those applications that make use of them.

The most basic way to apply a filter is by typing its name into the filter box at the top of the window. For example, type `dns` and you will see only DNS packets.

The following is a screenshot of the `dns` filter:

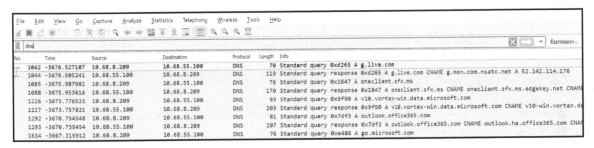

You can also click on the **Analyze** menu and select **Display Filters** to see the filters that are created by default.

In the following screenshot, we can see the display filters that we can apply when capturing packets with Wireshark:

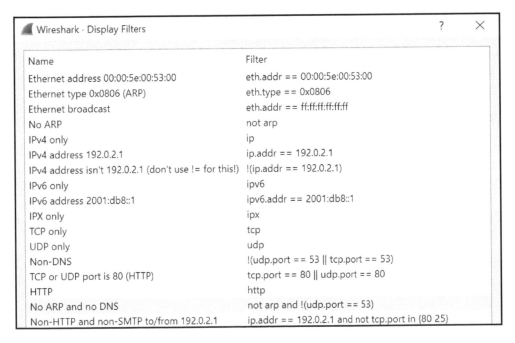

Filtering by protocol name

This filter is very powerful, but you will realize its full potential now that you are going to filter by protocol. Some of the filters include TCP, HTTP, POP, DNS, ARP, and SSL.

We can find out about HTTP requests by applying the HTTP filter. In this way, we can know about all of the GET and POST requests that have been made during the capture. Wireshark displays the HTTP message that was encapsulated in a TCP segment, which was encapsulated in an IP packet and encapsulated in an Ethernet frame:

```
>  Frame 4: 533 bytes on wire (4264 bits), 533 bytes captured (4264 bits)
>  Ethernet II, Src: Xerox_00:00:00 (00:00:01:00:00:00), Dst: fe:ff:20:00:01:00 (fe:ff:20:00:01:00)
>  Internet Protocol Version 4, Src: 145.254.160.237, Dst: 65.208.228.223
>  Transmission Control Protocol, Src Port: 3372, Dst Port: 80, Seq: 1, Ack: 1, Len: 479
v  Hypertext Transfer Protocol
   >  GET /download.html HTTP/1.1\r\n
      Host: www.ethereal.com\r\n
      User-Agent: Mozilla/5.0 (Windows; U; Windows NT 5.1; en-US; rv:1.6) Gecko/20040113\r\n
      Accept: text/xml,application/xml,application/xhtml+xml,text/html;q=0.9,text/plain;q=0.8,image/png,image/jpeg,image/gif;q=0.2,*/*;q=0.1\r\n
      Accept-Language: en-us,en;q=0.5\r\n

0060  65 72 65 61 6c 2e 63 6f  6d 0d 0a 55 73 65 72 2d   ereal.co m··User-
0070  41 67 65 6e 74 3a 20 4d  6f 7a 69 6c 6c 61 2f 35   Agent: M ozilla/5
0080  2e 30 20 28 57 69 6e 64  6f 77 73 3b 20 55 3b 20   .0 (Wind ows; U;
0090  57 69 6e 64 6f 77 73 20  4e 54 20 35 2e 31 3b 20   Windows  NT 5.1;
00a0  65 6e 2d 55 53 3b 20 72  76 3a 31 2e 36 29 20 47   en-US; r v:1.6) G
00b0  65 63 6b 6f 2f 32 30 30  34 30 31 31 33 0d 0a 41   ecko/200 40113··A
00c0  63 63 65 70 74 3a 20 74  65 78 74 2f 78 6d 6c 2c   ccept: t ext/xml,
00d0  61 70 70 6c 69 63 61 74  69 6f 6e 2f 78 6d 6c 2c   applicat ion/xml,
00e0  61 70 70 6c 69 63 61 74  69 6f 6e 2f 78 68 74 6d   applicat ion/xhtm
00f0  6c 2b 78 6d 6c 2c 74 65  78 74 2f 68 74 6d 6c 3b   l+xml,te xt/html;
```

In the preceding screenshot, we can see how a GET request has been sent to the URL that was requested from the browser. After this, the web server where the page is hosted has answered successfully (200 OK), encapsulating itself in an HTTP message where the html code contains the required path. It is the browser (application) that de-encapsulates the code and interprets it.

HTTP objects filter

As we can see, the filters provide us with a great traceability of communications and also serves as an ideal complement to analyze a multitude of attacks. An example of this is the http.content_type filter, thanks to which we can extract different data flows that take place in an HTTP connection (text/html, application/zip, audio/mpeg, image/gif). This will be very useful for locating malware, exploits, or other types of attacks that are embedded in such a protocol:

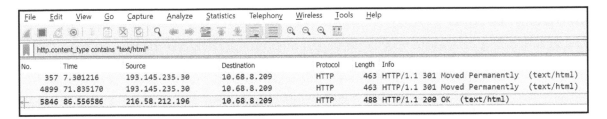

Wireshark contemplates two types of filters, that is, capture filters and display filters:

- Capture filters are those that are set to show only packets that meet the requirements indicated in the filter
- Display filters establish a filter criterion on the captured packages, which we are visualizing in the main screen of Wireshark

Capture filters

Capture filters are those that are set to show only the packages that meet the requirements indicated in the filter. If we do not establish any, Wireshark will capture all of the traffic and present it on the main screen. Even so, we can set the display filters to show us only the desired traffic:

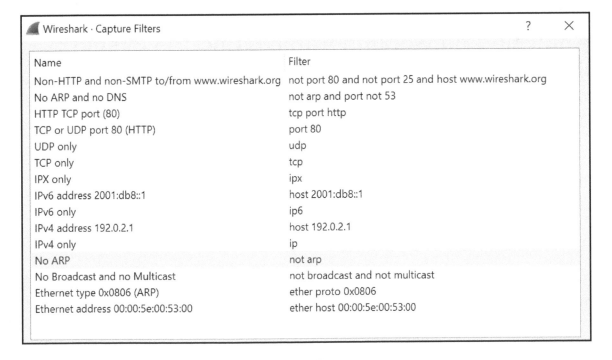

Display filters

The visualization filters establish a criterion of filter on the packages that we are capturing and that we are visualizing in the main screen of Wireshark. When you apply a filter on the Wireshark main screen, only the filtered traffic will appear through the display filter. We can also use it to filter the content of a capture through a `pcap` file:

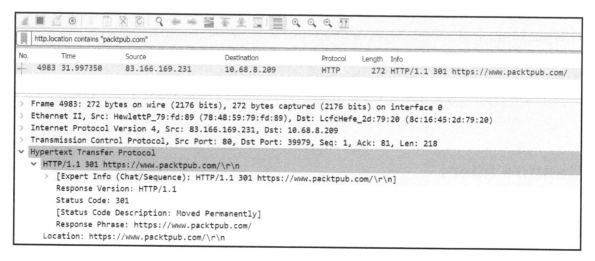

Analyzing networking traffic using the pyshark library

We can use the `pyshark` library to analyze the network traffic in Python, since everything Wireshark decodes in each packet is made available as a variable. We can find the source code of the tool in GitHub's repository: `https://github.com/KimiNewt/pyshark`.

In the PyPI repository, we can find the last version of the library, that is, `https://pypi.org/project/pyshark`, and we can install it with the `pip install pyshark` command.

In the documentation of the module, we can see that the main package for opening and analyzing a `pcap` file is `capture.file_capture`:

```
>>> help(pyshark.capture.file_capture)
Help on module pyshark.capture.file_capture in pyshark.capture:

NAME
    pyshark.capture.file_capture

CLASSES
    pyshark.capture.capture.Capture(builtins.object)
        FileCapture

    class FileCapture(pyshark.capture.capture.Capture)
     |  A class representing a capture read from a file.
     |
     |  Method resolution order:
     |      FileCapture
     |      pyshark.capture.capture.Capture
     |      builtins.object
     |
     |  Methods defined here:
     |
     |  __getitem__(self, packet_index)
     |      Gets the packet in the given index.
     |
     |      :param item: packet index
     |      :return: Packet object.
     |
     |  __init__(self, input_file=None, keep_packets=True, display_filter=None, only_summaries=False, decryption_
    key=None, encryption_type='wpa-pwk', decode_as=None, disable_protocol=None, tshark_path=None, override_prefs=None
    , use_json=False, output_file=None, include_raw=False, eventloop=None)
     |      Creates a packet capture object by reading from file.
```

Here's an example that was taken from pyshark's GitHub page. This shows us how, from the Python 3 command-line interpreter, we can read packets stored in a `pcap` file. This will give us access to attributes such as packet number and complete information for each layer, such as its protocol, IP address, mac address, and flags, where you can see if the packet is a fragment of another:

```
>> import pyshark
>>> cap = pyshark.FileCapture('http.cap')
>>> cap
>>> print(cap[0])
```

In the following screenshot, we can see the execution of the previous commands, and also see where we passed the `pcap` file path in the `FileCapture` method as a parameter:

```
>>> import pyshark
>>> cap = pyshark.FileCapture('http.cap')
>>> cap
<FileCapture http.cap>
>>> print(cap[0])
Packet (Length: 62)
Layer ETH:
        Destination: fe:ff:20:00:01:00
        Address: fe:ff:20:00:01:00
        .... ...1. .... .... .... .... = LG bit: Locally administered address (this is NOT the factory default)
        .... ...0 .... .... .... .... = IG bit: Individual address (unicast)
        Source: 00:00:01:00:00:00
        Type: IPv4 (0x0800)
        Address: 00:00:01:00:00:00
        .... ..0. .... .... .... .... = LG bit: Globally unique address (factory default)
        .... ...0 .... .... .... .... = IG bit: Individual address (unicast)
Layer IP:
        0100 .... = Version: 4
        .... 0101 = Header Length: 20 bytes (5)
        Differentiated Services Field: 0x00 (DSCP: CS0, ECN: Not-ECT)
        0000 00.. = Differentiated Services Codepoint: Default (0)
        .... ..00 = Explicit Congestion Notification: Not ECN-Capable Transport (0)
        Total Length: 48
        Identification: 0x0f41 (3905)
        Flags: 0x4000, Don't fragment
        0... .... .... .... = Reserved bit: Not set
        .1.. .... .... .... = Don't fragment: Set
        ..0. .... .... .... = More fragments: Not set
        ...0 0000 0000 0000 = Fragment offset: 0
        Time to live: 128
        Protocol: TCP (6)
```

We can apply a filter for DNS traffic only with the `display_filter` argument in the `FileCapture` method:

```
import pyshark
cap = pyshark.FileCapture('http.cap', display_filter="dns")
for pkt in cap:
  print(pkt.highest_layer)
```

In the following screenshot, we can see the execution of the previous commands:

```
Layer DNS:
        Transaction ID: 0x0023
        Flags: 0x0100 Standard query
        0... .... .... .... = Response: Message is a query
        .000 0... .... .... = Opcode: Standard query (0)
        .... ..0. .... .... = Truncated: Message is not truncated
        .... ...1 .... .... = Recursion desired: Do query recursively
        .... .... .0.. .... = Z: reserved (0)
        .... .... ...0 .... = Non-authenticated data: Unacceptable
        Questions: 1
        Answer RRs: 0
        Authority RRs: 0
        Additional RRs: 0
        Queries
        Name: pagead2.googlesyndication.com
        Name Length: 29
        Label Count: 3
        Type: A (Host Address) (1)
        Class: IN (0x0001)
        pagead2.googlesyndication.com: type A, class IN
```

FileCapture and LiveCapture in pyshark

As we saw previously, you can use the `FileCapture` method to open a previously saved trace file. You can also use `pyshark` to sniff from an interface in real time with the `LiveCapture` method, like so:

```
import pyshark
# Sniff from interface in real time
capture = pyshark.LiveCapture(interface='eth0')
capture.sniff(timeout=10)
<LiveCapture (5 packets)>
```

Once a `capture` object is created, either from a `LiveCapture` or `FileCapture` method, several methods and attributes are available at both the capture and packet level. The power of `pyshark` is that it has access to all of the packet decoders that are built into TShark.

Now, let's see what methods provide the returned capture object.

To check this, we can use the `dir` method with the capture object:

```
>>> dir(cap)
['DEFAULT_BATCH_SIZE', 'DEFAULT_LOG_LEVEL', 'SUMMARIES_BATCH_SIZE', 'SUPPORTED_ENCRYPTION_STANDARDS', '__class__',
'__del__', '__delattr__', '__dict__', '__dir__', '__doc__', '__eq__', '__format__', '__ge__', '__getattribute__',
'__getitem__', '__gt__', '__hash__', '__init__', '__init_subclass__', '__iter__', '__le__', '__len__', '__lt__',
'__module__', '__ne__', '__new__', '__reduce__', '__reduce_ex__', '__repr__', '__setattr__', '__sizeof__', '__str__',
'__subclasshook__', '__weakref__', '_capture_filter', '_cleanup_subprocess', '_close_async', '_closed', '_crea
ted_new_process', '_current_packet', '_decode_as', '_disable_protocol', '_display_filter', '_extract_packet_json_f
rom_data', '_extract_tag_from_data', '_get_json_separator', '_get_packet_from_stream', '_get_psml_struct', '_get_t
shark_path', '_get_tshark_process', '_go_through_packets_from_fd', '_log', '_only_summaries', '_output_file', '_ov
erride_prefs', '_packet_generator', '_packets', '_packets_from_tshark_sync', '_running_processes', '_setup_eventlo
op', '_stderr_output', 'apply_on_packets', 'clear', 'close', 'debug', 'encryption', 'eventloop', 'get_parameters',
'include_raw', 'input_filename', 'keep_packets', 'load_packets', 'loaded', 'next', 'next_packet', 'packets_from_t
shark', 'reset', 'set_debug', 'tshark_path', 'use_json']
```

The `display_filter`, `encryption`, and `input_filename` attributes are used for displaying parameters that are passed into `FileCapture` or `LiveCapture`.

Both methods offer similar parameters that affect packets that are returned in the capture object. For example, we can iterate through the packets and apply a function to each. The most useful method here is the `apply_on_packets()` method. `apply_on_packets()` is the main way to iterate through the packets, passing in a function to apply to each packet:

```
>>> cap = pyshark.FileCapture('http.cap', keep_packets=False)
>>> def print_info_layer(packet):
>>>     print("[Protocol:] "+packet.highest_layer+" [Source IP:]
"+packet.ip.src+" [Destination IP:]"+packet.ip.dst)
>>> cap.apply_on_packets(print_info_layer)
```

In the following screenshot, we can see the information that's returned when we are obtaining information for each packet pertaining to `Protocol`, `Source IP`, and `Destination IP`:

```
[Protocol:] TCP  [Source IP:] 145.254.160.237 [Destination IP:]65.208.228.223
[Protocol:] TCP  [Source IP:] 65.208.228.223 [Destination IP:]145.254.160.237
[Protocol:] TCP  [Source IP:] 145.254.160.237 [Destination IP:]65.208.228.223
[Protocol:] HTTP [Source IP:] 145.254.160.237 [Destination IP:]65.208.228.223
[Protocol:] TCP  [Source IP:] 65.208.228.223 [Destination IP:]145.254.160.237
[Protocol:] TCP  [Source IP:] 65.208.228.223 [Destination IP:]145.254.160.237
[Protocol:] TCP  [Source IP:] 145.254.160.237 [Destination IP:]65.208.228.223
[Protocol:] TCP  [Source IP:] 65.208.228.223 [Destination IP:]145.254.160.237
[Protocol:] TCP  [Source IP:] 145.254.160.237 [Destination IP:]65.208.228.223
[Protocol:] TCP  [Source IP:] 65.208.228.223 [Destination IP:]145.254.160.237
[Protocol:] TCP  [Source IP:] 65.208.228.223 [Destination IP:]145.254.160.237
[Protocol:] TCP  [Source IP:] 145.254.160.237 [Destination IP:]65.208.228.223
[Protocol:] DNS  [Source IP:] 145.254.160.237 [Destination IP:]145.253.2.203
[Protocol:] TCP  [Source IP:] 65.208.228.223 [Destination IP:]145.254.160.237
[Protocol:] TCP  [Source IP:] 145.254.160.237 [Destination IP:]65.208.228.223
[Protocol:] TCP  [Source IP:] 65.208.228.223 [Destination IP:]145.254.160.237
[Protocol:] DNS  [Source IP:] 145.253.2.203 [Destination IP:]145.254.160.237
```

We can also use the `apply_on_packets()` method for adding the packets to a list for counting or other processing means. Here's a script that will append all of the packets to a list and print the count. For this, create a text file called `count_packets.py`:

```python
import pyshark
packets_array = []

def counter(*args):
 packets_array.append(args[0])

def count_packets():
    cap = pyshark.FileCapture('http.cap', keep_packets=False)
    cap.apply_on_packets(counter, timeout=10000)
    return len(packets_array)

print("Packets number:"+str(count_packets()))

for packet in packets_array:
 print(packet)
```

We can use `only_summaries`, which will return packets in the capture object with just the summary information of each packet:

```python
>>> cap = pyshark.FileCapture('http.cap', only_summaries=True)
 >>> print cap[0]
```

This option makes capture file reading much faster, and with the `dir` method, we can check the attributes that are available in the object to obtain information about a specific packet.

In the following screenshot, we can see information about a specific packet and get all of the attributes that return not null information:

```
>>> import pyshark
>>> cap = pyshark.FileCapture('http.cap', only_summaries=True)
>>> dir(cap[0])
['__class__', '__delattr__', '__dict__', '__dir__', '__doc__', '__eq__', '__format__', '__ge__', '__getattr
ibute__', '__gt__', '__hash__', '__init__', '__init_subclass__', '__le__', '__lt__', '__module__', '__ne__'
, '__new__', '__reduce__', '__reduce_ex__', '__repr__', '__setattr__', '__sizeof__', '__str__', '__subclass
hook__', '__weakref__', '_field_order', '_fields', 'destination', 'info', 'length', 'no', 'protocol', 'sour
ce', 'summary_line', 'time']
>>> print(cap[0].destination)
145.254.160.237
>>> print(cap[0].info)
80 \xe2\x86\x92 3372 [SYN, ACK] Seq=0 Ack=1 Win=5840 Len=0 MSS=1380 SACK_PERM=1
>>> print(cap[0].length)
62
>>> print(cap[0].no)
2
>>> print(cap[0].protocol)
TCP
>>> print(cap[0].source)
65.208.228.223
>>> print(cap[0].summary_line)
2 0.91131 65.208.228.223 145.254.160.237 TCP 62 80 \xe2\x86\x92 3372 [SYN, ACK] Seq=0 Ack=1 Win=5840 Len=0
MSS=1380 SACK_PERM=1
>>> print(cap[0].time)
0.91131
>>> print(cap[0].__dict__)
{'_fields': {'No.': '2', 'Time': '0.91131', 'Source': '65.208.228.223', 'Destination': '145.254.160.237', '
Protocol': 'TCP', 'Length': '62', 'Info': '80 \\xe2\\x86\\x92 3372 [SYN, ACK] Seq=0 Ack=1 Win=5840 Len=0 MS
S=1380 SACK_PERM=1'}, '_field_order': ['No.', 'Time', 'Source', 'Destination', 'Protocol', 'Length', 'Info'
], 'no': '2', 'time': '0.91131', 'source': '65.208.228.223', 'destination': '145.254.160.237', 'protocol':
'TCP', 'length': '62', 'info': '80 \\xe2\\x86\\x92 3372 [SYN, ACK] Seq=0 Ack=1 Win=5840 Len=0 MSS=1380 SACK
```

The information you can see in the form of attributes is as follows:

- `destination`: The IP destination address
- `source`: The IP source address
- `info`: A summary of the application layer
- `length`: Length of the packet in bytes
- `no`: Index number of the packet
- `protocol`: The highest layer protocol that's recognized in the packet
- `summary_line`: All of the summary attributes in one string
- `time`: Time between the current packet and the first packet

Summary

In this chapter, we have completed an introduction to TCP/IP and how machines communicate in a network. We learned about the main protocols of the network stack and the different types of address for communicating in a network. We started with Python libraries for network programming and looked at socket and the `urlllib` and `requests` modules, and provided an example of how we can interact and obtain information from RFC documents. We also acquired some basic knowledge so that we are able to perform a network traffic analysis with Wireshark.

Wireshark is provided with innumerable functionalities, thanks to which we will be able to identify and analyze network traffic and identify communications in our network.

In the next chapter, you will learn how to use Python as an HTTP client so that you can make requests over the REST API and retrieve web resources with the `urllib` and `requests` modules.

Questions

1. What TCP/IP layer does user interaction with computers and services occur?
2. Why do we need to replace IPv4 with the IPv6 protocol?
3. What protocol allows you to dynamically configure IP addresses in the device's operating system?
4. What mechanism makes the traffic from the private network appear to be coming from a single valid public internet address and hides the private addresses from the internet?
5. What are the main options for installing Python packages on your localhost machine?
6. What is the main Python tool for creating virtual environments, which also includes a separate Python installation for the packages?
7. What are the main modules that we can find in Python to make HTTP requests at a high level?
8. What are the main modules that we can find in Python to make HTTP requests at a low level?
9. Which library can we use to analyze network traffic in Python that Wireshark decodes in each packet?
10. What method from the `pyshark` package can we use to iterate through the packets and apply a function to each one?

Further reading

By going to the following links, you will find more information about the tools and the official Python documentation that was mentioned in this chapter:

- This is the official documentation for the `socket` package: `https://docs.python.org/3/library/socket.html`
- This is the official documentation for downloading and installing Wireshark: `https://www.wireshark.org/`
- This is the official documentation for the `pyshark` package: `https://kiminewt.github.io/pyshark/`

Programming for the Web with HTTP

2

In the chapter, you will learn how to use Python as an HTTP client to make requests and retrieve web resources. You will be encouraged to try a series of example requests. We will compare urllib and the third-party requests library and show you the differences when working with forms and cookies. The third-party Requests package is a very popular alternative to urllib. It has an elegant interface and a powerful feature set, and it is a great tool for streamlining HTTP workflows. We also cover HTTP authentication mechanisms and how we can manage them with the Requests module.

The following topics will be covered in this chapter:

- Understanding the urllib package to query a REST API
- Understanding the Requests package to query a REST API
- Handling forms with urllib and requests with Python 3.7
- Handling cookies with urllib and requests with Python 3.7
- Handling HTTPS and HTTP Basic Authentication with requests

The urllib package is the recommended Python standard library package for HTTP tasks. The standard library also has a low-level module called HTTP. Although this offers access to almost all aspects of the protocol, it has not been designed for everyday use. The urllib package has a simpler interface, and it deals with everything that we are going to cover in this chapter.

The third-party Requests package is a very popular alternative to urllib. It has an elegant interface and a powerful feature set, and it is a great tool for streamlining HTTP workflows.

Technical requirements

The examples and source code for this chapter are available in the GitHub repository in the Chapter02 folder, at https://github.com/PacktPublishing/Learning-Python-Networking-Second-Edition.

You will need to install the Python distribution on your local machine and have some basic knowledge of the HTTP protocol.

Consuming web services in Python with urllib

In this section, we will learn how to use urllib and how we can build HTTP clients with this module.

The urllib module allows access to any resource published on the network (web page, files, directories, images, and so on) through various protocols (HTTP, FTP, SFTP). To start consuming a web service, we have to import the following libraries:

```python
#! /usr/bin/env python3
import urllib.request
import urllib.parse
```

There are four functions in urllib:

- request: Opens and reads the request's URL
- error: Contains the errors generated by the request
- parse: A tool to convert the URL
- robotparse: Converts the robots.txt files

The urllib.request module allows access to a resource published on the internet through its address. If we go to the documentation of the Python 3 module (https://docs.python.org/3/library/urllib.request.html#module-urllib.request), we will see all the functions that have this class. The main one is urlopen, which works in the following way.

A urlopen function is used to create an object similar to a file, with which to read from the URL. This object has methods such as read, readline, readlines, and close, which work exactly the same as in the file objects, although in reality, we are working with wrapper's methods that abstract us from using sockets at a low level.

The `urlopen` function has an optional data parameter with which to send information to HTTP addresses using the POST method, where parameters are sent in the request itself; for example, to respond to a form. This parameter is a properly encoded string:

```
urllib.request.urlopen (url, data = None, [timeout,] *, cafile = None,
capath = None, cadefault = False, context = None)
```

Retrieving the contents of a URL is a straightforward process when done using `urllib`. You can open the Python interpreter and execute the following instructions:

```
>>> from urllib.request import urlopen
>>> response = urlopen('http://www.packtpub.com')
>>> response
<http.client.HTTPResponse object at 0x7fa3c53059b0>
>>> response.readline()
```

We use the `urllib.request.urlopen()` function to send a request and receive a response for the resource at http://www.packtpub.com, in this case an HTML page. We will then print out the first line of the HTML we receive, with the `readline()` method from the response object.

This function also supports specifying a timeout for the request that represents the waiting time in the request; that is, if the page takes more than what we indicated, it will result in an error:

```
>>> print (urllib.request.urlopen("http://packtpub.com",timeout=30))
```

We can see from the preceding example that `urlopen()` returns an `http.client.HTTPResponse` instance. The response object gives us access to the data of the requested resource and the properties and the metadata of the response:

```
<http.client.HTTPResponse object at 0x03C4DC90>
```

If we get a response in JSON format, we can use the following Python `json` module:

```
>>> import json
>>> response = urllib.request.urlopen(url,timeout=30)
>>> json_response = json.loads(response.read())
```

In the variable response, we save the file that launches the request, and we use the `read()` function to read the content. Then we transform it into JSON format.

Status codes

HTTP responses provide us with a way to check the status of the response through status codes. We can read the status code of a response using its status property. The value of 200 is an HTTP status code that tells us that the request is OK:

```
>>> response.status
200
```

The 200 code informs us that everything went fine. There are a number of codes, and each one conveys a different meaning. According to their first digit, status codes are classified into the following groups:

- 100: Informational
- 200: Success
- 300: Redirection
- 400: Client error
- 500: Server error

Status codes help us to see whether our response was successful or not. Any code in the 200 range indicates a success, whereas any code in either the 400 range or the 500 range indicates failure in the server.

 The official list of status codes is maintained by IANA and can be found at https://www.iana.org/assignments/http-status-codes.

Handling exceptions

Status codes should always be checked so that our program can respond appropriately if something goes wrong. The urllib package helps us in checking the status codes by raising an exception if it encounters a problem.

Let's go through how to catch these and handle them usefully. We'll try this following command block. You can find the following code in the urllib_exceptions.py file:

```
import urllib.error
from urllib.request import urlopen
try:
    urlopen('http://www.ietf.org/rfc/rfc0.txt')
except urllib.error.HTTPError as e:
```

```
print('Exception', e)
print('status', e.code)
print('reason', e.reason)
print('url', e.url)
```

The output of the previous script is:

```
Exception HTTP Error 404: Not Found
status 404
reason Not Found
url https://www.ietf.org/rfc/rfc0.txt
```

In the previous script, we've requested an `rfc0.txt` document, which doesn't exist. So the server has returned a `404` status code, and `urllib` has captured this and raised an `HTTPError`. You can see that `HTTPError` provides useful attributes regarding the request. In the preceding example, we obtain the `status`, `reason`, and `url` attributes to get some information about the response.

HTTP headers

A request to the server consists of a request line that contains some basic information about the request, and various lines that constitute the headers. An example might be the following:

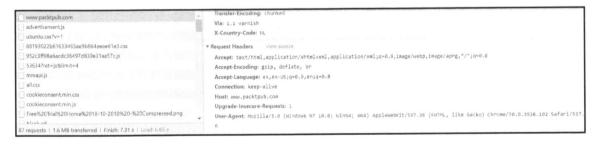

HTTP requests consist of two main parts: a header and a body. Headers are the lines of information that contain specific metadata about the response and tell the client how to interpret it. With this module, we can check whether the headers can provide information about the web server.

The HTTP headers are `Name: value` pairs; for example, **Host:** `www.packtpub.com`. These headers contain different information about the HTTP request and about the browser. For example, the **User-Agent** line provides information about the browser and operating system of the machine from which the request is made, and **Accept Encoding** informs the server if the browser can accept compressed data under formats such as **gzip**.

An important header is the host header. Many web server applications provide the ability to host more than one website on the same server using the same IP address. DNS aliases are set up for the various website domain names, so they all point to the same IP address. Effectively, the web server is given multiple hostnames, one for each website it hosts.

The following script will obtain the site headers through the response object's headers. For this task, we can use the `headers` property or the `getheaders()` method. The `getheaders()` method returns the headers as a list of tuples of the form (header name, header value).

You can find the following code in the `get_headers.py` file:

```
#!/usr/bin/env python3
import urllib.request
url = input("Enter the URL:")
http_response = urllib.request.urlopen(url)
if http_response.code == 200:
    print(http_response.headers)
    for key,value in http_response.getheaders():
        print(key,value)
```

In the following screenshot, we can see the script executing for the `packtpub.com` domain:

```
Enter the URL:http://www.packtpub.com
Server: nginx/1.4.5
Date: Mon, 26 Nov 2018 11:04:05 GMT
Content-Type: text/html; charset=utf-8
Transfer-Encoding: chunked
Connection: close
Expires: Sun, 19 Nov 1978 05:00:00 GMT
Cache-Control: public, s-maxage=172800
Age: 3661
Via: 1.1 varnish
X-Country-Code: NL
```

User agent

Another important request header is the `User-Agent` header. Any client that communicates using HTTP can be referred to as a user agent. RFC 7231 suggests that user agents should use the `User-Agent` header to identify themselves in every request. For example, the user agent if you are using the Chrome browser might be as follows:

```
User-Agent: Mozilla/5.0 (Windows NT 10.0; Win64; x64) AppleWebKit/537.36
(KHTML, like Gecko) Chrome/70.0.3538.102 Safari/537.36
```

Also, we can view the user agent used by the `urllib` Python version:

```
>>> from urllib.request import Request
>>> from urllib.request import urlopen
>>> req = Request('http://www.python.org')
 >>> urlopen(req)
<http.client.HTTPResponse object at 0x034AEBF0>
>>> req.get_header('User-agent')
 'Python-urllib/3.7'
```

Here, we have created a request and submitted it using `urlopen`, and `urlopen` added the user agent header to the request. We can examine this header by using the `get_header()` method. This header and its value are included in every request made by `urllib`, so every server we make a request to can see that we are using Python 3.7 and the `urllib` library.

Customizing requests with urllib

To make use of the functionality that headers provide, we add headers to a request before sending it. To do this, we need to follow these steps:

1. Create a `Request` object.
2. Add headers to the `Request` object.
3. Use `urlopen()` to send the `Request` object.

We're going to learn how to customize a request to retrieve a Netherlands version of the Debian home page. We will use the `Accept-Language` header, which tells the server our preferred language for the resource it returns.

First, we create a `Request` object:

```
>>> from urllib.request import Request,urlopen
 >>> req = Request('http://www.debian.org')
```

Next, we add the header:

```
>>> req.add_header('Accept-Language', 'nl')
```

The `add_header()` method takes the name of the header and the contents of the header as arguments. The `Accept-Language` header takes two-letter ISO 639-1 language codes. In this example, the code for Netherlands is `nl`.

Lastly, we submit the customized request with `urlopen()`:

```
>>> response = urlopen(req)
```

We can check if the response is in the Dutch language by printing out the first few lines:

```
>>> response.readlines()[:5]
```

In this screenshot, we can see that the language changed with the `Accept-language` header:

```
>>> from urllib.request import Request,urlopen
>>> req.add_header('Accept-Language', 'nl')
>>> from urllib.request import Request,urlopen
>>> req = Request('http://www.debian.org')
>>> req.add_header('Accept-Language', 'nl')
>>> response = urlopen(req)
>>> response.readlines()[:5]
[b'<!DOCTYPE HTML PUBLIC "-//W3C//DTD HTML 4.01//EN" "http://www.w3.org/TR/html4/
strict.dtd">\n', b'<html lang="nl">\n', b'<head>\n', b'  <meta http-equiv="Conten
t-Type" content="text/html; charset=utf-8">\n', b'  <title>Debian -- Het universe
le Besturingssysteem </title>\n']
```

The `Accept-Language` header has informed the server about our preferred language for the response's content. To view the headers present in a request, do the following:

```
>>> req = Request('http://www.debian.org')
 >>> req.add_header('Accept-Language', 'nl')
 >>> req.header_items()
[('Host', 'www.debian.org'), ('User-agent', 'Python-urllib/3.6'), ('Accept-
language', 'nl')]
```

Let's see how to add our own headers using the `User-agent` header as an example. The `User-agent` is a header used to identify the browser and operating system that we are using to connect to that URL. If we want to identify ourselves as using a Firefox browser, we could change the user agent.

To change the user agent, we have two alternatives. The first is using a headers dictionary parameter in the `Request` method. The second solution consists of using the `add_header()` method for adding headers at the same time that we create the `Request` object, as showing in the following example.

You can find the following code in the `add_headers_user_agent.py` file:

```
#!/usr/bin/env python3
from urllib.request import Request
USER_AGENT = 'Mozilla/5.0 (Windows NT 5.1; rv:20.0) Gecko/20100101
Firefox/20.0'
URL = 'http://www.debian.org'

def add_headers_user_agent():
```

```python
    headers = {'Accept-Language': 'nl','User-agent': USER_AGENT}
    request = Request(URL,headers=headers)
    #request.add_header('Accept-Language', 'nl')
    #request.add_header('User-agent', USER_AGENT)
    print ("Request headers:")
    for key,value in request.header_items():
        print ("%s: %s" %(key, value))
if __name__ == '__main__':
    add_headers_user_agent()
```

In this screenshot, we can see the request headers sent for the previous script:

```
Request headers:
Accept-language: nl
User-agent: Mozilla/5.0 (Windows NT 5.1; rv:20.0)
Gecko/20100101 Firefox/20.0
```

Getting headers with a proxy

We can use a proxy connection for the same task. If we need to specify a proxy in the code, we have to use an opener that contains the `ProxyHandler` handler. The default handler includes a `ProxyHandler` instance built by calling the initializer without parameters, which reads the list of proxies to use from the appropriate environment variable. However, we can also build a `ProxyHandler`, passing as a parameter a dictionary whose key is the HTTP protocol and the value is the proxy address or URL used for this protocol.

To install the opener once created, the `install_opener` function is used, which takes as a parameter the opener to be installed.

You can find the following code in the `proxy_web_request.py` file:

```python
import urllib.request, urllib.parse, urllib.error
URL = 'https://www.github.com'
# By Googling free proxy server
PROXY_ADDRESS = "165.24.10.8:8080"
if __name__ == '__main__':
    proxy = urllib.request.ProxyHandler({"http" : PROXY_ADDRESS})
    opener = urllib.request.build_opener(proxy)
    urllib.request.install_opener(opener)
    resp = urllib.request.urlopen(URL)
    print ("Proxy server returns response headers: %s " %resp.headers)
```

Content types

HTTP can be used as a method of transport for any type of file or data. The server can use the 'Content-Type' header in a response to inform the client about the type of data that it has sent in the body. This is the primary means with which an HTTP client determines how it should handle the body data that the server returns to it. To view the content type, we inspect the value of the response header, as shown here:

```
>>> response = urlopen('http://www.debian.org')
>>> response.getheader('Content-Type')
'text/html'
```

These values are called content types, internet media types, or MIME types. The full list can be found at http://www.iana.org/assignments/media-types.

Content type values can contain optional additional parameters that provide further information about the type. This is usually used to supply the character set that the data uses; for example, Content-Type: text/html; charset=utf-8.

In this screenshot, we can see many Content-Type instances depending on the requested URL:

```
>>> from urllib.request import urlopen
>>> response = urlopen('http://www.debian.org')
>>> response.getheader('Content-Type')
'text/html'
>>> response = urlopen('https://httpbin.org/get')
>>> response.getheader('Content-Type')
'application/json'
>>> response = urlopen('http://www.python.org')
>>> response.getheader('Content-Type')
'text/html; charset=utf-8'
```

Extracting links from a URL with urllib

In this script, we can see how to extract links using urllib and HTMLParser. HTMLParser is a module that allows us to parse text files formatted in HTML. You can get more information at https://docs.python.org/3/library/html.parser.html.

You can find the following code in the extract_links_parser.py file:

```
#!/usr/bin/env python3
from html.parser import HTMLParser
import urllib.request
```

```
class myParser(HTMLParser):
    def handle_starttag(self, tag, attrs):
        if (tag == "a"):
            for a in attrs:
                if (a[0] == 'href'):
                    link = a[1]
                    if (link.find('http') >= 0):
                        print(link)
                        newParse = myParser()
                        newParse.feed(link)

url = "http://www.packtpub.com"
request = urllib.request.urlopen(url)
parser = myParser()
parser.feed(request.read().decode('utf-8'))
```

In the following screenshot, we can see the script execution for the `packtpub.com` domain:

```
https://www.packtpub.com/account/password
https://hub.packtpub.com
https://www.packtpub.com/cart/checkout
https://mapt.io/free-trial/
https://www.packtpub.com/skill-up-2018/big-data-bundle
https://www.packtpub.com/skill-up-2018/blockchain-bundle
https://www.packtpub.com/skill-up-2018/business-intelligence-bundle
https://www.packtpub.com/ai-now/building-ai-powered-iot-systems
https://www.packtpub.com/skill-up-2018/core-c-sharp-programming-bundle
https://www.packtpub.com/skill-up-2018/c-sharp-web-development-bundle
https://www.packtpub.com/skill-up-2018/core-c-plus-plus-programming-bundle
https://www.packtpub.com/skill-up-2018/c-plus-plus-game-development-bundle
https://www.packtpub.com/skill-up-2018/high-performance-c-plus-plus-apps-bundle
https://www.packtpub.com/ai-now/creating-ai-systems-with-raspberry-pi
https://www.packtpub.com/skill-up-2018/devops-bundle
https://www.packtpub.com/ai-now/getting-started-with-machine-learning-on-the-cloud
https://www.packtpub.com/skill-up-2018/docker-bundle
https://www.packtpub.com/ai-now/everything-about-ai-bundle
https://www.packtpub.com/skill-up-2018/go-programming-bundle
https://www.packtpub.com/skill-up-2018/go-web-development-bundle
https://www.packtpub.com/skill-up-2018/hadoop-bundle
```

Another way to extract links from a URL is using the **regular expression (re)** module to find `href` elements in the target URL.

You can find the following code in the `urlib_link_extractor.py` file:

```
#!/usr/bin/env python3

from urllib.request import urlopen
import re

def download_page(url):
```

```
        return urlopen(url).read().decode('utf-8')

    def extract_links(page):
        link_regex = re.compile('<a[^>]+href=["\'](.*?)["\']',re.IGNORECASE)
        return link_regex.findall(page)

    if __name__ == '__main__':
        target_url = 'http://www.packtpub.com'
        packtpub = download_page(target_url)
        links = extract_links(packtpub)
        for link in links:
            print(link)
```

Getting images from a URL with urllib

In this example, we can see how to extract images using `urllib` and regular expressions. The easy way to extract images from a URL is to use the `re` module to find `img` elements in the target URL.

You can find the following code in the `extract_images_urllib.py` file:

```
#!/usr/bin/env python3

from urllib.request import urlopen, urljoin
import re

def download_page(url):
    return urlopen(url).read().decode('utf-8')

def extract_image_locations(page):
    img_regex = re.compile('<img[^>]+src=["\'](.*?)["\']',
    re.IGNORECASE)
    return img_regex.findall(page)

if __name__ == '__main__':
    target_url = 'http://www.packtpub.com'
    packtpub = download_page(target_url)
    image_locations = extract_image_locations(packtpub)
    for src in image_locations:
        print(urljoin(target_url, src))
```

In this screenshot, we can see the script execution for the `packtpub.com` domain:

```
http://www.packtpub.com
https://d255esdrn735hr.cloudfront.net/sites/default/files/BFH Front Compressed V3.png
https://dz13w8afd47il.cloudfront.net/sites/default/files/imagecache/featured_book_block/bookretailers/V10662_low.png
http://www.packtpub.com/sites/default/files/blank.gif
https://dz13w8afd47il.cloudfront.net/sites/default/files/imagecache/featured_book_block/bookretailers/V09066_low_0.png
http://www.packtpub.com/sites/default/files/blank.gif
https://d255esdrn735hr.cloudfront.net/sites/default/files/imagecache/featured_book_block/B10618.png
http://www.packtpub.com/sites/default/files/blank.gif
https://dz13w8afd47il.cloudfront.net/sites/default/files/imagecache/featured_book_block/B09048.png
http://www.packtpub.com/sites/default/files/blank.gif
https://dz13w8afd47il.cloudfront.net/sites/default/files/imagecache/featured_book_block/bookretailers/V09197_low_0.png
http://www.packtpub.com/sites/default/files/blank.gif
https://dz13w8afd47il.cloudfront.net/sites/default/files/imagecache/featured_book_block/B10120.png
http://www.packtpub.com/sites/default/files/blank.gif
https://d255esdrn735hr.cloudfront.net/sites/default/files/imagecache/featured_book_block/B09332.png
http://www.packtpub.com/sites/default/files/blank.gif
https://d255esdrn735hr.cloudfront.net/sites/default/files/imagecache/featured_book_block/B09991_New_cover.png
http://www.packtpub.com/sites/default/files/blank.gif
https://d255esdrn735hr.cloudfront.net/sites/default/files/imagecache/featured_book_block/cover_13.png
http://www.packtpub.com/sites/default/files/blank.gif
https://dz13w8afd47il.cloudfront.net/sites/default/files/imagecache/featured_book_block/bookretailers/V10068_Low.png
http://www.packtpub.com/sites/default/files/blank.gif
```

Working with URLs

Uniform Resource Locators (**URLs**) are fundamental to the way in which the web operates, and are formally described in RFC 3986. A URL represents a resource on a given host. URLs can point to files on the server, or the resources may be dynamically generated when a request is received.

Python uses the `urllib.parse` module for working with URLs. Let's use Python to break a URL into its component parts:

```
>>> from urllib.parse import urlparse
>>> result = urlparse('https://www.packtpub.com/tech/Python')
>>> result
ParseResult(scheme='http', netloc='www.packtpub.com', path='/tech/Python',
params='', query='', fragment='')
```

The `urllib.parse.urlparse()` function interprets our URL and recognizes HTTP as the scheme, `www.packtpub.com` as the network location, and `/tech/Python` as the path.

We can access these components as attributes of the `ParseResult`:

```
>>> from urllib.parse import urlparse
>>> result = urlparse('https://www.packtpub.com/tech/Python')
>>> result
ParseResult(scheme='https', netloc='www.packtpub.com', path='/tech/Python', params='', query='', fragment='')
>>> result.scheme
'https'
>>> result.netloc
'www.packtpub.com'
>>> result.path
'/tech/Python'
```

For almost all resources on the web, we'll be using the HTTP or HTTPS schemes. In these schemes, to locate a specific resource, we need to know the host that it resides on and the TCP port that we should connect to, and we also need to know the path to the resource on the host.

The path in a URL is anything that comes after the host and the port. Paths always start with a **forward slash** (/), and when a slash appears on its own, it's called the root.

RFC 3986 defines another property of URLs called query strings. They can contain additional parameters in the form of key-value pairs that appear after the path. They are separated from the path by a question mark. In this example, we can see how we can get URL parameters with the query argument:

```
>>> result = urlparse('https://search.packtpub.com/?query=python')
>>> result
ParseResult(scheme='https', netloc='search.packtpub.com', path='/',
params='', query='query=python', fragment='')
>>> result.query
'query=python'
```

Query strings are used for supplying parameters to the resource that we wish to retrieve, and this usually customizes the resource in some way. In the previous example, our query string tells the `packtpub` search page that we want to run a search for the term `python`. The `urllib.parse` module has a function called `parse_qs()` that reads the query string and then converts it into a dictionary:

```
>>> from urllib.parse import parse_qs
>>> result = urlparse('https://search.packtpub.com/?query=python')
>>> parse_qs(result.query)
{'query': ['python']}
```

The simplest way to code the string is to use the `urllib urlencode` method, which accepts a dictionary or a list of tuples (key, value) and generates the corresponding encoded string.

The `urlencode()` function is similarly intended for encoding query strings directly from dictionaries. Notice how it correctly percent-encodes our values and then joins them with &, so as to construct the query string:

```
>>> from urllib.parse import urlencode
>>> params = urllib.parse.urlencode({"user": "user", "password":
"password"})
>>> params
'user=user&password=password'
```

Consuming web services in Python with requests

In this section, we will learn how to use the `requests` library. How we interact with RESTful APIs based on HTTP is an increasingly common task in projects that use the Python programming language.

Introduction to requests

Requests allow you to send requests to an HTTP server and get responses and messages sent by the server. They're available as the Requests package on PyPI. This can either be installed through `pip` or be downloaded from `http://docs.python-requests.org`, which hosts the documentation. You can install the `requests` library on your system in an easy way with the `pip` command:

```
pip install requests
```

The `requests` library automates and simplifies many of the tasks that we've been looking at. The quickest way of illustrating this is by trying some examples. The commands for retrieving a URL with Requests are similar to retrieving a URL with the `urllib` package.

The `request.get()` function sends a request using the `get` method with the following syntax:

```
requests.get ('<URL>', params = <object type dict>)
>>> import requests
>>> response = requests.get('http://www.github.com')
```

The `requests.get()` method returns a `response` object, where you will find all the information corresponding to the response of our request. These are the main properties of the response object:

- `response.status_code`: This is the HTTP code returned by the server
- `response.content`: Here, we will find the content of the server response
- `response.json()`: If the answer is JSON, this method serializes the string and returns a dictionary structure with the corresponding JSON structure

We can look at the properties of the response object:

```
>>> response.status_code
200
```

```
>>> response.reason
'OK'
>>> response.url
'http://www.github.com/'
>>> response.headers['content-type']
'text/html; charset=utf-8'
```

We can also access the headers properties through the `response` object:

```
>>> response.request.headers
{'User-Agent': 'python-requests/2.19.1', 'Accept-Encoding': 'gzip,
deflate', 'Accept': '*/*', 'Connection': 'keep-alive'}
```

Notice that Requests is automatically handling compression for us. It's including `gzip` and `deflate` in an `Accept-Encoding` header. If we look at the `content-encoding` response, then we will see that the response was in fact `gzip` compressed, and Requests transparently decompressed it for us:

```
>>> response.headers['content-encoding']
'gzip'
```

We can look at the response content in many more ways. To get the same `bytes` object as we got from an `HTTPResponse` object, perform the following:

```
>>> response.text
'\n\n\n\n\n\n<!DOCTYPE html>\n<html lang="en">\n  <head>\n <meta
charset="utf-8">\n <link rel="dns-prefetch"
href="https://assets-cdn.github.com">\n  <link rel="dns-prefetch"
href="https://avatars0.githubusercontent.com">\n <link rel="dns-prefetch"
href="https://avatars1.githubusercontent.com">\n  <link rel="dns-prefetch"
href="https://avatars2.githubusercontent.com">\n
```

Checking HTTP headers

The `response.headers` statement provides the headers of the web server response. Basically, the response is an object dictionary, and with the `items()` method, we can iterate with the key-value format for access to the header's response.

You can find the following code in the `get_headers.py` file:

```
#!/usr/bin/env python3

import requests
response = requests.get('http://github.com')
try:
```

```
    for key,value in response.headers.items():
        print('%s: %s' % (key, value))
except Exception as error:
    print('%s' % (error))
```

In this screenshot, we can see the script execution for the `github.com` domain:

```
Content-Type: text/html; charset=utf-8
Transfer-Encoding: chunked
Server: GitHub.com
Status: 200 OK
Cache-Control: no-cache
Vary: X-PJAX, Accept-Encoding
Set-Cookie: has_recent_activity=1; path=/; expires=Thu, 22 Nov 2018 20:54:45 -0000, logged_in=no; domai
n=.github.com; path=/; expires=Mon, 22 Nov 2038 19:54:45 -0000; secure; HttpOnly, _gh_sess=a1ZTQW1HeHZo
NEdkR1liVzdMYjR5Nk9ZSEFqZnFTMEh1amloZzd2WXZzcVg1MORabwpReTMwMjZSNEErajJtQmRVaVFTak1BYUxJMnRtRWpVVTljVi8
zdG1nRnVJYXkwaTRoK0h6ekV4YW5LcWpPZDZPN2RMdzU1OGl1RU9mR01TL3c2bGIzaXlNYXNKLzdGRzEOdHltdwEvaWVEak84N2RzSn
1paohqUnpCam9NbFF3OC9zeDV5ZEtoS3V1S2tvdFBaYOpGVUd1Z3JRU0diRHBJYUtcGQT09LS1WZOtJbjdJT1lpZ013KOJIMjkxTOhnP
TO%3D--e6abe3a41b639f1bf2c2O2a24eff49d6bb6a4baa; path=/; secure; HttpOnly
X-Request-Id: bc39744d-bec4-4762-bf19-ef5ba7330838
Strict-Transport-Security: max-age=31536000; includeSubdomains; preload
X-Frame-Options: deny
X-Content-Type-Options: nosniff
X-XSS-Protection: 1; mode=block
Referrer-Policy: origin-when-cross-origin, strict-origin-when-cross-origin
Expect-CT: max-age=2592000, report-uri="https://api.github.com/_private/browser/errors"
```

We can also find browser add-ons or plugins that can help us in collecting information on the headers that are sent in the requests.

Among the available plugins for Firefox, we can suggest the **HTTP Header Live** add-ons:

With this plugin, we can get the headers for the request and response for a specific domain URL:

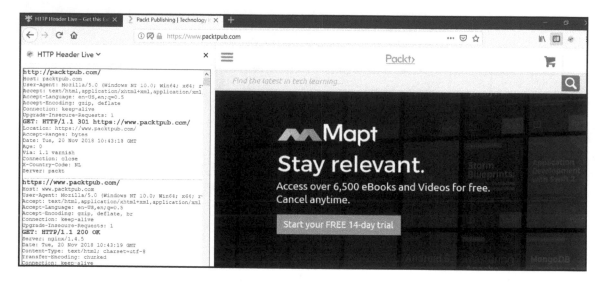

Proxy requests

An interesting feature offered by the Requests module is the possibility to make requests through a proxy or intermediate machine between our internal network and the external network. A proxy is defined in the following way:

```
>>> proxy = {"protocol":"ip:port", ...}
```

To make a Request through a proxy, the `proxies` attribute of the `get` method is used:

```
>>> response = requests.get(url,headers=headers,proxies=proxy)
```

The proxy parameter must be passed in the form of a dictionary; that is, you have to create a dictionary type where we specify the protocol with the IP address and the port where the proxy is listening:

```
>>> import requests
>>> http_proxy = "http://<ip_address>:<port>"
>>> proxy_dictionary = { "http" : http_proxy}
>>> requests.get("http://example.org", proxies=proxy_dictionary)
```

Get whois information

We can use the Requests module and the `whois.domaintools.com` service to get information about the domain we are analyzing, such as the IP address and location.

You can find the following code in the `get_whois_info.py` file:

```python
#!/usr/bin/env python3
from lxml.html import fromstring
import requests
domain = input("Enter the domain : ")
url = 'http://whois.domaintools.com/' + domain
headers = {'User-Agent': 'wswp'}
resp = requests.get(url, headers=headers)
html = resp.text
tree = fromstring(html)
info = tree.xpath('//*[@id="stats"]//table/tbody/tr//text()')
temp_list = []

for each in info:
    each = each.strip()
    if each == "":
        continue
    temp_list.append(each.strip("\n"))

ip_index = temp_list.index('IP Address')
print("IP address ", temp_list[ip_index + 1])
location = temp_list.index('IP Location')
location2 = temp_list.index('ASN')
print('Location : ', "".join(temp_list[location + 1:location2]))
```

In the output of the previous script, we can see information about the IP address and the location from the `packtpub.com` domain:

```
Enter the domain : http://www.packtpub.com
 IP address  83.166.169.231                        - 1 other site is
hosted on this server
 Location :   -England-Derby-Node4 Uk Hosting
```

Working with JSON

If we need to send JSON from a client to a server, the simplest way with the Requests module is using the `json` parameter, specifying a dictionary structure in key-value format.

The main advantage of using this parameter is that it is not necessary to specify `'Content-Type'` in the request. In the `json` response, we can see that it automatically returns this field with the `'application/json'` value:

```
>>> import requests
>>> response = requests.post('http://httpbin.org/post', json={"key":
"value"})
>>> response.status_code
200
>>> response.json()
{'args': {},
'data': '{"key": "value"}',
'files': {},
'form': {},
'headers': {'Accept': '*/*',
'Accept-Encoding': 'gzip, deflate',
'Connection': 'close',
'Content-Length': '16',
'Content-Type': 'application/json',
'Host': 'httpbin.org',
'User-Agent': 'python-requests/2.4.3 CPython/3.4.0',
'X-Request-Id': 'xx-xx-xx'},
'json': {'key': 'value'},
'origin': 'x.x.x.x',
'url': 'http://httpbin.org/post'}
```

Handling forms with urllib and requests with Python 3.7

In this section, we will learn how to use `urllib` and `requests` to interact with HTML forms.

Handling forms with urllib

When working with forms, it is useful to use the POST method to send data to the server. The POST method is used for submitting user input from HTML forms and for uploading files to a server.

When using POST, the data that we wish to send will go in the body of the request. We can put any bytes data in there and declare its type by adding a `Content-Type` header to our request with an appropriate MIME type.

Let's look at an example for sending some HTML form data to a server by using a POST request, just as browsers do when we submit a form on a website. The site at https:// httpbin.org offers a test server that returns certain data from requests. It will be used to exemplify some uses of the Requests module.

In the following example, we are using the form that corresponds with a POST method, http://httpbin.org/forms/post.

Suppose we have a service to register an order from a customer, where they must enter information such as their name, phone, email, and the desired pizza size:

This information would be passed through the data attribute through a dictionary structure. The POST method requires an extra field called data, in which we send a dictionary with all the elements that we will send to the server through the corresponding method.

The form data always consists of key-value pairs; urllib lets us work with regular dictionaries to supply the form data. We can create a data dictionary with the customer data, adding information such as their name, telephone, pizza size, and email address with the keys custname, custtel, size, and custemail respectively:

```
>>> data_dictionary = {'custname': 'customer','custtel': '323232', 'size':
'large','custemail': 'email@domain.com'}
```

When posting the HTML form data, the form values must be formatted in the same way as query strings are formatted in a URL, and must be URL encoded. A **Content-Type** header must also be set to the special MIME type of application/x-www-form-urlencoded.

In the **Request Headers**, we can see the **Content-Type** value when we send data with the POST method:

```
▼ Request Headers      view source
    Accept: text/html,application/xhtml+xml,application/xml;q=0.9,image/webp,image/apng,*/*;q=0.8
    Accept-Encoding: gzip, deflate
    Accept-Language: es,en-US;q=0.9,en;q=0.8
    Cache-Control: max-age=0
    Connection: keep-alive
    Content-Length: 92
    Content-Type: application/x-www-form-urlencoded
    Cookie: _gauges_unique_day=1; _gauges_unique_month=1; _gauges_unique_year=1; _gauges_unique=1
    Host: httpbin.org
    Origin: http://httpbin.org
    Referer: http://httpbin.org/forms/post
```

Since this format is identical to query strings, we can just use the `urlencode()` function in our dictionary to prepare the data:

```
>>> data = urlencode(data_dictionary).encode('utf-8')
b'custname=customer&custtel=323232&size=large&custemail=email%40domain.com'
```

Here, we also additionally encode the result to bytes, as it will be sent as the body of the request. In this case, we use the UTF-8 character set.

Next, we will construct our request:

```
>>> from urllib.request import Request
>>> req = Request('http://httpbin.org/post',data=data)
```

By adding our data as the data keyword argument, we are telling `urllib` that we want our data to be sent as the body of the request. This will make the request use the POST method, rather than the GET method. Next, we add the `Content-Type` header:

```
>>> req.add_header('Content-Type', 'application/x-www-form-
urlencode;charset=UTF-8')
```

Lastly, we submit the request and transform the response in a JSON dictionary with the `json` module.

In the response dictionary, we can see the data and `'Content-Type'` we established in the request:

```
>>> response = urlopen(req)
>>> response_dictionary = json.load(response)
>>> print(response_dictionary)
{'args': {}, 'data':
'custname=customer&custtel=323232&size=large&custemail=email%40domain.com',
'files': {}, 'form': {}, 'headers': {'Accept-Encoding': 'identity',
'Connection': 'close', 'Content-Length': '72', 'Content-Type':
'application/x-www-form-urlencode;charset=UTF-8', 'Host': 'httpbin.org',
'User-Agent': 'Python-urllib/3.6'}, '
```

Handling forms with requests

Typically, you want to send some form-encoded data. To do this, simply pass a dictionary to the data argument. Your data dictionary will automatically be form-encoded when the request is made. The `requests` library takes care of all the encoding and formatting for us.

In this example, we are going to simulate the sending of an HTML form through a POST request, just like browsers do when we send a form to a website. Form data is always sent in key-value dictionary format.

The `request.post()` function sends a request using the PUT method with the following syntax:

```
requests.post ('<URL>', data = <object>, json = <object type dict>)
```

You can find the following code in the `form_post_method.py` file:

```
import requests

data_dictionary = {'custname': 'customer','custtel': '323232',
'size': 'large','custemail': 'email@domain.com'}
response = requests.post("http://httpbin.org/post",data=data_dictionary)
# we then print out the http status_code
print("HTTP Status Code: " + str(response.status_code))
if response.status_code == 200:
    print(response.text)
```

In this screenshot, we can see the execution of the previous script:

```
HTTP Status Code: 200
{
  "args": {},
  "data": "",
  "files": {},
  "form": {
    "custemail": "email@domain.com",
    "custname": "customer",
    "custtel": "323232",
    "size": "large"
  },
  "headers": {
    "Accept": "*/*",
    "Accept-Encoding": "gzip, deflate",
    "Connection": "close",
    "Content-Length": "72",
    "Content-Type": "application/x-www-form-urlencoded",
    "Host": "httpbin.org",
    "User-Agent": "python-requests/2.19.1"
  },
  "json": null,
  "origin": "192.113.65.10",
  "url": "http://httpbin.org/post"
}
```

In the script response, we see how the information appears, that is being sent in the request data dictionary object in the form section data.

Handling cookies with urllib and requests with Python

In this section, we will learn about cookies and how we can use `urllib` and `requests` to get cookies when we are interacting with a site that supports identifying the user's action.

What are cookies?

A cookie is a file created by a website that contains small amounts of data and that is sent between a sender and a receiver. In the case of the internet, the sender would be the server where the web page is hosted, and the receiver is the browser that you use to visit any web page.

A cookie's main purpose is to identify the user by storing their activity history on a specific website, so that the most appropriate content according to their habits can be offered. This means that each time a website is visited for the first time, a cookie is saved in the browser with a little information. Then, when the same page is visited again, the server asks for the same cookie to fix the configuration of the site and make the visit as personalized as possible.

These cookies can have a simple purpose, such as knowing when the user last visited a certain web page, or something more important, as it is used to keep all the items placed in the shopping cart of a store—an action that is saved in real time.

There are several types of cookies, but the most common are called **session cookies**, which have a short lifespan since they are deleted when you close the browser. We also have **persistent cookies**, which are used to track the user by saving information about their behavior on a website for a certain period of time. Persistent cookies can be deleted by cleaning the browser data, but some have an expiration date.

Secure cookies store encrypted information to prevent the data stored in them from being vulnerable to malicious third-party attacks. They are used only in HTTPS connections.

Servers use cookies in various ways. They can add a unique ID to them, which enables them to track a client as they access different areas of a site. They can store a login token, which will automatically log the client in, even if the client leaves the site and then accesses it later. They can also be used for storing the client's user preferences or snippets of personalized information, and so on.

Cookies are necessary because the server has no other way of tracking a client between requests. HTTP is called a stateless protocol. It doesn't contain an explicit mechanism for a server to know for sure that two requests have come from the same client. Without cookies to allow the server to add some uniquely identifying information to the requests, things such as shopping carts would become impossible to build, because the server would not be able to determine which basket goes with which request.

Handling cookies with urllib

In order to work with cookies with `urllib`, we can use the `HTTPCookieProcessor` handler from the `urllib.request` package:

```
>>> import urllib
>>> cookie_processor = urllib.request.HTTPCookieProcessor()
```

If we want to access these cookies or be able to send our own cookies, we can pass a `CookieJar` object of the `cookielib` module as a parameter to the `HTTPCookieProcessor` initializer.

To read the cookies that the server sends us, just create an iterable object of the `CookieJar` class from the `http.cookiejar` package. This will automatically extract the cookies from the responses that we receive and then store them in our cookie jar:

```
>>> from http.cookiejar import CookieJar
>>> cookie_jar = CookieJar()
>>> cookie_processor = urllib.request.HTTPCookieProcessor(cookie_jar)
>>> opener = urllib.request.build_opener(cookie_processor)
>>> urllib.request.install_opener(opener)
```

We can use our opener to make an HTTP request:

```
>>> opener.open('http://www.github.com')
<http.client.HTTPResponse object at 0x00FFBD50>
```

Lastly, we can check that the server has sent us some cookies:

```
>>> len(cookie_jar)
3
```

Whenever we use the opener to make further requests, the `HTTPCookieProcessor` functionality will check our `cookie_jar` to see if it contains any cookies for that site and will then automatically add them to our requests. It will also add any further cookies that are received to the cookie jar.

Now, we are examining the cookies that GitHub sent us in the preceding section. You can see that we have three cookie objects with the names `'logged_in'`, `'_gh_sess'`, and `'has_recent_activity'`. Also, we can see information related to the GitHub domain as part of the mechanism that GitHub uses for finding out whether we've logged in.

The `expires` attribute or cookie's lifespan represents the amount of time that the server would like the client to hold on to the cookie for. Once the expiry date has passed, the client can throw the cookie away and the server will send a new one with the next request:

```
>>> cookies = list(cookie_jar)
>>> cookies
[Cookie(version=0, name='logged_in', value='no', port=None,
port_specified=False, domain='.github.com', domain_specified=True,
domain_initial_dot=True, path='/', path_specified=True, secure=True,
expires=2173978199, discard=False, comment=None, comment_url=None,
rest={'HttpOnly': None}, rfc2109=False), Cookie(version=0, name='_gh_sess',
value='cD1MVjFOdHM1djhLYWRGeGpPMTIxLytnRzdHN1RQT3VkUngxLzY2UkpmcGI1KzhNYVd4
```

```
TzBzb2VJK0cxcWZBeGdpOFA3ZE95RXd5Nnp0WDdDWlQ0dHpwSkYzQ0hOZ2o1R3JkOXBPZTdCCL0N
4dGVMZ0dHc0VKZ0RreW5raDdRNDcrS0tTT1ZiY1pOcGw5NkdkNDZBTnlQNTBiTDRzRTRIeVZPNV
Y2RWdUZ3VvYkFsczNqd3psQ0JBSld2R1k4d3QvQm5XRm1iSGtVeVpTdG9haVVzMFFhnQT09LS1pR
3NNNnN1VmRocVJ0RXpkaWhxK0JRPT0%3D-
-84304a9b84b7e8c2605efb9808c1b92a25fcc221', port=None,
port_specified=False, domain='github.com', domain_specified=False,
domain_initial_dot=False, path='/', path_specified=True, secure=True,
expires=None, discard=True, comment=None, comment_url=None,
rest={'HttpOnly': None}, rfc2109=False), Cookie(version=0,
name='has_recent_activity', value='1', port=None, port_specified=False,
domain='github.com', domain_specified=False, domain_initial_dot=False,
path='/', path_specified=True, secure=False, expires=1542829799,
discard=False, comment=None, comment_url=None, rest={}, rfc2109=False)]
```

Another interesting attribute is the HttpOnly flag, which indicates the client should only allow access to a cookie when the access is part of an HTTP request or response. The other methods should be denied access. This will protect the client from cross-site scripting attacks. This is an important security feature, and when the server sets it, our application should behaves accordingly. We can see that for cookies with the names 'logged_in' and '_gh_sess', the HTTPOnly flag is established to None value and the secure flag has the True value.

If the value is true, the secure flag indicates that the cookie should only ever be sent over a secure connection, such as HTTPS. Again, we should honor this if the flag has been set such that when our application sends requests containing this cookie, it only sends them to HTTPS URLs.

In this script, we can see how we can obtain cookies from a website. We are using the same methods we have reviewed, and for each cookie in the list, we print the name and the value. We can process the headers response to obtain other cookies related to the website.

You can find the following code in the extract_cookie_information.py file:

```
import http.cookiejar
import urllib
URL = 'https://github.com/'

def extract_cookie_info():
    # setup cookie jar
    cookie_j = http.cookiejar.CookieJar()
    # create url opener
    opener =
urllib.request.build_opener(urllib.request.HTTPCookieProcessor(cookie_j))
    # now access without any login info
    resp = opener.open(URL)
    for cookie in cookie_j:
```

```
        print ("Cookie: %s --> %s" %(cookie.name, cookie.value))
    print ("Headers: %s" %resp.headers)

if __name__ == '__main__':
    extract_cookie_info()
```

In this screenshot, we can see the execution of the previous script:

```
Cookie: logged_in --> no
Cookie: _gh_sess --> emFXNHFsYVZ1bWNtZWJpSzlyZndrRWduMTZNa01RMHJyYXh1b25kNlFYWWk2aGUzM3V1SXV
IRVFDMjd4djUxN3dETOppdW82eUtCdzd6aS9yMFRsR3FUMGxIRWNHaWhZS0zrOXdqYO1kY2ZiV24vTC9ST2ovYVB2MkF
MdTlXZHk2cHJQSTF4Yz1jYOsveGOrUDVwZl1uZTFpazhRWFJrcGhVSDJGenVKeWO3ekJRUENuMFIzdjdBRUprVldkN3Z
TaEpHZWhLWXE2WExpYYTlXR21jVmJFUT09LS1YTGhJSy9oQ1RHWmxzejE5ckxGcO9RPTO%3D--d00e1c111bcd9ebcfaf
3e7880a4b3b7ec4ffa662
Cookie: has_recent_activity --> 1
Headers: Date: Wed, 21 Nov 2018 18:39:49 GMT
Content-Type: text/html; charset=utf-8
Transfer-Encoding: chunked
Connection: close
Server: GitHub.com
Status: 200 OK
Cache-Control: no-cache
Vary: X-PJAX
Set-Cookie: has_recent_activity=1; path=/; expires=Wed, 21 Nov 2018 19:39:49 -0000
Set-Cookie: logged_in=no; domain=.github.com; path=/; expires=Sun, 21 Nov 2038 18:39:49 -000
0; secure; HttpOnly
Set-Cookie: _gh_sess=emFXNHFsYVZ1bWNtZWJpSzlyZndrRWduMTZNa01RMHJyYXh1b25kNlFYWWk2aGUzM3V1SXV
IRVFDMjd4djUxN3dETOppdW82eUtCdzd6aS9yMFRsR3FUMGxIRWNHaWhZS0zrOXdqYO1kY2ZiV24vTC9ST2ovYVB2MkF
MdTlXZHk2cHJQSTF4Yz1jYOsveGOrUDVwZl1uZTFpazhRWFJrcGhVSDJGenVKeWO3ekJRUENuMFIzdjdBRUprVldkN3Z
TaEpHZWhLWXE2WExpYYTlXR21jVmJFUT09LS1YTGhJSy9oQ1RHWmxzejE5ckxGcO9RPTO%3D--d00e1c111bcd9ebcfaf
3e7880a4b3b7ec4ffa662; path=/; secure; HttpOnly
X-Request-Id: 91aa5c7a-0518-49d5-ae26-a9de15536082
Strict-Transport-Security: max-age=31536000; includeSubdomains; preload
X-Frame-Options: deny
X-Content-Type-Options: nosniff
X-XSS-Protection: 1; mode=block
Referrer-Policy: origin-when-cross-origin, strict-origin-when-cross-origin
Expect-CT: max-age=2592000, report-uri="https://api.github.com/_private/browser/errors"
Content-Security-Policy: default-src 'none'; base-uri 'self'; block-all-mixed-content; conne
```

Cookie handling with requests

You can use the `requests` library to get cookies from the `response` object. With the cookies property from that object, you can access the cookies list through a `request.cookies.RequestsCookieJar` object:

```
>>> response = requests.get('http://www.github.com')
>>> print(response.cookies)
<<class 'requests.cookies.RequestsCookieJar'>
[<Cookie logged_in=no for .github.com/>,<Cookie
_gh_sess=NORTMHpreVk3cUk0N05qbFNpNncyajU3MVNZVWtINmZQVTUrdnlpQ11nYnZ6WGdXWU
1aQ0d2VXJQVk4wcE1IYWd4Nk54RHRrMWdjNXAwL010Oei9Jen1PeUJOeEZkcTRTST1wTWtvEt0e
i9XOW1WZGNwTXNzbmd6Tk93ekcrem9XZDduQzdjdjZXWVJEOXpNVUFXOTZRUWRYalZFay9mWDAv
```

c2NlREJSdEREb1hOUC9LR2prYi9ZQ3FoOH1ORHY3L0VvN3Z4MXk0WWJyWk1yMXZnSGJXQT09LS1
1Y1kzY1pWRXBnWU1ncjRaaUJacGhPT0%3D-
-85b693ec8eee1f743fcaa3dc382ee5048cfda6f1 for github.com/>, <Cookie
has_recent_activity=1 for github.com/>]>

Alternatively, you can use the `Session` class, `requests.Session`, and observe cookies from the request and the response:

```
>>> import requests
>>> session = requests.Session()
>>> print(session.cookies.get_dict())
{}
>>> response = session.get('http://github.com')
>>> print(session.cookies.get_dict())
{'logged_in': 'no', '_gh_sess':
'ekM5WmVnV1ZkMXBEcXY1ZkdFNXJuRnltdkRiajhGTExGRyt4NHNOQ1Eyc3VpOFh6VDgzRVFQZD
h5bU1rMFhYam81Qm9hYkphRUFLeUd6SHU4VCtSVS9ybUdMT21KaGhrMyttSTRCU09IckZvUUhkd
l1pWG10WFFJOGNTMVFxN1oxYWJqY20vVVVYR1BNN0pSMz14VkRaVDFCYS94WWFFS2NwNzlzMzV6
ajY0K2I5K1oyZmVLU0xJd1RjbTNvdFZnYmdXaEU5ej16TFFg0d09qTjA5Q3VaQT09LS1OWlhCOXB
neUdVN1JxVFBudVc0cmRBPT0%3D--c4f11645c3b08255c4667e264197c61cb02fe289',
'has_recent_activity': '1'}
```

The `Session` object has the same interface as the Requests module, so we use its `get()` method in the same way as we use the `requests.get()` method. Now, any cookies encountered are stored in the `Session` object.

In this script, we are going to extract cookies from the `github.com` domain. You can find the following code in the `get_cookies_github.py` file:

```python
#!/usr/bin/env python3
import requests

def check_httponly(c):
    if 'httponly' in c._rest.keys():
        return True
    else:
        return '\x1b[31mFalse\x1b[39;49m'

cookies = []
url = 'http://www.github.com'
response = requests.get(url)

for cookie in response.cookies:
    print('Name:', cookie.name)
    print('Value:', cookie.value)
    cookies.append(cookie.value)
    if not cookie.secure:
```

```
        cookie.secure = '\x1b[31mFalse\x1b[39;49m'
    print('HTTPOnly:', check_httponly(cookie), '\n')

  print(set(cookies))
```

In this screenshot, we can see the execution of the previous script:

```
Name: logged_in
Value: no
HTTPOnly: False

Name: _gh_sess
Value: c3RHUnB4MU01eVpqVVVsROVzcOJwQkh3d3FGMGVBRCs5SUJvK21FN1RzcC9ETVN1NnVVOWN
DUCsxQm9IbF14NnJ1aw94WnkybEMydTR1bnRxVEFpYzFuVm1pVlFBTHJ1Sm1iMGxXYmNHMXB6Z3VNO
Ep3WGVZKzIweUd5L3R3UXZMZ1d3TVNUaG5aFV1dUhvazkOdwlodDZvSnNGNEJncEdTcOZwVFNxYm1
wVmtiWjZibzZoYjVjQzdlS1hwdmRYMG1DSUddBUE95TVVNaWhqTDdDK2huUTO9LS1UOVNSMktuTHRmS
zRSV1pZWk1UTVpBPTO%3D--bde2a4b2048d7e45cee392ec9c3ca45576a4a1a5
HTTPOnly: False

Name: has_recent_activity
Value: 1
HTTPOnly: False

{'c3RHUnB4MU01eVpqVVVsROVzcOJwQkh3d3FGMGVBRCs5SUJvK21FN1RzcC9ETVN1NnVVOWNDUCsx
Qm9IbF14NnJ1aw94WnkybEMydTR1bnRxVEFpYzFuVm1pVlFBTHJ1Sm1iMGxXYmNHMXB6Z3VNOEp3WG
VZKzIweUd5L3R3UXZMZ1d3TVNUaG5aFV1dUhvazkOdwlodDZvSnNGNEJncEdTcOZwVFNxYm1wVmti
wjZibzZoYjVjQzdlS1hwdmRYMG1DSUddBUE95TVVNaWhqTDdDK2huUTO9LS1UOVNSMktuTHRmSzRSV1
pZWk1UTVpBPTO%3D--bde2a4b2048d7e45cee392ec9c3ca45576a4a1a5', 'no', '1'}
```

Also, we can send cookies to a server with the `cookies` parameter. In this example, we are using the service at `http://httpbin.org/cookies` to send the cookie with the `admin='True'` value.

You can find the following code in the `send_cookies.py` file:

```python
#!/usr/bin/env python3
import requests
cookies = []
url = 'http://httpbin.org/cookies'
cookies = dict(admin='True')
cookie_req = requests.get(url, cookies=cookies)
print(cookie_req.text)
```

Handling HTTP Basic and Digest Authentication with requests

In this section, we will learn about cookies and how we can use `urllib` and `requests` to get cookies when we are interacting with a site that supports identifying the user's action.

Introduction to authentication mechanisms

The authentication mechanisms supported natively in the HTTP protocol are HTTP basic and HTTP digest. Both mechanisms are supported in Python through the `requests` library. The HTTP Basic Authentication mechanism is based on forms and uses Base64 to encode the user composed with the password separated by a colon: `user: password`.

The HTTP Digest Authentication mechanism uses MD5 to encrypt the user, key, and realm hashes. The main difference between both methods is that basic only encodes without actually encrypting, while digest encrypts the user's information in MD5 format.

With the Requests module, we can connect with servers that support Basic and Digest Authentication. With Basic Authentication, the information about the user and password is sent in Base64 format, and with Digest the information about the user and password is sent as a hash using the MD5 or SHA1 algorithms.

HTTP Basic authentication

Basic access authentication assumes that the client will be identified by a username and a password. When the browser client initially accesses a site using this system, the server replies with a response of type 401, which contains the `WWW-Authenticate` tag with the `Basic` value and the name of the protected domain (such as `WWW-Authenticate: Basic realm = "www.domainProtected.com"`).

The browser responds to the server with an `Authorization` tag, which contains the `Basic` value and the concatenation in the Base64 encoding of the login, the colon punctuation mark `:`, and the password (for example, `Authorization : Basic b3dhc3A6cGFzc3dvcmQ =`). Assuming that we have a URL protected with this type of authentication, in Python, with the Requests module, we can use the `HTTPBasicAuth` class.

In this script, we are using the `HTTPBasicAuth` class and providing the user credentials as a tuple.

You can find the following code in the `basic_authentication.py` file:

```python
#!/usr/bin/env python3
import requests
from requests.auth import HTTPBasicAuth
requests.get('https://api.github.com/user', auth=HTTPBasicAuth('user',
'password'))
# requests provides a shorthand for this authentication method
response = requests.get('https://api.github.com/user', auth=('user',
'password'))
print('Response.status_code:'+ str(response.status_code))
if response.status_code == 200:
print('Login successful :'+response.text)
```

HTTP Digest authentication

HTTP Digest is a mechanism used to improve the Basic authentication process in the HTTP protocol. MD5 is normally used to encrypt the user information, key, and realm, although other algorithms, such as SHA, can also be used in its different variants, which improve security.

Digest access authentication extends Basic access authentication by using a one-way hashing cryptographic algorithm (MD5) to first encrypt authentication information, and then add a unique connection value.

This value is used by the client browser in the process of calculating the password response in the hash format. Although the password is obfuscated by the use of a cryptographic hash, and the use of the unique value prevents the threat of a replay attack, the login name is sent as plain text.

Assuming we have a URL protected with this type of authentication, in Python, it would be as follows:

```python
>>> import requests
>>> from requests.auth import HTTPDigestAuth
>>> response = requests.get(protectedURL, auth=HTTPDigestAuth(user,passwd))
```

We can use this script to test access to a protected-resource Digest Authentication. The script is similar to the previous one with Basic Authentication. The main difference is the part where we send the username and password over the protected URL, http://httpbin.org/digest-auth/auth/user/pass.

In this screenshot, we can see that with Digest Authentication, the authorization request header is established with the `username`, `realm`, and the `MD5` algorithm:

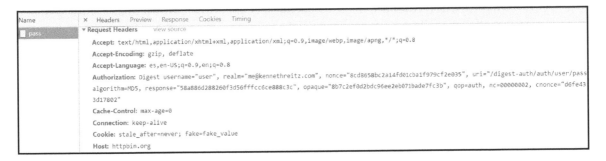

You can find the following code in the `digest_authentication.py` file:

```python
#!/usr/bin/env python3
import requests
from requests.auth import HTTPDigestAuth

url = 'http://httpbin.org/digest-auth/auth/user/pass'

response = requests.get(url, auth=HTTPDigestAuth('user', 'pass'))
print('Response.status_code:'+ str(response.status_code))
if response.status_code == 200:
    print('Login successful :'+str(response.json()))
```

Summary

In this chapter, we learned principles of the HTTP . We saw how to perform numerous fundamental tasks with the `urllib` standard library and the third-party Requests packages.

For each library, we learned about the structure of HTTP messages, HTTP status codes, the different headers that we may encounter in `requests` and `responses`, and how to interpret and use them to customize our requests. We also covered how to handle cookies and how to submit data to websites in the manner of submitting a form on a web page, and how to extract the parameters that we need from a page's source code.

In the next chapter, we'll be employing what we've learned here to carry out detailed interactions with different web services, query APIs for data, and upload our own objects to the web.

Questions

1. Which function from the `urllib` package is used to create an object similar to a file with which to read from the URL?
2. Which lines of information contain specific metadata about the response and tell the client how to interpret it?
3. Which header allows us to identify the browser we are using in every request?
4. Which modules allow us to extract links and parse text files formatted in HTML?
5. Which module and service can we use to get information about the domain we are analyzing, such as an IP address and location?
6. Which method can we use to define a proxy or intermediate machine between our internal network and the external network, using the Requests package?
7. What is the main purpose of using cookies?
8. Which object is used for working with cookies with the `urllib` package?
9. Which object is used for working with cookies with the Requests package?
10. Which mechanism is used to improve the Basic Authentication process by using a one-way hashing cryptographic algorithm (MD5)?

Further reading

You will find more information about the aforementioned tools and the official Python documentation for some of the modules discussed at the following links:

- The official documentation for the `urllib` package: `https://docs.python.org/3/library/urllib.request.html#module-urllib.request`
- Some more examples for the `urllib` package: `https://pythonspot.com/urllib-tutorial-python-3/`
- The official documentation for the HTML parser package: `https://docs.python.org/3/library/html.parser.html`
- The official documentation for the Requests package: `http://docs.python-requests.org/en/latest`
- The official documentation for the authentication package: `http://docs.python-requests.org/en/master/user/authentication/`

Section 2: Interacting with APIs, Web Scraping, and Server Scripting

2

In this section, you will learn how to interact with APIs, how to perform web scraping with BeautifulSoup and Scrapy, and how to use server scripting to interact with SMTP, SSH, FTP, SNMP, and LDAP servers.

This section contains the following chapters:

- Chapter 3, *Application Programming Interface in Action*
- Chapter 4, *Web Scraping with BeautifulSoup and Scrapy*
- Chapter 5, *Engaging with Email*
- Chapter 6, *Interacting with Remote Systems*

Application Programming Interface in Action

3

When we talk about APIs in relation to Python, we usually refer to the classes and the functions that a module presents to us for interact action. In this chapter, we'll be talking about something different, that is, web APIs.

A web API is a type of API that you interact with through the HTTP protocol. Nowadays, many web services provide a sct of HTTP calls, which are designed to be used programmatically by clients; they are meant to be used by machines rather than by humans. Through these interfaces, it's possible to automate interaction with the services and to perform tasks such as extracting data, configuring the service in some way, and uploading your own content to the service.

The following topics will be covered in this chapter:

- Introduction to REST APIs
- Introduction to JSON and the `json` module
- Interacting with a JSON hybrid-REST API (Twitter)
- Introduction to XML
- Working with XML and a full REST API (Amazon S3 bucket) with the Boto module

You will learn how to use Python to extract data from the major data formats found on the web: HTML, XML, and JSON. An example of pulling useful information from a downloaded web page will be used to illustrate HTML, while interactions with REST APIs will be used to guide you through the essentials of working with XML and JSON.

Technical requirements

Examples and source code for this chapter are available in the GitHub repository in the `Chapter03` folder: `https://github.com/PacktPublishing/Learning-Python-Networking-Second-Edition`.

You will need to install Python's version 3 distribution on your local machine and activate Twitter and Amazon Web Services accounts at the following links:

- `https://developer.twitter.com`
- `https://console.aws.amazon.com`

Introduction to REST APIs

REST is a fairly academic concept about how HTTP should be used for APIs. Although the properties that an API should possess so as to be considered RESTful are quite specific, in practice pretty much any API that is based on HTTP is now slapped with the RESTful label.

REST is any interface between systems that uses HTTP to obtain data or generate operations on that data in all possible formats, such as XML and JSON. It is a booming alternative to other standard data exchange protocols such as the **Simple Object Access Protocol** (**SOAP**), which has great capacity but also a lot of complexity. Sometimes a simpler data manipulation solution such as REST is preferable.

Advantages of using REST APIs

Some advantages of REST APIs are as follows:

- **Automation**: APIs enable and facilitate automatic processes with great ease. You can use an API of some web service in your own code to automate tasks such as checking your timeline, posting a message, and so on.
- **Separation between the client and the server**: The REST protocol completely separates the user interface of the server and the storage of data. That has some advantages when making developments. For example, it improves the portability of the interface to other platforms, increases the scalability of the projects, and allows the different components of the developments to evolve independently.

- **External database access**: APIs allow website visitors to access remote, password-protected databases. Your API password and username authorizes permission for information to be exchanged between your website and the API's database-driven resources.
- **Visibility, reliability, and scalability**: The separation between client and server has an evident advantage: any development team can scale the product without excessive problems. You can migrate to other servers or make all kinds of changes in the database, as long as the data of each of the requests is sent correctly. This separation makes it easier to have the frontend and backend on different servers, and that makes the applications more flexible when it comes to working.
- **The REST API is always independent of the type of platform or language**: The REST APIs always adapt to the type of syntax or platforms with which they are working, which offers great freedom when changing or testing new environments during development. With a REST API you can have PHP, Java, Python, or Node.js servers. The only thing that is essential is that the responses to requests are always made in the information exchange language used, usually XML or JSON.

Introduction to JSON and the JSON module

In this section, we will learn how to work with the JSON data format, how to convert Python objects into the JSON data format, and how to convert them back to Python objects in Python 3.7.

JSON corresponds to the way in which objects are defined in JavaScript. JSON is a standard way of representing simple objects, such as lists and dictionaries, in the form of text strings. Although it was originally developed for JavaScript, JSON is language-independent and most languages can work with it. It's lightweight, yet flexible enough to handle a broad range of data. This makes it ideal for exchanging data over HTTP, and a large number of web APIs use this as their primary data format.

Encoding and decoding with the JSON package

We use the `json` module for working with JSON in Python. The `json` package allows you to transform a Python object into a character string that represents those objects in JSON format. Let's create a `json` representation of a Python list by using the following commands:

```
>>> import json
>>> books = ['book1', 'book2', 'book3']
>>> json.dumps(books)
'["book1", "book2", "book3"]'
```

The `json.dumps()` function allows you to transform a dictionary-type object as the first parameter into a text string in JSON format. In this case, we can see the JSON string appears to be identical to Python's own representation of a list, but note that this is a string. You can confirm this by executing the following commands:

```
>>> string_books = json.dumps(['book1', 'book2', 'book3'])
>>> type(string_books)
<class 'str'>
```

The `json.loads()` function transforms a character string that contains information in JSON format and transforms it into a dictionary Python-type object. Typically, we will receive a JSON string as the body of an HTTP response, which can simply be decoded using `json.loads()` to provide immediately usable Python objects:

```
>>> books = '["book1", "book2", "book3"]'
>>> list = json.loads(books)
>>> list
['book1', 'book2', 'book3']
>>> list[1]
'book2'
```

We can also use the load method to extract the Python object whose representation in JSON format is in the `books.json` file. In the output, we can see that the type returned is a dictionary when reading a JSON file.

You can find the following code in the `read_books_json.py` file:

```
import json
with open("books.json", "rt") as file:
    books = json.load(file)

print(books)

print(type(books))
```

The following is the output for the execution of the previous script:

```
{'title': 'Learning Python 3', 'author': 'author', 'publisher': 'Packt
Publishing', 'pageCount': 500, 'numberOfChapters': 12, 'chapters':
[{'chapterNumber': 1, 'chapterTitle': 'Python Fundamentals', 'pageCount':
30}, {'chapterNumber': 2, 'chapterTitle': 'Chapter 2', 'pageCount': 25}]}
 <class 'dict'>
```

Using dict with JSON

JSON natively supports a mapping-type object, which is equivalent to a Python dictionary. This means that we can work directly with dict through JSON. In this example, we import the json package and we display the contents of the dictionary-type object called books in JSON format:

```
>>> import json
>>> books = {'A':'Book1', 'B':'Book2', 'C':'Book3'}
>>> type(books)
<class 'dict'>
>>> books['A']
'Book1'
>>> books['B']
'Book2'
>>> books['C']
'Book3'
>>> books['D']
Traceback (most recent call last):
 File "<stdin>", line 1, in <module>
KeyError: 'D'
>>> json.dumps(books)
'{"A": "Book1", "B": "Book2", "C": "Book3"}'
Now the text string resulting from the conversion will be linked to the
name books_json.
>>> books_json = json.dumps(books)
>>> print(books_json)
 {"A": "Book1", "B": "Book2", "C": "Book3"}
The string with the representation of an object in JSON format will be
transformed to a Python object.
>>> json.loads(books_json)
 {'A': 'Book1', 'B': 'Book2', 'C': 'Book3'}
```

Interacting with a JSON hybrid-REST API (Twitter)

In this section, we will learn how to manage and interact with the Twitter API in Python 3.7.

The Twitter API

The Twitter API provides access to all the functions that we may want a Twitter client to perform. With the Twitter API, we can create clients that search for recent Tweets, find out what's trending, look up user details, follow users' timelines, and even act on behalf of users by posting tweets and sending direct messages for them.

The Twitter module is based on the Twitter REST API located at `https://developer.twitter.com/en/docs/tweets/search/api-reference.html`.

You can install it with the `pip install twitter` command:

```
Collecting twitter
 Downloading
https://files.pythonhosted.org/packages/85/e2/f602e3f584503f03e0389491b2514
64f8ecfe2596ac86e6b9068fe7419d3/twitter-1.18.0-py2.py3-none-any.whl (54kB)
    100% |████████████████████████████████| 61kB 655kB/s
 Installing collected packages: twitter
 Successfully installed twitter-1.18.0
```

Now we can import the `twitter` module and show information about it with the `help` function:

```
>>> import twitter
>>> help(twitter)
```

This gives us the following output:

```
>>> help(twitter)
Help on package twitter:

NAME
    twitter - The minimalist yet fully featured Twitter API and Python toolset.

DESCRIPTION
    The Twitter and TwitterStream classes are the key to building your own
    Twitter-enabled applications.


    The Twitter class
    -----------------

    The minimalist yet fully featured Twitter API class.

    Get RESTful data by accessing members of this class. The result
    is decoded python objects (lists and dicts).

    The Twitter API is documented at:

      https://dev.twitter.com/overview/documentation

    The list of most accessible functions is listed at:

      https://dev.twitter.com/rest/public
```

Also, we can see some examples of using the API:

```
Examples::

    from twitter import *

    t = Twitter(
        auth=OAuth(token, token_secret, consumer_key, consumer_secret))

    # Get your "home" timeline
    t.statuses.home_timeline()

    # Get a particular friend's timeline
    t.statuses.user_timeline(screen_name="billybob")

    # to pass in GET/POST parameters, such as `count`
    t.statuses.home_timeline(count=5)

    # to pass in the GET/POST parameter `id` you need to use `_id`
    t.statuses.oembed(_id=1234567890)

    # Update your status
    t.statuses.update(
        status="Using @sixohsix's sweet Python Twitter Tools.")

    # Send a direct message
    t.direct_messages.new(
        user="billybob",
        text="I think yer swell!")
```

Registering your application for the Twitter API

We need to create a Twitter account and register our application with the account. Then we will receive the authentication credentials for our app. To create an account, go to `http://www.twitter.com` and complete the signup process. Do the following to register your application once you have a Twitter account:

1. Log in to `http://apps.twitter.com` with your main Twitter account, and then select **Create New App**.
2. Fill out the new app form. Note that Twitter application names need to be unique globally.
3. Go to the app's settings and then change the app permissions to have read and write access. You may need to register your mobile number to enable this.

Now we need to get our access credentials by following the next steps:

1. Go to the **Keys** and **Access tokens** section and then note the **Consumer key** and the **Access Secret**
2. Generate an **Access token**
3. Note down the **Access token** and the **Access token secret** (**Access token secret** is generated form the **Consumer key** and **Access secret**)

Authenticating requests with OAuth

We now have enough information for authenticating requests. Twitter uses an authentication standard called OAuth, version 2.0. It's described in detail at `http://oauth.net/`.

OAuth credentials comprise of two main elements, consumer and access. The consumer element identifies our application and the access element proves that the account the access credentials came from authorized our app to act on its behalf. Twitter lets us acquire the access credentials directly from the `dev.twitter.com` interface.

The OAuthLib library (`https://oauthlib.readthedocs.io/en/latest`) is a library that allows authentication to a server using the OAuth protocol. Sites such as Facebook, Twitter, LinkedIn, GitHub, and Google, among others, use this protocol.

The Requests module has a library called `requests-oauthlib` (`http://requests-oauthlib.readthedocs.io/en/latest`), which can handle most of the complexity for us. This is available on PyPI, so we can download and install it with `pip`. This library allows access to sites that use this protocol using OAuthLib:

```
$ pip install requests-oauthlib
```

This authentication process is demonstrated in the Requests-OAuthlib documentation, which can be found at: `https://requests-oauthlib.readthedocs.org/en/latest/oauth1_workflow.html`.

Collecting information from Twitter

Twitter has a REST API that allows you to control an account and perform very specific searches using several types of filters. To make queries, it is necessary to have an application on Twitter linked to an account and a series of values that correspond to the OAuth authentication tokens.

The Twitter API has a fairly broad list of functions that can be invoked from any client, be it a custom-developed program or even a web browser, since being an API REST, it uses the HTTP protocol as a transfer protocol.

The documentation on the Twitter API is available at `https://dev.twitter.com/rest/public`:

Search Tweets

Use the Search API to find historical Tweets. Free to enterprise versions available.

Learn more

Filter realtime Tweets

Get only the Tweets you need by using advanced filtering tools with the realtime streaming API.

Learn more

Account Activity API

Have 15+ account activities delivered to you in realtime via a webhook connection.

Learn more

Direct Message API

Build personalized customer experiences with our Direct Message platform.

Learn more

In addition to the REST API, there are also some other libraries, such as the streaming API and Twitter for websites. More details about these and other libraries can be found at the following link: `https://dev.twitter.com/overview/documentation`.

A Twitter client

In this example, we will connect to the Twitter API, which uses the OAuth protocol. You'll need to provide a credentials file with the keys you have taken down from the Twitter app configuration. This is the format of `credentials.txt` file, where we use a new line for each key or token:

- CONSUMER_KEY
- CONSUMER_SECRET
- OAUTH_TOKEN
- OAUTH_TOKEN_SECRET

You can find the following code in the `twitter_connect.py` file:

```python
!/usr/bin/python3

import requests, requests_oauthlib, sys

def init_auth(file):
    (CONSUMER_KEY,CONSUMER_SECRET,OAUTH_TOKEN,OAUTH_TOKEN_SECRET) =
open(file, 'r').read().splitlines()
    auth_obj = requests_oauthlib.OAuth1(CONSUMER_KEY,
CONSUMER_SECRET,OAUTH_TOKEN, OAUTH_TOKEN_SECRET)
    if verify_credentials(auth_obj):
        print('Validated credentials OK')
        return auth_obj
    else:
        print('Credentials validation failed')
        sys.exit(1)

def verify_credentials(auth_obj):
    url = 'https://api.twitter.com/1.1/account/verify_credentials.json'
    response = requests.get(url, auth=auth_obj)
    return response.status_code == 200

if __name__ == '__main__':
    auth_obj = init_auth('credentials.txt')
```

In the previous script, we create the OAuth1 authentication instance, `auth_obj`, in the `init_auth()` function by using our access credentials. We pass this to Requests whenever we need to make an HTTP Request, and through it, Requests handles the authentication. You can see an example of this in the `verify_credentials()` function.

In the `verify_credentials()` function, we test whether Twitter recognizes our credentials. The URL that we're using here is an endpoint that Twitter provides for testing whether our credentials are valid. It returns an HTTP 200 status code if they are valid or a 401 status code if not.

Retrieving tweets from a timeline

In the previous script, we can add a `get_mentions()` function for checking and retrieving new tweets from our mentions timeline. For this task, we can use the timeline endpoint at `https://developer.twitter.com/en/docs/tweets/timelines/api-reference/get-statuses-mentions_timeline.html`.

You can find the following code in the `twitter_mentions.py` file:

```
#! /usr/bin/python3
import requests
import requests_oauthlib
import sys
import json

def init_auth(file):
    (CONSUMER_KEY,CONSUMER_SECRET,OAUTH_TOKEN,OAUTH_TOKEN_SECRET) =
open(file, 'r').read().splitlines()
    auth_obj = requests_oauthlib.OAuth1(CONSUMER_KEY, CONSUMER_SECRET,
    OAUTH_TOKEN, OAUTH_TOKEN_SECRET)
    if verify_credentials(auth_obj):
        print('Validated credentials OK')
        return auth_obj
    else:
        print('Credentials validation failed')
        sys.exit(1)

def verify_credentials(auth_obj):
    url = 'https://api.twitter.com/1.1/account/verify_credentials.json'
    response = requests.get(url, auth=auth_obj)
    return response.status_code == 200

def get_mentions(since_id, auth_obj):
    params = {'count': 200, 'since_id': since_id,'include_rts': 0,
'include_entities': 'false'}
```

```
    url = 'https://api.twitter.com/1.1/statuses/mentions_timeline.json'
    response = requests.get(url, params=params, auth=auth_obj)
    #Checking if the request is successful.
  #It will raise an HTTPError if the request returned an unsuccessful status
code.
    response.raise_for_status()
    return json.loads(response.text)

if __name__ == '__main__':
    auth_obj = init_auth('credentials.txt')
    since_id = 1
    for tweet in get_mentions(since_id, auth_obj):
        print(tweet['text'])
```

Using `get_mentions()`, we check for and download any tweets that mention our app account by connecting to the `statuses/mentions_timeline.json` endpoint. We supply a number of parameters, which Requests passes on as a query string. These parameters are specified by Twitter and they control how the tweets will be returned to us. They are as follows:

- `'count'`: This specifies the maximum number of tweets that will be returned. Twitter will allow 200 tweets to be received by a single request made to this endpoint.
- `'include_entities'`: This is used for trimming down some extraneous information from the tweets retrieved.
- `'include_rts'`: This tells Twitter not to include any retweets. We don't want the user to receive another time update if someone retweets our reply.
- `'since_id'`: This tells Twitter to only return the tweets with IDs above this value. Every tweet has a unique 64-bit integer ID, and later tweets have higher value IDs than earlier tweets. By remembering the ID of the last tweet we processed and then passing it as this parameter, Twitter will filter out the tweets that we've already seen.

Searching tweets

In the previous script, we can add a `search()` function to search for and retrieve tweets from a specific search parameter. In this example, we are using the `'q'` parameter with the `'python'` value as search term. For this task, we can use the search endpoint at https://developer.twitter.com/en/docs/tweets/search/api-reference/get-search-tweets.html. The endpoint (https://api.twitter.com/1.1/search/tweets.json) requires the search term as a mandatory parameter.

You can find the following code in the `twitter_search_tag.py` file:

```python
#! /usr/bin/python3

import requests
import requests_oauthlib
import sys
import json

def verify_credentials(auth_obj):
    url = 'https://api.twitter.com/1.1/account/verify_credentials.json'
    response = requests.get(url, auth=auth_obj)
    return response.status_code == 200

def search(auth_obj):
    params = {'q': 'python'}
    url = 'https://api.twitter.com/1.1/search/tweets.json'
    response = requests.get(url, params=params, auth=auth_obj)
    return response

if __name__ == '__main__':
    auth_obj = init_auth('credentials.txt')
    response = search(auth_obj)
    print (json.dumps(response.json(),indent = 2))
```

In this screenshot, we can see the execution of the previous script:

```
Validated credentials OK
{
  "statuses": [
    {
      "created_at": "Tue Dec 04 18:02:08 +0000 2018",
      "id": 1070015412702732289,
      "id_str": "1070015412702732289",
      "text": "My workflow for developing Python packages is *completely* different from how I approach data analysis.\n\nI'd never\u
26 https://t.co/uMFa6JVo8p",
      "truncated": true,
      "entities": {
        "hashtags": [],
        "symbols": [],
        "user_mentions": [],
        "urls": [
          {
            "url": "https://t.co/uMFa6JVo8p",
            "expanded_url": "https://twitter.com/i/web/status/1070015412702732289",
            "display_url": "twitter.com/i/web/status/1\u2026",
            "indices": [
              116,
              139
            ]
          }
        ]
      },
      "metadata": {
        "iso_language_code": "en",
        "result_type": "recent"
      },
```

Consuming the Twitter REST API with Python

REST services can be used with standard HTTP Requests and, in any case, if the service requires it, the requests must contain specific headers that allow authentication and authorization processes.

Starting with this, there are several possibilities to create a Python script that can consume a REST service, for example using the `urllib` module or other libraries written by third parties such as `urllib3` or `requests`.

There are other modules for working with Twitter from Python, such as **Tweepy** (`https://github.com/tweepy/tweepy`) and **Python-Twitter** (`https://github.com/bear/python-twitter`).

To access the Twitter API, it is necessary to have developer credentials. These credentials can be obtained from `https://apps.twitter.com` when creating a new application. The data that will be used includes the following:

- Consumer key
- Consumer secret
- OAuth token
- OAuth token secret

These keys will be needed to make the connection with the API through OAuth and allow our application to use our account, since to access certain functionalities of the API we will have to be logged in.

After ensuring the necessary authentication values correspond to the application previously created, the next step is to use the library to consume some of the REST services available in the Twitter API. To do this, the first step is to create a `twitter.oauth.OAuth` object.

If the authentication values are correct, the instance of the API class will contain all the methods necessary to consume the Twitter rest services.

Connecting with the Twitter API

To be able to use the Twitter API, it is necessary to create an object based on the `twitter.Twitter` class, which will result in an object capable of interacting with the Twitter API that must be defined using the `auth` parameter:

```
>>> twitter.Twitter (auth = <object twitter.oauth.OAuth>)
```

The argument for the auth parameter must be an instantiated object of the twitter.oauth.OAuth class for which the Twitter access credentials must be entered:

```
>>>
twitter.oauth.OAuth(CONSUMER_KEY, CONSUMER_SECRET, ACCESS_TOKEN, ACCESS_TOKEN_
SECRET)
```

For example, this function allows you to read the credentials from a file whose path will be entered as a parameter and to return a twitter.Twitter object with an active connection to the Twitter API:

```
def twitter_connection(path_file):
    with open(path_file, 'r') as file:
        (CONSUMER_KEY,
        CONSUMER_SECRET,
        ACCESS_TOKEN,
        ACCESS_TOKEN_SECRET) = archivo.read().splitlines()
        auth = twitter.oauth.OAuth(ACCESS_TOKEN,
                            ACCESS_TOKEN_SECRET,
                            CONSUMER_KEY,
                            CONSUMER_SECRET)
        return twitter.Twitter(auth=auth)
```

In this case, the credentials will be read from the data/credentials.txt file. We can invoke the previous function with the credentials file as a parameter:

```
>>> twitter = twitter_connection("data/credentials.txt")
```

From here, you can create scripts that allow you to extract information of interest, such as taking a list of tweets from a specific account or searching for a specific hashtag.

The following example allows you to extract the first 10 tweets that match the "#python" hashtag. You can find the following code in the get_info_account.py file:

```
import twitter

def get_info_twitter(tw):
    if tw is not None:
        query = tw.search.tweets(q="#python", lang="en",
count="10")["statuses"]
        for q in query:
            for key,value in q.items():
                if(key=='text'):
                    print(value+'\n')

def main():
    try:
```

```
        tw = twitter_connection("credentials.txt")
        get_info_twitter(tw)
    except Exception as e:
        print(str(e))

if __name__ == "__main__":
    main()
```

In this screenshot, we can see the execution of the previous script:

```
RT @SecurityTube: @ppolstra #windowsForensics Book https://t.co/2r1RwbIaWD Learn to create, mount &amp; analyze filesystem images wi
#python…

RT @Real_Shit_News: weather sent by #RaspberryPi, #Python and #Yahoo weather API. Yahoo API is pretty good.

RT @Real_Shit_News: #RaspberryPI and #Python weather App. #Twython

#RaspberryPI and #Python weather App. #Twython

weather sent by #RaspberryPi, #Python and #Yahoo weather API. Yahoo API is pretty good.

RT @Ronald_vanLoon: #MachineLearning Is Not Magic: It's All About Math, Stats, Data, and Programming
  by @janakiramm @thenewstack |

Read f…

@ppolstra #windowsForensics Book https://t.co/2r1RwbIaWD Learn to create, mount &amp; analyze filesystem images with… https://t.co/N
SqhVlD

Python Game Development™ : Build 11 Total Games

⎘ https://t.co/u5OPMHBRj3

#python #GameDevelopment https://t.co/bLO1FOBuEY
```

Accessing Twitter API resources

The created object has access to the GET and POST resources of the Twitter API, which are listed in the reference index: https://developer.twitter.com/en/docs/api-reference-index.

The Twitter package transforms the responses of the Twitter API, of JSON format, to a Python object. The Twitter API uses the JSON format by default to transmit information, but the Twitter module transforms the information into a dictionary-type object. This query returns the last two tweets related to Python in the English language:

```
>>> search= twitter.search.tweets(q="python", lang="en", count="2")
>>> for item in search.keys():
>>>     print(item)
```

In this script, we can see an example of an application that consumes the Twitter API, gets a search term from the user input, and saves the results in a JSON file. You can find the following code in the `twitter_search.py` file:

```
#! /usr/bin/python3
import twitter, json
```

```
def twitter_connection(file):
    '''Create the object from which the Twitter API will be
consumed, reading the credentials from a file, defined in path parameter.'''
    (CONSUMER_KEY,CONSUMER_SECRET,OAUTH_TOKEN,OAUTH_TOKEN_SECRET) =
open(file, 'r').read().splitlines()
    auth =
twitter.oauth.OAuth(OAUTH_TOKEN,OAUTH_TOKEN_SECRET,CONSUMER_KEY,CONSUMER_SE
CRET)
    return twitter.Twitter(auth=auth)

def recently_tweets(tw, search_term):
    '''Get the last 10 tweets in English from a specific search.'''
    search = tw.search.tweets(q=search_term, lang="en",
count="10")["statuses"]
    print(search)
    return search

def save_tweets(tweets, file):
    '''Store the tweets in JSON format in the specified file.'''
    with open(file, "w") as f:
        json.dump(tweets, f, indent=1)

def main(file='tweets.json'):
    try:
        search_term = input("Enter the search term in twitter : ")
        tw = twitter_connection("credentials.txt")
        tweets = recently_tweets(tw, search_term)
        save_tweets(tweets, file)
    except Exception as e:
        print(str(e))

if __name__ == "__main__":
    main()
```

Streaming APIs with Tweepy

We can use the `tweepy` library to connect to the Twitter API. In this example, we will use a streaming API to process data in real time.

In the same way as we have done before with the Twitter module, we can create our function for connecting with OAuth credentials:

```
def twitter_connection(file):
    '''Create the object from which the Twitter API will be consumed,
    reading the credentials from a file, defined in path parameter.'''
    (CONSUMER_KEY,CONSUMER_SECRET,OAUTH_TOKEN,OAUTH_TOKEN_SECRET) =
```

```
open(file, 'r').read().splitlines()
    # We instanced the authorization manager
    auth = tweepy.OAuthHandler(CONSUMER_KEY,CONSUMER_SECRET)
    auth.set_access_token(OAUTH_TOKEN,OAUTH_TOKEN_SECRET)
    return (tweepy.API(auth), auth)
```

The first thing we can do is create a class inherited from `tweepy.StreamListener`. This will be the class that is listening the flow of tweets and will process a tweet that matches the term we are looking for:

```
class StreamListener(tweepy.StreamListener):
    '''When a Tweet matches our targetTerms it will be passed to this
function'''
    def on_data(self, data):
        data = json.loads(data)
        print(data['text'])
        return True

    # If we reach the limit of calls alert and wait 10 "
    def on_limit(self, track):
        print('[!] Limit: {0}').format(track)
        sleep(10)

    # In case of an error, interrupt the listener
    # https://dev.twitter.com/overview/api/response-codes
    def on_error(self, status):
        print('[!] Error: {0}').format(status)
            return False
```

We can create a function that uses the Tweepy API to extract information about trending topics from Twitter:

```
def getTrendingTopics(woeid=1):
    trends = api.trends_place(1)[0]['trends']
    # We extract the name of the trends and return them as a list
    trendList = [trend['name'] for trend in trends]
    return trendList
```

To tell the listener what our keywords will be and for it to be able to use them, we will add the following function to our project:

```
def streamAPI(auth):
    # instantiate our listener
    l = StreamListener()
    # We start the streamer with the OAuth object and the listener
    streamer = tweepy.Stream(auth=auth, listener=l)
    # We define the terms that we want to track
    targetTerms = ['python']
```

```
#We start the streamer, passing it our trackTerms
streamer.filter(track=targetTerms)
```

We'll call it, passing it our authentication `auth` object in the following way:

```
try:
    streamAPI(auth)
except KeyboardInterrupt, e:
    exit(1)
```

In this screenshot, we can see the execution of the `twitter_stream.py` script used to track Python terms when they appear in the Twitter timeline, and tweets tagged with Python:

Introduction to XML

In this section, we will learn how to work with XML documents, parse them, and extract data from them by using the ElementTree API in Python 3.7. We're going to start by introducing how XML is used in Python, and then we will explain an XML-based API called the Amazon S3 API.

Getting started with XML

XML corresponds to a general standard to serialize data of diverse types in a structured way. The XML standard was published in 1996 by W3C and is used intensively to define data structures.

An XML document is known as an element and contains data structures based on content delimited by markers (markups). These markers correspond to labels (tags) that indicate the beginning and end of the structure they delimit.

The XML is a way of representing hierarchical data in a standard text format. When working with XML-based web APIs, we'll be creating XML documents and sending them as the bodies of HTTP Requests and receiving XML documents as the bodies of responses.

The XML APIs

There are two main approaches to working with XML data:

- Reading a whole document and creating an object-based representation of it, then manipulating it by using an object-oriented API
- Processing the document from start to end, and performing actions as specific tags are encountered

For now, we're going to focus on the object-based approach by using a Python XML API called ElementTree. The second so-called pull or event-based approach (also often called SAX, as SAX is one of the most popular APIs in this category) is more complicated to set up, and is only needed for processing large XML files.

Processing XML with ElementTree

The `xml` package is part of the Python standard library and contains in turn a series of packages and modules specializing in the management and manipulation of keyed documents.

The `xml.etree.ElementTree` package specializes in XML documents and contains various classes and functions that can be used for that purpose.

Let's see how we may create the previously mentioned example XML document by using `ElementTree`. Open a Python interpreter and run the following commands:

```
>>> import xml.etree.ElementTree as ET
>>> root = ET.Element('root')
>>> ET.dump(root)
<root />
```

We start by creating the root element, that is, the outermost element of the document. The `<root />` representation is an XML shortcut for `<root></root>`. It's used to show an empty element, that is, an element with no data and no child tags.

We create the `<root>` element by creating a new `ElementTree.Element` object. You'll notice that the argument we give to `Element()` is the name of the tag that is created. Our `<root>` element is empty at the moment, so let's put something in it:

```
>>> book = ET.Element('book')
>>> root.append(book)
>>> ET.dump(root)
<root><book /></root>
```

Now we have an element called `<book>` in our `<root>` element. When an element is directly nested inside another, then the nested element is called a child of the outer element, and the outer element is called the parent. Similarly, elements that are at the same level are called siblings.

Let's add another element, and this time let's give it some content. Add the following commands:

```
>>> name = ET.SubElement(book, 'name')
>>> name.text = 'Book1'
>>> ET.dump(root)
<root><book><name>Book1</name></book></root>
```

Now our document is starting to shape up. We do two new things here: first, we use the shortcut class method `ElementTree.SubElement()` to create the new <name> element and insert it into the tree as a child of <book> in a single operation. Second, we give it some content by assigning some text to the element's text attribute.

We can remove elements by using the `remove()` method on the parent element, as shown in the following commands:

```
>>> temp = ET.SubElement(root, 'temp')
>>> ET.dump(root)
<root><book><name>Book1</name></book><temp /></root>
>>> root.remove(temp)
>>> ET.dump(root)
<root><book><name>Book1</name></book></root>
```

Pretty printing

It would be useful for us to be able to produce output in a more legible format, such as the example shown at the beginning of this section. To do this, we can use another XML API, `minidom`, provided by the standard library.

We can use the following commands to print some nicely formatted XML:

```
>>> import xml.dom.minidom as minidom
>>> print(minidom.parseString(ET.tostring(root)).toprettyxml())
<?xml version="1.0" ?>
<root>
        <book>
                <name>Book1</name>
        </book>
</root>
```

Reading an XML file

The `xml.etree.ElementTree` module contains the `Element` class, which allows you to inspect an XML document by accessing its methods and attributes, as well as the indexing of its elements.

In this example, we are reading an XML file called `books.xml`:

```
<?xml version="1.0" encoding="UTF-8"?>
<root>
 <book id="book1" name="Learning Python 2">
 <title>Learning Python 2</title>
```

```
<publisher>Packt Publishing</publisher>
<numberOfChapters>13</numberOfChapters>
<pageCount>500</pageCount>
<author>Author1</author>
<chapters>
<chapter>
<chapterNumber>1</chapterNumber>
<chapterTitle>Chapter1</chapterTitle>
<pageCount>30</pageCount>
</chapter>
<chapter>
<chapterNumber>2</chapterNumber>
<chapterTitle>Chapter2</chapterTitle>
<pageCount>25</pageCount>
</chapter>
</chapters>
</book>
<book id="book2" name="Learning Python 3">
<title>Learning Python 3</title>
<publisher>Packt Publishing</publisher>
<numberOfChapters>10</numberOfChapters>
<pageCount>400</pageCount>
<author>Author2</author>
<chapters>
<chapter>
<chapterNumber>1</chapterNumber>
<chapterTitle>Chapter1</chapterTitle>
<pageCount>30</pageCount>
</chapter>
<chapter>
<chapterNumber>2</chapterNumber>
<chapterTitle>Chapter2</chapterTitle>
<pageCount>25</pageCount>
</chapter>
</chapters>
</book>
</root>
```

We can use the parse method from the ElementTree module for reading an XML file, passing as an argument the path of the XML file. This is the definition of the parse method:

```
Elementtree.parse('<path_xml_file>')
```

In this example we are using the parse method to process the books.xml file:

```
>>> import xml.etree.ElementTree as ET
>>> books = ET.parse("books.xml")
```

With the `getroot()` method, we can access the node root:

```
>>> root = books.getroot()
>>> print(root)
<Element 'root' at 0x02F5DA20>
```

With the `tag` property, we can access the string identifying what kind of data this element represents:

```
>>> print(root.tag)
root
```

By iterating over each element, we can access attributes with the `attrib` property and access the text of a final element:

```
>>> for child in root:
>>>     print(child.tag, child.attrib)
>>>     for element in child:
>>>         print(element.tag, element.text)
```

This is the output of the previous commands, where we can see the values of each `book` element:

```
book {'id': 'book1', 'name': 'Learning Python 2'}
 title Learning Python 2
 publisher Packt Publishing
 numberOfChapters 13
 pageCount 500
 author Author1

book {'id': 'book2', 'name': 'Learning Python 3'}
 title Learning Python 3
 publisher Packt Publishing
 numberOfChapters 10
 pageCount 400
 author Author2
```

If we need access to the contents of a specific attribute, we can use the form `child.attrib['name_attribute']`:

```
>>> for child in root:
>>> print(child.tag, child.attrib['id'],child.attrib['name'])
book book1 Learning Python 2
book book2 Learning Python 3
```

In the following script we can see how we can iterate over the `books.xml` file. You can find the following code in the `books_iterate_xml.py` file:

```python
from xml.etree.cElementTree import iterparse

def books(file):
    for event, elem in iterparse(file):
        if event == 'start' and elem.tag == 'root':
            books = elem
        if event == 'end' and elem.tag == 'book':
            print('{0}, {1}, {2}, {3}, {4}'. format(elem.findtext('title'),
elem.findtext('publisher'), elem.findtext('numberOfChapters'),
elem.findtext('pageCount'),elem.findtext('author')))
        if event == 'end' and elem.tag == 'chapter':
            print('{0}, {1}, {2}'. format(elem.findtext('chapterNumber'),
elem.findtext('chapterTitle'), elem.findtext('pageCount')))

if __name__ == '__main__':
    books(open("books.xml"))
```

This is the output of the previous script, where we can see the values of each book element and the chapter elements for each book:

```
1,Chapter1,30
2,Chapter2,25
Learning Python 2,Packt Publishing,13,500,Author1
1,Chapter1,30
2,Chapter2,25
Learning Python 3,Packt Publishing,10,400,Author2
```

Working with XML and a full REST API (Amazon S3 bucket) with the Boto module

In this section, we will learn how to manage and interact with Amazon S3 bucket in Python 3.7 with the S3 API and the `boto3` package.

The Amazon S3 API

Amazon S3 is a data storage service that provides a simple API for automated access. It's one of the many cloud services in the growing AWS portfolio.

You'll notice that in the S3 documentation and elsewhere, the S3 web API is referred to as a REST API. The S3 API is actually among the most RESTful high-profile APIs, because it appropriately uses a good range of the HTTP methods.

Registering with AWS

Before we can access S3, we need to register with AWS. It is the norm for APIs to require registration before allowing access to their features. You can use either an existing Amazon account or create a new one at `https://console.aws.amazon.com`.

When you register with Amazon you will get a lot of services. In this section, we will focus on the S3 Storage service:

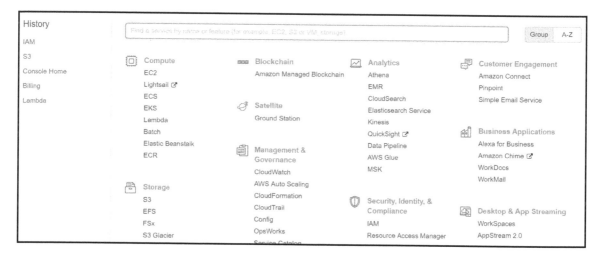

Authentication with AWS

Most web APIs we use will specify a way of supplying authentication credentials that allow requests to be made to them, and typically every HTTP Request we make must include authentication information. APIs require this information for the following reasons:

- To ensure that others can't abuse your application's access permissions
- To apply per-application rate limiting
- To manage the delegation of access rights, so that an application can act on the behalf of other users of a service or other services
- Collection of usage statistics

All of the AWS services use an HTTP Request-signing mechanism for authentication. To sign a request, we hash and sign unique data in an HTTP Request using a cryptographic key, then add the signature to the request as a header. By recreating the signature on the server, AWS can ensure that the request has been sent by us, and that it doesn't get altered in transit.

The AWS signature-generation process is currently on its fourth version, and an involved discussion would be needed to cover it, so we're going to employ a third-party library, that is, `requests-aws4auth`. This is a library for the Requests module that automatically handles signature generation for us. It's available at PyPI. So, install it on a command line with the help of `pip`:

```
$ pip install requests-aws4auth
```

Once you are logged in to the Amazon console at `https://console.aws.amazon.com`, you need to perform the steps shown here:

1. Click on your name in the top-right, and then choose **Security Credentials**.
2. Click on **Users**, which is in the list on the left-hand side of the screen, and then click on the **Create New Users** button at the top.
3. Type in the username, and make sure that **Generate an Access Key** for each user has been checked, and then click on the **Create** button in the bottom right-hand corner.
4. You'll see a new page saying that the user has been created successfully. Click on the **Download credentials** button at the bottom-right corner to download a CSV file, which contains the **Access ID** and **Access Secret** for this user. These are important because they will help in authenticating to the S3 API.
5. In the **Policies** section, a list of policy templates will appear. The policy we are going to use is the **AmazonS3FullAccess**:

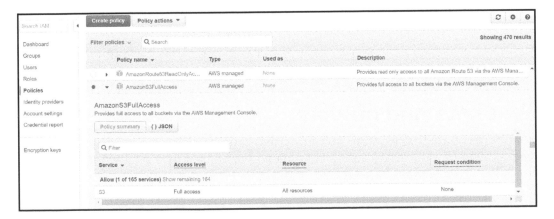

6. Scroll down this list and select the **AmazonS3FullAccess** policy, as shown in the following screenshot:

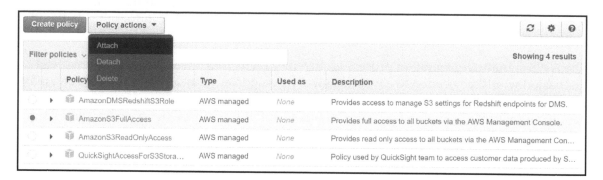

7. Finally, select the user or the user group and click on the **Attach** policy button. Now, our selected user or the user group has full access to the S3 service:

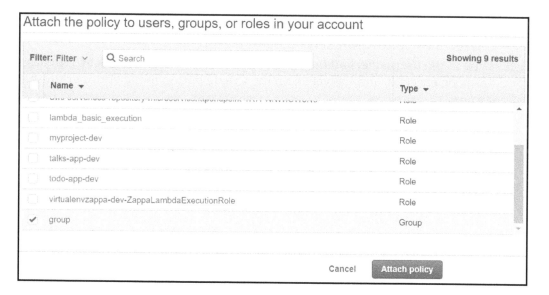

S3 buckets and objects

S3 organizes the data that we store in it using two concepts: buckets and objects. An object is the equivalent of a file, that is, a blob of data with a name, and a bucket is equivalent to a directory. Every bucket has its own URL of the form http://s3.<region>.amazonaws.com/<bucketname>.

In the URL, `<bucketname>` is the name of the bucket and `<region>` is the AWS region where the bucket is present, for example **eu-west-2**. The bucket name and region are set when we create the bucket.

Bucket names are shared globally among all S3 users, and so they must be unique. If you own a domain, then a subdomain of that will make an appropriate bucket name.

Objects are named when we first upload them. We access objects by adding the object name to the end of the bucket's URL as a path. For example, if we have a bucket called **mybucket** in the **eu-west-2** region containing the object `Python.png`, then we can access it by using `https://s3.eu-west-2.amazonaws.com/mybucket/Python.png`.

Let's create our first bucket through the AWS Console. We can perform most of the operations that the API exposes manually through this web interface, and it's a good way of checking that our API client is performing the desired tasks:

1. Log into the console at `https://console.aws.amazon.com`.
2. Go to the S3 service. You will see a page, which will prompt you to **Create bucket**.
3. Click on the **Create bucket** button.
4. Enter a bucket name, pick a region, and then click on **Create**:

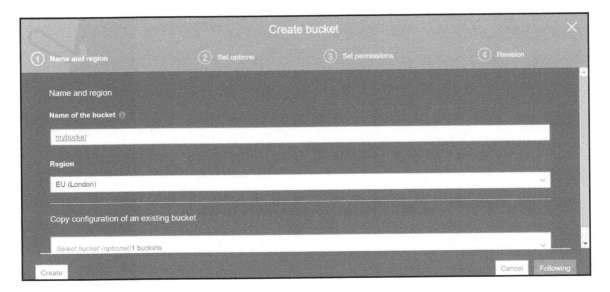

Creating a bucket with the S3 API

In this section, we are going to write a script that will enable us to interact with the service and create a bucket with the S3 API. To create a bucket, you'll need to use the `requests_aws4auth` package and the `aws4auth` method with your AWS credentials, <ACCESS_ID> and <ACCESS_KEY>. Also, you need to specify the <REGION> with the AWS region of your choice:

```
>>> import requests
>>> import requests_aws4auth
>>> auth = requests_aws4auth.AWS4Auth('<ACCESS_ID>', '<ACCESS_KEY>', 'eu-west-2', 's3')
```

Whenever we write a client for an API, our main point of reference is the API documentation. The documentation tells us how to construct the HTTP Requests for performing operations.

`http://docs.aws.amazon.com/AmazonS3/latest/API/RESTBucketPUT.html` provides the details of bucket creation. This documentation tells us that to create a bucket, we need to make an HTTP Request to our new bucket's endpoint by using the HTTP `PUT` method:

---

create_bucket(**kwargs)

Creates a new bucket.

See also: AWS API Documentation

Request Syntax

```
response = client.create_bucket(
    ACL='private'|'public-read'|'public-read-write'|'authenticated-read',
    Bucket='string',
    CreateBucketConfiguration={
        'LocationConstraint': 'EU'|'eu-west-1'|'us-west-1'|'us-west-2'|'ap-south-1'|'ap-
    },
    GrantFullControl='string',
    GrantRead='string',
    GrantReadACP='string',
    GrantWrite='string',
    GrantWriteACP='string',
    ObjectLockEnabledForBucket=True|False
)
```

We'll use this in conjunction with Requests to add AWS authentication to our API requests. The ns variable is a string that represents the namespace, which we'll need to work with XML from the S3 API:

```
ns = 'http://s3.amazonaws.com/doc/2006-03-01/'
```

You can see that the script will create a bucket from the command-line arguments and so calls the create_bucket() function, passing myBucket as an argument.

You can find the following code in the s3_create_bucket.py file:

```python
import xml.etree.ElementTree as ET

def create_bucket(bucket):
    print(bucket)
    XML = ET.Element('CreateBucketConfiguration')
    XML.attrib['xmlns'] = ns
    location = ET.SubElement(XML, 'LocationConstraint')
    location.text = auth.region
    data = ET.tostring(XML, encoding='utf-8')
    url = 'http://{}.{}'.format(bucket,endpoint)
    xml_pprint(data)
    response = requests.put(url, data=data, auth=auth)
    print(response)
    if response.ok:
        print('Created bucket {} OK'.format(bucket))
    else:
        xml_pprint(response.text)
```

We can create a method for printing the XML output:

```python
import xml.dom.minidom as minidom

def xml_pprint(xml_string):
    print(minidom.parseString(xml_string).toprettyxml())
```

For creating a bucket, we can see that it creates an XML tree with the format that is available in the S3 documentation. If you run the script, then you will see the XML shown here:

```
$ python3 s3_create_bucket.py mybucket
<?xml version="1.0" ?>
 <CreateBucketConfiguration
xmlns="http://s3.amazonaws.com/doc/2006-03-01/">
        <LocationConstraint>eu-west-2</LocationConstraint>
 </CreateBucketConfiguration>
```

This matches the format specified in the documentation. You can see that we've used the `ns` variable to fill the `xmlns` attribute. This is the code that executes the `put` request:

```
url = 'http://{}.{}'.format(bucket, endpoint)
response = requests.put(url, data=data, auth=auth)
if response.ok:
    print('Created bucket {} OK'.format(bucket))
else:
    xml_pprint(response.text)
```

The first line shown here will generate the full URL from our bucket name and endpoint. The second line will make the `put` request to the S3 API. Also, note that we have supplied our `auth` object to the call. This will allow Requests to handle all the S3 authentication for us.

If all goes well, then we print out a message. In case everything does not go as expected, we print out the response body. S3 returns error messages as XML in the response body. So we use our `xml_pprint()` function to display it.

When we refresh the S3 Console in our browser, we will see that our bucket has been created:

Uploading and downloading file

Now that we've created a bucket, we can upload and download some files. Writing a function for uploading a file is similar to creating a bucket. We check the documentation to see how to construct our HTTP Request, figure out what information should be collected at the command line, and then write the function.

We need to use an HTTP PUT again. We need the name of the bucket that we want to store the file in and the name that we want the file to be stored under in S3. The body of the request will contain the file data. At the command line, we'll collect the bucket name, the name we want the file to have in the S3 service, and the name of the local file to upload.

Note that we open the local file in binary mode. The file could contain any type of data, so we don't want text transforms applied. We could pull this data from anywhere, such as a database or another web API. Here, we just use a local file for simplicity.

The URL is the same endpoint that we constructed in `create_bucket()` with the S3 object name appended to the URL path. Later, we can use this URL to retrieve the object.

You can find the following code in the `s3_upload_download_file.py` file. This is the function we can use to upload a file to a specific bucket:

```python
def upload_file(bucket, local_path):
    data = open(local_path, 'rb').read()
    url = 'http://{}/{}/{}'.format(endpoint, bucket, local_path)
    print('upload file '+url)
    response = requests.put(url, data=data, auth=auth)
    if response.ok:
        print('Uploaded {} OK'.format(local_path))
    else:
        xml_pprint(response.text)
```

You'll need to replace bucket with your own bucket name. Once the file gets uploaded, you will see it in the S3 Console. Downloading a file through the S3 API is similar to uploading it. We simply take the bucket name, the S3 object name, and the local filename again with `GET` request instead of a `put` request, and then write the data received to disk. This is the function we can use to download a file from a specific bucket:

```python
def download_file(bucket, s3_name):
    url = 'http://{}/{}/{}'.format(endpoint, bucket, s3_name)
    print('download file '+url)
    response = requests.get(url, auth=auth)
    print(response)
    if response.ok:
        open(s3_name, 'wb').write(response.content)
```

```
        print('Downloaded {} OK'.format(s3_name))
    else:
        xml_pprint(response.text)
```

The complete script is available in the `s3_upload_download_file.py` file. We can execute it, passing the bucket name and the file we want to upload and download as arguments:

```
$python s3_upload_download_file.py bucket-aux Python.png
upload file http://s3.eu-west-2.amazonaws.com/bucket-aux/Python.png
 Uploaded Python.png OK
 download file http://s3.eu-west-2.amazonaws.com/bucket-aux/Python.png
 <Response [200]>
 Downloaded Python.png OK
```

Listing buckets

To list buckets, we need to do a get request with the AWS authentication data. Then we get the response in XML format and get the `response.text` content:

```
>>> endpoint = 's3.eu-west-2.amazonaws.com'
>>> auth = aws4auth.AWS4Auth(access_id, access_key, region, 's3')
>>> response = requests.get("http://"+endpoint, auth=auth)
>>> print(response.text)<ListAllMyBucketsResult
xmlns="http://s3.amazonaws.com/doc/2006-03-01/"><Owner><ID>e6c7c8b59da10019
0ebe74cf53f402506382c4c2889d64c426f8cfa8026e2f29</ID></Owner><Buckets><Buck
et><Name>bucket-
aux</Name><CreationDate>2018-12-11T18:33:03.000Z</CreationDate></Bucket><Bu
cket><Name>zappa-0esu8ehc9</Name><CreationDate>2018-07-23T11:19:50.000Z</Cr
eationDate></Bucket></Buckets></ListAllMyBucketsResult>
```

Now we can process our XML and convert it into an `ElementTree` tree:

```
>>> import xml.etree.ElementTree as ET
>>> root = ET.fromstring(r.text)
```

We now have an `ElementTree` instance in the `root` variable and we can extract such information from XML easily way.

The simplest way of navigating the tree is by using the elements as iterators. Iterating over the root returns each of its child elements, and then we print out the tag of an element by using the tag attribute:

```
>>> for element in root:
>>>     print('Tag: ' + element.tag)
```

You can find the following code in the s3_list_buckets.py file. This is the function we can use to list buckets to a specific AWS account:

```
def list_buckets():
    print(endpoint)
    response = requests.get("http://"+endpoint, auth=auth)
    print(response.text)
    xml_pprint(response.text)
    if response.ok:
        root = ET.fromstring(response.text)
        for element in root:
            print('Tag: ' + element.tag)
```

In this screenshot, we can see the output of the previous script execution:

```
s3.eu-west-2.amazonaws.com
<?xml version="1.0" encoding="UTF-8"?>
<ListAllMyBucketsResult xmlns="http://s3.amazonaws.com/doc/2006-03-01/"><Owner><ID>e6c7c8b59da10
0190ebe74cf53f402506382c4c2889d64c426f8cfa8026e2f29</ID></Owner><Buckets><Bucket><Name>bucket-au
x</Name><CreationDate>2018-12-11T18:33:03.000Z</CreationDate></Bucket><Bucket><Name>zappa-0esu8e
hc9</Name><CreationDate>2018-07-23T11:19:50.000Z</CreationDate></Bucket></Buckets></ListAllMyBuc
ketsResult>
<?xml version="1.0" ?>
<ListAllMyBucketsResult xmlns="http://s3.amazonaws.com/doc/2006-03-01/">
        <Owner>
                <ID>e6c7c8b59da100190ebe74cf53f402506382c4c2889d64c426f8cfa8026e2f29</ID>
        </Owner>
        <Buckets>
                <Bucket>
                        <Name>bucket-aux</Name>
                        <CreationDate>2018-12-11T18:33:03.000Z</CreationDate>
                </Bucket>
                <Bucket>
                        <Name>zappa-0esu8ehc9</Name>
                        <CreationDate>2018-07-23T11:19:50.000Z</CreationDate>
                </Bucket>
        </Buckets>
</ListAllMyBucketsResult>

Tag: {http://s3.amazonaws.com/doc/2006-03-01/}Owner
Tag: {http://s3.amazonaws.com/doc/2006-03-01/}Buckets
```

Parsing XML and handling errors

S3 embeds error messages in the XML, returned in the response body, and until now we've just been dumping the raw XML to the screen. We can improve on this and pull the text out of the XML. First, let's generate an error message so that we can see what the XML looks like. In `s3_list_buckets.py`, if we replace the access secret with an empty string, then it will produce an error.

This is the function we can use for handling errors:

```python
def handle_error(response):
    output = 'Status code: {}\n'.format(response.status_code)
    root = ET.fromstring(response.text)
    code = root.find('Code').text
    output += 'Error code: {}\n'.format(code)
    message = root.find('Message').text
    output += 'Message: {}\n'.format(message)
    print(output)
```

In you try to execute the `s3_list_buckets.py` with an empty string in the access secret, it will tell you that it can't authenticate the request because you have set a blank access secret.

In this screenshot, we can see the XML error related to `AuthorizationHeaderMalformed`:

```
<?xml version="1.0" encoding="UTF-8"?>
<Error><Code>AuthorizationHeaderMalformed</Code><Message>The authorization header is malformed
; a non-empty Access Key (AKID) must be provided in the credential.</Message><RequestId>B41C17
BDF7235401</RequestId><HostId>Mn1tkDj8gOsBunsRItjTa6SKG+/rYXsr3sAwaq5Wh3QWxzUeNK1CeAJ3MhZXDSSs
Ja7C9rD4gbA=</HostId></Error>
<?xml version="1.0" ?>
<Error>
        <Code>AuthorizationHeaderMalformed</Code>
        <Message>The authorization header is malformed; a non-empty Access Key (AKID) must be
provided in the credential.</Message>
        <RequestId>B41C17BDF7235401</RequestId>
        <HostId>Mn1tkDj8gOsBunsRItjTa6SKG+/rYXsr3sAwaq5Wh3QWxzUeNK1CeAJ3MhZXDSSsJa7C9rD4gbA=</
HostId>
</Error>

Status code: 400
Error code: AuthorizationHeaderMalformed
Message: The authorization header is malformed; a non-empty Access Key (AKID) must be provided
 in the credential.
```

Connecting to S3 with the Python Boto package

We've discussed working directly with the S3 REST API, and this has given us some useful techniques that will allow us to program similar APIs in the future.

In many cases, this will be the only way in which we can interact with a web API. However, some APIs, including AWS, have ready-to-use packages that expose the functionality of the service without having to deal with the complexities of the HTTP API. These packages generally make the code cleaner and simpler, and they should be used for production work if they're available.

The AWS package for connecting from Python is called **Boto3**. The `boto3` package is available in PyPI, so we can install it with `pip` and with the following command:

```
pip install boto3
```

Now, open a Python shell and let's try it out. We need to connect to the service first:

```
>>> import boto3
>>> s3 = boto3.client('s3')
```

Use the following to display a list of the buckets:

```
>>> buckets = s3.list_buckets()
>>> buckets = [bucket['Name'] for bucket in response['Buckets']]
```

Now, let's create a bucket:

```
>>> s3.create_bucket('mybucket')
```

This creates the bucket in the default standard US region. We can supply a different region, as shown here:

```
>>> conn.create_bucket('mybucket',
CreateBucketConfiguration={'LocationConstraint': 'eu-west-2'})
```

We can see a list of acceptable region names in the official documentation at https://boto3.amazonaws.com/v1/documentation/api/latest/reference/services/s3.html#S3.Client.create_bucket.

In this screenshot, we can see the documentation for the create_bucket function and the parameters we can use:

```
create_bucket(**kwargs)
    Creates a new bucket.

    See also: AWS API Documentation

    Request Syntax


    response = client.create_bucket(
        ACL='private'|'public-read'|'public-read-write'|'authenticated-read',
        Bucket='string',
        CreateBucketConfiguration={
            'LocationConstraint': 'EU'|'eu-west-1'|'us-west-1'|'us-west-2'|'ap-south-1'|'ap-
        },
        GrantFullControl='string',
        GrantRead='string',
        GrantReadACP='string',
        GrantWrite='string',
        GrantWriteACP='string',
        ObjectLockEnabledForBucket=True|False
    )
```

To upload a file, we can use the upload_file() method from the S3 object, passing as parameters the bucket name and the filename for upload. To download a file, first we need to get a reference to the bucket from which we want to extract the file, and then we can use the download_file() method, passing as parameter the file we want to download and the name of the file when it is stored in your system folder.

In the following script we can see how we implement two methods for doing this tasks. You can find the following code in the s3_upload_download_file_boto.py file:

```python
import sys
import boto3
import botocore

# Create an S3 client
s3 = boto3.client('s3')

# Create an S3 bucket
s3_bucket = boto3.resource('s3')
```

```
def download_file(bucket, s3_name):
    try:
        s3_bucket.Bucket(bucket).download_file('Python.png',
'Python_download.png')
    except botocore.exceptions.ClientError as e:
        if e.response['Error']['Code'] == "404":
            print("The object does not exist.")
        else:
            raise

def upload_file(bucket_name, filename):
    # Uploads the given file using a managed uploader, which will split up
large
    # files automatically and upload parts in parallel.
    s3.upload_file(filename, bucket_name, filename)

if __name__ == '__main__':
    upload_file(sys.argv[1], sys.argv[2])
    download_file(sys.argv[1], sys.argv[2])
```

This script uploads and downloads the `Python.png` S3 object in the bucket, passed as a parameter, and then stores it in the `Python.png` local file. For the execution of the previous script we can pass as arguments the bucket name and the file we want to upload to the bucket:

```
$ python s3_upload_download_file_boto.py mybucket Python.png
```

I'll leave you to further explore the Boto package's functionality with the help of the tutorial, which can be found at `https://boto.readthedocs.org/en/latest/s3_tut.html`.

Summary

In this chapter, we reviewed the JSON data format, how to convert Python objects into the JSON data format, and how to convert them back to Python objects. We then explored the Twitter API and wrote an on-demand search service using tag names. We also explored other modules, such as Tweepy, which is used for processing tweets in real time.

We learned about XML, and how to construct documents, parse them, and extract data from them by using the ElementTree API. We looked at both the Python ElementTree implementation and lxml. We looked at the Amazon S3 service and wrote a client that lets us perform basic operations, such as listing and creating buckets, and uploading and downloading files through the S3 REST API and the Boto package.

In the next chapter, we will review the web scraping process as a technique for extracting information from websites. We will use Python packages such as BeautifulSoup and Scrapy for this purpose.

Questions

1. Which function from the `json` package allows you to transform a dictionary-type object as the first parameter into a text string in JSON format?
2. Which function from the `json` package transforms a character string that contains information in JSON format and transforms it into a dictionary Python-type object?
3. Which authentication mechanism uses Twitter, where credentials are composed of two main elements, consumer and access?
4. Which library inside the requests module can handle most of the complexity of the OAuth protocol for us?
5. Which information do we need to provide at the credentials level to connect with the Twitter API from Python?
6. Which library can we use from Python to connect with the Twitter API and process data in real time using the streaming API?
7. Which `xml` package is part of the Python standard library and contains in turn a series of packages and modules specializing in the management and manipulation of XML documents?
8. Which AWS policy provides access to the Amazon S3 service?
9. Which package can we use for AWS authentication from Python?
10. Which format does S3 use to organize the data and buckets that we store in it?

Further reading

You will find more information about the mentioned tools and the official Python documentation for some of the commented modules at the following links:

- `orjson`, a faster `json` library than the `json` default module: `https://github.com/ijl/orjson`
- Official documentation for the requests package: `http://requests-oauthlib.readthedocs.io/en/latest`
- Official GitHub repository for the `tweepy` module: `https://github.com/tweepy/tweepy`.
- Official GitHub repository for the Python Twitter module: `https://github.com/bear/python-twitter`
- Official documentation for the Amazon S3 API: `http://docs.aws.amazon.com/AmazonS3/latest/API/`
- AWSBucketDump, a tool for enumerating AWS S3 buckets: `https://github.com/jordanpotti/AWSBucketDump`

4
Web Scraping with BeautifulSoup and Scrapy

When we want to extract the content of a web page by automating the extraction of information, we often find that the website does not offer any API to obtain the data you need and it is necessary to resort to scraping techniques to recover data automatically. Some of the most powerful tools can be found in Python 3.7, among which we shall highlight BeautifulSoup and Scrapy.

Scrapy is a framework written in Python for the extraction of data in an automated way that can be used for a wide range of applications, such as the processing of data mining.

The following topics will be covered in this chapter:

- Introduction to web scraping
- Extracting information from web pages and parsing HTML with BeautifulSoup
- Introduction to Scrapy components and architecture
- Scrapy as a framework for performing web crawling processes and data analysis
- Working with Scrapy in the cloud

Technical requirements

Examples and source code for this chapter are available in the GitHub repository in the `Chapter04` folder: `https://github.com/PacktPublishing/Learning-Python-Networking-Second-Edition`.

You will need to install Python 3 distribution on your local machine. For the last section, *Working with Scrapy in the cloud*, you will need an active Scrapinghub account, which you can install with the following link: `https://app.scrapinghub.com`.

Introduction to web scraping

In this section, we will learn about how we can extract the content of a web page by automating the extraction of information.

Web content extraction

Among the techniques available to extract content from the web, we can highlight the following:

- **Screen scraping**: A technique that allows you to obtain information by moving around the screen, registering user pulsations.
- **Web scraping**: The aim is to obtain the information of a resource, such as a web page in HTML, and process that information to extract relevant data.
- **Report mining**: A technique that also tries to obtain information, but in this case from a file (HTML, RDF, CSV, and so on). So, with this approach, we can create a simple and fast mechanism without the need to write an API. A main characteristic is that we can indicate that the system does not need a connection, since it is possible to extract the information offline and without using any API when working from a file. With this technique, it is possible to facilitate the analysis while avoiding the excessive use of equipment and computing time, and increase the efficiency and speed for a prototype and the development of customized reports.
- **Spiders**: Scripts that follow specific rules to move around the website and gather information imitating the interaction a user would perform with the website. The idea is that developers only need to write the rules for managing the data and leave automated tools such as Scrapy to get the contents of the website for you.
- **Crawlers**: Processes that automatically parse and extract content from a website and provide that content to search engine providers for building their page indexes.

In this chapter, we will focus on the web scraping and spiders techniques that allow the collection or extraction of data from web pages automatically. They are very active and developing fields that share objectives with the semantic web, automatic word processing, artificial intelligence, and human-computer interaction.

What is web scraping?

Web scraping is a technique that allows the extraction of information from websites, transforming unstructured data such as data in HTML format into structured data.

In this section, we will review the BeautifulSoup Python library. We complement this library by using the requests library to open the URL and download the HTML code. BeautifulSoup will receive that content to parse the website's HTML and extract the data.

HTML parsers

For parsing HTML, the recommended third-party package is lxml, which is primarily an XML parser. However, it does include a very good HTML parser. It's quick, it offers several ways of navigating documents, and it is tolerant of broken HTML.

The `lxml` library can be installed on Debian and Ubuntu distributions through the `python-lxml` package. If you need an up-to-date version, then `lxml` can be installed through `pip` with the `pip install lxml` command.

Another option is to use BeautifulSoup. BeautifulSoup is pure Python, so it can be installed with `pip`, and it should run anywhere. Although it has its own API, it's a well-respected and capable library, and it can, in fact, use `lxml` as a `backend` library.

Parsing HTML with lxml

The lxml parser (`https://lxml.de`) is the main module for analysis of XML documents and `libxslt`.

The main module features are as follows:

- Support for XML and HTML
- An API based on ElementTree
- Support to selected elements of the document through XPath expressions

The installation of the XML parser can be done through the official repository:

```
pip install lxml
```

lxml.etree is a submodule within the lxml library that provides methods such as XPath(), which supports expressions with XPath selector syntax. With this example, we see the use of the parser to read an HTML file and extract the text from the title tag through an XPath expression:

```
from lxml import html,etree
simple_page = open('data/simple.html').read()
parser = etree.HTML(simple_page)
result = etree.tostring(parser,pretty_print=True, method="html")
find_text = etree.XPath("//title/text()", smart_strings=False)
text = find_text(parser)[0]
print(text)
```

Before we start parsing HTML, we need something to parse. We can obtain the version and codename of the latest stable Debian release from the Debian website. Information about the current stable release can be found at https://www.debian.org/releases/stable/index.en.html. The information that we want is displayed in the page title and in the first sentence.

Let's open a Python shell and get to parsing. First, we'll download the page with the requests package:

```
>>> import requests
>>> response =
requests.get('https://www.debian.org/releases/stable/index.en.html')
```

Next, we parse the source into an ElementTree tree. This is the same as parsing XML with the standard library's ElementTree, except here we will use the lxml specialist HTMLParser:

```
>>> from lxml.etree import HTML
>>> root = HTML(response.content)
```

The HTML() function is a shortcut that reads the HTML that is passed to it, and then it produces an XML tree. Notice that we're passing response.content and not response.text. The lxml library produces better results when it uses the raw response rather than the decoded Unicode text.

The lxml library's ElementTree implementation has been designed to be 100% compatible with the standard library's, so we can start exploring the document in the same way as we did with XML:

```
>>> [e.tag for e in root]
['head', 'body']
>>> root.find('head').find('title').text
'Debian -- Debian "stretch" Release Information '
```

In the preceding code, we have printed out the text content of the document's `<title>` element. We can already see it contains the codename that we want.

Let's inspect the HTML source of the page, and see what we're dealing with. For this, either use **View source** in a web browser, or save the HTML to a file and open it in a text editor. The page's source code is also included in the source code download for this book. Search for text Debian 9.6 in the text, so that we are taken straight to the information we want.

In this screenshot, we can see how it looks as a block of code:

```
<div id="content">
<h1>Debian &ldquo;stretch&rdquo; Release Information</h1>
<p>Debian 9.6 was
released November 10th, 2018.
Debian 9.0 was initially released on June 17th, 2017.
The release included many major
changes, described in
our <a href="../../News/2017/20170617">press release</a> and
the <a href="releasenotes">Release Notes</a>.</p>
```

From the preceding image, we can see that we want the contents of the `<p>` tag child of the `<div>` element. If we navigated to this element by using the ElementTree functions, which we have used before, then we'd end up with something like the following:

```
>>> root.find('body').findall('div')[1].find('p').text
'Debian 9.6 was\nreleased November 10th, 2018.\nDebian 9.0 was initially
released on June 17th, 2017.\nThe release included many major\nchanges,
described in\nour '
```

The main problem with this way is that it depends quite heavily on the HTML structure. A change, such as a `<div>` tag being inserted before the one that we needed, would break it. Also, in more complex documents, this can lead to horrendous chains of method calls, which are hard to maintain.

Our use of the `<title>` tag in the previous section to get the codename is an example of a good technique, because there is always only one `<head>` tag and one `<title>` tag in a document. A better approach to finding our `<div>` tag would be to make use of the `id="content"` attribute it contains.

It's a common web page design pattern to break a page into a few top-level `<divs>` tag for the major page sections such as header, footer, and the content, and to give the `<divs>` ID attributes that identify them as such.

Since version 2, lxml has by default installed a dedicated Python submodule to work with HTML, `lxml.html`: `http://lxml.de/lxmlhtml.html`.

In this example, we make a request to the DuckDuckGo search engine and obtain the form that is used to perform the searches. To do this, we access the forms object that will be contained within the URL response.

You can find the following code in the `duckduckgo.py` file inside the `lxml` folder:

```
from lxml.html import fromstring, tostring
from lxml.html import parse, submit_form

import requests
response = requests.get('https://duckduckgo.com')
form_page = fromstring(response.text)
form = form_page.forms[0]
print(tostring(form))

page = parse('http://duckduckgo.com').getroot()
page.forms[0].fields['q'] = 'python'
result = parse(submit_form(page.forms[0])).getroot()
print(tostring(result))
```

This is the output of the first part of the script, where we can see the form object from DuckDuckGo:

```
b'<form id="search_form_homepage" class="search search--home js-search-
form" name="x" method="POST" action="/html">\n\t\t\t<input
id="search_form_input_homepage" class="search__input js-search-input"
type="text" autocomplete="off" name="q" tabindex="1"
value="">\n\t\t\t<input id="search_button_homepage" class="search__button
js-search-button" type="submit" tabindex="2" value="S">\n\t\t\t<input
id="search_form_input_clear" class="search__clear empty js-search-clear"
type="button" tabindex="3" value="X">\n\t\t\t<div
id="search_elements_hidden" class="search__hidden js-search-
hidden"></div>\n\t\t</form>\n\n\t\t\t\t\t\t'
```

Searching with XPath

In order to avoid exhaustive iteration and the checking of every element, we need to use XPath, which is a query language that was developed specifically for XML, and is supported by lxml.

To get started with XPath, use the Python shell from the last section, and do the following:

```
>>> root.xpath('body')
[<Element body at 0x4477530>]
```

This is the simplest form of XPath expression; it searches for children of the current element that have tag names that match the specified tag name. The current element is the one we call xpath() on—in this case, root. The root element is the top-level <html> element in the HTML document, and so the returned element is the <body> element.

XPath expressions can contain multiple levels of elements. The searches start from the node the xpath() call is made on and work down the tree as they match successive elements in the expression. We can use this to find just the <div> child elements of <body>:

```
>>> root.xpath('body/div')
[<Element div at 0x447a1e8>, <Element div at 0x447a210>, <Element div at 0x447a238>]
```

In body and div expression means, match the <div> children of the <body> children of the current element. Elements with the same tag can appear more than once at the same level in an XML document, so an XPath expression can match multiple elements, hence the xpath() function always returns a list.

The preceding queries are relative to the element that we call xpath() on, but we can force a search from the root of the tree by adding a slash to the start of the expression. We can also perform a search over all the descendants of an element, with the help of a double-slash. To do this, try the following:

```
>>> root.xpath('//h1')
[<Element h1 at 0x447aa58>]
```

The real power of XPath lies in applying additional conditions to the elements in the path:

```
>>> root.xpath('//div[@id="content"]')
[<Element div at 0x3d6d800>]
```

The square brackets after div, [@id="content"], form a condition that we place on the <div> elements that we're matching. The @ sign before id keyword means that id refers to an attribute, so the condition means: only elements with an id attribute equal to "content". This is how we can find our content <div> tag.

Before we employ this to extract our information, let's just touch on a couple of useful things that we can do with conditions. We can specify just a tag name, as shown here:

```
>>> root.xpath('//div[h1]')
[<Element div at 0x3d6d800>]
```

This returns all the <div> elements that have an <h1> child element. Also try the following:

```
>>> root.xpath('body/div[2]')
 [<Element div at 0x3d6d800>]
```

Putting a number as a condition will return the element at that position in the matched list. In this case, this is the second <div> child element of <body>. Note that these indexes start at 1, unlike Python indexing which starts at 0. There's a lot more that XPath can do: the full specification is a **World Wide Web Consortium (W3C)** standard. The latest version can be found at: http://www.w3.org/TR/xpath-3.

Now, let's finish up by writing a script to get our Debian version information.

You can find the following code in the get_debian_version.py file in the lxml folder:

```
import re
import requests

from lxml.etree import HTML
response =
requests.get('https://www.debian.org/releases/stable/index.en.html')
root = HTML(response.content)

title_text = root.find('head').find('title').text

if re.search('\u201c(.*)\u201d', title_text):
    release = re.search('\u201c(.*)\u201d', title_text).group(1)
    p_text = root.xpath('//div[@id="content"]/p[1]')[0].text
    version = p_text.split()[1]
    print('Codename: {}\nVersion: {}'.format(release, version))
```

Here, we have downloaded and parsed the web page by pulling out the text that we want with the help of XPath. We have used a regular expression to pull out stretch version name, and a split to extract the version 9.6. Finally, we print it out. So, run it as shown here:

```
$ python get_debian_version.py
 Codename: stretch
 Version: 9.6
```

XPath is a language that allows you to select nodes from an XML document and calculate values from their content. There are several XPath versions approved by the W3C. In this URL, you can see documentation and all XPath versions: https://www.w3.org/TR/xpath/all/.

In this example, we are using XPath expressions to get images and links from a URL. For extracting images, we use the `'//img/@src'` XPath expression and for extracting links we use the `'//a/@href'` expression.

You can find the following code in the `get_links_images.py` file in the `lxml` folder:

```python3
#!/usr/bin/env python3

import os
import requests
from lxml import html

class Scraping:
    def scrapingImages(self,url):
        print("\nGetting images from url:"+ url)
        try:
            response = requests.get(url)
            parsed_body = html.fromstring(response.text)
            # regular expresion for get images
            images = parsed_body.xpath('//img/@src')
            print('Found images %s' % len(images))
            #create directory for save images
            os.system("mkdir images")
            for image in images:
                if image.startswith("http") == False:
                    download = url + "/"+ image
                else:
                    download = image
                print(download)
                # download images in images directory
                r = requests.get(download)
                f = open('images/%s' % download.split('/')[-1], 'wb')
                f.write(r.content)
                f.close()
        except Exception as e:
            print("Connection error in " + url)
            pass
```

In the previous code block, we define the `scrapingImages` function for extracting images from a URL using the regular expression `'//img/@src'`. In the next code block, in a similar way, we define the `scrapingLinks` function for extracting links from a URL using the regular expression `'//a/@href'`:

```python
    def scrapingLinks(self,url):
        print("\nGetting links from url:"+ url)
        try:
            response = requests.get(url)
```

```
            parsed_body = html.fromstring(response.text)
            # regular expression for get links
            links = parsed_body.xpath('//a/@href')
            print('Found links %s' % len(links))
            for link in links:
                print(link)
        except Exception as e:
            print("Connection error in " + url)
            pass

if __name__ == "__main__":
    target = "https://news.ycombinator.com"
    scraping = Scraping()
    scraping.scrapingImages(target)
    scraping.scrapingLinks(target)
```

Extracting information from web pages and parsing HTML with BeautifulSoup

In this section, we will explore BeautifulSoup as a Python package that allows us to extract information from web pages and parse HTML in Python 3.7.

BeautifulSoup introduction

The BeautifulSoup package contains a library specialized in analyzing and searching data within an HTML file by means of various types of criteria such as the following:

- Searches of HTML elements by means of the structure of the DOM
- Searches through selectors
- Tag searches

BeautifulSoup is a library used to perform web scraping operations from Python, focused on the parsing of web content such as XML, HTML, and JSON.

This tool is not intended directly for web scraping. Instead, the purpose of this tool is to provide an interface that allows access in a very simple way to the content of a web page, which makes it ideal to extract information from the web.

Among the main features, we can highlight the following:

- Parses and allows the extraction of information from HTML documents
- Supports multiple parsers in processing XML documents and HTML (lxml, html5lib)
- Generates a tree structure with all the elements of the paired document
- Very easily allows the user to search HTML elements, such as links, forms, or any HTML tag

To use it, you have to install the specific module that can be found in the official repository (https://www.crummy.com/software/BeautifulSoup/bs4/doc/) using the following command:

```
pip install BeautifulSoup4
```

You can also see the latest version of the module on the official Python page: https://pypi.python.org/pypi/beautifulsoup4.

Once installed, the name of the package is bs4. The first thing to use the library for is to import the BeautifulSoup package from the bs4 module:

```
>>> from bs4 import BeautifulSoup
```

To be able to perform operations with an HTML document, it is necessary to create an object from the bs4.BeautifulSoup class by entering a str type object containing the HTML code and selecting the type of analyzer to be used as second parameter: bs4.BeautifulSoup (<object type str>, <analyzer type>).

> To learn more about the analyzer options, you can query the documentation: https://www.crummy.com/software/BeautifulSoup/bs4/doc/#installing-a-parser.

To create an instance of BeautifulSoup, it is necessary to pass the parameters of the HTML document and the parser that we want to use (lxml or html5lib):

```
>>> bs= BeautifulSoup(contents,'lxml')
```

In this way, we managed to create an instance of the BeautifulSoup class, passing the HTML content of the page and the parser to be used as parameters. In the bs object we have all the information to navigate through the document and access each of the labels that are included in it. For example, if we want to access the title tag of the document, simply execute bs.title.

Access to elements through DOM

DOM is the acronym for **Document Object Model** and is the way in which a browser interprets an HTML document inside a window.

The DOM presents a structure similar to that of the trunk of a tree from which branches are emerge. It is said that the HTML element that contains other elements is the father of these:

```
parent
 | children
 ├── Element
 ├── brother (sibling)
```

When searching through the DOM, BeautifulSoup returns the first item with the matching HTML tag. An interesting feature of the library is that it allows the user to search for specific elements in the structure of the document; in this way, we can search for meta tags, form, and links.

`bs.find_all()` is a method that allows us to find all the HTML elements of a certain type and returns a list of tags that match the search pattern.

For example, to search for all meta tags in an HTML document, use the following code:

```
>>> meta_tags = bs.find_all("meta")
>>> for tag in meta_tags:
 >>>   print(tag)
```

To search all the forms of an HTML document, use the following code:

```
>>> form_tags = bs.find_all("form")
>>> for form in form_tags:
 >>>   print (form)
```

To search all links in an HTML document, use the following code:

```
>>> link_tags = bs.find_all("a")
>>> for link in link_tags:
 >>>   print (link)
```

The `findAll` function returns all the elements of the collection that match the argument specified. If you want to return a single element, you can use the `find` function, which only returns the first element of the collection.

In this example, we extract all the links of a certain URL. The idea is to make the request with `requests` and with BeautifulSoup to parse the data that the request returns.

You can find the following code in the `extract_links_from_url.py` file inside the `beautifulSoup` folder:

```python3
#!/usr/bin/env python3

from bs4 import BeautifulSoup
import requests

url = input("Enter a website to extract the URL's from: ")

headers = {'User-Agent': 'Mozilla/5.0 (Macintosh; Intel Mac OS X 10_10_1)
AppleWebKit/537.36 (KHTML, like Gecko) Chrome/39.0.2171.95 Safari/537.36'}
response = requests.get("http://" +url, headers = headers)
data = response.text
soup = BeautifulSoup(data,'lxml')
for link in soup.find_all('a'):
    print(link.get('href'))
```

In this screenshot, we can see the output of the previous script:

```
Enter a website to extract the URL's from: www.packtpub.com
/account
#
/register
https://account.packtpub.com/
/logout
https://www.packtpub.com/account/password
/register
#
/
/all
/tech
/
/books/content/support
https://subscribe.packtpub.com
https://www.packtpub.com/cart/checkout
https://search.packtpub.com/?refinementList[released][0]=Available&refinementList[category][0]=Data
https://search.packtpub.com/?refinementList[released][0]=Available&refinementList[category][0]=Business%20%26%20Other
https://search.packtpub.com/?refinementList[released][0]=Available&refinementList[category][0]=Cloud%20%26%20Networking
https://search.packtpub.com/?refinementList[released][0]=Available&refinementList[category][0]=Game%20Development
https://search.packtpub.com/?refinementList[released][0]=Available&refinementList[category][0]=IoT%20%26%20Hardware
https://search.packtpub.com/?refinementList[released][0]=Available&refinementList[category][0]=Mobile
https://search.packtpub.com/?refinementList[released][0]=Available&refinementList[category][0]=Programming
https://search.packtpub.com/?refinementList[released][0]=Available&refinementList[category][0]=Security
https://search.packtpub.com/?refinementList[released][0]=Available&refinementList[category][0]=Web Development
https://search.packtpub.com/?refinementList%5Bproduct_type%5D%5B0%5D=Book&refinementList%5Breleased%5D%5B0%5D=Available
https://search.packtpub.com/?refinementList%5Bproduct_type%5D%5B0%5D=Video&refinementList%5Breleased%5D%5B0%5D=Availablehttps://www.
ktpub.com/bestsellers
https://search.packtpub.com/?refinementList%5Breleased%5D%5B0%5D=Available&refinementList%5Btool%5D%5B0%5D=Android
https://search.packtpub.com/?refinementList%5Breleased%5D%5B0%5D=Available&refinementList%5Btool%5D%5B0%5D=Angular
https://search.packtpub.com/?refinementList[released][0]=Available&refinementList[concept][0]=Artificial%20Intelligence
```

We can also extract images directly with BeautifulSoup, in the same way that we extracted the images with the `lxml` module in the previous section.

In this example, we make the request to the URL passed by the parameter with the requests module. Later, we build the BeautifulSoup object from which we will extract those tags that are `<img>`. If the URL is correct, the image is downloaded again using the `requests` package.

You can find the following code in the download_images.py file inside the beautifulSoup folder:

```python
#!/usr/bin/env python3

import requests
from bs4 import BeautifulSoup
import urllib.parse
import sys
import os

response =
requests.get('http://www.freeimages.co.uk/galleries/transtech/informationte
chnology/index.htm')
parse = BeautifulSoup(response.text,'lxml')

# Get all image tags
image_tags = parse.find_all('img')

# Get urls to the images
images = [ url.get('src') for url in image_tags]

# If no images found in the page
if not images:
    sys.exit("Found No Images")

# Convert relative urls to absolute urls if any
images = [urllib.parse.urljoin(response.url, url) for url in images]
print('Found %s images' % len(images))
```

In the previous code block, we have obtained images' URLs using BeautifulSoup and a lxml parser. Now we are going to create the folder for storing images and download images in that folder using the request package.

```python
#create download_images folder if not exists

file_path = "download_images"
directory = os.path.dirname(file_path)

if not os.path.exists(directory):
    try:
        os.makedirs(file_path)
        print ("Creation of the directory %s OK" % file_path)
    except OSError:
        print ("Creation of the directory %s failed" % file_path)
else:
    print ("download_images directory exists")
```

```
# Download images to downloaded folder
for url in images:response = requests.get(url)
    file = open('download_images/%s' % url.split('/')[-1], 'wb')
    file.write(response.content)
    file.close()
    print('Downloaded %s' % url)
```

In this screenshot, we can see the output of the previous script:

```
Found 79 images
Creation of the directory download_images OK
Downloaded http://www.freeimages.co.uk/galleries/transtech/informationtechnology/thumbs/beige_keyboard.jpg
Downloaded http://www.freeimages.co.uk/galleries/transtech/informationtechnology/thumbs/blue_screen.jpg
Downloaded http://www.freeimages.co.uk/galleries/transtech/informationtechnology/thumbs/chiclet_keyboard.jpg
Downloaded http://www.freeimages.co.uk/galleries/transtech/informationtechnology/thumbs/computer_blank_screen.jpg
Downloaded http://www.freeimages.co.uk/galleries/transtech/informationtechnology/thumbs/computer_dollar_key.jpg
Downloaded http://www.freeimages.co.uk/galleries/transtech/informationtechnology/thumbs/computer_help_key.jpg
Downloaded http://www.freeimages.co.uk/galleries/transtech/informationtechnology/thumbs/computer_memory.jpg
Downloaded http://www.freeimages.co.uk/galleries/transtech/informationtechnology/thumbs/computer_memory_dimm.jpg
Downloaded http://www.freeimages.co.uk/galleries/transtech/informationtechnology/thumbs/computer_typing.jpg
Downloaded http://www.freeimages.co.uk/galleries/transtech/informationtechnology/thumbs/CPU_chip_and_scoket.jpg
Downloaded http://www.freeimages.co.uk/galleries/transtech/informationtechnology/thumbs/designer_keyboard.jpg
Downloaded http://www.freeimages.co.uk/galleries/transtech/informationtechnology/thumbs/end_button.jpg
Downloaded http://www.freeimages.co.uk/galleries/transtech/informationtechnology/thumbs/enter_key.jpg
Downloaded http://www.freeimages.co.uk/galleries/transtech/informationtechnology/thumbs/ethernet_router.jpg
Downloaded http://www.freeimages.co.uk/galleries/transtech/informationtechnology/thumbs/floppy_disks.jpg
Downloaded http://www.freeimages.co.uk/galleries/transtech/informationtechnology/thumbs/forward_stop_buttons.jpg
Downloaded http://www.freeimages.co.uk/galleries/transtech/informationtechnology/thumbs/green_network_plug.jpg
Downloaded http://www.freeimages.co.uk/galleries/transtech/informationtechnology/thumbs/handy_scanner.jpg
```

In this example, we are going to extract titles and links from the following hacker news domain: https://news.ycombinator.com. In this case, we are using the findAll function to obtain elements that match with a specific style, later we use the find function for getting elements that match with the href tag.

You can find the following code in the extract_links_hacker_news.py file inside the beautifulSoup folder:

```python
#!/usr/bin/env python3
import requests
from bs4 import BeautifulSoup

def get_front_page():
    target = "https://news.ycombinator.com"
    frontpage = requests.get(target)
    if not frontpage.ok:
        raise RuntimeError("Can't access hacker news, you should go
outside")
    news_soup = BeautifulSoup(frontpage.text,"lxml")
    return news_soup
```

```python
def find_interesting_links(soup):
    items = soup.findAll('td', {'align': 'right', 'class': 'title'})
    links = []
    for i in items:
        try:
            siblings = list(i.next_siblings)
            post_id = siblings[1].find('a')['id']
            link = siblings[2].find('a')['href']
            title = siblings[2].text
            links.append({'link': link, 'title': title,'post_id':post_id})
        except Exception as e:
            pass
    return links


if __name__ == '__main__':
    soup = get_front_page()
    results = find_interesting_links(soup)
    for r in results:
        if r is not None:
            print(r['link'] +" "+(r['title']))
```

In this screenshot, we can see the output of the previous script:

```
https://plt.eecs.northwestern.edu/snapshots/current/pdf-doc/racklog.pdf Racklog: Pr
olog Style Logic Programming [pdf] (northwestern.edu)
https://graydon2.dreamwidth.org/263429.html Rust 2019 and beyond: limits to some gr
owth (graydon2.dreamwidth.org)
http://www.daemonology.net/blog/2018-12-26-the-many-ways-to-launch-FreeBSD-in-EC2.h
tml The many ways to launch FreeBSD in EC2 (daemonology.net)
http://antitrust.slated.org/www.iowaconsumercase.org/011607/8000/PX08875.pdf Micros
oft Word for Windows 1.0 Postmortem (1989) [pdf] (slated.org)
https://oaklandmofo.com/blog/block-stringray-devices How to Block Stringray Devices
 (oaklandmofo.com)
https://www.nytimes.com/2018/12/26/sports/antarctica-race-colin-obrady.html Colin O
'Brady Completes Crossing of Antarctica with Final 32-Hour Push (nytimes.com)
item?id=18767767 Ask HN: What do you use for authentication and authorization?
http://tech.paulcz.net/blog/future-of-kubernetes-is-virtual-machines/ The future of
 Kubernetes is virtual machines (paulcz.net)
https://fastmail.blog/2018/12/27/jmap-is-on-the-home-straight/ JMAP is on the home
straight (fastmail.blog)
https://www.nytimes.com/2018/05/08/science/alan-turing-desalination.html Alan Turin
g and the mathematics of pattern formation in nature (nytimes.com)
https://www.facebook.com/notes/daniel-colascione/buttery-smooth-emacs/1015531344006
6102/ Buttery smooth Emacs (2016) (facebook.com)
https://www.cnet.com/news/this-man-spent-5000-of-his-own-money-to-put-zimbabwe-on-s
treet-view Spending $5k to put Zimbabwe on Street View (cnet.com)
https://github.com/linux-noah/noah Noah: Bash on Ubuntu on macOS (github.com)
https://www.lockhaven.edu/~dsimanek/puzzles/puzzles.htm Physics puzzles (lockhaven.
edu)
https://www.braze.com/perspectives/article/building-braze-job-queues-resiliency Res
iliency with Queues: Building a System That Never Skips a Beat in a Billion (braze.
com)
https://github.com/arun1729/road-network Show HN: QuadTree model for generating ran
dom road networks (github.com)
```

Extracting labels using regex

We can use regex package to identify common patterns such as emails and URLs. With BeautifulSoup, you can specify regular expression patterns to match specific tags. In this script, we are extracting email addresses that match a specific pattern.

You can find the following code in the `extract_emails_from_url.py` file inside the `beautifulSoup` folder:

```
import requests
import re
from bs4 import BeautifulSoup

url = input("Enter the URL: ")
response = requests.get(url)
html_page = response.text
email_pattern=re.compile(r'\b[\w.-]+?@\w+?\.\w+?\b')

for match in re.findall(email_pattern,html_page):
    print(match)
```

Handling URL exceptions and not found tags

It is also important to verify if the label is returned when we use the find method. We may have written an incorrect label or try to get a label that is not on the page and this will return the None object, so we must verify if the object is None. This can be done using a simple conditional statement such as the one in this example.

You can find the following code in the `handling_exceptions_tags.py` file inside the `beautifulSoup` folder:

```
from urllib.request import urlopen
from urllib.error import HTTPError
from urllib.error import URLError
from bs4 import BeautifulSoup

try:
    html = urlopen("https://www.packtpub.com/")
except HTTPError as e:
    print(e)
except URLError:
    print("Server down or incorrect domain")
else:
    res = BeautifulSoup(html.read(),"html5lib")
    if res.title is None:
```

```
        print("Tag not found")
    else:
        print(res.title.text)
```

There are some other third-party packages available that can speed up scraping and form submission. Two popular ones are mechanize and Scrapy.

You can check them at `http://wwwsearch.sourceforge.net/mechanize` and `http://scrapy.org`.

Introduction to Scrapy components and architecture

In this section, we will learn about Scrapy components and architecture. We will review Scrapy architecture and XPath expressions from Scrapy shell.

What is Scrapy?

Scrapy (`https://scrapy.org/`) is an open source collaborative platform that allows us to extract data from web pages used for a series of applications such as data mining, information processing, and historical registration.

This framework also allows us to expand its functionality and is portable because it is written in Python, which can be interpreted on Linux, Macintosh, and Windows systems.

Although the main objective of Scrapy is the extraction of data from web pages, this can also be used to extract data through the use of APIs, obtain the structure of the web, or simply as a general purpose extractor. Scrapy has the following features:

- **Fast and powerful**: You write the rules to extract the data and Scrapy does the work for us
- **Easily extensible**: Given its configuration, it can generate new functionality without having to modify the source code
- **Portable**: It is written in Python and can run on Linux, Windows, Mac, and BSD

Since it is a framework, Scrapy has a series of powerful tools to scrape or extract information from websites easily and efficiently. These tools include the following:

- Support to extract and select data from HTML/XML sources using CSS selectors and XPath expressions, with help methods to extract using regular expressions
- An interactive console in IPython to test CSS and XPath expressions to extract data, which is very useful when building your own methods
- Support for exporting records in multiple formats such as JSON, CSV, and XML
- Support for handling foreign statements, non-standards, and broken codes
- Strong extensibility, since it allows you to connect your own functionality using signals, extensions, and pipelines

To get started in Scrapy, we recommend installing Scrapy as shown in this *Installation Guide*: `https://doc.scrapy.org/en/latest/intro/install.html#intro-install`.

Scrapy architecture

Scrapy allows us to recursively scan the contents of a website and apply a set of rules on said contents to extract information that may be useful to us. These are the main architecture elements:

- **Interpreter**: Allows quick tests, as well as the creation of projects with a defined structure.
- **Spiders**: Code routines that are responsible for making HTTP requests to a list of domains given by the client and applies rules in the form of regular expressions or XPath on the content returned from HTTP requests.
- **XPath expressions**: With XPath expressions, we can get to a fairly detailed level of the information we want to extract. For example, if we want to extract the download links from a page, it is enough to obtain the XPath expression of the element and access the `href` attribute.
- **Items**: Scrapy uses a mechanism based on XPath expressions called *Xpath selectors*. These selectors are responsible for applying XPath rules defined by the developer and composing Python objects that contain the information extracted. The items are such as containers of information and allow us to store the information that the rules that we apply return on the contents that we are obtaining.

In this image, you can see an overview of the Scrapy architecture:

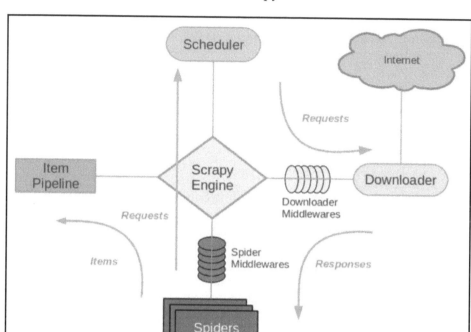

As you can see in the preceding image, the spiders use the items to pass the data to the item. Scrapy can have several spiders—the spiders do the requests, which are scheduled in the scheduler, and these are what make the requests to the server. Finally, when the server responds, these responses are sent back to the spiders, so that the spider is fed back with each request.

XPath expressions

To use Scrapy, it is necessary to define rules that Scrapy will use for extracting information. These rules can be XPath expressions. Scrapy has an interpreter that allows you to test XPath expressions on a website, which facilitates the debugging and development of web spiders. For example, if we want to extract the text corresponding to the title of the page, we can do with the '//title/text()' XPath expression:

```
>>> fetch('http://www.scrapy.org')
 >>> response.xpath('//title/text()').extract()
 >>> ['Scrapy | A Fast and Powerful Scraping and Web Crawling Framework']
```

In the following screenshot, you can see the result of the execution of the `fetch` command in the Scrapy shell and extract the title of the page with the XPath expression:

```
[s] Available Scrapy objects:
[s]   crawler    <scrapy.crawler.Crawler object at 0x042138D0>
[s]   item       {}
[s]   request    <GET http://scrapy.org>
[s]   response   <200 http://scrapy.org>
[s]   settings   <scrapy.settings.Settings object at 0x029A8750>
[s]   spider     <Spider 'default' at 0x4498c30>
[s] Useful shortcuts:
[s]   shelp()          Shell help (print this help)
[s]   fetch(req_or_url) Fetch request (or URL) and update local objects
[s]   view(response)   View response in a browser

>>> response.xpath('//title/text()').extract()
[u'Scrapy | A Fast and Powerful Scraping and Web Crawling Framework']
```

Scrapy as a framework for performing web crawling processes and data analysis

In this section, we will explore Scrapy as a framework for Python that allows us to perform web scraping tasks and web crawling processes and data analysis. Also, we will explain the structure that a Scrapy project presents and how to create our own project, and we will create a spider to track a web page and extract the data that interests us. We will review Scrapy components, creating a project for configuring pipelines.

Installation of Scrapy

There are diverse tools and techniques that allow a developer or analyst to access, consume, and extract content based on the web. The Scrapy project offers a tool that enables automated and rapid web scraping of large amounts of web-based content. Scrapy has very good documentation, which can be accessed from the following URL: `https://doc.scrapy.org/en/latest`.

Scrapy was created from Twisted (`https://twistedmatrix.com/`), so it is capable of performing thousands of queries simultaneously. Similarly, Scrapy makes use of tools such as BeautifulSoup and the Python XML package to facilitate content searches.

Scrapy needs lxml and OpenSSL as prerequisite packages for the installation. You can install Scrapy using `pip` with the `pip install scrapy` command.

Scrapinghub maintains official `conda` packages for Linux, Windows, and OS X at the following URL: `https://anaconda.org/anaconda/scrapy`.

To install Scrapy using `conda`, run the following code:

```
conda install -c scrapinghub scrapy
```

Once installed, it is possible to use the `scrapy` command from the command line, using subcommands at the same time.

In this screenshot, we can see all available `scrapy` subcommands:

```
Scrapy 1.5.1 - no active project

Usage:
  scrapy <command> [options] [args]

Available commands:
  bench         Run quick benchmark test
  fetch         Fetch a URL using the Scrapy downloader
  genspider     Generate new spider using pre-defined templates
  runspider     Run a self-contained spider (without creating a project)
  settings      Get settings values
  shell         Interactive scraping console
  startproject  Create new project
  version       Print Scrapy version
  view          Open URL in browser, as seen by Scrapy

  [ more ]      More commands available when run from project directory

Use "scrapy <command> -h" to see more info about a command
```

Creating a project with Scrapy

Before starting with Scrapy, you have to start a project where you want to store your code. To create a project with Scrapy, you have to execute the command from the console:

```
scrapy startproject helloProject
```

This command will create a `helloProject` directory with the following contents:

```
helloProject/
  scrapy.cfg # deploy configuration file
  helloProject/ # project's Python module, you'll import your code from here
      __init__.py
      items.py # project items file
      pipelines.py # project pipelines file
```

```
settings.py # project settings file
spiders/ # a directory where you'll later put your spiders
    __init__.py
```

Each project consists of the following:

- `items.py`: We define the elements to extract
- `spiders`: The heart of the project, here we define the extraction procedure
- `Pipelines.py`: The elements to analyze what has been obtained—data validation and cleaning of HTML code

Once the project is created, we have to define the items that we want to extract, or rather the class where the data extracted by `scrapy` will be stored. Basically, in `items.py` we create the fields of the information that we are going to extract.

Scrapy item class

Scrapy provides the item class to define the output data format. Item objects are containers used to collect the extracted data and specify metadata for the field used to characterize that data. For more details, see `https://doc.scrapy.org/en/1.5/topics/items.html`.

Create a file named `MyItem.py` and add the following code into it:

```
import scrapy
from scrapy.loader.processors import TakeFirst

class MyItem(scrapy.Item):
    # define the fields for your item here like:
    name = scrapy.Field(output_processor=TakeFirst(),)
```

The next step is to describe how the information can be extracted using XPath expressions so that Scrapy can differentiate it from the rest of the HTML code on the page of each book.

To start the crawling process, it is necessary to import the `CrawlerProcess` class. We instantiate the class by passing it through the parameters of the configuration that we want to apply:

```
# setup crawler
from scrapy.crawler import CrawlerProcess
crawler = CrawlerProcess(settings)
# define the spider for the crawler
crawler.crawl(MySpider())
# start scrapy
print("STARTING ENGINE")
```

```
crawler.start()
# printed at the end of the crawling process
print("ENGINE STOPPED")
```

We import the necessary modules to carry out the crawling process:

```
from scrapy.spiders import CrawlSpider, Rule
from scrapy.linkextractors.lxmlhtml import LxmlLinkExtractor
from scrapy.selector import HtmlXPathSelector
```

- `Rule`: Allows us to establish the rules by which the crawler will be based to navigate through different links.
- `LxmlLinkExtractor`: Allows us to define a callback function and regular expressions to tell the crawler which links to go through. It allows us to define the navigation rules between the links that we want to obtain.
- `HtmlXPathSelector`: Allows us to apply XPath expressions.

Spiders

Spiders are classes that define the way to navigate through a specific site or domain and how to extract data from those pages; that is, we define in a personalized way the behavior to analyze the pages of a particular site.

The cycle that follows a spider is the following:

- First, we start generating the initial request (Requests) to navigate through the first URL and we specify the `backward` function to be called with the response (Response) downloaded from that request
- The first request to be made is obtained by calling the `start_request()` method, which by default generates the request for the specific URL in the `start_urls` starting addresses and the function of `backward` for the requests

These requests will be made by downloading by Scrapy and their responses manipulated by the `backward` functions. In the `backward` functions, we analyze the content typically using the selectors (XPath selectors) and generate the items with the content analyzed. Finally, the items returned by the spider can be passed to an item pipeline.

Creating our spider

This is the code for our first spider. Save it in a file named `MySpider.py` under the `spiders` directory in your project:

```
from scrapy.contrib.spiders import CrawlSpider, Rule
from scrapy.linkextractors.lxmlhtml import LxmlLinkExtractor
from scrapy.selector import HtmlXPathSelector
from scrapy.item import Item

class MySpider(CrawlSpider):
    name = 'example.com'
    allowed_domains = ['example.com']
    start_urls = ['http://www.example.com']
    rules = (Rule(LxmlLinkExtractor(allow=())))

    def parse_item(self, response):
        hxs = HtmlXPathSelector(response)
        element = Item()
        return element
```

`CrawlSpider` provides a mechanism that allows you to follow the links that follow a certain pattern. Apart from the inherent attributes of the `BaseSpider` class, this class has a new rules attribute with which we can indicate to the spider the behavior that it should follow.

Pipelines items and export formats

The items pipelines could be called the channels or pipes of the items. They are elements of Scrapy and the information that arrives to them are Items that have been previously obtained and processed by some spider. They are classes in themselves that have a simple objective—to re-process the item that arrives to them, being able to reject it for some reasons or let it pass through this channel.

The typical uses of pipelines are as follows:

- Cleaning data in HTML
- Validation of scraped data checking that the items contain certain fields
- Checking duplicate items
- Storage of the data in a database

For each element that is obtained, it is sent to the corresponding pipeline, which will process it either to save it in the database or to send it to another pipeline. For detail, you can go to official documentation: `https://doc.scrapy.org/en/latest/topics/item-pipeline.html`.

An item pipeline is a Python class that overrides some specific methods and needs to be activated on the settings of the Scrapy project. When creating a Scrapy project with the `scrapy startproject myproject`, you'll find a `pipelines.py` file already available for creating your own pipelines. It isn't mandatory to create your pipelines in this file, but it would be good practice. We'll be explaining how to create a pipeline using the `pipelines.py` file.

These objects are Python classes that must implement the `process_item (item, spider)` method and must return an item type object (or a subclass of it) or, if it does not return it, it must throw an exception of a `DropItem` type to indicate that item will not continue to be processed. An example of this component is as follows:

```python
#!/usr/bin/python
# -*- coding: utf-8 -*-
from scrapy.exceptions import DropItem
class MyPipeline(object):
    def process_item(self, item, spider):
        if item['key']:
            return item
        else:
            raise DropItem("Element not exists: %s" % item['key'])
```

One more point to keep in mind is that when we create an object of this type, we must enter in the `settings.py` file of the project a line like the following to activate the pipe. Now, to enable it you need to specify it is going to be used in your settings. Go to your `settings.py` file and search (or add) the `ITEM_PIPELINES` variable. Update it with the path to your pipeline class and its priority over other pipelines:

```python
ITEM_PIPELINES = {
 'myproject.pipelines.MyPipeline': 300,
}
```

Scrapy settings

Before starting Scrapy, is recommended that you modify the settings and limit the speed at which the data is accessed, so as not to create a DOS attack. For doing this task, we need to configure settings.py with the DOWNLOAD_DELAY property:

```
# Scrapy settings for scrapy project
#
# For simplicity, this file contains only the most important settings by
# default. All the other settings are documented here:
#
# http://doc.scrapy.org/en/latest/topics/settings.html
#
BOT_NAME = 'hacker_news'
SPIDER_MODULES = ['hacker_news.spiders']
NEWSPIDER_MODULE = 'hacker_news.spiders'
# Configure a delay for requests for the same website (default: 0)
# See
http://scrapy.readthedocs.org/en/latest/topics/settings.html#download-delay
DOWNLOAD_DELAY = 60
```

Executing Scrapy

With Scrapy, we can collect the information and save it in a file in one of the supported formats (XML, JSON, or CSV), or even directly in a database using a pipeline. In this case, we are executing the scrapy command passing as argument the JSON format:

```
$ scrapy crawl <crawler_name> -o items.json -t json
```

The last parameters indicate that the extracted data is stored in a file called items.json and that the exporter uses for JSON format. It can be done in the same way to export to CSV and XML formats.

The option -o items.csv provides as a parameter the name of the output file that will contain the data you have extracted. You can also extract information as JSON format by using the -t json option.

With the -t csv option, we will obtain a CSV file with the crawling process result:

```
$ scrapy crawl <crawler_name> -o items.csv -t csv
```

With the `-t json` option, we will obtain a JSON file with the crawling process result:

```
$ scrapy crawl <crawler_name> -o items.json -t json
```

With the `-t xml` option, we will obtain an XML file with the crawling process result:

```
$ scrapy crawl <crawler_name> -o items.xml -t xml
```

The `runspider` command tells `scrapy` to run your spider from your spider template:

```
$ scrapy runspider spider-template.py
```

Scrapy execution tips and tricks

When executing Scrapy, we can follow these rules for managing the crawler execution:

- If the scraping process fails, you can look in the console log for lines that include `[scrapy] DEBUG`.
- If you want to stop Scrapy while it is still processing, just press the key combination *Ctrl+C*.
- When Scrapy has finished processing data, it will display the following information in the log `console: [scrapy] INFO: Spider closed (finished)`.
- By default, Scrapy will append new data to the end of the output file if it already exists. If the file does not exist, it will create one. So, if you want to only get new data, then you should first remove the old file.

EuroPython project

In this section, we are going to build a project with Scrapy that allows us to extract the data of the sessions of the EuroPython conference following the pattern from the following URL: `http://ep{year}.europython.eu/en/events/sessions`. You can try with years from 2015 to 2018: for example we can try with the following URL: `https://ep2018.europython.eu/events/sessions/`.

To create a project with `scrapy`, we can execute the following command:

```
scrapy startproject europython
```

In this screenshot, we can see the result of creating a Scrapy project:

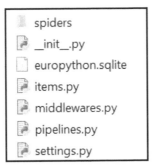

`items.py` is where we define the fields and the information that we are going to extract:

```
import scrapy
class EuropythonItem(scrapy.Item):
    # define the fields for your item here like:
    title = scrapy.Field()
    author = scrapy.Field()
    description = scrapy.Field()
    date = scrapy.Field()
    tags = scrapy.Field()
```

In the `settings.py` file, we define the name of the `'europython.spiders'` module and the pipelines defined among which we highlight one that allows exporting the data in XML format—`EuropythonXmlExport`—and another that saves the data in a database SQLite—`EuropythonSQLitePipeline`.

You can find the following code in the `settings.py` file:

```
# Scrapy settings for europython project
#
# For simplicity, this file contains only the most important settings by
# default. All the other settings are documented here:
#
# http://doc.scrapy.org/en/latest/topics/settings.html
#
BOT_NAME = 'europython'
SPIDER_MODULES = ['europython.spiders']
NEWSPIDER_MODULE = 'europython.spiders'
# Configure item pipelines
# See http://scrapy.readthedocs.org/en/latest/topics/item-pipeline.html
ITEM_PIPELINES = {
'europython.pipelines.EuropythonXmlExport': 200,
'europython.pipelines.EuropythonSQLitePipeline': 300,
```

```
    }
DOWNLOADER_MIDDLEWARES = {
'scrapy.downloadermiddlewares.httpproxy.HttpProxyMiddleware': 110,
#'europython.middlewares.ProxyMiddleware': 100,
    }
```

In the `pipelines.py` file we define the class that will process the results and store them in an SQLite file. For this task, we can create an entity called `EuropythonSession` that extends from `db`. Entity class available in pony ORM package (https://ponyorm.com). You need to install the pony package with the `pip install pony` command.

You can find the following code in the `pipelines.py` file:

```
from pony.orm import *

db = Database("sqlite", "europython.sqlite", create_db=True)

class EuropythonSession(db.Entity):
    """ Pony ORM model of the europython session table """
    id = PrimaryKey(int, auto=True)
    author = Required(str)
    title = Required(str)
    description = Required(str)
    date = Required(str)
    tags = Required(str)
```

Also, we need to define a `EuropythonSQLitePipeline` class for processing data about author, title, description, date, tags, and storing items in the database:

```
class EuropythonSQLitePipeline(object):

@classmethod
  def from_crawler(cls, crawler):
    pipeline = cls()
    crawler.signals.connect(pipeline.spider_opened, signals.spider_opened)
    crawler.signals.connect(pipeline.spider_closed, signals.spider_closed)
    return pipeline

  def spider_opened(self, spider):
    db.generate_mapping(check_tables=True, create_tables=True)

def spider_closed(self, spider):
    db.commit()

  # Insert data in database
  @db_session
  def process_item(self, item, spider):
```

```
    # use db_session as a context manager
    with db_session:
    try:
        strAuthor = str(item['author'])
        strAuthor = strAuthor[3:len(strAuthor)-2]
        strTitle = str(item['title'])
        strTitle = strTitle[3:len(strTitle)-2]
        strDescription = str(item['description'])
        strDescription = strDescription[3:len(strDescription)-2]
        strDate = str(item['date'])
        strDate = strDate[3:len(strDate)-2]
        strDate = strDate.replace("[u'", "").replace("']",
"").replace("u'", "").replace("',", ",")
        strTags = str(item['tags'])
        strTags = strTags.replace("[u'", "").replace("']",
"").replace("u'", "").replace("',", ",")
        europython_session =
EuropythonSession(author=strAuthor,title=strTitle,
 description=strDescription,date=strDate,tags=strTags)
    except Exception as e:
        print("Error processing the items in the DB %d: %s" % (e.args[0],
e.args[1]))
    return item
```

In the `europython_spider.py` file we define the `EuropythonSpyder` class. In this class, the spider is defined, which will track the links it finds from the starting URL depending on the indicated pattern, and for each entry it will obtain the corresponding data for each session (title, author, description, date, and tags).

You can find the following code in the `europython_spider.py` file:

```python
import scrapy

from scrapy.spiders import CrawlSpider, Rule
from scrapy.linkextractors import LinkExtractor
from scrapy.linkextractors.lxmlhtml import LxmlLinkExtractor
from scrapy.selector import HtmlXPathSelector

from europython.items import EuropythonItem

class EuropythonSpyder(CrawlSpider):
    def __init__(self, year='', *args, **kwargs):
        super(EuropythonSpyder, self).__init__(*args, **kwargs)
        self.year = year
        self.start_urls =
['http://ep'+str(self.year)+".europython.eu/en/events/sessions"]
        print('start url: '+str(self.start_urls[0]))
```

```
    name = "europython_spyder"
    allowed_domains = ["ep2015.europython.eu","ep2016.europython.eu",
"ep2017.europython.eu","ep2018.europython.eu"]

    # Pattern for entries that match the conference/talks format
    rules =
[Rule(LxmlLinkExtractor(allow=['conference/talks']),callback='process_respo
nse')]
    def process_response(self, response):
        item = EuropythonItem()
        print(response)
        item['title'] = response.xpath("//div[contains(@class,
'grid-100')]//h1/text()").extract()
        item['author'] = response.xpath("//div[contains(@class, 'talk-
speakers')]//a[1]/text()").extract()
        item['description'] = response.xpath("//div[contains(@class,
'cms')]//p//text()").extract()
        item['date'] = response.xpath("//section[contains(@class, 'talk
when')]/strong/text()").extract()
        item['tags'] = response.xpath("//div[contains(@class, 'all-
tags')]/span/text()").extract()
        return item
```

Executing EuroPython spider

We can execute our spider with the following command:

```
scrapy crawl europython_spider -o europython_items.json -t json
```

At the end of the process, we obtain the following as output files:

- europython_items.json
- europython_items.xml
- europython.sqlite

Each of these files are generated in the classes that are defined in the pipelines.py file and the JSON file is generated automatically by the spider.

Another interesting option is that spiders can manage arguments that are passed in the crawl command using the -a option. For example, the following command will extract the data of the sessions of the EuroPython 2018 from the following URL: http://ep2018.europython.eu/en/events/sessions:

```
scrapy crawl europython_spider -a year=2018 -o europython_items.json -t
json
```

In this screenshot, we can see the JSON file generated after the execution of the previous command:

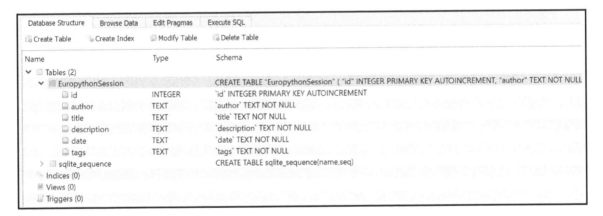

```
[
{"title": ["Citizen Science with Python"], "author": ["Ian Ozsvald"], "description": ["You could make a difference in the world with a lit
{"title": ["Creating a Culture of Software Craftsmanship\u202f"], "author": ["Keith Harrison"], "description": ["This time it\u2019ll be d
{"title": ["CatBoost - the new generation of Gradient Boosting"], "author": ["Anna Veronika Dorogush"], "description": ["Gradient boosting
{"title": ["Code Review Skills for Pythonistas"], "author": ["Nina Zakharenko"], "description": ["As teams and projects grow, code review
{"title": ["Creating Solid APIs"], "author": ["Rivo Laks"], "description": ["Increasingly, our apps are used not by humans but by other ap
{"title": ["Building a Question Answering System using Deep Learning Techniques "], "author": ["Kricha Jalota"], "description": ["Question
{"title": ["Change music in two epochs"], "author": ["Marcel Raas"], "description": ["This talk is about applying deep learning to music.
{"title": ["Building new NLP solutions with spaCy and Prodigy"], "author": ["Matthew Honnibal"], "description": ["Commercial machine learn
{"title": ["Bytecodes and stacks: A look at CPython\u2019s compiler and its execution model"], "author": ["Petr Viktorin"], "description":
{"title": ["Automating testing and deployment with Github and Travis"], "author": ["Alex Gr\u00f6nholm"], "description": ["Maintaining an
{"title": ["Asyncio in Python 3.7 and 3.8."], "author": ["Yury Selivanov"], "description": ["The talk is aimed to give attendees a clear p
{"title": ["Bad hotel again? Find your perfect match!"], "author": ["Elisabetta Bergamini"], "description": ["For most travellers, online
{"title": ["Asyncio in production"], "author": ["Hrafn Eiriksson"], "description": ["Much has been written about asynchronous programming
{"title": ["Bridging the Gap: from Data Science to Production"], "author": ["Florian Wilhelm"], "description": ["A recent but quite common
{"title": ["Building a Naive Bayes Text Classifier with scikit-learn"], "author": ["Obiamaka Agbaneje"], "description": ["Machine learning
{"title": ["Autism in development"], "author": ["Ed Singleton"], "description": ["Autism is a condition that correlates with engineering.
{"title": ["The pytest/tox/devpi help desk"], "author": ["Oliver Bestwalter"], "description": ["We\u2019ll try to help everyone with their
{"title": ["OpenStack Help Desk"], "author": ["Daniel Abad"], "description": ["Come and chat with us about OpenStack! The free and open-so
{"title": ["Help desk: choosing (or not) the right NoSQL database"], "author": ["Alexys Jacob"], "description": ["During this ", "help des
```

Also, we can see that it generates a SQLite file that we can open with the SQLite browser tool and see the structure of the generated table:

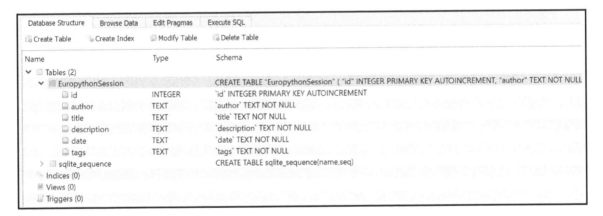

Working with Scrapy in the cloud

In this section, we will explore Scrapy for deploying spiders and crawlers in the cloud.

Scrapinghub

The first step is register in the Scrapinghub service, which can be done at the following URL: `https://app.scrapinghub.com/account/login/`.

Scrapy Cloud is a platform for running web crawlers and spiders, where spiders are executing in cloud servers and scale on demand: `https://scrapinghub.com/scrapy-cloud`.

To deploy projects into Scrapy Cloud, you will need the Scrapinghub command-line client, called `shub`, and it can be installed with the `pip` install command. You can check if you have the latest version:

```
$ pip install shub --upgrade
```

The next step is to create a project in Scrapinghub and deploy your Scrapy project:

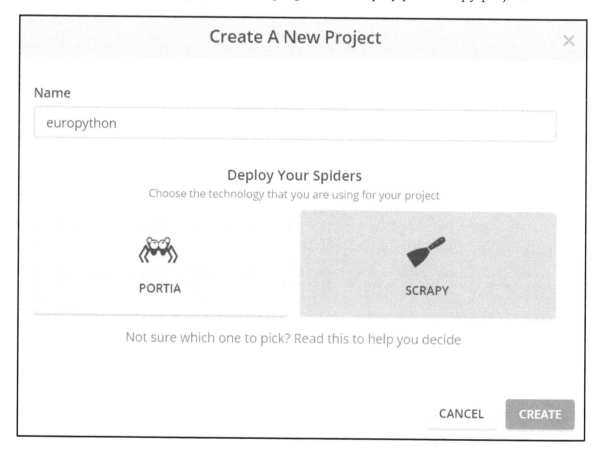

When you create a Scrapy Cloud project, you will see information related with API key and the ID on your project's **Code & Deploys** page:

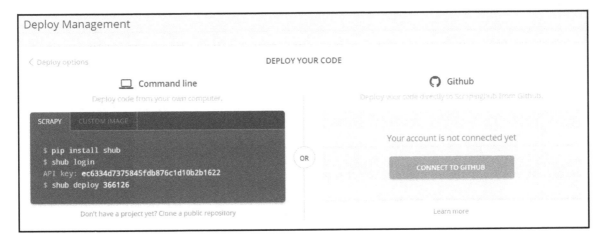

When spider is deployed, you can go to your project page and schedule or run the spider there:

When you run the spider, you will be redirected to the project dashboard for checking the state of your spider, items, and data extracted. Once the process is finished, the job created will be automatically moved to completed jobs:

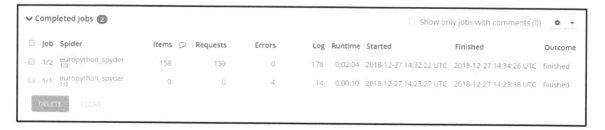

We can also see job details where we can see extracted data in the job items section:

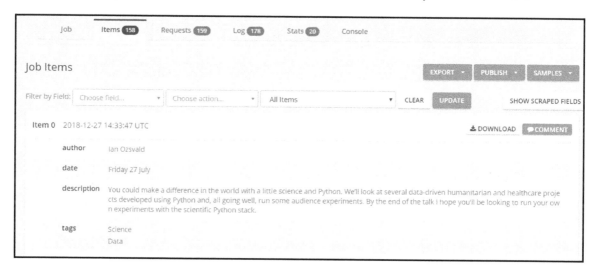

Portia

Portia is a visual web scraping tool available in the Scrapinghub platform: `https://github.com/scrapinghub/portia`.

Portia is a tool that allows you to visually scrape websites annotating a web page to identify the data you wish to extract. Portia will understand how to scrape data from similar pages based on these annotations.

Documentation can be found from reading the docs in the URL: `https://portia.readthedocs.io/en/latest/getting-started.html`.

You can run and deploy Portia in your local machine through some environments such as Docker, Vagrant, and Ubuntu virtual machine following the official documentation: `https://portia.readthedocs.io/en/latest/installation.html`. Also, you can access this Portia service at `https://portia.scrapinghub.com`, following is the screenshot to run and deploy Portia:

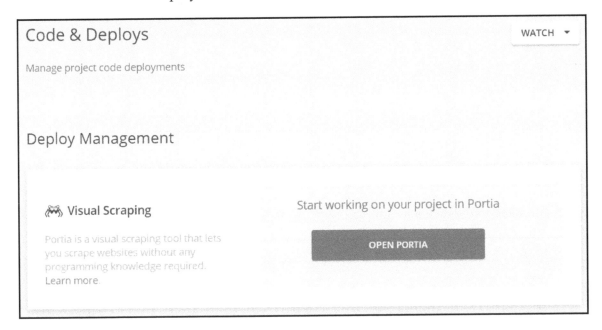

Portia has the capacity to find similar items for each page. This process will continue until it has finished checking every page or has reached the limit of your Scrapinghub plan.

The first step is set up the website that you want to scrape in the Portia site:

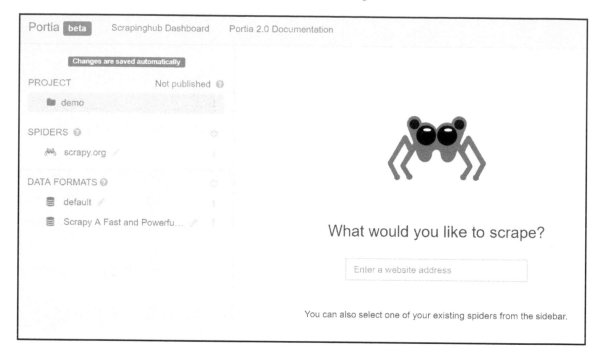

Next, you need to create a new spider:

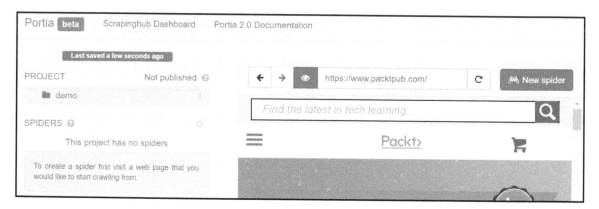

Portia has the capacity to add the page's URL as a start page automatically. The crawling process will start with start pages and Portia will visit them to find more links when the spider is executed.

In this example, we are extracting the titles of the books from the `packtpub.com` domain:

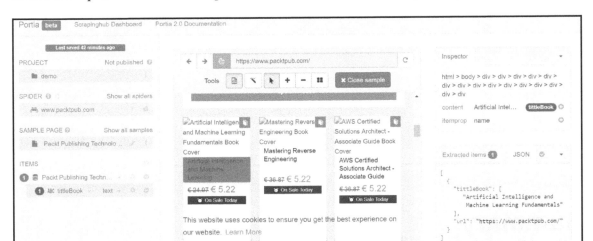

Start pages and link crawling

Portia will use start pages for starting crawling. Under the **LINK CRAWLING** section, you can choose how Portia will follow links and in the **LINK CRAWLING** section you can add and remove start pages.

These are the many options for link crawling:

- **Follow all in-domain links**: Allow it to follow links under the same domain and subdomain
- **Don't follow links**: Allow it to only follow start pages
- **Configure URL pattern**: Ensure that the URL pattern is defined using regular expressions

In this screenshot, we can see the methods Portia uses for link crawling:

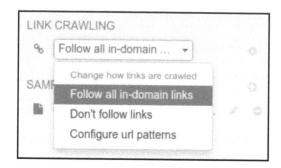

Summary

One of the objectives of this chapter has been to learn about the modules that allow the automatic extraction of data on a specific domain. One of the best tools for web scraping in Python is Scrapy. In this tool, we simply create a class that represents the information that we want to get from the web and Scrapy itself is responsible for connecting to the website, extracting information, and creating the objects of our class.

In the next chapter, we will learn how to use Python to compose, send, and retrieve email with SMTP, POP3, and IMAP protocols.

Questions

1. What library does Scrapy use to extract content from web pages as if they were regular expressions?
2. What XPath expression could we use to extract the images of a certain URL from which the HTML code has been extracted?
3. What XPath expression could we use to extract the links of a certain URL from which the HTML code has been extracted?
4. What method of the BeautifulSoup module allows you to obtain all the elements of a certain label?
5. What basic elements at the level of files and folders can we find in a Scrapy project?
6. In which part of our Scrapy project do we define the extraction procedure for each of the items?

7. In which part of our Scrapy project do we define the classes that allow us to validate the data or save the extracted data in some databases?
8. What is the main Scrapy class that allows us to define our spider?
9. What is the main method you must implement when building an item pipeline?
10. What is the main platform for deploying spiders in the cloud and what are the commands for doing this task?

Further reading

In these links, you will find more information about the mentioned tools and the official Python documentation for some of the modules that we've discussed:

- This is the official documentation for the BS4 package: `http://www.crummy.com/software/BeautifulSoup/bs4/doc`
- This is the official documentation for the Scrapy package: `http://doc.scrapy.org/en/latest`
- This is the official documentation for the mechanize package: `http://wwwsearch.sourceforge.net/mechanize`
- `scrapy` commands: `https://doc.scrapy.org/en/latest/topics/commands.html`
- Comparison between Portia and ParseHub: `https://www.parsehub.com/blog/portia-vs-parsehub-comparison-which-alternative-is-the-best-option-for-web-scraping/`
- Twint: `https://github.com/twintproject/twint`

5
Engaging with Email

Email is one of the most popular forms of digital communication. Python has a rich number of built-in libraries for dealing with emails. In this chapter, you will learn how to use Python to compose, send, and retrieve emails with the **Simple Mail Transfer Protocol (SMTP)**, **Post Office Protocol 3 (POP3)**, and **Internet Message Access Protocol (IMAP)** protocols. Practical code examples in Python 3.7 will illustrate most of these concepts in detail.

The following topics will be covered in this chapter:

- Learning about and understanding email protocols
- Sending emails with SMTP through the `smtplib` library
- Learning the POP3 protocol and retrieving emails with `poplib`
- Retrieving emails on the email server using IMAP with `imapclient` and `imaplib`

Technical requirements

The examples and source code for this chapter are available in this book's GitHub repository in the `Chapter05` folder: `https://github.com/PacktPublishing/Learning-Python-Networking-Second-Edition`.

You will need to install Python's version 3 distribution on your local machine and have active Twitter and Gmail accounts for testing examples that are related to Gmail servers.

Introduction to email protocols

Often, end users use software or a graphical user interface (GUI) to write, send and receive emails., Also known as email clients, for example, Mozilla Thunderbird, Microsoft Outlook, etc., are customers of e-mail. The same tasks can be done through a web interface, that is, a web mail client interface. Some common examples of these are: Gmail, Yahoo mail and Hotmail

The mail you send from your client's interface travels through a series of specialized email servers that internally run software called the Mail Transfer Agent (MTA), and their main job is to route the email to destinations appropriate by analyzing the mail header.

Subsequently, the mail arrives at the recipient's mail server, which can be retrieved using his email client.

In this section we will review the main communication protocols that are used to send and receive emails, among which we can highlight:

- **SMTP**: The SMTP protocol is used for sending emails from one host to another and allows you to transfer files between mail servers.
- **Simple Mail Transfer Protocol Secure (SMTPS)**: This encrypts communications while the email is being transferred between mail servers.
- **POP3**: The POP3 protocol provides a standardized way for users to download messages from mailboxes to their computers. When using the POP3 protocol, your email messages will be downloaded from the **internet service provider (ISP)** mail server to your local computer. You can also leave copies of your emails on the ISP server.
- **IMAP**: The IMAP protocol provides a standardized way of accessing your emails from your ISP. As this requires only a small data transfer, this scheme works well even over a slow connection, such as a mobile phone network. If you send a request to read a specific email, that email message will be downloaded from the ISP. You can also do some other interesting things, such as creating and manipulating folders or mailboxes on the server, and deleting messages. A mail client also pulls emails from the mail server, but has more functionality than POP3 since a copy of the message is retained on the mail server.
- **Secure/Multipurpose Internet Mail Extensions(S/MIME)**: This uses a **public key infrastructure (PKI)** to either encrypt the email or digitally sign the email to prove the integrity of the message. It is very cumbersome as it requires each user to exchange their public key and does not scale very well.

Python has three modules, smtplib, poplib, and imaplib, which support SMTP, POP3, and the IMAP protocols, respectively. Each module has options for transmitting the information securely by using the **Transport Layer Security** (**TLS**) protocol. Each protocol also uses some form of authentication for ensuring the confidentiality of the data.

Sending emails with SMTP through the smtplib library

In this section, we will learn about the SMTP protocol and introduce smtplib, a Python module that's used to send emails. We will also demonstrate how to send different types of email, such as simple text messages, emails with attachments, and emails with HTML content. We will also explore how to work with emails with SMTP authentication in Python 3.7.

SMTP protocol

SMTP is a set of rules for the transmission of messages from their origin to the destination and is used to transmit email messages to mail servers. SMTP uses port 25 to send or transmit mail messages. Email servers need to have this port open to listen for incoming connections.

In the connection between the client and server, the client sends the first **SYN** message to the server to start the connection through port 25. The server accepts the connection by sending the **SYN_ACK** message.

After this exchange of messages, the server sends the client a message with identifier **220**, indicating that the server is ready to carry out transactions so that it can proceed and send emails. Subsequently, the client identifies the server message through **HELO**, which is used to read the messages.

The following image shows the client and server's communication through the SMTP protocol:

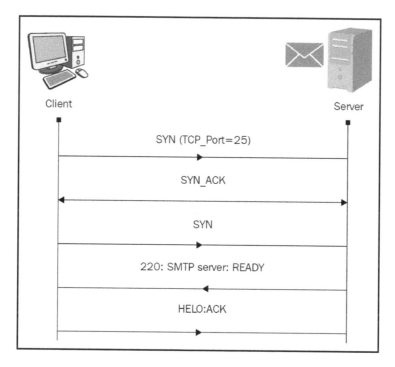

In this diagram we can see the first phase of the communication where the client sends a SYN packet to the server using the port 25. If the connection is established, a series of confirmation packets SYN_ACK are exchanged between them. Finally,the server it returns the STMP server: READY packet to the client indicating that server its ready to receive connections.

Working with smtplib

Python provides the smtplib module for working with the SMTP protocol. You can transmit messages by calling the sendmail() method of SMTP objects. Let's look at how we can using it to send an email with this module:

1. Create a smtplib.SMTP object that will receive as a parameter of its constructor method, that is, the host (localhost)
2. Create a mail message
3. Send the message through a call to the sendmail method of the SMTP object

The syntax for creating a SMTP object is as follows:

```
import smtplib
smtpObj = smtplib.SMTP([host[,port[,local_hostname]]])
```

Let's look at what each parameter in the preceding code in more detail:

- `host`: This is the IP address or domain of the SMTP server host
- `port`: The default value is `25` and, if you provide a host parameter, you need to specify the port number that's used by the SMTP server
- `local_hostname`: You need to specify the localhost server address if your SMTP server is located on your local machine `sendmail` has the following syntax and parameters:

```
SMTP.sendmail(from_addr, to_addrs, msg[, mail_options,
rcpt_options])
```

Let's look at these parameters in detail:

- `from_addr`: The sender's email address
- `to_addrs`: A list of chains; sends an email
- `msg`: Sends a message

Sending a basic message

These are the basic steps we can follow for sending a basic message with `smtplib`:

1. To begin, we need to import the necessary classes: `import smtplib`.
2. The SMTP class represents a connection to an SMTP server. Next, we specify our email address, destination, and the message:

```
from_address = "from_user@domain.com"
to_address = "to_user@domain.com"
message = "Message"
```

3. To begin with the message format, we need to import the necessary classes:

```
from email.mime.text import MIMEText
```

4. These messages use the MIME standard, and so we must use the MIMEText class to build a plain text email. We implement an instance of the MIMEText class to build the message:

```
mime_message = MIMEText(message, "plain")
mime_message["From"] = from_address
mime_message["To"] = to_address
mime_message["Subject"] = "Subject"
```

5. In case the message contains Unicode characters, consider specifying the encoding:

```
mime_message = MIMEText(message, "plain", _charset="utf-8")
```

6. You can modify the visual aspect of the message using HTML:

```
message = "<em>Hello</em>, <strong>python</strong>!"mime_message =
MIMEText(message, "html", _charset="utf-8")
```

7. Once the message has been elaborated, we must make the connection to the SMTP server:

```
import smtplib
smtp = SMTP("smtp_server")
```

8. We can use the server address provided by your hosting provider for this. In the case of the most important services, the server addresses are `smtp.live.com` (Outlook/Hotmail), `smtp.mail.yahoo.com` (Yahoo!), and `smtp.gmail.com` (Gmail).

9. We then need to enter the data for authentication, that is, the username (usually, this is an email address) and password:`smtp.login(from_address, "password")`

10. Finally, we send the email and close the connection with the `quit()` method:

```
smtp.sendmail(from_address, to_address, mime_message.as_string())
smtp.quit()
```

In the following script, we are using a basic example for sending email using `smtplib`.

You can find the following code in the `smtp_basic.py` file:

```
#!/usr/bin/env python3

import smtplib
```

```
smtp = smtplib.SMTP('smtp_server')

try:
    smtp.sendmail('from@fromdomain.com', ['to@todomain.com'], "This is a
test email message.")
except SMTPException as exception:
    print("Error: unable to send email: "+exception)
finally:
    smtp.quit()
```

In this script, we are using a SMTP object to connect to the SMTP server and then using the `sendmail()` method, passing from address, the destination address, and the message as parameters.

If you are using a webmail service (such as Gmail), your email provider must have provided you with outgoing mail server details that you can supply them with, as follows:

```
smtplib.SMTP('mail.server.domain', 25)
```

Here, we must point out that the third argument, message, is a string representing the email. We know that a message is usually composed of a header, sender, recipient, message content, and attachments.

In the following script, we are reviewing a way to send an email by using `MIMeText` for the message format. You can find the following code in the `smtp_message_format.py` file:

```
#!/usr/bin/env python3

import smtplib
from email.mime.text import MIMEText
from email.header import Header

sender = 'sender@domain.com'
receiver = 'receiver@domain.com'

mail_host="smtp.domain.com"
mail_user="user"
mail_password="password"

message = MIMEText('Python', 'plain', 'utf-8')
message['From'] = Header(sender, 'utf-8')
message['To'] = Header(receiver, 'utf-8')

subject = 'Python SMTP message'
message['Subject'] = Header(subject, 'utf-8')

smtp = smtplib.SMTP()
```

```
try:
    smtp.connect(mail_host, 25)
    smtp.login(mail_user,mail_password)
    smtp.sendmail(sender, receiver, message.as_string())
except smtplib.SMTPException as exception:
    print("Error:"+exception)
finally:
    smtp.quit()
```

If you get `smtplib.SMTPNotSupportedError: SMTP AUTH`, then the extension is not supported by the server. When you're trying this with a Gmail server, it's important to mention that Gmail requires TLS (which we will review in the following examples).

Sending messages in HTML format

The library provides you with an option to send a message in HTML format. In this way, while sending an email message, you can specify a MIME version, content type, and character set, thanks to the `MiMEText` constructor. In this example, we are using the `'html'` content type and the `'utf-8'` character set:

```
mail_message = """
 <p>Python</p>
 <p><a href="http://www.python.org">python</a></p>
 """
 message = MIMEText(mail_message , 'html', 'utf-8')
```

In this way we can provide a message in HTML format following utf-8 encoding.

Sending emails to multiple recipients

To send an email to multiple recipients, it will only be necessary to generate a list with the email receivers.

```
receivers = ['receiver1@domain.com', 'receiver2@domain.com']
```

In this example, we are declaring an array with two receivers.

Sending an email with attachments

To send messages with attachments, you must create an object instance of the `MimeMultipart()` class. If there are multiple attachments, these can be built sequentially. In this example, we are attaching two text files to the message:

```
from email.mime.multipart import MIMEMultipart
from email.mime.text import MIMEText

message = MIMEMultipart()
message['From'] = Header("Sender", 'utf-8')
message['To'] =  Header("Receiver", 'utf-8')
message['Subject'] = Header('Python SMTP', 'utf-8')

message.attach(MIMEText('Python SMTP', 'plain', 'utf-8'))

file1 = MIMEText(open('file1.txt', 'rb').read(), 'base64', 'utf-8')
file1["Content-Type"] = 'application/octet-stream'
file1["Content-Disposition"] = 'attachment; filename="file1.txt"'
message.attach(file1)

file2 = MIMEText(open('file2.txt', 'rb').read(), 'base64', 'utf-8')
file2["Content-Type"] = 'application/octet-stream'
file2["Content-Disposition"] = 'attachment; filename="file2.txt"'
message.attach(file2)
```

In this script we are using the attach() method from MIMEMultipart class for attaching two files with the message. Each file is declared as MIMEText object and defined as application/octet-stream in the Content-Type property.

Authentication with TLS

The SMTP class also has the capacity to manage authentication and TLS encryption. First, we need to determine whether the server supports TLS encryption. To do this, we can use the ehlo() method to identify our computer to the server and query what extensions are available. Then, we can call has_extn() to check the results. Once TLS is started, you must call ehlo() again to re-identify yourself over TLS connection.

If you want to do SMTP authentication with TLS instead of SSL, you simply have to change the port to 587 and execute smtp.starttls() in the following way:

```
smtp.connect('smtp.mail.server', 587)
smtp.ehlo()
if smtp.has_extn('STARTTLS'):
    smtp.starttls()
    smtp.ehlo()
smtp.login('user@domain', 'password')
```

In this section we have reviewed how we can manage authentication and TLS encryption.

Establishing a connection with a Gmail SMTP server

It is possible to take advantage of the free Gmail SMTP server to send emails. It can be the definitive solution for those who cannot use the SMTP server that's provided by their ISP or their host, as well as those who experience several problems with sending emails. In this section, you will learn how to use the free Gmail SMTP server.

To establish a connection with `smtp.gmail.com`, we can use the following instructions:

```
mailServer = smtplib.SMTP('smtp.gmail.com',587)
mailServer.ehlo()
mailServer.starttls()
mailServer.ehlo()
mailServer.login("user@gmail.com","password")
```

Basically, we indicate `smtp.gmail.com` as the mail server name and the connection as port `587`. Then, we establish the `starttls()` protocol, sending an `ehlo()` message beforehand to accept it. Finally, we enter the session with `user@gmail.com` and the corresponding password, once again sending an `ehlo()` message beforehand.

You can see all of these features in the `smtp_login_tls.py` file:

```python
#!/usr/bin/env python3

import sys, smtplib, socket

# this invokes the secure SMTP protocol (port 465, uses SSL)
from smtplib import SMTP_SSL as SMTP
from email.mime.text import MIMEText

try:
    msg = MIMEText("Test message", 'plain')
    msg['Subject']= "Sent from Python"
    msg['From'] = "user@gmail.com"
```

In the previous code block we import necessary packages and define our message object using MIMEText class.In the next code block we create smtp session and if the server it supports SSL encryption,establish a secure connection with the server.

```python
# create smtp session
smtp = smtplib.SMTP("smtp.gmail.com", 587)
#debug active
smtp.set_debuglevel(True)
# identify ourselves to smtp gmail client
smtp.ehlo()
# Check if we can encrpt this session
if smtp.has_extn('STARTTLS'):
```

```
# secure our email with tls encryption
smtp.starttls()
# re-identify ourselves as an encrypted connection
smtp.ehlo()
```

Once we have created our SMTP session and checked whether we can encrypt this session, we can use the login method for authenticating our user credentials and send an email with the `sendmail` method:

```
try:
    smtp.login("user@gmail.com", "password")
except smtplib.SMTPException as e:
    print("Authentication failed:", e)
    sys.exit(1)

    try:
        smtp.sendmail('user@gmail.com', ['user@gmail.com'],
msg.as_string())
    except (socket.gaierror, socket.error,
socket.herror,smtplib.SMTPException) as e
        print(e)
        sys.exit(1)
    finally:
        smtp.quit()

except (socket.gaierror, socket.error, socket.herror,smtplib.SMTPException)
as e:
    print(e)
    sys.exit(1)
```

In the next section, we are going to review the configuration for sending emails with the Gmail SMTP service.

Using an external SMTP service

Although most hosts and ISP providers offer support for SMTP, there are some benefits of using an external SMTP service:

- They can guarantee a better delivery of emails
- You will not have to configure your own server (if you use VPS)

You can find the details of Google SMTP in the following parameters:

- **SMTP server:** smtp.gmail.com
- **SMTP user:** Your complete Gmail user (email), for example, user@gmail.com

- **SMTP password**: Your Gmail password
- **SMTP port**: The default Gmail SMTP server port is `465` for SSL and `587` for TSL
- **TLS/SSL**: Required

To send an email through the Gmail SMTP server, you need to configure it through the following service by activating the **Allow less secure apps: ON** option with your Google account at `https://www.google.com/settings/security/lesssecureapps`:

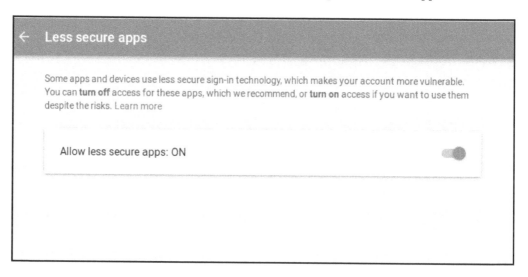

Now, we can proceed and send emails from Python. We will follow these steps to achieve this process:

1. Create an SMTP object for the server connection
2. Log in to your account
3. Define the headers of your messages and login credentials
4. Create a `MIMEMultipart` message object and attach the corresponding headers
5. Attach the message to the `MIMEMultipart` object message
6. Send the message

You can find the following code in the `send_text_mail_from_gmail.py` file:

```
#!/usr/bin/env python3

from email.mime.multipart import MIMEMultipart
from email.mime.text import MIMEText
import smtplib
```

```
# create message object instance
message = MIMEMultipart()

# setup the parameters of the message
message['From'] = "user@domain"
message['To'] = "user@domain"
message['Subject'] = "Subject"

# add in the message body
message.attach(MIMEText("message", 'plain'))
```

In the previous code block we have created the message object instance and setup the parameters of the message.In the next code block we are going to create the connection with the smtp server, login with user credentials and send email with sendmail method.

```
#create server
server = smtplib.SMTP('smtp.gmail.com: 587')
server.starttls()

# Login Credentials for sending the mail
server.login(message['From'], "password")

 # send the message via the server.
server.sendmail(message['From'], message['To'], message.as_string())
print("successfully sent email to %s:" % (message['To']))
server.quit()
```

In the previous example we have reviewed how to send an email using the Gmail SMTP server.You can test it changing the parameters of the message using your user and setting your password in the login() method credentials.

Creating and sending an email with an attachment

Now, we will be sending an image attachment. This is a similar process to sending a plain text email. The only difference is that, here, we are using the MIMEImage class to create MIME message objects of image types. Follow these steps to get started:

1. Create an SMTP object for the connection to the server
2. Log in to your account
3. Define the headers of your messages and login credentials
4. Create a MIMEMultipart message object and attach the corresponding headers, that is, from, to, and subject
5. Read and attach the image to the MIMEMultipart object message
6. Finally, send the message

You can find the following code in the `send_attachment_mail_from_gmail.py` file:

```python
from email.mime.multipart import MIMEMultipart
from email.MIMEImage import MIMEImage
from email.mime.text import MIMEText
import smtplib

# create message object instance
message = MIMEMultipart()

# setup the parameters of the message
message['From'] = "user@domain"
message['To'] = "user@domain"
message['Subject'] = "sending images as attachment"

# attach image to message body
message.attach(MIMEImage(file("image.jpg").read()))
```

In the previous code block we have created the message object instance and setup the parameters of the message,including attached image to message body. In the next code block we are going to create the connection with the smtp server, login with user credentials and send email with sendmail method.

```python
# create server
server = smtplib.SMTP('smtp.gmail.com:587')
server.starttls()

# Login Credentials for sending the mail
server.login(message['From'], "password")

# send the message via the server.
server.sendmail(message['From'], message['To'], message.as_string())
server.quit()
print("successfully sent email to %s:" % (message['To']))
```

In the previous example we have reviewed how to send an email with attached image using the Gmail SMTP server. You can test it changing the parameters of the message using your user and setting your password in the login() method credentials.

Learning the POP3 protocol and retrieving emails with poplib

In this section, we will learn about the POP3 protocol and explore the `poplib` library and how to work with emails with POP3 in Python 3.7.

Understanding the POP3 protocol

POP3 is a protocol that allows email clients to obtain email messages that are stored on a remote server. It is an application-level protocol in the OSI model. The stored email messages can be downloaded and read by the local computer. The POP3 protocol can be used to download these messages from the email server.

POP3 is designed to receive emails, not to send them; it allows users with intermittent or very slow connections (such as modem connections) to download their emails while they have a connection and later check them when they are disconnected. It should be mentioned that most mail clients include the option to leave messages on the server so that a client using POP3 connects, obtains all messages, stores them on the user's computer as new messages, removes them from the server, and finally disconnects.

The following diagram shows the client and server communicating through the POP3 protocol:

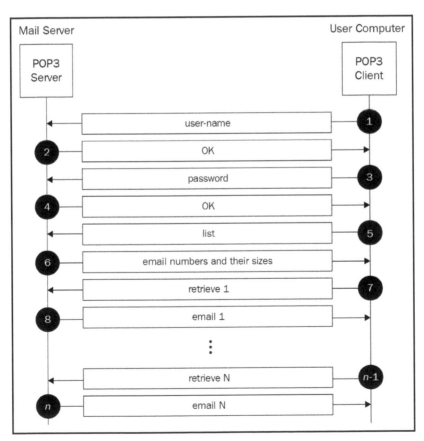

The client establishes a connection to the server on TCP port 110. They then send their username and password to access the mailbox. Once the connection has been established, the user can obtain the email messages individually.

 If you want to read a little more, here is a link to your corresponding RFC: `https://tools.ietf.org/html/rfc1725.html`.

Introduction to poplib

Accessing an email address from Python is very simple if you have POP3 enabled. For this task, can use the `poplib` library. As an example, I will use Gmail. If you want to try this out for yourself, remember to enable POP3 on the Gmail website. To do this, you need to enter the configuration section inside a Gmail account. You can review *Gmail account configuration* section of this chapter.

This module defines a class called POP3 that encapsulates a connection to a POP3 server. This class also supports encrypted communication with the TLS protocol.

This module provides two high-level classes:

- POP()
- POP3_SSL()

Both classes implement the POP3 and POP3S protocols, respectively. The class constructor for each one accepts three arguments: host, port, and timeout. The optional timeout parameter determines the number of seconds of the connection timeout at the server.

Basically, this module will allow us to connect to a POP3 server, and then authenticate and read the emails. In addition, this module provides a POP3_SSL class, which provides support for connecting to POP3 servers that use SSL as the underlying protocol layer.

As we can see in the documentation on `poplib` (`https://docs.python.org/3/library/poplib.html`), the `poplib` module has two classes with the following constructors:

```
class poplib.POP3(host[, port[, timeout]])
class poplib.POP3_SSL(host[, port[, keyfile[, certfile]]])
```

These are the more relevant methods:

- `POP3.user(username)`: This establishes a user in the connection.
- `POP3.pass_(password)`: This establishes a password in the connection. Note that the mailbox on the server is locked until the `quit()` method is called.
- `POP3.getwelcome()`: This returns the welcome string that's returned by the POP3 server.
- `POP3.stat()`: This gets the status of the mailbox. The result is a tuple of two integers (message count and mailbox size).
- `POP3.list([which])`: This requests a list of messages. The result is in the form (response, ['mesg_num octets', ...], octets). If it is configured, it is the message to list.
- `POP3.retr(which)`: This retrieves the complete message number and configures your view banner.
- `POP3.dele(which)`: This marks the message number that will be deleted. On most servers, deletions are not carried out until the `quit()` method is called.
- `POP3.quit()`: This allows you to confirm the changes, unlock the mailbox, and release the connection.
- `POP3.top (which, number)`: This retrieves the header of the message, plus the number of lines of the message after the header of the message number.

To summarize, we have the `poplib.POP3` and `poplib.POP3_SSL` classes to connect to the server (we use the second one if the server has SSL implemented) and the `user` and `pass_` methods to authenticate us. Finally, we have the `getwelcome` method, which captures the welcome message from the server.

Retrieving emails with SSL

`POP3_SSL()` is the secure version of `POP3()`. This class takes additional parameters, such as `keyfile` and `certfile`, which are used for supplying the SSL certificate files, namely the private key and certificate chain file. Writing for a POP3 client is also very straightforward. To do this, instantiate a mailbox object by initializing the `POP3()` or `POP3_SSL()` classes. Then, invoke the `user()` and `pass_()` methods to login to the server by using the following command:

```
mailbox = poplib.POP3_SSL("POP3_SERVER", "SERVER_PORT")
mailbox.user('username')
mailbox.pass_('password')
```

You can see the basic POP3 example from the documentation: `http://docs.python.org/library/poplib.html#pop3-example`.

 We can retrieve all of the messages from an email account with the `retr` method. The following link provides documentation about this method: `https://docs.python.org/3/library/poplib.html#poplib.POP3.retr`.

Here is a minimal example that opens a mailbox and retrieves all of its messages. First, we create a `POP3_SSL` object (Gmail works with SSL) and enter our username and password. From here, we can manage our emails with the functions that are provided by the `poplib` library. In this example, we obtain the list of messages with the `list()` method. The last message is chosen from the response and the server is requested through `retr(msgid)`.

You can find the following code in the `mailbox_basic.py` file:

```python3
#!/usr/bin/env python3

import poplib

mailbox = poplib.POP3_SSL("pop.gmail.com",995)
mailbox.user("user")
mailbox.pass_("password")

print(mailbox.getwelcome())

messages = len(mailbox.list()[1])

for index in range(messages):
    for message in mailbox.retr(index+1)[1]:
        print(message)

mailbox.quit()
```

In this example, we have the same functionality from the previous script—the only difference is how we get the `params` server, port, user, and password from the command line.

You can find the following code in the `mailbox_basic_params.py` file:

```python3
#!/usr/bin/env python3

import poplib
import argparse
```

```
def main(hostname,port,user,password):

  mailbox = poplib.POP3_SSL(hostname,port)
  try:
    mailbox.user(user)
    mailbox.pass_(password)
    response, listings, octet_count = mailbox.list()
    for listing in listings:
      number, size = listing.decode('ascii').split()
      print("Message %s has %s bytes" % (number, size))
  except poplib.error_proto as exception:
    print("Login failed:", exception)

  finally:
    mailbox.quit()
```

In the previous code block we have defined our function that accepts as parameters the hostname,port,user and password and establish the connection with this configuration.In the next code block we use the argparse module for setting the parameters used by the main() method.

```
if __name__ == '__main__':
    parser = argparse.ArgumentParser(description='MailBox basic params')
    parser.add_argument('--hostname', action="store", dest="hostname")
    parser.add_argument('--port', action="store", dest="port")
    parser.add_argument('--user', action="store", dest="user")
    given_args = parser.parse_args()
    hostname = given_args.hostname
    port = given_args.port
    user = given_args.user
    import getpass
    password = getpass.getpass(prompt='Enter your password:')
    main(hostname,port,user,password)
```

Let's see how we can read out the email messages by accessing Google's secure POP3 email server. By default, the POP3 server listens on port 995 securely. The following is an example of fetching an email by using POP3.

Get the total number of messages:

```
(messagesNumber, size) = mailbox.stat()
```

Get a specific message by using your mailbox number:

```
response, headerLines, bytes = mailbox.retr(i+1)
```

You can find the following code in the `poplib_gmail.py` file:

```python
#!/usr/bin/env python3

import poplib
import getpass

mailbox = poplib.POP3_SSL ('pop.gmail.com', 995)
username = input('Enter your username:')
password = getpass.getpass(prompt='Enter your password:')

mailbox.user(username)
mailbox.pass_(password)

EmailInformation = mailbox.stat()
print("Number of new emails: %s ", EmailInformation)
numberOfMails = EmailInformation[0]

num_messages = len(mailbox.list()[1])
```

In the previous code block we initialize the connection with pop3 server mail and store information about connection in mailbox object, later we get information about stats and the messages number. In the next code block we use the mailbox object to retrieve information about each message contained in the mailbox.

```python
for i in range (num_messages):
    print("\nMessage number "+str(i+1))
    print("-------------------")
    # read message
    response, headerLines, bytes = mailbox.retr(i+1)
    #for header in headerLines:
        #print(str(header))
    print('Message ID', headerLines[1])
    print('Date', headerLines[2])
    print('Reply To', headerLines[4])
    print('To', headerLines[5])
    print('Subject', headerLines[6])
    print('MIME', headerLines[7])
    print('Content Type', headerLines[8])

mailbox.quit()
```

In this example we have extracted mails from our mailbox server using the list() method.For each message we can print all information available in headerLines array .Also we can get information in that array accessing specific index like headerLines[1] for get Message ID or headerLines[5] for get mail destination.

Establishing a connection with Gmail for reading emails

Now, we are going to go into detail regarding the code of the previous script. For reading, we first establish the connection to the Gmail pop server, using the `getpass` module to request the password:

```
# Connection is established with the gmail pop server
mailbox = poplib.POP3_SSL ('pop.gmail.com', 995)

import getpass
username = input('Enter your username:')
password = getpass.getpass(prompt='Enter your password:')

mailbox.user(username)
mailbox.pass_(password)
```

Here, we used `poplib.POP3_SSL`, passing the name of the server, that is, `pop.gmail.com`, and the connection port, `995`. Then, we have set the username and password of Gmail. The method to do this is `pass_()`, with an underscore at the end.

Gmail account configuration

In the POP/IMAP configuration of your account, you can find the following options.

In the following screenshot, we can see the Gmail settings page for the POP protocol:

In the **Settings** page, you can configure the POP protocol and enable it for all emails or only emails that arrive from now on.

Unread messages

To see how many unread messages you have, you can call the `list()` method from the mailbox object. Use the following code to find out how many unread messages you have:

```
number_messages = len(mailbox.list()[1])
```

With this, we just have to loop and get the messages one by one to analyze them:

```
for i in range (num_messages):
    print("Message number "+str(i+1))
    print("-------------------")
    # read message
    response, headerLines, bytes = mailbox.retr(i+1)
```

The `retr(i+1)` method brings the message from the server whose number is indicated and marks it on the server as read. It is set to `i+1` because the `retr()` method starts at `1` and not at zero. This method returns the server response, the message, and a few bytes related to the message that we are reading. The important thing is `headerLines`, which in some way contains all of the lines of the message.

Manipulating and retrieving emails on the server email using IMAP with imapclient and imaplib

In this section, we will learn about the IMAP protocol and explore the `imapclient` and `imaplib` modules for working with emails with IMAP in Python 3.7.

IMAP protocol

The IMAP protocol does not download messages to your computer—both the messages and the folders that we have created are kept on the server.

The IMAP protocol is the most advisable when we access our emails from various devices, or when we are mobile. As a precaution, we must periodically delete the contents of our account so that it does not exceed the space that's granted. The drawback of this protocol is that we must always have an internet connection, even to access and work with old messages.

This protocol has the advantage that, when we connect to read our emails from different devices, for example, our laptop or smartphone, we know that we can always access all of our messages, and that the mailbox will be updated. It is also interesting to preserve our privacy when we read our emails from a public or shared computer, as it does not store information on the local machine.

For starters, like POP, this protocol is only intended to read emails, not to send them. The main advantage over this is that you are also prepared to manage them: being able to organize them in folders or search in the server are inherent capabilities of the protocol.

Another differential aspect is the architecture that's designed to be accessed from different computers while keeping copies of our emails synchronized. If, in POP, we said that the common thing was to erase the messages as we downloaded them, in IMAP, those messages are kept on the server until we request their deletion explicitly.

This distributed synchronization is based on the UID that represents a unique identifier for a given message sequence number, which allows several clients to access it simultaneously and understand what messages they are manipulating. To round off this distributed support, clients can access any of the following connection modes:

- **Offline mode**: It periodically connects to the server to download new messages and synchronize any changes that may have happened in the different folders. We have the ability to delete the messages as we download them, following a function that's very similar to POP3.
- **Online mode**: It has access to the copy of the server messages exactly when we need to, synchronizing the changes practically on the fly.
- **Disconnected mode**: Do not confuse this with offline mode. In this case, the client works with a local copy while they do not have access to the internet, where they can create/delete/read their emails. The next time you connect to the internet, these changes will be synchronized with the master copy of the server.

Since it is based on a model in which messages are normally stored on the server after being read, IMAP defines an easy way to manage them—with mail trays, that is, with folders. These follow a tree-like hierarchy, which we are used to in conventional filesystems. Following the standard we always have, the inbox will be the main source, but we can create other folders with different attributes. For example, there are attributes to specify that a folder contains only emails, (\Noinferiors), or only folders, (\Noselect), but they can also have other attributes that indicate whether or not new messages exist since the last time we opened it with (\Marked) and (\Unmarked).

A similar kind of label can have the emails we receive or send. One of the most used is the one that indicates whether it has been read or not (\Seen), but there are also others that indicate that the message has been answered (\Answered), that the message has been highlighted (\Flagged), which is a draft (\ Draft), and so on. All of this information is saved directly on the server and not on the client as we are used to, which allows you to perfectly synchronize this metadata between several clients.

Technically, at a low level, IMAP works very similarly to POP3—a connection is opened to port 143 of the server, and a conversation begins in ASCII. Following the custom, Gmail uses another port 993, which is the alternative port of IMAP if we want the connection to be encrypted under SSL. Once that connection is created, the client starts sending commands and receiving responses.

On an IMAP server, email messages are grouped into folders, some of which will come predefined by an IMAP provider. Once a folder has been selected, messages can be listed and fetched. Instead of having to download every message, the client can ask for particular information from a message, such as a few headers and its message structure, to build a display or summary for the user to click on, hence pulling message parts and downloading attachments from the server on demand.

Retrieving emails with imaplib

As we mentioned earlier, accessing emails over the IMAP protocol doesn't necessarily download them onto the local device.

Python provides a library called imaplib, which can be used for accessing messages over the IMAP protocol. This library provides the IMAP4() class, which takes the host and port for implementing this protocol as arguments. The default port is 143.

The IMAP4_SSL() class has the capacity to connect over an SSL encrypted socket and provides a secure version of the IMAP4 protocol by using 993 as the default port.

A typical example of what an IMAP client looks like can be seen here:

```
mailbox = imaplib.IMAP4_SSL("IMAP_SERVER", "SERVER_PORT")
mailbox.login('username', 'password')
mailbox.select('Inbox')
```

The previous code will try to initiate an IMAP4 encrypted client session. After the login() method is successful, you can apply the various methods on the created object. In the previous code snippet, the select() method has been used. This will select a user's mailbox. The default mailbox is called inbox.

> A full list of methods that are supported by this mailbox object is available on the Python standard library documentation page, which can be found at https://docs.python.org/3/library/imaplib.html.

Here, we would like to demonstrate how you can search the mailbox by using the search() method. It accepts a character set and search criterion parameter. The character set parameter can be None, where a request for no specific character will be sent to the server. However, at least one criterion needs to be specified. For performing an advanced search for sorting the messages, you can use the sort() method.

We can use a secure IMAP connection for connecting to the server by using the IMAP4_SSL() class.

If you are using a Gmail account and want to store all of your emails messages in your Gmail Sent folder, go to the **Forwarding and POP/IMAP** tab and enable IMAP.

In the following screenshot, we can see the Gmail configuration for the IMAP protocol:

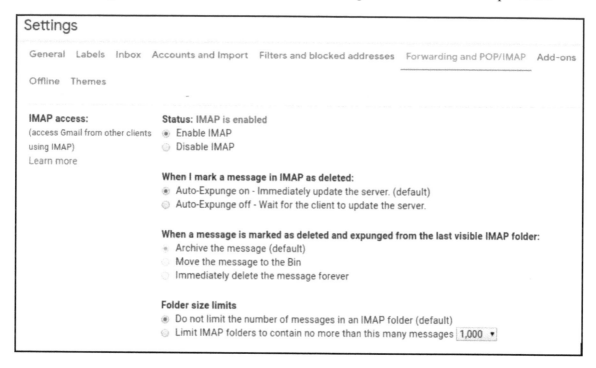

You can find the following code in the `check_remote_email_imaplib.py` file:

```python
#!/usr/bin/env python3

import argparse
import imaplib

def check_email(username,password):
    mailbox = imaplib.IMAP4_SSL('imap.gmail.com', '993')
    mailbox.login(username, password)
    mailbox.select('Inbox')
    type, data = mailbox.search(None, 'ALL')
    for num in data[0].split():
        type, data = mailbox.fetch(num, '(RFC822)')
        print ('Message %s\n%s\n' % (num, data[0][1]))
    mailbox.close()
    mailbox.logout()
```

In the previous code block we define `check_email()` method that establish the connection with imap gmail server with username and password parameters, select the inbox for recover messages and search for specific RFC number protocol inside the mailbox. In the next code block we define our main program that request information about username and password used for establish the connection.

```
if __name__ == '__main__':
    parser = argparse.ArgumentParser(description='Email Download IMAP')
    parser.add_argument('--username', action="store", dest="username")
    given_args = parser.parse_args()
    username = given_args.username
    import getpass
    password = getpass.getpass(prompt='Enter your password:')
    check_email(username, password)
```

In this example, an instance of `IMPA4_SSL()`, that is, the `mailbox` object, has been created. Here, we have taken the server address and port as arguments. Upon successfully logging in with the `login()` method, you can use the `select()` method to choose the `mailbox` folder that you want to access. In this example, the `inbox` folder has been selected. To read the messages, we need to request the data from the inbox. One way to do that is by using the `search()` method. Upon successful reception of some email metadata, we can use the `fetch()` method to retrieve the email message envelope part and data. In this example, the RFC 822 type of standard text message has been sought with the help of the `fetch()` method.

We can use the Python pretty print or the `print` module for showing the output on the screen. Finally, apply the `close()` and the `logout()` methods to the mailbox object.

Retrieving emails with imapclient

IMAPClient is a complete IMAP client library written in Python that uses the `imaplib` module from the Python standard library. It provides an API for creating a connection and reads messages from the `inbox` folder.

You can install `imapclient` with the following command:

```
$ pip install imapclient
```

The `IMAPClient` class is the core of the IMAPClient API. You can create a connection to an IMAP account by instantiating this class and interacting with the server calling methods on the IMAPClient instance.

The following script shows how to interact with an IMAP server, displaying all of the messages in the inbox folder and the information related to the message ID, subject, and date of the message.

You can find the following code in the `folder_info_imapclient.py` file:

```python
#!/usr/bin/env python3

from imapclient import IMAPClient
import getpass

username = input('Enter your username:')
password = getpass.getpass(prompt='Enter your password:')

server = IMAPClient('imap.gmail.com', ssl=True)
server.login(username, password)
select_info = server.select_folder('INBOX',readonly=True)
for k, v in list(select_info.items()):
    print('%s: %r' % (k, v))

server.logout()
```

In this script, we open an IMAP connection with the `IMAPClient` and get information about its capabilities and mailboxes.

You can find the following code in the `listing_mailbox_imapclient.py` file:

```python
#!/usr/bin/env python3

import sys
from imapclient import IMAPClient
import getpass

username = input('Enter your username:')
password = getpass.getpass(prompt='Enter your password:')

server = IMAPClient('imap.gmail.com', ssl=True)

try:
    server.login('user', 'password')
except server.Error as e:
    print('Could not log in:', e)
    sys.exit(1)

print('Capabilities:', server.capabilities())
print('Listing mailboxes:')
data = server.list_folders()
for flags, delimiter, folder_name in data:
```

```
        print(' %-30s%s %s' % (' '.join(str(flags)), delimiter, folder_name))

server.logout()
```

This could be the output of the previous script, where we can see capabilities and mailboxes that are available in your Gmail account:

```
Capabilities: ('UNSELECT', 'IDLE', 'NAMESPACE', 'QUOTA',
'XLIST','AUTH=XOAUTH')
 Listing mailboxes:
 \Noselect \HasChildren / [Gmail]
 \HasChildren \HasNoChildren / [Gmail]/All Mail
 \HasNoChildren / [Gmail]/Drafts
 \HasChildren \HasNoChildren / [Gmail]/Sent Mail
 \HasNoChildren / [Gmail]/Spam
 \HasNoChildren / [Gmail]/Starred
 \HasChildren \HasNoChildren / [Gmail]/Trash
```

In this section we have reviewed the `imapclient` and `imaplib` modules which provide the methods can for accessing emails with IMAP protocol.

Summary

This chapter demonstrated how Python can interact with the three major email handling protocols, that is, SMTP, POP3, and IMAP. In each of these cases, you learned how to work with the client code. Finally, an example for using SMTP in Python's logging module was shown.

In the next chapter, you will learn how to use Python to work with remote systems to perform various tasks, such as administrative tasks, by using SSH, file transfer through FTP, Samba, and so on. Some remote monitoring protocols, such as SNMP, and authentication protocols, such as LDAP, will be reviewed.

Questions

1. What is the main difference between the `pop` and `imap` protocols?
2. What method can you use to send emails with `smtplib`?
3. What is the class and method from `smtplib` for sending an email message where you can specify a MIME version, content type, and character set?
4. What is the class and method from `smtplib` for sending messages with attachments?
5. What is the method from the `poplib` package that gets the status of the mailbox?
6. What is the class from the `poplib` package that allows you to retrieve emails in a secure way with SSL?
7. How we can get a specific message with your mailbox number with `poplib`?
8. What is the main advantage of the IMAP protocol if we were to compare it with SMTP and POP?
9. Which class from the `imaplib` package provides a secure version of the IMAP4 protocol?
10. How can you open an IMAP connection with `IMAPClient` and list folder information?

Further reading

In the following links, you will find more information about the tools and the official Python documentation that was covered in this chapter:

- Other `smtplib` examples: `https://pymotw.com/2/smtplib/`
- Python module for connecting with an Outlook email account: `https://github.com/awangga/outlook`

6
Interacting with Remote Systems

In this chapter, you'll learn about the different modules that allow us to interact with the FTP, SSH, SNMP, and LDAP servers. You'll also learn how to use Python to work with remote systems to perform administrative tasks. Then, you'll get to explore several network protocols and Python libraries, which are used to interact with remote systems, and understand how you can access a few services through the Python scripts and modules, such as `ftplib`, `paramiko`, `pysnmp`, and `python-ldap`.

The following topics will be covered in this chapter:

- Understanding the SSH protocol
- SSH terminal and running commands with paramiko
- Understanding the FTP protocol for transferring files
- Reading and interacting with SNMP servers
- Reading and interacting with LDAP servers

Technical requirements

The examples and source code for this chapter are available in the GitHub repository in the `Chapter06` folder: `https://github.com/PacktPublishing/Learning-Python-Networking-Second-Edition/tree/master/chapter6`.

This chapter requires quite a few third-party packages, such as `paramiko` and `pysnmp`. You can use your operating system's package management tool to install them. If we are working with Python 3 in Debian and Ubuntu Unix distributions, all of the modules that are required for understanding the topics will be covered in this chapter.

We can use the following commands to install the required modules in a Debian distribution:

- `sudo apt-get install python3`
- `sudo apt-get install python3-setuptools`
- `sudo easy_install3 paramiko`
- `sudo easy_install3 python3-ldap`
- `sudo easy_install3 pysnmp`

Understanding the SSH protocol

In this section, you will be introduced to the SSH protocol.

SSH introduction

Secure shell (**SSH**) is a protocol that facilitates secure communications between two systems using a client/server architecture and allows users to connect to a host remotely. Unlike other remote communication protocols, such as FTP or Telnet, SSH encrypts the connection session, making it impossible for anyone to obtain unencrypted passwords.

SSH is a protocol that was built with the aim of offering a secure alternative to other commands for remote connection from another machine, and allows you to authenticate a user through a secure channel.

For Mac and Linux users, the `ssh` command comes installed by default. The SSH command consists of three different parts:

```
ssh {user}@{host}
```

The following are the three different parts of a SSH command:

- The `ssh` key command tells your system that you want to open a secure and encrypted shell connection.
- `{user}` represents the account you wish to access. For example, you can use the root user to authenticate with full permissions on the server.
- `{host}` refers to the server IP address or domain you need to access.

When you press *Enter*, you will be asked to enter the password for the requested account. When you write it, nothing will appear on the screen, but your password, in fact, is being transmitted. Once you have finished typing the password, press the *Enter* key again, even though you will not see the password you introduced in the console. If your password is correct, you will receive a remote Terminal window.

This is the output you will receive when you try to connect with the `192.168.0.1` IP address using the `ssh root@192.168.0.1` command:

```
The authenticity of host '192.168.0.1  (192.168.0.1 )' can't be
established.
 ECDSA key fingerprint is
SHA256:NW6uvRVer4uKQAQt+USwpeFwjz0NDqvflzbwM9c5SR4.
 Are you sure you want to continue connecting (yes/no)? yes
 Warning: Permanently added '192.168.0.1 ' (ECDSA) to the list of known
hosts.
 root@192.168.0.1 's password:
 Last login: Fri Mar 8 14:31:58 2019 from 192.168.0.1
```

 Details of the SSH protocol can be found in the RFC4251-RFC4254 documents, available at `http://www.rfc-editor.org/rfc/rfc4251.txt`

Using SSH to encrypt sessions

When you access a remote server through the SSH protocol, the security risks are considerably reduced. In the case of the client and of the system itself, security is improved thanks to encryption; secure shell is responsible for encrypting all sessions. Thus, it is impossible for anyone to access the passwords, the customer's access data, or what the client has written. When a connection is made through the Secure Shell protocol, the remote user is authenticated by the system. Then, we proceed to transfer this information from the host client and return the data to the client.

How the SSH protocol works

The operation of this protocol can be summarized in the following steps:

1. The client initiates a TCP connection on port 22 of the service. This port is the one that uses the protocol by default, although as we will see in the following steps, it can be modified.

2. The client and the server agree on the version of the protocol to be used, as well as the encryption algorithm used for the exchange of information.

3. The server, which has two keys (one private and one public), sends its public key to the client.

4. When the client receives the key sent by the server, it compares it with the one stored to verify its authenticity. The SSH protocol requires the client to confirm it the first time.

5. With the public key of the server in its possession, the client generates a random session key, creating a message that contains that key and the algorithm that was selected for the encryption of the information. All this information is sent to the server, which makes use of the public key that was sent in an earlier step in an encrypted form.

6. If everything is correct, the client is authenticated, initiating the session to communicate with the server.

SSH service features

The secure shell protocol offers a series of interesting features, which has become the most-used protocol by all users who manage some type of Linux server, either in the cloud or dedicated. Let's highlight some of its features:

- The use of SSH encrypts the registration session, which prevents anyone from getting non-encrypted passwords.
- The encryption keys that are used are only known by those who issue the information and receive it.
- Modifying the key could modify the original message, which means that if a third-party obtains the key, it cannot access the complete message.
- The user can verify that they are still connected to the same server that was initially connected.
- When a user authenticates, an encrypted secure channel is created between them and the server to exchange the information with total guarantee.
- The data that's sent and received through the use of SSH is done through encryption algorithms, where the recommended minimum key size is 1,024 bits, which makes it very difficult to decipher and read.
- The client can use applications securely from the server's command interpreter, which allows them to manage the machine as if they were in front of it.
- The use of SSH is also used as an encrypted channel to protect protocols that do not use default encryption, such as port-forwarding techniques.

From a security point of view, the SSH protocol provides the following types of protection:

- Once the client has established the initial connection, it is possible to check whether it is connecting to the same server it was initially connected to.
- The client uses a robust encryption, 128-bit, to send authentication information to the server.
- All traffic that is sent and received during communication is transferred through a 128-bit encryption.

Configuring the SSH protocol to make it more secure

Although we have been talking about the use of the SSH protocol being completely safe, this does not mean that it is oblivious to suffer some kind of attack that puts our information at risk. For this reason, users have the option to modify the default configuration of this protocol to make it even more secure, such as changing the default port or the maximum number of retries to connect to the server. Let's see how we can improve the security of our SSH.

First, we need to locate the configuration file, `sshd_config`. This file is usually in the `/etc/ssh` path.

The following configuration could be the default content of the file:

```
Port 22
Protocol 2
LoginGraceTime 30
PermitRootLogin no
MaxAuthTries 2
MaxStartups 3
```

These are the parameters we can modify in this file configuration:

- **Change the default port**: By default, SSH uses port `22`, so when a hacker launches an attack, it usually does so on this port. If we change the port number, the service will not respond to the port by default, and we will have created a new obstacle for anyone trying to get our information. To make this happen, just change the value of the `port` field in the configuration file to the value you want.

- **Disable root access**: Every server is assigned a root user, which has privileges to do any kind of action on the machine. A good practice to improve security is to prevent access to the server through this root user and force access through any of the users we have created who do not have root privilege. Once logged in with our user, we can become a root user through the `sudo` command. To prevent access by the root user, we must set the `PermitRootLogin` variable to `no`.

- **Limit the number of retries**: By means of the `MaxAuthTries` variable, we can indicate the number of times that we can make a mistake when entering the username or password. Once the number that we have indicated is exceeded, the connection will be lost and the connection process will have to start again. With this, we will avoid attacks of persistence of the connection. If we want to enable a maximum of five attempts, we would have to indicate it in the following way: `MaxAuthTries 5`.

- **Limit the number of login screens**: We can limit the number of simultaneous login windows that we can have active from the same IP in order to avoid divided attacks. Once the user is logged in, it will not be possible to have a higher number of SSH terminals open than indicated in this variable. If we just want a single login screen over the IP, we should do it in the following way: `MaxStartups 1`.

- **Limit the time that the login screen will be available**: Through the `LoginGraceTime` instruction, we indicate the time in seconds that the login screen will be available to enter our credentials. After that time, the screen will disappear and you will have to start the process again. With this, we prevent the use of a script to access the system. If we want to put a duration of 15 seconds, we would do it in the following way: `LoginGraceTiem 15`.

- **Indicate the users that can access via SSH**: By means of the `AllowUser` directive, we can indicate the users that will be able to access the server via SSH, as well as from what IP address they will be able to do so. Let's see some examples of how to indicate it:
    - **Indicate only the name of the users who will have access**: Using `AllowUser user1 user2`, we are indicating that only users `user1` and `user2` will have access to the system via SSH, regardless of the computer and the IP address from which they are connected.

- **Access of a user from a certain IP address**: Using `AllowUser user@<ip_address>`, we can indicate that the `user` user can access the machine via SSH, but only from the IP address that we specify.
- **Access of a user from a given network indicated**: Using `AllowUser user@<network_ip>.*`, we indicate that the user will be able to access from any IP address that forms part of the indicated network.

SSH terminals and running commands with paramiko

In this section, you will learn how to establish an SSH connection to transfer files and run commands with the paramiko python package.

Installing paramiko

Python's paramiko library (`http://www.paramiko.org/`) provides very good support for SSH-based network communication. You can use Python scripts to benefit from the advantages of SSH-based remote administration, such as the remote command-line login, command execution, and the other secure network services between two networked computers. You may also be interested in using the `pysftp` module, which is based on paramiko.

 More details regarding this package can be found at PyPI: `https://pypi.python.org/pypi/pysftp`.

The recommendation is always to install `paramiko` using `pip`, as follows:

```
pip install paramiko
```

Establishing an SSH connection with paramiko

SSH is a client/server protocol. Both of the parties use the SSH key-pairs to encrypt the communication. Each key-pair has one private and one public key. The public key can be published to anyone who may be interested in it. The private key is kept private from everyone except the owner of the key.

We can use the paramiko module to create an SSH client and then connect it to the SSH server. This module will supply the SSHClient() class.

You can use the SSHClient class to create an SSH client with the paramiko module:

```
ssh_client = paramiko.SSHClient()
```

By default, the instance of this client class will reject the unknown host keys. So, you can set up a policy to accept the unknown host keys. The built-in AutoAddPolicy() class will add the host keys as and when they are discovered. Run the set_missing_host_key_policy() method, along with the following argument, on the ssh_client object:

```
ssh_client.set_missing_host_key_policy(paramiko.AutoAddPolicy())
```

If you need to restrict accepting connections only to specific hosts, you can use the load_system_host_keys() method to add the system host keys and system fingerprints:

```
ssh_client.load_system_host_keys()
```

Before executing a command on our server via ssh, we need to create an object of the SSHClient type, which will be responsible for sending all our requests to the server and handling the responses that are returned. You can wrap this code in a function called get_connection(), as follows:

```
import paramiko

def get_connection():
    # start SSH client
    ssh = paramiko.SSHClient()
    # We add the list of known hosts
    ssh.load_system_host_keys()
    #If it does not find the host, it automatically adds it
    ssh.set_missing_host_key_policy(paramiko.AutoAddPolicy())
    # need to use the domain name resolved through DNS query
    ssh.connect('domain', username='user', password='password')
    return ssh
```

Running commands with paramiko

Now that we are connected to the remote host with paramiko, we can run commands on the remote host using this connection. To connect, we can simply call the `connect()` method, along with the target hostname and the SSH login credentials. To run any command on the target host, we need to invoke the `exec_command()` method by passing the command as its argument:

```
ssh_client.connect(hostname, port, username, password)
stdin, stdout, stderr = ssh_client.exec_command(cmd)
    for line in stdout.readlines():
        print(line.strip())
ssh.close()
```

The following code listing shows how to do an SSH login to a target host and then run the command the user introduced in the prompt. You can find the following code in the `ssh_execute_command.py` file:

```
#!/usr/bin/env python3

import getpass
import paramiko

HOSTNAME = 'ssh_server'
PORT = 22

def run_ssh_cmd(username, password, command, hostname=HOSTNAME,port=PORT):
    ssh_client = paramiko.SSHClient()
    ssh_client.set_missing_host_key_policy(paramiko.AutoAddPolicy())
    ssh_client.load_system_host_keys()
    ssh_client.connect(hostname, port, username, password)
    stdin, stdout, stderr = ssh_client.exec_command(command)
    print(stdout.read())
    stdin.close()
    for line in stdout.read().splitlines():
        print(line)

if __name__ == '__main__':
    username = input("Enter username: ")
    password = getpass.getpass(prompt="Enter password: ")
    command = input("Enter command: ")
    run_ssh_cmd(username, password, command)
```

Running an interactive shell with paramiko

If you want to run several commands on the remote host using paramiko, but you encounter the problem that the ssh session is closed when you execute a command, give an exception related with SSH session not active:

paramiko.ssh_exception.SSHException: SSH session not active

To solve this, you can implement an interactive shell using paramiko; that way, the channel does not close after a command is executed in the remote shell.

After creating the SSH client, using connect, you can use the invoke_shell() method, and it will open a channel that it doesn't close after you send something through it.

You can find the following code in the ssh_interactive_shell.py file:

```python
#!/usr/bin/env python3

import paramiko
import re

class ShellHandler:
    def __init__(self, host, user, psw):
        self.ssh = paramiko.SSHClient()
        self.ssh.set_missing_host_key_policy(paramiko.AutoAddPolicy())
        self.ssh.connect(host, username=user, password=psw, port=22)
        # we use this method for getting a shell in the host
        channel = self.ssh.invoke_shell()
        self.stdin = channel.makefile('wb')
        self.stdout = channel.makefile('r')
    def __del__(self):
        self.ssh.close()

    @staticmethod
    def _print_exec_out(cmd, out_buf, err_buf, exit_status):
        print('command executed: {}'.format(cmd))
        print('STDOUT:')
        for line in out_buf:
            print(line, end="")
        print('end of STDOUT')
        print('STDERR:')
        for line in err_buf:
            print(line, end="")
        print('end of STDERR')
        print('finished with exit status: {}'.format(exit_status))
        print('----------------------------------')
        pass
```

In the previous code block, we declared the ShellHandler class with the init method constructor and static method to print the output of the executed command. We continue declaring the method to execute a command that's passed as a parameter, as well as our main program that instantiates an object of this class. For each command available in command list, it calls the execute method:

```
def execute(self, cmd):
""":param cmd: the command to be executed on the remote computer
:examples: execute('ls')
execute('finger')
execute('cd folder_name')
"""
    cmd = cmd.strip('\n')
    self.stdin.write(cmd + '\n')
    finish = 'end of stdOUT buffer. finished with exit status'
    echo_cmd = 'echo {} $?'.format(finish)
    self.stdin.write(echo_cmd + '\n')
    shin = self.stdin
    self.stdin.flush()

    shout = []
    sherr = []
    exit_status = 0

    for line in self.stdout:
        if str(line).startswith(cmd) or str(line).startswith(echo_cmd):
        # up for now filled with shell junk from stdin
            shout = []
        elif str(line).startswith(finish):
        # our finish command ends with the exit status
            exit_status = int(str(line).rsplit(maxsplit=1)[1])
            if exit_status:
                # stderr is combined with stdout.
                # thus, swap sherr with shout in a case of failure.
                sherr = shout
                shout = []
            break
        else:
        # get rid of 'coloring and formatting' special characters
            shout.append(re.compile(r'(\x9B|\x1B\[)[0-?]*[ -/]*[@-
~]').sub('', line).replace('\b', '').replace('\r', '').replace('\n', ''))

    # first and last lines of shout/sherr contain a prompt
    if shout and echo_cmd in shout[-1]:
        shout.pop()
    if shout and cmd in shout[0]:
        shout.pop(0)
```

```
    if sherr and echo_cmd in sherr[-1]:
        sherr.pop()
    if sherr and cmd in sherr[0]:
        sherr.pop(0)

    self._print_exec_out(cmd=cmd, out_buf=shout,
err_buf=sherr,exit_status=exit_status)
    return shin, shout, sherr

commands = ["ls","whoami","pwd"]
host="localhost"
name="user"
pwd="password"

shell_connection = ShellHandler(host,name,pwd)
for command in commands:
    shell_connection.execute(command)
```

SFTP with paramiko

SSH can be used to securely transfer files between two computer nodes. The protocol that's used in this case is the **secure file transfer protocol** (**SFTP**). The Python `paramiko` module will supply the classes that are required to create the SFTP session. This session can then perform a regular SSH login:

```
ssh_transport = paramiko.Transport(hostname, port)
ssh_transport.connect(username='username', password='password')
```

The SFTP session can be created from the SSH transport. The paramiko working in the SFTP session will support the normal FTP commands, such as the `get()` command:

```
sftp_session = paramiko.SFTPClient.from_transport(ssh_transport)
sftp_session.get(source_file, target_file)
```

As you can see, the SFTP `get` command requires the source file's path and the target file's path. In the following example, the script will download a `test.txt` file that's located in the server, which is located on the user's home directory through SFTP.

You can find the following code in the `ssh_download_sftp.py` file:

```
#!/usr/bin/env python3

import getpass
import paramiko
```

```
HOSTNAME = 'ssh_server'
PORT = 22
FILE_PATH = '/tmp/test.txt'

def sftp_download(username, password, hostname=HOSTNAME,port=PORT):
    ssh_transport = paramiko.Transport(hostname, port)
    ssh_transport.connect(username=username, password=password)
    sftp_session = paramiko.SFTPClient.from_transport(ssh_transport)
    file_path = input("Enter filepath: ") or FILE_PATH
    target_file = file_path.split('/')[-1]
    sftp_session.get(file_path, target_file)
    print("Downloaded file from: %s" %file_path)
    sftp_session.close()

if __name__ == '__main__':
    hostname = input("Enter the target hostname: ")
    port = input("Enter the target port: ")
    username = input("Enter your username: ")
    password = getpass.getpass(prompt="Enter your password: ")
    sftp_download(username, password, hostname, int(port))
```

In this example, a file has been downloaded with the help of SFTP. Notice how paramiko has created the SFTP session by using the `SFTPClient.from_transport(ssh_transport)` class.

Paramiko alternatives

In the Python ecosystem, there are other interesting solutions that act as a paramiko wrapper to connect to ssh servers and execute command remotely, such as the **fabric solution**.

Fabric

Fabric is a Python library and a command-line tool that's designed to simplify application deployment and perform system administration tasks through the SSH protocol. It provides tools to execute arbitrary shell commands (either as a normal login user, or via `sudo`), upload and download files, and so on.

Fabric (`http://www.fabfile.org`) is a high-level Python (2.7, 3.4+) library that's designed to execute shell commands remotely over SSH so that we can control a group of SSH servers in parallel. It is possible to use Fabric directly from the command line by executing the fab utility or with the API that contains all the classes and decorators that are needed to declare a set of SSH servers, as well as the tasks that we want to execute on them.

One of the main dependencies that must be met before installing Fabric is having the paramiko library installed; this library is responsible for making the connections to the SSH servers using the appropriate authentication mechanism according to each case (auth by password or auth by public key).

Fabric is available in the official Python repository (https://pypi.org/project/Fabric/). We can install `Fabric` simply by running the following command:

```
pip install Fabric
```

The fundamental element of Fabric from version 2 is the connections. These objects represent the connection to another machine, and we can use it to do the following:

- Execute commands in the shell of the other machine, which you can run using `sudo`
- Download files from the remote machine to local using `get`
- Upload files from local to remote using `put`
- Do forwarding using `forward_local`, `forward_remote`

To start a connection, we need the address of the machine and some way to identify ourselves. In the whole issue of Fabric authentication, it delegates the work in paramiko, which supports a wide variety of options, including the option to use gateways.

Let's look at an example; in this case, we are requesting the IP address and the password for authentication in the remote host:

```
>>> from getpass import getpass
  >>> ip_address= prompt="Enter remote host ip address:")
>> password = getpass(prompt="Enter Password for Connecting with remote host: ")
  >>> connection=
Connection(host=ip_address,user="user",connect_kwargs={"password" : password})
```

We can execute commands with the `run()` and `sudo()` methods. If we want to obtain the result of the command, we can simply assign a variable for the evaluation of the run commands:

```
>>> def isLinux(connection):
>>>     result = connection.run("uname -s")
>>>     return result.stdout.strip() == "Linux"
>>> isLinux(connection)
```

Fabric is very powerful tool, but as soon as we have many machines, we will often do the same tasks. We can use a simple `for` loop, but Fabric brings us an abstraction called group. Basically, we can join connections in a single group and execute the actions that we ask. There are two types of groups:

- `SerialGroup`: Executes the operations sequentially
- `ThreadGroup`: Executes the operations in parallel

In this example, we are launching the `sudo apt update` command in parallel over hosts defined in the `ThreadingGroup` constructor:

```
>>> from fabric import ThreadingGroup
 >>> def update(cxn):
 >>>     cxn.run("sudo apt update")
>>> pool = ThreadingGroup("user1@host1", "user2@host2")
 >>> update(pool)
```

Understanding the FTP protocol for transferring files

In this section, you will be introduced to the FTP protocol for transferring files and the `ftplib` package for interacting with Python.

The File Transfer Protocol

The **File Transfer Protocol** (**FTP**) protocol allows us to make file transfers through a connection in a network. This is the protocol that we use to connect remotely to servers and manipulate files. Port `21` is usually used.

The protocol design is defined in such a way that it is not necessary for the client and server to run on the same platform; any client and any FTP server can use a different operating system and use the primitives and commands defined in the protocol to transfer files.

To interact with this protocol, we need two things. The first is a server that is available for our network—it can be on the same network or maybe on the internet. The second is a client that can send and receive information from said server; this client must have the capacity to be able to use the ports specified by the service and the established authentication.

Introduction to ftplib

Unlike SFTP, FTP uses the plaintext file transfer method. This means any username or password transferred through the wire can be detected by an unrelated third party. Even though FTP is a very popular file transfer protocol, people frequently use this to transfer a file from their PCs to remote servers.

FTPlib is a Python library that will allow us to connection to an FTP server from a script. To begin, we must have installed Python in our operating system and the FTPLib package. We can install them on a Linux system in two ways:

```
pip install ftplib
apt-get install python-ftplib
```

In Python, ftplib is a built-in module that's used to transfer files to and from the remote machines. You can create an anonymous FTP client connection with the FTP() class:

```
ftp_client = ftplib.FTP(path, username, email)
```

Then, you can invoke the normal FTP commands, such as the CWD command, to list the files in a specific directory. To download a binary file, you need to create a file handler, such as the following:

```
file_handler = open(DOWNLOAD_FILE_NAME, 'wb')
```

To retrieve the binary file from the remote host, the syntax shown here can be used, along with the RETR command:

```
ftp_client.retrbinary('RETR remote_file_name', file_handler.write)
```

In the following script, we are trying to connect to the FTP server, ftp.free.fr, to get get a list of directories with the dir() method, and download a specific file on that server. To download a file through the ftplib libraries, we will use the retrbinary method. We need to pass two things to it as an input parameter: the retr command with the name of the file and a callback function that will be executed every time a block of data is received. In this case it will write it in a file of the same name.

You can find the following code in the ftp_download_file.py file:

```
!/usr/bin/env python3

import ftplib

FTP_SERVER_URL = 'ftp.free.fr'
DOWNLOAD_DIR_PATH = '/mirrors/ftp.kernel.org/linux/kernel/Historic/'
```

```
DOWNLOAD_FILE_NAME = 'linux-0.01.tar.gz'

def ftp_file_download(path, username):
    # open ftp connection
    ftp_client = ftplib.FTP(path, username)
    print("Welcome:", ftp_client.getwelcome())
    # list the files in the download directory
    ftp_client.cwd(DOWNLOAD_DIR_PATH)
    print("Current working directory:", ftp_client.pwd())
    print("File list at %s:" %path)
    files = ftp_client.dir()
    print(files)
    # download a file
    try:
        file_handler = open(DOWNLOAD_FILE_NAME, 'wb')
        ftp_cmd = 'RETR %s' %DOWNLOAD_FILE_NAME
        ftp_client.retrbinary(ftp_cmd, file_handler.write)
        file_handler.close()
        ftp_client.quit()
    except Exception as exception:
        print('File could not be downloaded:', exception)

    if __name__ == '__main__':
        ftp_file_download(path=FTP_SERVER_URL, username='anonymous')
```

The preceding code illustrates how an anonymous FTP can be downloaded from
`ftp.free.fr`, which hosts the first Linux kernel version. The `FTP()` class takes three
arguments, such as the initial filesystem path on the remote server, the username, and the
email address of the ftp user. The `FTP.cwd()` function is used to change the directory or
folder (change the working directory). In this case, after accessing as an anonymous user,
change the location to the `kernel/Historic` folder.

For anonymous downloads, no username and password is required. So, the script can be
downloaded from the `linux-0.01.tar.gz` file, which can be found on the
`/mirrors/ftp.kernel.org/linux/kernel/Historic/` path.

In the following screenshot, we can see the execution of the previous script:

```
Welcome: 220 Welcome to ProXad FTP server
Current working directory: /.mirrors17/ftp.kernel.org/linux/kernel/Historic
File list at ftp.free.fr:
-r--r--r--   1 ftp      ftp         73091 Oct 30  1993 linux-0.01.tar.gz
-r--r--r--   1 ftp      ftp           665 Aug 08  2013 linux-0.01.tar.sign
drwxr-sr-x   5 ftp      ftp          4096 Mar 20  2003 old-versions
-rw-r--r--   1 ftp      ftp           969 May 11  2017 sha256sums.asc
drwxr-sr-x   2 ftp      ftp          4096 Dec 10  2007 v0.99
```

Another way to get information about the files and folders in the current location is to use the `retrlines()` method, which can indicate the commands to execute. `LIST` is a command that's defined by the protocol, as well as others that can also be applied in this function as `RETR`, `NLST`, or `MLSD`.

 For more information on these commands, see RFC 959: `http://tools.ietf.org/html/rfc959.html`.

The second parameter is the `callback` function, which is called for each piece of received data:

```
def callback(info):
    print info
...
ftp.retrlines('LIST', callback)
```

In this example, instead of using the `ntransfercmd()` method to apply a `RETR` command, we receive data in a byte array. We execute the `RETR` command to download the file in binary mode.

You can find the following code in the `ftp_download_file_bytes.py` file:

```
#!/usr/bin/env python3

import os, sys
from ftplib import FTP

f = FTP('ftp.free.fr')
f.login()

f.cwd('/mirrors/ftp.kernel.org/linux/kernel/Historic/')
f.voidcmd("TYPE I")

datasock, size = f.ntransfercmd("RETR linux-0.01.tar.gz")
bytes_so_far = 0
fd = open('linux-0.01.tar.gz', 'wb')

while 1:
    buf = datasock.recv(2048)
    if not buf:
        break
    fd.write(buf)
    bytes_so_far += len(buf)
    print("\rReceived", bytes_so_far, end=' ')
```

```
    if size:
        print("of %d total bytes (%.1f%%)" % (
        size, 100 * bytes_so_far / float(size)),end=' ')
    else:
        print("bytes", end=' ')
  sys.stdout.flush()

print()
fd.close()
datasock.close()
f.voidresp()
f.quit()
```

In this example, we are going to list versions that are available in the Linux kernel ftp with the dir() method.

You can find the following code in the list_kernel_versions.py file:

```
#!/usr/bin/env python3

from ftplib import FTP

entries = []
f = FTP('ftp.free.fr')
f.login()
f.cwd('/mirrors/ftp.kernel.org/linux/kernel/')
f.dir(entries.append)
print("%d entries:" % len(entries))
for entry in entries:
    print(entry)
f.quit()
```

In the following screenshot, we can see the execution of the previous script:

```
28 entries:
drwxr-sr-x     4 ftp      ftp         4096 Mar 20  2003 Historic
drwxr-sr-x     2 ftp      ftp         4096 Jun 26  2017 SillySounds
drwxr-sr-x     5 ftp      ftp         4096 Nov 24  2001 crypto
drwxr-sr-x     2 ftp      ftp       299008 Jan 10 04:13 next
drwxr-sr-x   547 ftp      ftp        16384 Dec 13 00:17 people
drwxr-sr-x     6 ftp      ftp         4096 Mar 13  2003 ports
drwxr-sr-x     7 ftp      ftp         4096 Sep 18  2012 projects
drwxr-sr-x     3 ftp      ftp         4096 Feb 14  2002 testing
drwxr-sr-x     3 ftp      ftp         4096 Oct 03 20:58 tools
drwxr-sr-x     2 ftp      ftp         4096 Mar 20  2003 uemacs
drwxr-sr-x     2 ftp      ftp         4096 Mar 20  2003 v1.0
drwxr-sr-x     2 ftp      ftp        20480 Mar 20  2003 v1.1
drwxr-sr-x     2 ftp      ftp         4096 Mar 20  2003 v1.2
drwxr-sr-x     2 ftp      ftp        40960 Mar 20  2003 v1.3
drwxr-sr-x     3 ftp      ftp        20480 Feb 08  2004 v2.0
drwxr-sr-x     2 ftp      ftp        49152 Mar 20  2003 v2.1
drwxr-sr-x     3 ftp      ftp        12288 Mar 24  2004 v2.2
drwxr-sr-x     2 ftp      ftp        24576 Mar 20  2003 v2.3
drwxr-sr-x     5 ftp      ftp        20480 May 01  2013 v2.4
drwxr-sr-x     4 ftp      ftp        32768 Jul 14  2003 v2.5
drwxr-sr-x    10 ftp      ftp        57344 Aug 08  2013 v2.6
drwxr-sr-x     2 ftp      ftp         4096 Apr 16  2018 v2018.x
lrwxrwxrwx     1 ftp      ftp            4 Nov 23  2012 v3.0 -> v3.x
drwxr-sr-x     4 ftp      ftp       299008 Dec 21 13:11 v3.x
drwxr-sr-x     2 ftp      ftp         4096 Apr 16  2018 v3000.x
drwxr-sr-x     4 ftp      ftp       221184 Jan 09 17:02 v4.x
drwxr-sr-x     2 ftp      ftp         4096 Apr 16  2018 v5.x
drwxr-sr-x     2 ftp      ftp         4096 Apr 16  2018 v6.x
```

Other ftplib functions

These are the main ftplib functions we can use to execute ftp operations:

- `FTP.getwelcome()`: Gets the welcome message
- `FTP.mkd(route)`: Creates a directory; it is passed as an input argument to the route
- `FTP.rmd(path)`: Deletes the directory that we pass
- `FTP.delete(file)`: Deletes the file that we passed as an input parameter
- `FTP.pwd()`: (Print Working Directory) Returns the current directory where it is located
- `FTP.cwd(path)`: (Change Working Directory) Changes directory

- `FTP.dir(path)`: Returns a list of directories
- `FTP.nlst(path)`: Returns a list with the file names of the directory
- `FTP.size(file)`: Returns the size of the file we passed to it

In this example, we are going to list the versions that are available in the Linux kernel FTP with the `nlst()` method.

You can find the following code in the `list_kernel_versions_nslt.py` file:

```python
!/usr/bin/env python3

from ftplib import FTP

f = FTP('ftp.free.fr')
f.login()
f.cwd('/mirrors/ftp.kernel.org/linux/kernel/')
entries = f.nlst()
entries.sort()
print(len(entries), "entries:")
for entry in entries:
    print(entry)
f.quit()
```

Inspecting FTP packets with Wireshark

If we capture the FTP session in Wireshark on port 21 of the public network interface, we can see how the communication happens in plaintext. In the following example, we can see that after successfully establishing a connection with a client, the server sends the `230 Welcome to mirror.as35701.net` banner message. Following this, the client will anonymously send a request for login.

In this example, we are using the `ftplib` module to build a script to determine whether a server offers anonymous logins.

You can find the following code in the `checkFTPanonymousLogin.py` file:

```python
import ftplib

def ftpListDirectory(ftp):
    try:
        dirList = ftp.nlst()
        print(dirList)
    except:
        dirList = []
```

```
                print('[-] Could not list directory contents.')
                print('[-] Skipping To Next Target.')
                return
        retList = []
        for fileName in dirList:
            fn = fileName.lower()
            if '.php' in fn or '.htm' in fn or '.asp' in fn:
                print('[+] Found default page: ' + fileName)
                retList.append(fileName)
        return retList


    def anonymousLogin(hostname):
        try:
            ftp = ftplib.FTP(hostname)
            ftp.login('anonymous', '')
            print(ftp.getwelcome())
            ftp.set_pasv(1)
            print(ftp.dir())
            print('\n[*] ' + str(hostname) +' FTP Anonymous Logon Succeeded.')
            return ftp
        except Exception as e:
            print(str(e))
            print('\n[-] ' + str(hostname) +' FTP Anonymous Logon Failed.')
            return False


    host = 'ftp.be.debian.org'
    ftp = anonymousLogin(host)
    ftpListDirectory(ftp)
```

The anonymousLogin() function takes a hostname and returns a Boolean that describes the availability of anonymous logins. This function tries to create an FTP connection with anonymous credentials. If successful, it returns the True value.

In the following screenshot, we can see an example of executing the previous script over a server that allows anonymous login:

```
220 ProFTPD 1.3.5b Server (mirror.as35701.net) [::ffff:195.234.45.114]
lrwxrwxrwx   1 ftp      ftp            16 May 14  2011 backports.org -> debian-backports
drwxr-xr-x   9 ftp      ftp          4096 Jan 14 09:01 debian
drwxr-sr-x   5 ftp      ftp          4096 Mar 13  2016 debian-backports
drwxr-xr-x   5 ftp      ftp          4096 Nov 11 03:00 debian-cd
drwxr-xr-x   7 ftp      ftp          4096 Jan 13 22:32 debian-security
drwxr-sr-x   5 ftp      ftp          4096 Jan  5  2012 debian-volatile
drwxr-xr-x   5 ftp      ftp          4096 Oct 13  2006 ftp.irc.org
-rw-r--r--   1 ftp      ftp           419 Nov 17  2017 HEADER.html
drwxr-xr-x  10 ftp      ftp          4096 Jan 14 12:05 pub
drwxr-xr-x  18 ftp      ftp          4096 Jan 14 12:14 video.fosdem.org
-rw-r--r--   1 ftp      ftp           377 Nov 17  2017 welcome.msg
None

[*] ftp.be.debian.org FTP Anonymous Logon Succeeded.
['debian-backports', 'backports.org', 'debian-security', 'pub', 'HEADER.html', 'debian', 'welcome.msg', 'ftp.irc.org', '
debian-volatile', 'video.fosdem.org', 'debian-cd']
[+] Found default page: HEADER.html
```

In the following screenshot, we can see packets that are exchanged in the ftp communication:

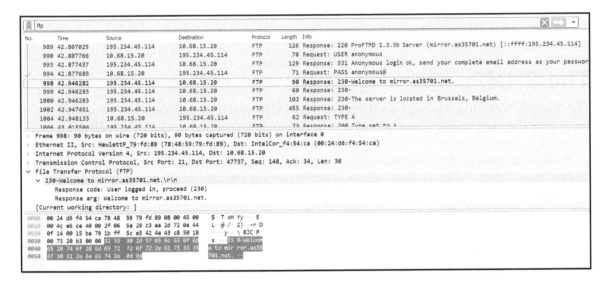

In the following screenshot, we can see packets and the request command for listing files in the ftp server:

Reading and interacting with SNMP servers

In this section, you will learn about the SNMP protocol and examine Python libraries for dealing with SNMP packets.

The SNMP

The **Simple Network Management Protocol** (**SNMP**) is an application layer protocol that facilitates the exchange of management information between network devices. This protocol is part of the set of TCP/IP protocols and allows administrators to manage performance, find and solve problems, and plan the future growth of the network.

SNMP is used to monitor and control the status of devices connected to the internet, especially routers, although it can be used in any type of host that allows the snmpd process to be executed. SNMP operates at the application level using the TCP/IP transport protocol, so it ignores the specific aspects of the hardware on which it operates. The management is carried out at the IP level, so you can control devices that are connected in any network that's accessible from the internet, and not only those located in the local network itself.

For the SNMP protocol, the network is a set of basic elements. The fundamental elements of a network that employs SNMP are as follows:

- **Managed devices:** In each one, an agent is executed
- **Administrator (manager):** The device from which the network is administered
- **Management Information Base, MIB:** A namespace organized hierarchically in the form of a tree, containing the information that can be read and/or written

Here are the five types of SNMP messages that are exchanged between Agents and Administrators:

- **Get Request:** A request from the Administrator to the Agent to send the values contained in the MIB (database)
- **Get Next Request:** A request from the Administrator to the Agent to send the values contained in the MIB, referring to the object
- **Get Response:** The Agent's response to the information request that's launched by the Administrator
- **Set Request:** A request from the Administrator to the Agent to change the value contained in the MIB, referring to a specific object

- **Trap:** A spontaneous message sent by the Agent to the Administrator, upon detecting a predetermined condition, such as the connection/disconnection of a station or an alarm

The SNMP protocol is composed of two elements: the agent and the manager. It is a client-server architecture, in which the agent plays the role of the server and the manager acts as the client.

The agent is a program that must be executed in each network node that you want to manage or monitor. It offers an interface of all the elements that can be configured. These elements are stored in data structures called **Management Information Base** (**MIB**). It represents part of the server, insofar as it has the information that you want to manage and expects commands from the client.

The manager is the software that runs in the station responsible for monitoring the network; its task is to consult the different agents that are in the nodes of the network and data they have been obtaining.

In essence, SNMP is a very simple protocol since all operations are performed under the load-and-store paradigm, which allows for a reduced set of commands. A manager can perform only two types of operations on an agent: read or write the value of a variable in the agent's MIB. These two operations are known as a **read request** (get request) and a **write request** (set-request). There is a command to respond to a read request, called **read-response**, which is used only by the agent.

The possibility of extending the protocol is directly related to the ability of the MIB to store new elements. If a manufacturer wants to add a new command to a device, such as a router, they simply add the corresponding variables to its database (MIB).

MIB – a broad base of information

A MIB is a hierarchical database of objects and their values, stored in an SNMP agent.

Generally, the objects of the MIB are referenced by an identifier. For example, the internet object is referred to by 1.3.6.1, or `iso-ccitt.identified-organization.dod.internet`.

Through the MIB, you have access to the information for management, which is contained in the internal memory of the device in question. MIB is a complete and well-defined database, with a tree structure, and is suitable for handling various groups of objects, with unique identifiers for each object.

The SNMP architecture operates with a small group of objects that are defined in detail in the RFC 1066 Management information base for network management over TCP/IP.

The 8 groups of objects that are usually handled by MIB, which define a total of 114 objects (recently, with the introduction of MIB-II, are defined up to a total of 185 objects), are as follows:

- **System:** Includes the identity of the vendor and the time since the last reinitialization of the management system
- **Interfaces**: Single or multiple interfaces, local or remote
- **ATT (Address Translation Table):** Contains the address of the network and the equivalences with the physical addresses
- **IP (Internet Protocol):** Provides the route tables, and keeps statistics on the received IP datagrams
- **ICMP (Internet Communication Management Protocol):** Counts the number of received ICMP messages and errors
- **TCP (Transmission Control Protocol):** Provides information about TCP connections and retransmissions
- **UDP (User Datagram Protocol):** Counts the number of UDP datagrams sent, received, and delivered
- **EGP (Exterior Gateway Protocol):** Collects information on the number of EGP messages that are received and generated

SNMP is a client/server-based network protocol. The server daemon provides the requested information to the clients. If you are working with a Debian-based distribution, you can install snmp in your local machine with the `apt-get install snmp` command. This will provide some snmp commands. In your machine, if SNMP has been installed and configured properly, you can use the `snmpwalk` utility command to query the basic system information by using the following syntax:

```
# snmpwalk -v2c -c public localhost
```

Here is the output of the execution of the `snmpwalk` command, where we can see information being returned by the SNMP agent:

```
iso.3.6.1.2.1.1.1.0 = STRING: "Linux debian6box 2.6.32-5-686 #1 SMP
Tue Jan 15 15:00:01 UTC 2019 i686"
iso.3.6.1.2.1.1.2.0 = OID: iso.3.6.1.4.1.8072.3.2.10
iso.3.6.1.2.1.1.3.0 = Timeticks: (88855240) 10 days, 6:49:12.40
iso.3.6.1.2.1.1.4.0 = STRING: "Me <me@example.org>"
iso.3.6.1.2.1.1.5.0 = STRING: "debian6box"
iso.3.6.1.2.1.1.6.0 = STRING: "Sitting on the Dock of the Bay"
```

The output of the preceding command will show the MIB number and its values. For example, the `iso.3.6.1.2.1.1.1.0` MIB number shows that it's a string type value, such as `Linux debian6box 2.6.32-5-686 #1 SMP Tue Jan 15 15:00:01 UTC 2019 i686`.

Introduction to pysnmp

PySNMP is a cross-platform, pure Python SNMP engine implementation (`https://github.com/etingof/pysnmp`) that abstracts a lot of SNMP details for developers, and supports both Python 2 and Python 3.

You can install the `pysnmp` module by using the `pip` command:

```
$ pip install pysnmp
```

ASN.1 (`https://asn1js.org`) is a standard and notation that describes rules and structures to represent, encode, transmit, and decode data in telecommunication and computer networking. PySNMP also requires the PyASN1 package. PyASN1 (`https://github.com/etingof/pyasn1`) conveniently provides a Python wrapper around ASN.

This module provides a useful wrapper for the snmp commands. Let's learn how to create an `snmpwalk` command. To begin, import a command generator:

```
from pysnmp.entity.rfc3413.oneliner import cmdgen
cmd_generator = cmdgen.CommandGenerator()
```

Then, define the necessary default values for the connection, assuming that the snmpd daemon has been running on port 161 in **public SNMP simulator at demo.snmplabs.com** and that the community string has been set to public:

```
SNMP_HOST = 'demo.snmplabs.com'
SNMP_PORT = 161
SNMP_COMMUNITY = 'public'
```

We can perform SNMP using the `getCmd()` method. The result is unpacked into various variables. The output of this command consists of a four-value tuple. Out of those, three are related to the errors that are returned by the command generator, and the fourth one (`varBinds`) is related to the actual variables that bind the returned data and contains the query result:

```
error_notify, error_status, error_index, var_binds =
  cmd_generator.getCmd(
  cmdgen.CommunityData(SNMP_COMMUNITY),
  cmdgen.UdpTransportTarget((SNMP_HOST, SNMP_PORT)),
```

```
cmdgen.MibVariable('SNMPv2-MIB', 'sysDescr', 0),
lookupNames=True, lookupValues=True
```

You can see that cmdgen takes the following parameters:

- CommunityData(): Sets the community string as public.
- UdpTransportTarget(): This is the host target, where the snmp agent is running. This is specified in a pair of the hostname and the UDP port.
- MibVariable: This is a tuple of values that includes the MIB version number and the MIB target string (which is sysDescr; this refers to the description of the system).

The output of this command consists of a four-value tuple. Out of those, three are related to the errors returned by the command generator, and the fourth is related to the actual variables that bind the returned data. The following example shows how the preceding method can be used to fetch the SNMP host description string from a running SNMP daemon.

You can find the following code in the snmp_get_information.py file:

```python
#!/usr/bin/env python3

from pysnmp.hlapi import *
import sys

def get_info_snmp(host, oid):
    for (errorIndication,errorStatus,errorIndex,varBinds) in
nextCmd(SnmpEngine(),
    CommunityData('public'),UdpTransportTarget((host, 161)),ContextData(),
ObjectType(ObjectIdentity(oid)),lookupMib=False,lexicographicMode=False):

if errorIndication:
    print(errorIndication, file=sys.stderr)
    break
elif errorStatus:
    print('%s at %s' % (errorStatus.prettyPrint(),errorIndex and
varBinds[int(errorIndex) - 1][0] or '?'), file=sys.stderr)
    break
else:
    for varBind in varBinds:
        print('%s = %s' % varBind)

get_info_snmp('demo.snmplabs.com', '1.3.6.1.2.1.1.9.1.2')
```

Polling information from the SNMP agent

An interesting tool to check for connections with SNMP servers and obtain the value of the SNMP variable is `snmp-get`, which is available for both Windows and Unix environments: `https://snmpsoft.com/shell-tools/snmp-get/`.

Other tools, such as `snmpwalk` (available at `https://snmpsoft.com/shell-tools/snmp-walk/`), allow us to obtain information about SNMP servers.

This is the syntax you can use to request information about a specific host:

```
snmpwalk -c:community -v:2c -r:host -os:[oid]
```

In the following screenshot, we can see the usage for the `snmpwalk` command:

```
Description:
    Lists existing SNMP variables on any network device that supports SNMP.
    SNMP is widely used for administration and monitoring purposes.

Usage:
    SnmpWalk.exe [-q] -r:host [-p:port] [-t:timeout] [-v:version] [-c:community]
        [-ei:engine_id] [-sn:sec_name] [-ap:auth_proto] [-aw:auth_passwd]
        [-pp:priv_proto] [-pw:priv_passwd] [-ce:cont_engine] [-cn:cont_name]
            [-os:start_oid] [-op:stop_oid] [-csv]

    -q                  Quiet mode (suppress header; print variable values only).
    -r:host             Name or network address (IPv4/IPv6) of remote host.
    -p:port             SNMP port number on remote host. Default: 161
    -t:timeout          SNMP timeout in seconds (1-600). Default: 5
    -v:version          SNMP version. Supported version: 1, 2c or 3. Default: 1
    -c:community        SNMP community string for SNMP v1/v2c. Default: public
    -ei:engine_id       Engine ID. Format: hexadecimal string. (SNMPv3).
    -sn:sec_name        SNMP security name for SNMPv3.
    -ap:auth_proto      Authentication protocol. Supported: MD5, SHA (SNMPv3).
    -aw:auth_passwd     Authentication password (SNMPv3).
    -pp:priv_proto      Privacy protocol. Supported: DES, IDEA, AES128, AES192,
                        AES256, 3DES (SNMPv3).
    -pw:priv_passwd     Privacy password (SNMPv3).
    -cn:cont_name       Context name. (SNMPv3)
    -ce:cont_engine     Context engine. Format: hexadecimal string. (SNMPv3)
    -os:start_oid       Object ID (OID) of first SNMP variable to walk. Default:.1
    -op:stop_oid        Object ID (OID) of last SNMP variable to walk.
                        Default: walk to the very last variable.
    -csv                Output in CSV (Comma Separated Values) format.
```

At `http://snmplabs.com/snmpsim/public-snmp-agent-simulator.html#examples`, you can see some examples of executing the `snmpalk` command using the SNMP simulation service at `demo.snmplabs.com`.

Reading and interacting with LDAP servers

In this section, you will learn about the LDAP protocol and examine the Python libraries that deal with LDAP packets.

The LDAP protocol

LDAP is a protocol based on the X.500 standard, which is used to access information that is stored through a centralized directory that contains the information of our organization.

LDAP has a client/server architecture, where the server can use a variety of databases to store a directory, each optimized for fast, high-volume read operations. When a client application is connected to an LDAP server, most of the time it will be for queries, although it is also possible to make changes to the directory entries. If the client application is trying to modify the information in an LDAP directory, the server will try to verify that the user has the necessary permissions to update the information.

The biggest advantage of LDAP is that you can consolidate information for an entire organization within a central repository. For example, instead of managing user lists for each group within an organization, you can use LDAP as a central directory, which is accessible from anywhere in the network. Since LDAP supports **Secure Connection Layer** (**SSL**) and **Transport Layer Security** (**TLS**), confidential data can be protected from hackers.

Another advantage of LDAP is that your company can access the LDAP directory from almost any computing platform, from any of the applications that is readily available for LDAP. It is also easy to customize your internal business applications to add LDAP support.

LDAP terminology

LDAP stands for **Lightweight Directory Access Protocol**. It is an application-level protocol that allows queries about a directory service to search for information.

LDAP defines the way to access that directory, that is, it is optimized to carry out read operations on the directory, such as validating authenticated access to a user stored in the directory.

A directory service runs the client-server model, so if a client computer wants to access the directory, it does not access the database directly; instead contacts a process on the server. The process queries the directory and returns the result of the operation to the client. Among the main terms when we work with LDAP, let's highlight the following:

- **Classes**: The objects and their characteristics are defined in classes. For example, the type of object to be defined and the attributes that it will contain depend on the type of object. In the scheme, each class is defined with the attributes that will be obligatory and optional for each created entry.
- **Objects**: Entries in the directory. Objects are instances that are created from a certain class or several, depending on the attributes required for an object. The entire directory will be composed of objects (such as users, groups, or organizational units).
- A **directory service** is like a database where we organize and store information with objects of different classes. This hierarchically-organized structure of the objects is achieved with the implementation of LDAP.
- **entry**: A unit in an LDAP directory. Each entry is identified by its unique **distinguished name (DN)**.
- **DN**: The distinguished name to uniquely identify a specific object in the directory. That is, each entry defined is unique throughout the directory. As we can see, the DN of that object (user type) will be unique throughout the directory and will uniquely identify you.
- **Attributes**: Pieces of information directly associated with the input. For example, an organization can be represented as an LDAP entry. The attributes associated with the organization can be your fax number or your address, for example. In an LDAP directory, the entries can also be people, with common attributes such as their telephone number and email addresses. Some attributes are mandatory while others are optional.
- **The LDAP Data Exchange Format (LDIF)**: An ASCII text representation of LDAP entries. The files used to import data to the LDAP servers must be in LDIF format.

Introduction to python-ldap

Python's `python-ldap` (https://www.python-ldap.org/en/latest/) third-party package provides the necessary functionality to interact with an LDAP server.

You can install this package with the `pip` command:

```
$ pip install python-ldap
```

It is also possible to install `python-ldap` distributions based on Debian or Ubuntu with the following commands:

```
sudo apt-get update
sudo apt-get install python-ldap
```

To begin, you will have to initialize the LDAP connection, where we can replace `ldap_server` with the IP address of the server and the port number:

```
import ldap
ldap_client = ldap.initialize("ldap://<ldap_server>:port_number/")
```

This method initializes a new connection object to access the given LDAP server, and return an LDAP object that's used to perform operations on that server. The next step is bind/authenticate with a user with appropriate rights:

```
ldap_client.simple_bind(user,password)
```

Then, you can perform an `ldap` search. It requires you to specify the necessary parameters, such as base DN, filter, and attributes. Here is an example of the syntax that is required to search for users on an LDAP server:

```
ldap_client.search_s( base_dn, ldap.SCOPE_SUBTREE, filter, attrs)
```

Here is a complete example to find user information using the LDAP protocol. It demonstrates how to open a connection to an LDAP server using the `ldap` module and invoke a synchronous subtree search.

You can find the following code in the `connect_python_ldap.py` file:

```python
#!/usr/bin/env python3
import ldap

LDAP_SERVER ="ldap://52.57.162.88:389"
LDAP_BASE_DN = 'ou=ldap3-tutorial,dc=demo1,dc=freeipa,dc=org'
LDAP_FILTER = '(objectclass=person)'
LDAP_ATTRS = ["cn", "dn", "sn", "givenName"]

def main():
    try:
        # Open a connection
        ldap_client = ldap.initialize(LDAP_SERVER)
        # Set LDAPv3 option
        ldap_client.set_option(ldap.OPT_PROTOCOL_VERSION,3)
        # Bind/authenticate with a user with appropriate rights
        ldap_client.simple_bind("admin",'Secret123')
        # Get user attributes defined in LDAP_ATTRS
```

```
        result =
ldap_client.search_s(LDAP_BASE_DN,ldap.SCOPE_SUBTREE,LDAP_FILTER,
LDAP_ATTRS)
        print(result)
    except ldap.INVALID_CREDENTIALS as exception:
        ldap_client.unbind()
        print('Wrong username or password. '+exception)
    except ldap.SERVER_DOWN as exception:
        print('LDAP server not available. '+exception)

if __name__ == '__main__':
    main ()
```

The previous script verifies credentials for the username and password against a LDAP server. It returns some of the user attributes on success, or a string that describes the error on failure. The script will search the LDAP directory subtree with the `ou=ldap3-tutorial,dc=demo1,dc=freeipa,dc=org` base DN. The search is limited to person objects.

We need to define some global variables so that we can establish the URL of the LDAP server, that is, the base DN to search for users within the LDAP directory and the user attributes that you want to recover.

First, we need to initialize an instance of the `ldap` class and define the options that are required for the connection. Then, try to connect to the server using the `simple_bind` function. In case of success, the user's attributes are retrieved using the `search_s` function.

The LDAP FreeIPA server

FreeIPA (`https://www.freeipa.org/page/Demo`) is a fully-featured identity management solution that provides LDAP server. We can find a free public instance of the FreeIPA server at `https://ipa.demo1.freeipa.org`. The FreeIPA domain is configured with the following users (the password is `Secret123` for all of them):

- **admin**: This user has all the privileges and is considered the administrator account
- **helpdesk**: A regular user with the helpdesk role
- **employee**: A regular user with no special permissions
- **manager**: A regular user, set as the manager of the employee user

In the following screenshot, we can see the active users that are available:

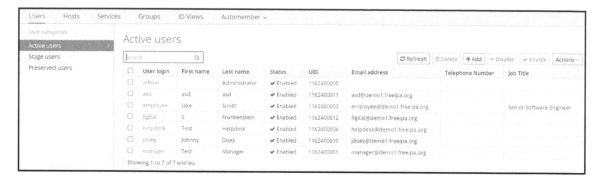

In the following screenshot, we can see the IPA Server configuration:

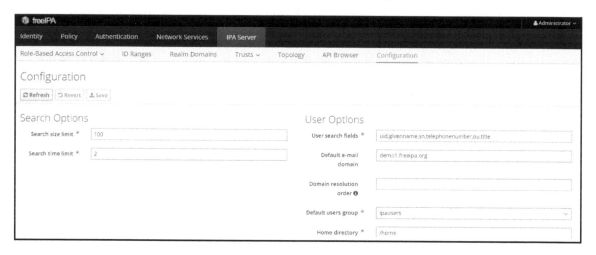

In the following screenshot, we can see the default user object classes inside the IPA Server configuration:

Working with LDAP3

`ldap3` is a fully-compliant Python LDAP v3 client library. It's written from scratch to be compatible with Python 2 and Python 3, and can be installed via its Standard Library with the following command:

```
pip install ldap3
```

Accessing the LDAP server

Using `ldap3` is straightforward—you define a `Server` object and a `Connection` object. All the importable objects are available in `ldap3 namespace`. You need to at least import the `Server` and the `Connection` object, and any additional constants you will use in your LDAP connection:

```
>>> from ldap3 import Server, Connection, ALL
```

In this example, we are accessing the LDAP server with an anonymous bind. The `auto_bind=True` parameter forces the Bind operation to execute after creating the Connection object. You can get information with the info property of the **Server object**.

You can find the following code in the `connect_ldap_server.py` file:

```python
#!/usr/bin/env python3

import argparse
from ldap3 import Server, Connection, ALL

def main(address):
    # Create the Server object with the given address.
    # Get ALL information.
    server = Server(address, get_info=ALL)
    #Create a connection object, and bind with auto bind set to true.
    conn = Connection(server, auto_bind=True)
    # Print the LDAP Server Information.
    print('*****************Server Info**************')
    print(server.info)

if __name__ == '__main__':
    parser = argparse.ArgumentParser(description='Query LDAP Server')
    parser.add_argument('--address', action="store", dest="address",
default='ipa.demo1.freeipa.org')
    given_args = parser.parse_args()
    address = given_args.address
    main(address)
```

The following is the output of the previous script. From this response, we know that this server is a standalone LDAP server that can hold entries in the `dc=demo1`, `dc=freeipa`, and `dc=org` contexts:

```
DSA info (from DSE):
 Supported LDAP Versions: 2, 3
 Naming Contexts:
 cn=changelog
 dc=demo1,dc=freeipa,dc=org
```

```
o=ipaca
Alternative Servers: None
Supported Controls:
 1.2.840.113556.1.4.319 - LDAP Simple Paged Results - Control - RFC2696
 1.2.840.113556.1.4.473 - Sort Request - Control - RFC2891
 1.3.6.1.1.13.1 - LDAP Pre-read - Control - RFC4527
 1.3.6.1.1.13.2 - LDAP Post-read - Control - RFC4527
 1.3.6.1.4.1.1466.29539.12 - Chaining loop detect - Control - SUN
microsystems
 1.3.6.1.4.1.42.2.27.8.5.1 - Password policy - Control - IETF DRAFT behera-
ldap-password-policy
 1.3.6.1.4.1.42.2.27.9.5.2 - Get effective rights - Control - IETF DRAFT
draft-ietf-ldapext-acl-model
 1.3.6.1.4.1.42.2.27.9.5.8 - Account usability - Control - SUN microsystems
 1.3.6.1.4.1.4203.1.9.1.1 - LDAP content synchronization - Control -
RFC4533
 1.3.6.1.4.1.4203.666.5.16 - LDAP Dereference - Control - IETF DRAFT draft-
masarati-ldap-deref
 2.16.840.1.113730.3.4.12 - Proxied Authorization (old) - Control -
Netscape
 2.16.840.1.113730.3.4.13 - iPlanet Directory Server Replication Update
Information - Control - Netscape
 2.16.840.1.113730.3.4.14 - Search on specific database - Control -
Netscape
 2.16.840.1.113730.3.4.15 - Authorization Identity Response Control -
Control - RFC3829
 2.16.840.1.113730.3.4.16 - Authorization Identity Request Control -
Control - RFC3829
 2.16.840.1.113730.3.4.17 - Real attribute only request - Control -
Netscape
 2.16.840.1.113730.3.4.18 - Proxy Authorization Control - Control - RFC6171
 2.16.840.1.113730.3.4.19 - Chaining loop detection - Control - Netscape
 2.16.840.1.113730.3.4.2 - ManageDsaIT - Control - RFC3296
 2.16.840.1.113730.3.4.20 - Mapping Tree Node - Use one backend [extended]
- Control - openLDAP
 2.16.840.1.113730.3.4.3 - Persistent Search - Control - IETF
 2.16.840.1.113730.3.4.4 - Netscape Password Expired - Control - Netscape
 2.16.840.1.113730.3.4.5 - Netscape Password Expiring - Control - Netscape
 2.16.840.1.113730.3.4.9 - Virtual List View Request - Control - IETF
 2.16.840.1.113730.3.8.10.6 - OTP Sync Request - Control - freeIPA
Supported Extensions:
 1.3.6.1.4.1.1466.20037 - StartTLS - Extension - RFC4511-RFC4513
 1.3.6.1.4.1.4203.1.11.1 - Modify Password - Extension - RFC3062
 1.3.6.1.4.1.4203.1.11.3 - Who am I - Extension - RFC4532
 2.16.840.1.113730.3.5.10 - Distributed Numeric Assignment Extended Request
- Extension - Netscape
 2.16.840.1.113730.3.5.12 - Start replication request - Extension -
Netscape
```

```
  2.16.840.1.113730.3.5.3 - Transaction Response Extended Operation -
Extension - Netscape
  2.16.840.1.113730.3.5.4 - iPlanet Replication Response Extended Operation
- Extension - Netscape
  2.16.840.1.113730.3.5.5 - iPlanet End Replication Request Extended
Operation - Extension - Netscape
  2.16.840.1.113730.3.5.6 - iPlanet Replication Entry Request Extended
Operation - Extension - Netscape
  2.16.840.1.113730.3.5.7 - iPlanet Bulk Import Start Extended Operation -
Extension - Netscape
  2.16.840.1.113730.3.5.8 - iPlanet Bulk Import Finished Extended Operation
- Extension - Netscape
  2.16.840.1.113730.3.5.9 - iPlanet Digest Authentication Calculation
Extended Operation - Extension - Netscape
  2.16.840.1.113730.3.6.5 - Replication CleanAllRUV - Extension - Netscape
  2.16.840.1.113730.3.6.6 - Replication Abort CleanAllRUV - Extension -
Netscape
  2.16.840.1.113730.3.6.7 - Replication CleanAllRUV Retrieve MaxCSN -
Extension - Netscape
  2.16.840.1.113730.3.6.8 - Replication CleanAllRUV Check Status - Extension
- Netscape
  2.16.840.1.113730.3.8.10.1 - KeyTab set - Extension - FreeIPA
  2.16.840.1.113730.3.8.10.3 - Enrollment join - Extension - FreeIPA
  2.16.840.1.113730.3.8.10.5 - KeyTab get - Extension - FreeIPA
  Supported SASL Mechanisms:
  EXTERNAL, GSS-SPNEGO, GSSAPI, DIGEST-MD5, CRAM-MD5, PLAIN, LOGIN,
ANONYMOUS
  Schema Entry:
  cn=schema
  Vendor name: 389 Project
  Vendor version: 389-Directory/1.3.3.8 B2015.036.047
  Other:
  dataversion:
  020150912040104020150912040104020150912040104
  changeLog:
  cn=changelog
  lastchangenumber:
  3033
  firstchangenumber:
  1713
  lastusn:
  8284
  defaultnamingcontext:
  dc=demo1,dc=freeipa,dc=org
  netscapemdsuffix:
  cn=ldap://dc=ipa,dc=demo1,dc=freeipa,dc=org:389
  objectClass:
  top
```

Finding entries in LDAP

To find entries in the ldap directory, you must use the search operation. This operation has a number of parameters, but only two of them are mandatory:

conn.search(search_base,search_filter, attributes)

The following are the parameters:

- search_base: The location in the ldap directory where the search will start
- search_filter: A string that describes what you are searching for
- attributes: Attributes to extract

In this script, we are going to search all users in the FreeIPA demo LDAP server. You can find the following code in the entries_ldap_server.py file:

```python
#!/usr/bin/env python3

from ldap3 import Server, Connection, ObjectDef, AttrDef, Reader, Writer,
ALL

LDAP_SERVER ="ipa.demo1.freeipa.org"
LDAP_USER ="uid=admin,cn=users,cn=accounts,dc=demo1,dc=freeipa,dc=org"
LDAP_PASSWORD ="Secret123"
LDAP_FILTER = '(objectclass=person)'
LDAP_ATTRS = ["cn", "dn", "sn", "givenName"]

def main():
    # Create the Server object with the given address.
    server = Server(LDAP_SERVER, get_info=ALL)
    #Create a connection object, and bind with the given DN and password.
    try:
        conn = Connection(server, LDAP_USER, LDAP_PASSWORD, auto_bind=True)
        print('LDAP Bind Successful.')
        # Perform a search for a pre-defined criteria.
        # Mention the search filter / filter type and attributes.
        conn.search('dc=demo1,dc=freeipa,dc=org', LDAP_FILTER ,
attributes=LDAP_ATTRS)
        # Print the resulting entries.
        for entry in conn.entries:
            print(entry)
    except core.exceptions.LDAPBindError as e:
    # If the LDAP bind failed for reasons such as authentication failure.
        print('LDAP Bind Failed: ', e)

if __name__ == '__main__':
    main()
```

This is the execution of the previous script. Here, you request all the entries of person class , starting from the `dc=demo1`, `dc=freeipa`, and `dc=org` contexts with the default subtree scope:

```
[DN: uid=admin,cn=users,cn=accounts,dc=demo1,dc=freeipa,dc=org
, DN: uid=manager,cn=users,cn=accounts,dc=demo1,dc=freeipa,dc=org
, DN: uid=employee,cn=users,cn=accounts,dc=demo1,dc=freeipa,dc=org
, DN: uid=helpdesk,cn=users,cn=accounts,dc=demo1,dc=freeipa,dc=org
]
```

Summary

In this chapter, we encountered several network protocols and Python libraries that are used to interact with remote systems. SSH and SFTP are used to securely connect and transfer files to the remote hosts. We also examined Python libraries to work with remote systems to perform various tasks, such as administrative tasks by using SSH, and file transfer through FTP and Samba. Finally, we reviewed some remote monitoring protocols, such as SNMP, and authentication protocols, such as LDAP.

In the next chapter, we will discuss one of the most common networking protocols: DNS and IP. We will also explore TCP/IP networking using Python scripts.

Questions

1. What is the file configuration for ssh connections and where is it located in a Unix machine?
2. What is the encryption type that's used by the `ssh` protocol to establish communication between the client and server?
3. How we can prevent access by the root user to a SSH server by a configuration established in `sshd_config` file?
4. How should you run several commands on the remote host using `paramiko` when you encounter the problem that the SSH session is closed?
5. How does `paramiko` create an SFTP session to download files in a secure way from the SSH server?
6. Which command do we use to download a binary file from the `ftp` server with the `ftplib` package?
7. Which method from the `ftplib` package returns a list with the filenames of the directory?

8. Which Python module provides a useful wrapper for the `snmp` commands, and how we can create a command to connect with an `snmp` server?

9. What is the name of the database where we can organize and store information with objects of different classes in the `ldap` server?

10. Which method from `python-ldap` initializes a new connection object to access the given LDAP server, and returns an LDAP object that's used to perform operations on that server?

Further reading

Check out the following links for more information on the topics that were covered in this chapter:

- To learn more about the `ftplib` module, you can query the official documentation: `http://docs.python.org/library/ftplib.html`

- The complete distribution of `paramiko` comes with many good examples in the GitHub repository: `https://github.com/paramiko/paramiko/tree/master/demos`

- SNMP Link: a collection of SNMP resources: `http://www.snmplink.org/`

- Net-SNMP: SNMP Open Source Tools: `http://net-snmp.sourceforge.net/`

- To learn more about the `pysnmp` module, you can query the official documentation: `http://snmplabs.com/pysnmp/index.html`

- The Python 3 script to perform LDAP queries and enumerate users, groups, and computers from Windows Domains: `https://github.com/m8r0wn/ldap_search`

- To learn more about the Python `ldap` module, you can query the official documentation: `https://www.python-ldap.org/en/latest/reference/ldap.html`

- A tutorial and examples for `ldap3`: `https://ldap3.readthedocs.io/tutorial_intro.html`

3
Section 3: IP Address Manipulation and Network Automation

In this section, you will learn about the Python modules for IP address manipulation, how to get DNS and geolocation information from servers, and what tools are available in Python for network automation with Ansible.

This section contains the following chapters:

Working with IP and DNS 7

In this chapter, you will learn how to work with IP, DNS networking, and geolocation in Python. Through practical examples, you will learn how to determine the IP address of your own computer and look up other computers in the network. You will also learn how to extract information from DNS servers with the `dnspython` module and extract information about geolocation IP addresses.

The following topics will be covered in this chapter:

- Principles of the IP protocol
- Retrieving the network configuration of a local machine
- Using Python to manipulate IP addresses and perform CIDR calculations
- The DNS Python module as a tool for extracting information from DNS servers
- GeoIP lookups with `pygeoip` and `python-geoip`

Technical requirements

The examples and source code for this chapter are available in the GitHub repository in the `Chapter07` folder: `https://github.com/PacktPublishing/Learning-Python-Networking-Second-Edition/tree/master/chapter7`.

You will need to install a Python distribution on your local machine and have some basic knowledge of the IP and TCP protocols to work through this chapter.

Principles of the IP protocol

In this section, you will learn how to resolve and validate an IP address with the socket package.

Resolving the IP address with the socket package

If you would like to see the local machine IP, you can do so using the `ifconfig` command in Linux and the `ipconfig` command in Windows. Here, we'll do this in Python using the `built-in` function:

```
>>> import socket
>>> socket.gethostbyname('python.org')
 '10.0.2.15'
```

This process is known as a host file-based name resolution. You can send a query to a DNS server and ask for the IP address of a specific host. If the name has been registered properly, you will get a response from the server.

Here are some useful methods for gathering this kind of information:

- `socket.gethostbyaddr(address)`: This allows us to obtain a domain name from the IP address.
- `socket.gethostbyname(hostname)`: This method converts a hostname into IPv4 address format. The IPv4 address is returned in the form of a string. This method is equivalent to the `nslookup` command that we can find in many operating systems.

Validating the IP address with the socket package

We can use also the socket package to validate an IP address in both IPv4 and IPv6.

You can find the following code in the `check_ip_address.py` file:

```python
import socket

def is_valid_ipv4_address(address):
    try:
        socket.inet_pton(socket.AF_INET, address)
    except AttributeError:
        try:
            socket.inet_aton(address)
        except socket.error:
            return False
        return address.count('.') == 3
    except socket.error:  # not a valid address
        return False

    return True
```

```
def is_valid_ipv6_address(address):
    try:
        socket.inet_pton(socket.AF_INET6, address)
    except socket.error:  # not a valid address
        return False
    return True

print("IPV4 127.0.0.1 OK:"+ str(is_valid_ipv4_address("127.0.0.1")))
print("IPV4 127.0.0.0.1 NOT OK:"+
str(is_valid_ipv4_address("127.0.0.0.1")))

print("IPV6 ::1 OK:"+ str(is_valid_ipv6_address("::1")))
print("IPV6 127.0.0.0 NOT OK:"+ str(is_valid_ipv6_address("127.0.0.0.1")))
```

This is the execution of the previous script, where we can see that `127.0.0.1` is a valid
IPv4 address and `::1` is a valid IPv6 address:

```
IPV4 127.0.0.1 OK:True
IPV4 127.0.0.0.1 NOT OK:False
IPV6 ::1 OK:True
IPV6 127.0.0.0 NOT OK:False
```

Retrieving the network configuration of a local machine

In this section, you will learn how to retrieve the network configuration with
the `netifaces` package, and understand the standard Python libraries for IP address
manipulation.

Gathering information with the netifaces package

Now, we are going to discover some more information about the network interface and the
gateway machine of your network.

In every LAN, a host is configured to act as a gateway, which talks to the outside world. To
find the network address and the `netmask`, we can use a Python third-party
library, `netifaces`. For example, you can call `netifaces.gateways()` to find the
gateways that are configured to the outside world. Similarly, you can enumerate the
network interfaces by calling `netifaces.interfaces()`. If you would like to know all the
IP addresses of a particular interface, `eth0`, then you can call
`netifaces.ifaddresses('eth0')`.

The following code listing shows the way in which you can list all the gateways and IP addresses of a local machine.

You can find the following code in the `local_network_config.py` file:

```python
!/usr/bin/env python3

import socket
import netifaces

# Find host info
host_name = socket.gethostname()
ip_address = socket.gethostbyname(host_name)
print("Host name: {0}".format(host_name))

# Get interfaces list
ifaces = netifaces.interfaces()

for iface in ifaces:
    ipaddrs = netifaces.ifaddresses(iface)
    #for each ipaddress
    if netifaces.AF_INET in ipaddrs:
        ipaddr_desc = ipaddrs[netifaces.AF_INET]
        ipaddr_desc = ipaddr_desc[0]
        print("Network interface: {0}".format(iface))
        if 'addr' in ipaddr_desc:
            print("\tIP address: {0}".format(ipaddr_desc['addr']))
        if 'netmask' in ipaddr_desc:
            print("\tNetmask: {0}".format(ipaddr_desc['netmask']))

# Find the gateway
gateways = netifaces.gateways()
print("Default
gateway:{0}".format(gateways['default'][netifaces.AF_INET][0]))
```

If you run this code in a Windows operating system, it will print a summary of the local network configuration, which will be similar to the following:

```
Network interface: {40EE5A9D-737D-40AA-BBFC-4F5833D17C0E}
        IP address: 10.80.92.139
        Netmask: 255.255.255.0
Network interface: {361548CA-A87A-40B1-9E88-EAAC3B1B91B1}
        IP address: 192.168.56.1
        Netmask: 255.255.255.0
Network interface: {7641A251-28A7-46E8-A6E1-781D95CE9477}
        IP address: 169.254.204.194
        Netmask: 255.255.0.0
Network interface: {E1722BC0-6333-11E7-BB0C-806E6F6E6963}
        IP address: 127.0.0.1
        Netmask: 255.0.0.0
Default gateway:10.68.14.1
```

Using Python to manipulate IP addresses and perform CIDR calculations

In this section, you will explore TCP/IP networking using Python scripts.

The Python ipaddress module

The ipaddress module simplifies working with IPv4 and IPv6 addresses in Python. In this section, we will focus on IPv4 and will work primarily with the following three class types:

- IPv4Address: Represents a single IPv4 address
- IPv4Network: Represents an IPv4 network
- IPv4Interface: Represents an IPv4 interface

You can get more information about this module with the help command from the Python interpreter:

```
>>> import ipaddress
>>> help(ipaddress)
Help on module ipaddress:

NAME
    ipaddress - A fast, lightweight IPv4/IPv6 manipulation library in Python.

DESCRIPTION
    This library is used to create/poke/manipulate IPv4 and IPv6 addresses
    and networks.

CLASSES
    builtins.ValueError(builtins.Exception)
        AddressValueError
        NetmaskValueError
    _BaseAddress(_IPAddressBase)
        IPv4Address(_BaseV4, _BaseAddress)
            IPv4Interface
        IPv6Address(_BaseV6, _BaseAddress)
            IPv6Interface
    _BaseNetwork(_IPAddressBase)
        IPv4Network(_BaseV4, _BaseNetwork)
        IPv6Network(_BaseV6, _BaseNetwork)
    _BaseV4(builtins.object)
        IPv4Address(_BaseV4, _BaseAddress)
            IPv4Interface
        IPv4Network(_BaseV4, _BaseNetwork)
```

`IPv4Address` is the class that represents and manipulates single IPv4 addresses:

```
class IPv4Address(_BaseV4, _BaseAddress)
    Represent and manipulate single IPv4 Addresses.

    Method resolution order:
        IPv4Address
        _BaseV4
        _BaseAddress
        _IPAddressBase
        builtins.object

    Methods defined here:

    __init__(self, address)
        Args:
            address: A string or integer representing the IP

            Additionally, an integer can be passed, so
            IPv4Address('192.0.2.1') == IPv4Address(3221225985).
            or, more generally
            IPv4Address(int(IPv4Address('192.0.2.1'))) ==
                IPv4Address('192.0.2.1')

        Raises:
            AddressValueError: If ipaddress isn't a valid IPv4 address.
```

The `class` represents an IPv4 address or network. To create these objects in Python, the module provides some basic `factory` functions:

```
import ipaddress
from ipaddress import IPv4Address, IPv4Network, IPv4Interface
```

After you create an IPv4/IPv6 object, you can get a lot information from the class, for example, whether it is a multicast address or a private address, the prefix length, and netmask.

In the following screenshot, we can see the methods that are used to check these use cases:

```
is_link_local
    Test if the address is reserved for link-local.

    Returns:
        A boolean, True if the address is link-local per RFC 3927.

is_loopback
    Test if the address is a loopback address.

    Returns:
        A boolean, True if the address is a loopback per RFC 3330.

is_multicast
    Test if the address is reserved for multicast use.

    Returns:
        A boolean, True if the address is multicast.
        See RFC 3171 for details.

is_private
    Test if this address is allocated for private networks.

    Returns:
        A boolean, True if the address is reserved per
        iana-ipv4-special-registry.

is_reserved
    Test if the address is otherwise IETF reserved.

    Returns:
        A boolean, True if the address is within the
        reserved IPv4 Network range.
```

From Python 3.3, the best way to check whether an IPv6 or IPv4 address is correct is to use the Python standard library module, ipaddress.

 Check out https://docs.python.org/3/library/ipaddress.html for the complete documentation.

If you're using Python 3.3 or later, you can use the `ipaddress` module to validate the IP address:

```
>>> import ipaddress
>>> ipaddress.ip_address('127.0.0.1')
IPv4Address('127.0.0.1')
>>> ipaddress.ip_address('500.500.0.1')
Traceback (most recent call last):
 File "<stdin>", line 1, in <module>
 File "/usr/lib/python3.7/ipaddress.py", line 54, in ip_address
   address)
ValueError: '500.500.0.1' does not appear to be an IPv4 or IPv6 address
```

In this example, we use this method to validate both IPv4 and IPv6. You can find the following code in the `validate_ip_address.py` file:

```
!/usr/bin/env python3

import ipaddress
import sys

try:
    ip = ipaddress.ip_address(sys.argv[1])
    print('%s is a correct IP%s address' % (ip, ip.version))
except ValueError:
    print('address/netmask is invalid: %s' % sys.argv[1])
except:
    print('Usage : %s  ip' % sys.argv[0])
```

If you execute the previous script with an IP address as a parameter, it will validate in both IPv4 and IPv6 versions:

```
$ python validate_ip_address.py 127.0.0.1
 127.0.0.1 is a correct IP4 address
$ python validate_ip_address.py ::1
 ::1 is a correct IP6 address
```

Manipulating IP addresses

Often, you will need to manipulate IP addresses and perform some sort of operations on them. Python 3 has a built-in `ipaddress` module to help you carry out this task. It has convenient functions for defining the IP addresses and the IP networks, and for finding lots of useful information. For example, if you would like to know how many IP addresses exist in a given subnet, for instance, `10.0.1.0/255.255.255.0` or `10.0.1.0/24`, you can find them with the help of the following command.

This module will provide several classes and `factory` functions for working with both IPv4 and IPv6 versions.

IP network objects

Let's import the `ipaddress` module and define a `net4` network:

```
>>> import ipaddress
>>> net4 = ipaddress.ip_network('10.0.1.0/24')
```

Now, we can find some useful information, such as `netmask` and the network/broadcast address, of `net4`:

```
>>> net4.netmask
 IP4Address(255.255.255.0)
```

The `netmask` properties of `net4` will be displayed as an `IP4Address` object. If you are looking for its string representation, then you can call the `str()` method, as shown here:

```
>>> str(net4.netmask)
 '255.255.255.0'
```

Similarly, you can find the network and the broadcast addresses of `net4` by using the following code:

```
>>> str(net4.network_address)
 10.0.1.0
>>> str(net4.broadcast_address)
 10.0.1.255
```

We can get the number of addresses `net4` can hold with the following command:

```
>>> net4.num_addresses
 256
```

So, if we subtract the network and the broadcast addresses, the total available IP addresses will be 254. We can call the `hosts()` method on the `net4` object. This will produce a Python generator, which will supply all the hosts as `IPv4Address` objects:

```
>>> net4.hosts()
>>> <generator object _BaseNetwork.hosts at 0x02F25FC0>
 >>> all_hosts = list(net4.hosts())
 >>> len(all_hosts)
 254
>>> print(all_hosts)
>>> [IPv4Address('10.0.1.1'), IPv4Address('10.0.1.2'),
```

```
IPv4Address('10.0.1.3'),
IPv4Address('10.0.1.4'),......,IPv4Address('10.0.1.253'),
IPv4Address('10.0.1.254')]
```

Subnetting in Python

Another use case is an IP subnetting application, which gives you the required IP subnets based on required network size or amount of networks per location. We can also find the subnet information from the `IPv4Network` objects, as follows:

```
>>> net4.subnets()
 <generator object _BaseNetwork.subnets at 0x02F2C0C0>
>>> subnets = list( net4.subnets())
>>> subnets
 [ IPv4Network('10.0.1.0/25'), IPv4Network('10.0.1.128/25') ]
```

The `ipaddress` module includes many functions to create subnets and supernets; for example, we can use these methods to check whether a network overlaps with another:

```
>>> ipnet = ipaddress.IPv4Network("10.2.0.0/16")
>>> list(ipnet.subnets())
 [IPv4Network('10.2.0.0/17'), IPv4Network('10.2.128.0/17')]
```

The `subnets(prefixlen_diff=1, new_prefix=None)` method also has the capacity to generate subnets with additional host bits or with a specific amount of network bits. In the following example, we use the `new_prefix` argument in the `subnets` method to define the number of network bits for the new network mask:

```
# new_prefix = number of network bits for the new mask
>>> list(ipnet.subnets(new_prefix=20))
 [IPv4Network('10.2.0.0/20'), IPv4Network('10.2.16.0/20'),
IPv4Network('10.2.32.0/20'), IPv4Network('10.2.48.0/20'),
IPv4Network('10.2.64.0/20'), IPv4Network('10.2.80.0/20'),
IPv4Network('10.2.96.0/20'), IPv4Network('10.2.112.0/20'),
IPv4Network('10.2.128.0/20'), IPv4Network('10.2.144.0/20'),
IPv4Network('10.2.160.0/20'), IPv4Network('10.2.176.0/20'),
IPv4Network('10.2.192.0/20'), IPv4Network('10.2.208.0/20'),
IPv4Network('10.2.224.0/20'), IPv4Network('10.2.240.0/20')]
```

Any `IPv4Network` object can tell, which is the opposite of the `subnet` by looking at its parent supernet:

```
>>> net4.supernet()
 IPv4Network('10.0.0.0/23')
```

Network interface objects

In the `ipaddress` module, we have a convenient class to represent an interface's IP configuration in detail: `IPv4Interface`. It takes an arbitrary address and behaves like a network address object:

```
>>> import ipaddress
>>> eth0 = ipaddress.IPv4Interface('192.168.0.1/24')
>>> eth0.ip
IPv4Address('192.168.0.1')
>>> eth0.with_prefixlen
'192.168.0.1/24'
>>> eth0.with_netmask
'192.168.0.1/255.255.255.0'
>>> eth0.network
IPv4Network('192.168.0.0/24')
>>> eth0.is_private
True
>>> eth0.is_reserved
False
>>> eth0.is_multicast
False
>>>
```

As you can see, a network interface, `eth0`, with the `IPv4Address` class, has been defined. It has some interesting properties, such as IP and network address. In the same way as the network objects, you can check whether the address is `private`, `reserved`, or `multicast`.

IP address objects

In this example, the `loopback` interface is defined with the `127.0.0.1` IP address. As you can see, the `is_loopback` property returns `True`:

```
>>> loopback = ipaddress.IPv4Interface('127.0.0.1')
>>> loopback.is_private
True
>>> loopback.is_reserved
False
>>> loopback.is_multicast
False
>>> loopback.is_loopback
True
```

The IP address classes have many more interesting properties. You can perform some arithmetic and logical operations on those objects. For example, we can check whether an IP address is part of a network.

In this example, we are checking whether an IP address is part of a specific network. Here, a network called net has been defined by the network address, which is 192.168.1.0/24, and the membership of eth0 and eth1 has been tested to see if these IP addresses are part of the network:

```
>>> eth0 = ipaddress.IPv4Interface('192.168.1.1')
>>> eth1 = ipaddress.IPv4Interface('192.168.2.1')
>>> net = ipaddress.ip_network('192.168.1.0/24')
>>> eth0 in net
 True
>>> eth1 in net
 False
```

Planning IP addresses for your local area network

If you are wondering how to pick up a suitable IP subnet, try the ipaddress module. The following code snippet shows an example of how to choose a specific subnet, based on the number of necessary host IP addresses for a small private network.

Suppose you have a CIDR network address, such as 192.168.0.0/24, and you want to generate a range of all the IP addresses that it represents (192.168.0.1 to 192.168.0.254). The ipaddress module can be easily used to perform such calculations:

```
>>> import ipaddress
>>> net = ipaddress.ip_network('192.168.0.0/24')
>>> net
IPv4Network('192.168.0.0/24')
>>> for a in net:
...     print(a)
...
192.168.0.1
192.168.0.2
192.168.0.3
...
192.168.0.254
```

In this example, we are using the `ip_network` method from the `ipaddress` module to generate a range of all the IP addresses that represent the network.

You can find the following code in the `net_ip_planner.py` file:

```
!/usr/bin/env python3

import ipaddress as ip

CLASS_C_ADDR = '192.168.0.0'

mask = input("Enter the mask len (24-30): ")
mask = int(mask)
if mask not in range(23, 31):
    raise Exception("Mask length must be between 24 and 30")

net_addr = CLASS_C_ADDR + '/' + str(mask)
print("Using network address:%s " %net_addr)

try:
    network = ip.ip_network(net_addr)
except:
    raise Exception("Failed to create network object")

print("This mask will give %s IP addresses" %(network.num_addresses))
print("The network configuration will be:")
print("\t network address: %s" %str(network.network_address))
print("\t netmask: %s" %str(network.netmask))
print("\t broadcast address: %s" %str(network.broadcast_address))
first_ip, last_ip = list(network.hosts())[0], list(network.hosts())[-1]
print("\t host IP addresses: from %s to %s" %(first_ip,last_ip))
```

The following is the execution of the previous script for some masks and the C class IP address, `192.168.0.0`:

- Execution with mask `24`:

```
Enter the mask len (24-30): 24
 Using network address:192.168.0.0/24
 This mask will give 256 IP addresses
 The network configuration will be:
        network address: 192.168.0.0
        netmask: 255.255.255.0
        broadcast address: 192.168.0.255
        host IP addresses: from 192.168.0.1 to 192.168.0.254
```

- Execution with mask 30:

```
Enter the mask len (24-30): 30
 Using network address:192.168.0.0/30
 This mask will give 4 IP addresses
 The network configuration will be:
        network address: 192.168.0.0
        netmask: 255.255.255.252
        broadcast address: 192.168.0.3
        host IP addresses: from 192.168.0.1 to 192.168.0.2
```

The dnspython module as a tool for extracting information from DNS servers

In this section, you will learn how to obtain information from DNS servers with the dnspython module.

Working with dnspython

The IP address can be translated into human-readable strings called domain names. DNS is a big topic in the world of networking. In this section, we will create a DNS client in Python, and see how this client will talk to the server using Wireshark.

A few DNS client libraries are available from PyPI. We will focus on the dnspython library, which is available at http://www.dnspython.org.

You can install this library by using either the easy_install command or the pip command:

```
$ pip install dnspython
```

In this practical example, we will use dnspython to execute queries on several types of DNS records, such as IPv4 (A), IPv6 (AAAA), **name servers** (**NS**), and **mail exchange** (**MX**).

The main utility of dnspython regarding other DNS query tools, such as dig, fierce, or nslookup, is that you can control the result of queries from Python, and then that information can be used for other purposes in a script.

You can also install it from its source code, which is available on its official website: http://www.dnspython.org.

Now, we are going to review some interesting queries, such as the examples that appear at http://www.dnspython.org/examples.html.

Making a simple query regarding the IP address of a host is very simple. You can use the dns.resolver submodule, as follows. You can find the following code in the dns_basic.py file:

```
import dns.resolver
answers = dns.resolver.query('dnspython.org', 'A')
for rdata in answers:
    print('IP', rdata.to_text())
```

Determining the destination of an MX record and its preference

With the dns.resolver submodule, we can access the information stored in the ExChange mail exchange records to see which hosts have priority when exchanging emails via the internet.

You can find the following code in the dns_mx.py file:

```
import dns.resolver

answers = dns.resolver.query('dnspython.org', 'MX')
for rdata in answers:
    print('Host', rdata.exchange, 'has preference', rdata.preference)
```

This is the output of the previous script:

```
Host alt1.aspmx.1.google.com. has preference 20
Host alt2.aspmx.1.google.com. has preference 20
Host aspmx2.googlemail.com. has preference 30
Host aspmx3.googlemail.com. has preference 30
Host aspmx.1.google.com. has preference 10
```

Manipulating domain names

In this example, we are checking the properties of a specific domain and checking whether a domain is a suddomain or superdomain from another.

You can find the following code in the `dns_domains.py` file:

```
import dns.name

domain1= dns.name.from_text('www.dnspython.org')
domain2 = dns.name.from_text('dnspython.org')
print(domain2 .is_subdomain(domain1))
print(domain2 .is_superdomain(domain1))
```

Converting IPv4 and IPv6 addresses into their DNS reverse map names

With this script, we can convert an IP address into a name object, whose value will be the reverse map domain name of the address. Using the following command, we can find out which domain name corresponds to each of the specified addresses, that is, whether they are IPv4 or IPv6.

If you want to make a reverse lookup, you need to use the `dns.reversename` submodule.

You can find the following code in the `dns_reverse.py` file:

```
!/usr/bin/env python3

import argparse
import dns.reversename
import dns.resolver

def main(address):
    name = dns.reversename.from_address(address)
    print(name)
    print(dns.reversename.to_address(name))

    try:
        # Pointer records (PTR) maps a network interface (IP) to the host
name.
        domain = str(dns.resolver.query(name,"PTR")[0])
        print(domain)
    except Exception as e:
        print ("Error while resolving %s: %s" %(address, e))


if __name__ == '__main__':
    parser = argparse.ArgumentParser(description='DNS Python')
    parser.add_argument('--address', action="store", dest="address",
default='127.0.0.1')
```

```
given_args = parser.parse_args()
address = given_args.address
main(address)
```

This is the output of the previous script with the IP address from the Google name server domain:

```
$ python dns_reverse.py --address 8.8.8.8
 8.8.8.8.in-addr.arpa.
 8.8.8.8
google-public-dns-a.google.com
```

Now, let's create an interactive DNS client script that will do a complete lookup of the possible records, as shown here.

You can find the following code in the dns_details.py file:

```
#!/usr/bin/env python3

import argparse
import dns.zone
import dns.resolver

def main(domain):
    # IPv4 DNS Records
    answer = dns.resolver.query(domain, 'A')
    for i in range(0, len(answer)):
        print("IPV4 address: ", answer[i])

    # IPv6 DNS Records
    try:
        answer6 = dns.resolver.query(domain, 'AAAA')
        for i in range(0, len(answer6)):
            print("IPv6: ", answer6[i])
    except dns.resolver.NoAnswer as e:
        print("Exception in resolving the IPv6 Resource Record:", e)
```

In the previous code block, we defined our main function, which accepts the domain as a parameter and gets information about the IPv4 and IPv6 DNS records. Now, we can use the resolver.query function to obtain information about the mail exchange and name server's records, as follows:

```
    # MX (Mail Exchanger) Records
    try:
        mx = dns.resolver.query(domain, 'MX')
        print('Mail Servers: %s' % mx.response.to_text())
        for data in mx:
```

```
                print('Mailserver', data.exchange.to_text(), 'has preference',
    data.preference)
        except dns.resolver.NoAnswer as e:
            print("Exception in resolving the MX Resource Record:", e)

        # NS (Name servers) Records
        try:
            ns_answer = dns.resolver.query(domain, 'NS')
            print('Name Servers: %s' %[x.to_text() for x in ns_answer])
        except dns.resolver.NoAnswer as e:
            print("Exception in resolving the NS Resource Record:", e)

    if __name__ == '__main__':
        parser = argparse.ArgumentParser(description='DNS Python')
        parser.add_argument('--domain', action="store", dest="domain",
    default='dnspython.org')
        given_args = parser.parse_args()
        domain = given_args.domain
        main(domain)
```

If you run this script with the `python.org` domain, you will get an output similar to the following:

```
$ python dns_details.py --domain python.org
IPV4 address:  23.253.135.79
 IPv6:  2001:4802:7901:0:e60a:1375:0:6
 Mail Servers: id 40709
 opcode QUERY
 rcode NOERROR
 flags QR RD RA
 ;QUESTION
 python.org. IN MX
 ;ANSWER
 python.org. 195 IN MX 50 mail.python.org.
 ;AUTHORITY
 ;ADDITIONAL
 mail.python.org. 16396 IN A 188.166.95.178
 mail.python.org. 3195 IN AAAA 2a03:b0c0:2:d0::71:1
 Mailserver mail.python.org. has preference 50
 Name Servers: ['ns1.p11.dynect.net.', 'ns2.p11.dynect.net.',
 'ns3.p11.dynect.net.', 'ns4.p11.dynect.net.']
```

Inspecting the DNS client and server communication

Throughout this book we've captured network packets between the client and the server using Wireshark. Here, we look at an example of session capturing while Python is executing the script where we obtain DNS details from a domain.

In Wireshark, you can specify port 53 by navigating to **Capture** | **Options** | **Capture filter**. This will capture all the DNS packets that were sent to/from your machine. We can also filter with the dns keyword.

In the following screenshot, we can see how the client and the server have several request/response cycles with the DNS records. It was started with a standard request for the host's address and it was followed by a suitable response:

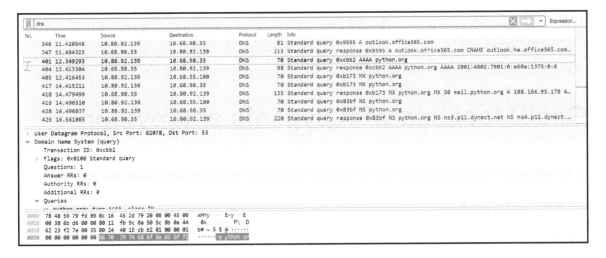

If you look deep inside the packet, you can see the request format of the response from the server:

No.	Time	Source	Destination	Protocol	Length	Info
401	12.349293	10.80.92.139	10.68.98.35	DNS	70	Standard query 0xcbb2 AAAA python.org
404	12.413304	10.68.98.35	10.80.92.139	DNS	98	Standard query response 0xcbb2 AAAA python.org AAAA 2001:4802:7901:0:e60a:1375:0:6
405	12.416453	10.80.92.139	10.68.55.100	DNS	70	Standard query 0xb173 MX python.org
417	14.415211	10.80.92.139	10.68.98.35	DNS	70	Standard query 0xb173 MX python.org
418	14.479499	10.68.98.35	10.80.92.139	DNS	135	Standard query response 0xb173 MX python.org MX 50 mail.python.org A 188.166.95.178 A...
419	14.496510	10.80.92.139	10.68.55.100	DNS	70	Standard query 0x83bf NS python.org
428	16.496837	10.80.92.139	10.68.98.35	DNS	70	Standard query 0x83bf NS python.org
429	16.561085	10.68.98.35	10.80.92.139	DNS	220	Standard query response 0x83bf NS python.org NS ns3.p11.dynect.net NS ns4.p11.dynect...

```
        Name Server: ns1.p11.dynect.net
   v python.org: type NS, class IN, ns ns2.p11.dynect.net
        Name: python.org
        Type: NS (authoritative Name Server) (2)
        Class: IN (0x0001)
        Time to live: 2119
        Data length: 6
        Name Server: ns2.p11.dynect.net
 v Additional records
    v ns3.p11.dynect.net: type A, class IN, addr 208.78.71.11
        Name: ns3.p11.dynect.net
        Type: A (Host Address) (1)
        Class: IN (0x0001)
        Time to live: 19712
        Data length: 4
        Address: 208.78.71.11
    v ns4.p11.dynect.net: type A, class IN, addr 204.13.251.11
        Name: ns4.p11.dynect.net
        Type: A (Host Address) (1)
```

GeoIP lookups with pygeoip and python-geoip

In this section, we will explore how to get geolocation information for an IP address or domain.

Introduction to geolocation

One way to obtain the geolocation from an IP address or domain is by using a service that provides this kind of information. Among the services that provide this information, we can highlight `hackertarget.com` (https://hackertarget.com/geoip-ip-location-lookup/). With `hackertarget.com`, we can get a geolocation from an IP address:

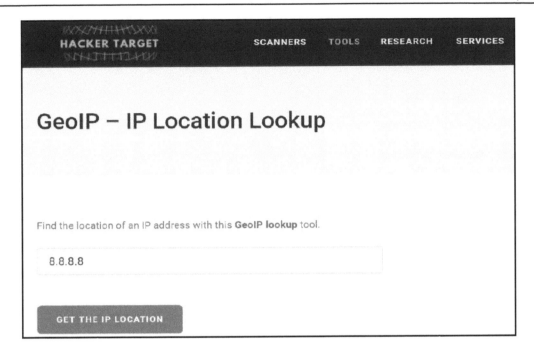

This service also provides a REST API for obtaining a geolocation from an IP address: `https://api.hackertarget.com/geoip/?q=8.8.8.8`.

Another service is `api.hostip.info`, which provides a query by the IP address:

```
// http://api.hostip.info/get_json.php?ip=8.8.8.8&position=true

{
   "country_name": "UNITED STATES",
   "country_code": "US",
   "city": "Mountain View, CA",
   "ip": "8.8.8.8",
   "lat": "37.402",
   "lng": "-122.078"
}
```

In the following script, we are using this service and the requests module to obtain a JSON response with the information for geolocation. You can find the following code in the `ip_to_geo.py` file:

```
import requests

class IPtoGeo(object):
```

```
        def __init__(self, ip_address):
            # Initialize objects to store
            self.latitude = ''
            self.longitude = ''
            self.country = ''
            self.city = ''
            self.ip_address = ip_address
            self._get_location()

    def _get_location(self):
        json_request = requests.get('http://api.hostip.info/get_json.php
ip=%s&position=true' % self.ip_address).json()
        if 'country_name' in json_request:
            self.country = json_request['country_name']
        if 'country_code' in json_request:
            self.country_code = json_request['country_code']
        if 'city' in json_request:
            self.city = json_request['city']
        if 'lat' in json_request:
            self.latitude = json_request['lat']
        if 'lng' in json_request:
            self.longitude = json_request['lng']

if __name__ == '__main__':
    geolocation = IPtoGeo('8.8.8.8')
    print(geolocation .__dict__)
```

This is the output of the previous script:

```
{'latitude': '37.402', 'longitude': '-122.078', 'country': 'UNITED STATES',
'city': 'Mountain View, CA', 'ip_address': '8.8.8.8', 'country_code': 'US'}
```

Introduction to pygeoip

pygeoip is one of the modules that's available in Python that allows you to retrieve geographic information from an IP address. It is based on GeoIP databases, which are distributed in several files depending on their type (city, region, country, ISP). The module contains several functions to retrieve data, such as the country code, time zone, or complete registration with all the information related to a specific address.

pygeoip can be downloaded from the official GitHub repository: http://github.com/appliedsec/pygeoip.

To build the object, we use a constructor that accepts a file as a database by parameter. An example of this file can be downloaded from `http://dev.maxmind.com/geoip/legacy/geolite`.

In the following script, we have two methods: `geoip_city(domain,ipaddress)`, to obtain information about the location, and `geoip_country(domain,ipaddress)` to obtain the country, both from the IP address and domain. In both methods, we must first instantiate a GeoIP class with the path of the file that contains the database. Next, we will query the database for a specific record, specifying the IP address or domain. This returns a record that contains fields for city, that is, `region_name`, `postal_code`, `country_name`, `latitude`, and `longitude`.

You can find the following code in the `pygeoip_test.py` file in the `geopip` folder:

```python
!/usr/bin/env python3

import pygeoip
import argparse

def geoip_city(domain,ipaddress):
    path = 'GeoLiteCity.dat'
    gic = pygeoip.GeoIP(path)
    print(gic.record_by_addr(ipaddress))
    print(gic.region_by_name(domain))

def geoip_country(domain,ipaddress):
    path = 'GeoIP.dat'
    gi = pygeoip.GeoIP(path)
    print(gi.country_code_by_name(domain))
    print(gi.country_name_by_addr(ipaddress))

if __name__ == '__main__':
 parser = argparse.ArgumentParser(description='Get geolocation from domain
and ip address')
 parser.add_argument('--domain', action="store", dest="domain",
default='www.packtpub.com')
 parser.add_argument('--ipaddress', action="store", dest="ipaddress",
default='83.166.169.231')
 given_args = parser.parse_args()
 domain = given_args.domain
 ipaddress = given_args.ipaddress
 geoip_city(domain,ipaddress)
 geoip_country(domain,ipaddress)
```

This is the output of the previous script with the default parameters:

```
{'dma_code': 0, 'area_code': 0, 'metro_code': None, 'postal_code': 'RH15',
'country_code': 'GB', 'country_code3': 'GBR', 'country_name': 'United
Kingdom', 'continent': 'EU', 'region_code': 'P6', 'city': 'Burgess Hill',
'latitude': 50.9667, 'longitude': -0.13329999999999131, 'time_zone':
'Europe/London'}
{'country_code': 'GB', 'region_code': 'P6'}
GB
United Kingdom
```

This is the output of the previous script with the `amazon.com` domain:

```
$ python pygeoip_test.py --domain www.amazon.com --ipaddress 143.204.191.30

{'dma_code': 819, 'area_code': 206, 'metro_code': 'Seattle-Tacoma, WA',
'postal_code': '98109', 'country_code': 'US', 'country_code3': 'USA',
'country_name': 'United States', 'continent': 'NA', 'region_code': 'WA',
'city': 'Seattle', 'latitude': 47.6344, 'longitude': -122.34219999999999,
'time_zone': 'America/Los_Angeles'}
{'country_code': 'US', 'region_code': 'WA'}
US
United States
```

Introduction to python-geoip

There is a third-party library called `python-geoip`, which has a robust interface to answer your IP location query.

You can find more information about this package on the developer's website: `http://pythonhosted.org/python-geoip`. You can install the package directly from the Python repository.

If you are working with Python 3, you need to install `python-geoip-python3` (`https://pypi.org/project/python-geoip-python3`). This is a fork of `python-geoip` with Python 3 support. We also need to install the `geolite2` module with the `pip install python-geoip-geolite2` command:

```
pip install python-geoip-python3
```

In the following script, we can see an example of how to use the `python-geoip` package. You can find the following code in the `geoip_lookup.py` file:

```python
!/usr/bin/env python3

import socket
from geoip import geolite2
import argparse
import json

# Setup commandline arguments
parser = argparse.ArgumentParser(description='Get IP Geolocation info')
parser.add_argument('--hostname', action="store", dest="hostname",
required=True)

# Parse arguments
given_args = parser.parse_args()
hostname = given_args.hostname
ip_address = socket.gethostbyname(hostname)

print("IP address: {0}".format(ip_address))

match = geolite2.lookup(ip_address)

if match is not None:
  print('Country: ',match.country)
  print('Continent: ',match.continent)
  print('Time zone: ', match.timezone)
  print('Location: ', match.location)
```

This script will show an output similar to the following:

```
$ python geoip_lookup.py --hostname=amazon.co.uk
IP address: 176.32.98.166
Country:   US
Continent:  NA
Time zone:  None
Location:  (38.0, -97.0)
```

The MaxMind database in Python

There are other Python modules that use the MaxMind database:

- geoip2: Provides access to the GeoIP2 web services and databases
  (https://github.com/maxmind/GeoIP2-python)
- maxminddb-geolite2: Provides a simple MaxMind DB reader extension
  (https://github.com/rr2do2/maxminddb-geolite2)

In the following script, we can see an example of how to use the maxminddb-geolite2 package.

You can find the following code in the geoip_reader.py file:

```
#!/usr/bin/env python3

import socket
from geolite2 import geolite2
import argparse
import json

# Setup commandline arguments
parser = argparse.ArgumentParser(description='Get IP Geolocation info')
parser.add_argument('--hostname', action="store", dest="hostname",
required=True)

# Parse arguments
given_args = parser.parse_args()
hostname = given_args.hostname
ip_address = socket.gethostbyname(hostname)

print("IP address: {0}".format(ip_address))

# Call geolite2
reader = geolite2.reader()
response = reader.get(ip_address)
print (json.dumps(response,indent=4))
print (json.dumps(response['continent']['names']['en'],indent=4))
print (json.dumps(response['country']['names']['en'],indent=4))
print (json.dumps(response['location']['latitude'],indent=4))
print (json.dumps(response['location']['longitude'],indent=4))
print (json.dumps(response['location']['time_zone'],indent=4))
```

In the following screenshot, we can see the output of the previous script in JSON format, along with the amazon.com domain:

```
    },
    "location": {
        "accuracy_radius": 1000,
        "latitude": 39.0481,
        "longitude": -77.4728,
        "metro_code": 511,
        "time_zone": "America/New_York"
    },
    "postal": {
        "code": "20149"
    },
    "registered_country": {
        "geoname_id": 6252001,
        "iso_code": "US",
        "names": {
            "de": "USA",
            "en": "United States",
            "es": "Estados Unidos",
            "fr": "\u00c9tats-Unis",
            "ja": "\u30a2\u30e1\u30ea\u30ab\u5408\u8846\u56fd",
            "pt-BR": "Estados Unidos",
            "ru": "\u0421\u0428\u0410",
            "zh-CN": "\u7f8e\u56fd"
        }
    },
```

Summary

In this chapter, we discussed the standard Python libraries for IP address manipulation. Two third-party dnspython libraries and geoip have been presented to interact with the DNS servers and get geolocation from an IP address. As we can see, when it comes to working with IP addresses, Python provides you with a series of modules that can be useful for checking IP addresses or converting values related to IP addresses and networks.

In the next chapter, we will introduce the IPv6 protocol and explore the best Python modules for working with IPv6 networking.

Questions

1. Which Python module allows us to retrieve geographic information from an IP address?
2. Which method from the `netifaces` module can you use to enumerate the network interfaces of your local machine?
3. Which port do DNS servers use to resolve requests for mail server names?
4. Which method from the `ipaddress` module method has the capacity to generate subnets with additional host bits or with a specific amount of network bits?
5. Which method within the `pygeoip` module allows us to obtain the value of the country name from the IP address passed by the parameter?
6. Which method within the `pygeoip` module allows us to obtain a structure in the form of a dictionary with the geographic data (country, city, area, latitude, longitude) from the IP address?
7. Which method within the `pygeoip` module allows us to obtain the name of the organization from the domain name?
8. Which method should be called and what parameters should be passed to obtain the IPv6 address records with the `dnspython` module?
9. Which method should be called and what parameters should be passed to obtain the records for mail servers with the `dnspython` module?
10. Which method should be called and what parameters should be passed to obtain the records for name servers with the `dnspython` module?

Further reading

Check out the following link for more information on the topics that were covered in this chapter:

- The official Python 3.7 documentation: `https://docs.python.org/3.7/howto/ipaddress.html#ipaddress-howto`

8

Implementing IPv6 and Address Manipulation

In this chapter, you will learn how to work with IPv6 and address manipulation with Python through practical tasks such as determining the IP address of your own computer and looking up other computers. Also, we will review the IPv6 protocol and standard Python libraries for IPv6 address manipulation. We will study three third-party libraries, ipaddress, netifaces, and netaddr, for working with IPv6 and address manipulation with Python. Finally, we will review the socket module for implementing the client-server application for sending messages.

The following topics will be covered in this chapter:

- Learning about and understanding the IPv6 protocol
- Creating an echo client and server with IPv6
- Understanding the netifaces module that allows checking of IPv6 support on your network
- The netaddr module as a network-address manipulation library for Python
- Understanding the ipaddress module as an IPv4 and IPv6 manipulation library

Technical requirements

Examples and source code for this chapter are available in the GitHub repository in the Chapter08 folder: https://github.com/PacktPublishing/Learning-Python-Networking-Second-Edition.

You will need to install Python distribution on your local machine and have some basic knowledge about the IP and TCP protocols.

Learning and understanding the IPv6 protocol

In this section, you will learn about the IPv6 protocol and how to resolve IP addresses in Python with this protocol.

The IPv6 protocol

The history of IPv6 begins with a real need we have today. When IPv4 was conceived, in the 1970s, the creators could not imagine the great success that it would have throughout the world. Due to the lack of addresses, the research team called **Internet Engineering Task Force (IETF)** began to look for a substitute for IPv4, which in principle was called **Internet Protocol Next Generation (IPng)**, but finally took the name of IPv6.

The IPv4 protocol has a 32-bit address space, which means that to calculate the total number of possible addresses, we can do it by taking 2 raised to 32, making a total of 4, 294, 967, 296 addresses.

The IPv6 protocol has expanded the address space to 128 bits, making a total of 340, 282, 366, 920, 938, 463, 374, 607, 431, 768, 211, 456 addresses available.

The main characteristics of the IPv6 protocol are as follows:

- Greater address space
- Plug-and-play auto-configuration
- Security included in the protocol core (IPsec)
- **Quality of Service (QoS)** and **Class of Service (CoS)**
- Multicast, which sends a single package to a group of receivers
- Anycast, which sends a packet to a receiver within a group
- Efficient and extensible IP packets, there is no packet fragmentation in the routers, aligned to 64 bits (optimal processing with 64-bit processors), and with a fixed-length, simpler header, which allows faster processing by routers
- Possibility of packages with payload (data) of more than 65,535 bytes (jumbograms)
- More efficient routing in the backbone of the network, due to a hierarchy of addressing based on aggregation

- Compensation and multi-homing, which facilitates the change of service provider
- Mobility characteristics

It is necessary to say that many of these features are standards that are still in the implementation phase. IPv6 addressing is still in a phase of evolution and it will take several years for some functionalities to be completed.

IPv6 addresses

In this section, we will discuss the different categories and types of addresses that exist in IPv6. The types of IPv6 addresses can be identified taking the ranges defined by the first bits of each address. Among the main types of IPv6 addresses, we can highlight the following:

- **Unicast**: These addresses uniquely identify an interface.
- **Multicast:** These are addresses that identify a set of interfaces. A packet that is sent to a multicast address is forwarded to all interfaces identified by this address.
- **Anycast**: These types of addresses identify a set of interfaces. A packet that is sent to an anycast address is forwarded to one of the interfaces identified by this address, being the closest one according to the routing protocol used.
- **Link-local**: These types of addresses are created automatically and exclusively used in local subnets, therefore they are not routable. This type of address starts with the `fe80 :: / 64` prefix. The link-local IP address is created automatically by adding the Mac address of the interface in IPv6 format to the previous prefix. In this way, a Mac of the `AE: 3E: 7B: 33: 5F: B0` type will have an IPv6 address of the `fe80 :: ac3e: 7bff: fe33: 5fb0` link-local type.
- **Unique Local Addresses (ULA) (RFC 4193)**: These types of addresses are the equivalent of private networks in IPv4. They are non-routable addresses in IPv6 to the internet. The routers with IPv6 support are responsible for discarding the packets coming from these addresses. This type of address has an address space of the `fc00 :: / 7` type, which in turn is divided into two networks with an 8-bit mask – `fc00 ::: / 8` (pending definition, and reserved) and `fd00 :: / 8`, which is what can be used to create the network.
- **Global**: An address with an unlimited scope.

Representation of IPv6 addresses

The size of an IPv6 address is 128 bits. Because the IPv6 addresses are so large, they are difficult to represent in decimal notation as we do in IPv4. That is why to represent an IPv6 address it was decided to use 8 groups of 16 bits in hexadecimal notation, separating each group by the colon character, :. Here, we will see an example of IPv6 address:

```
fe80: 0000: 0000: 0000: ac3e: 7bff: fe33: 5fb0
```

Among the different rules that IPv6 has for representation, one of them is that you can suppress the leading zeros in each group to represent the address in the following way:

```
fe80: 0: 0: 0: ac3e: 7bff: fe33: 5fb0
```

In addition to this simplification, there is another one that indicates that several groups of consecutive zeros can be replaced by two colons, : :, and this can only be done once in the complete address. Therefore, the previous example could be summarized in:

```
fe80 :: ac3e: 7bff: fe33: 5fb0
```

To determine in IPv6 which part of the IP address corresponds to the network and the host, the address must be divided into two 64-bit parts, leaving the previous IP address as follows:

```
Network address -> fe80 ::
Host address -> ac3e: 7bff: fe33: 5fb0
```

It should be noted that, in IPv6, the part of the address that corresponds to the host address is fixed. In link-local, as we reviewed before, the host address corresponds to the Mac address of the interface in EUI-64 format.

Reserved IPv6 addresses

There are a number of IP addresses that cannot be used for conventional unicast addresses. We have seen how addresses types can be link-local or ULA addresses, but there are some more that will be summarized in the following points:

- :: / 128: An unspecified address, equivalent to 0.0.0.0 in IPv4
- :: 1/128: Represents the loopback address, such as 127.0.0.1 in IPv4
- fc00 :: / 7: Belongs to the range of ULA addresses

- fc00 :: / 8: Still pending definition and reserved
- fd00 :: / 8: Defines a range of ULA addresses. IP addresses are constructed by generating a random 40-bit string, and by adding the prefix to make a 64-bit network address
- ff00 :: / 8: Multicast addresses, equivalent to the 224.0.0.0/4 IPv4 range
- fe80 :: / 10: Belongs to the link-local addresses, equivalent to the 169.254.0.0/16 range in IPv4

First steps with IPv6 – link-local

By default in Linux, in the new distributions, the IPv6 protocol is already activated and, therefore, already in the subnet where the machine is located and it can communicate with others devices using its link-local address. To find out the IPv6 address, use the ifconfig command or the ip command with the following options:

```
# ip -6 a l dev eth0
 2: eth0: <BROADCAST,MULTICAST,UP,LOWER_UP> mtu 1500 qlen 1000
 inet6 fe80::bc6c:91ff:feb7:be0a/64 scope link
 valid_lft forever preferred_lft forever

# ip -6 addr show
 1: lo: <LOOPBACK,UP,LOWER_UP> mtu 16436
 inet6 ::1/128 scope host
 valid_lft forever preferred_lft forever
 2: eth0: <BROADCAST,MULTICAST,UP,LOWER_UP> mtu 1500 qlen 1000
 inet6 fe80::bc6c:91ff:feb7:be0a/64 scope link
 valid_lft forever preferred_lft forever
```

We can see that the address is of the link-local type, using the network prefix fe80. If we have several machines, we can communicate with each other with the ping6 command, but when executing the command, it is necessary to indicate the interface where the ping has to be made. This is because all the interfaces have a link-local address, therefore they have the same prefix and there is no way of knowing which one will be available in one or another interface. In IPv4 the ARP tables were in charge of this, but in IPv6, the concept of ARP does not exist. Therefore, to perform the ping, we use the following command:

```
# ping6 -I eth0 fe80::ac3e:7bff:fe33:5fb0
 PING fe80::ac3e:7bff:fe33:5fb0(fe80::ac3e:7bff:fe33:5fb0) from
fe80::bc6c:91ff:feb7:be0a eth0: 56 data bytes
 64 bytes from fe80::ac3e:7bff:fe33:5fb0: icmp_seq=1 ttl=64 time=0.966 ms
 64 bytes from fe80::ac3e:7bff:fe33:5fb0: icmp_seq=2 ttl=64 time=0.294 ms
 ^C
 --- fe80::ac3e:7bff:fe33:5fb0 ping statistics ---
```

```
2 packets transmitted, 2 received, 0% packet loss, time 1001ms
rtt min/avg/max/mdev = 0.294/0.630/0.966/0.336 ms
```

This address can already be used as any IPv4 address, so if a web server is running and has a service with IPv6 support, you can establish the connection through this IP address.

In the following example, we can see how to resolve IP addresses from the `https://www.python.org/` domain with IPv4 and IPv6 formats.

You can find the following code in the `getaddrinfoIPv4_IPv6.py` file:

```python
!/usr/bin/env python3

import socket

def getaddrinfoIPv4(host, port=80, family=0, type=0, proto=0, flags=0):
    return socket.getaddrinfo(host=host, port=port,
 family=socket.AF_INET, type=type, proto=proto, flags=flags)

def getaddrinfoIPv6(host, port=80, family=0, type=0, proto=0, flags=0):
    return socket.getaddrinfo(host=host, port=port,
 family=socket.AF_INET6, type=type, proto=proto, flags=flags)


print(getaddrinfoIPv4("www.python.org"))

print(getaddrinfoIPv6("www.python.org"))
```

This is the output of the previous script where we can obtain IP addresses in the IPv4 and IPv6 formats:

```
[(<AddressFamily.AF_INET: 2>, 0, 0, '', ('151.101.120.223', 80))]
[(<AddressFamily.AF_INET6: 23>, 0, 0, '', ('2a04:4e42:1d::223', 80, 0, 0))]
```

Create an echo client and server with IPv6

In this section, we will see how to create a basic example of a client-server application in Python using the IPv6 protocol instead of IPv4.

Working with sockets

To create communication between two programs, we will use sockets. Sockets are an abstract concept. With them, two programs can communicate. These programs can be on the same machine or run on different devices. To be able to use sockets, we must import them, both on the server and on the client.

The socket server

First, we define the necessary variables for the connection, that is, the IP address for localhost in IPv6 format and the maximum number of connections from clients:

```
IPV6_ADDRESS = '::1'
# Up to 5 clients can connect
maxConnections = 5
```

Next, since we have the necessary data, we create the server. It is a socket-type object that is listening in a specific port using IPv6 and TCP/IP:

```
# Creating the server with ipv6 support
# socket.AF_INET6 to indicate that we will use Ipv6
# socket.SOCK_STREAM to use TCP/IP

server_socket = socket.socket(socket.AF_INET6,socket.SOCK_STREAM)
dataConection = (host,port)
server_socket.bind(dataConection)
```

Our socket is already created. Now we must accept connections from it:

```
print("Waiting connections in %s:%s" %(host, port))
connection, address = server_socket.accept()
print ('Connected to', address)
```

The `socket.accept()` method will remain listening until you receive a request. Then, in a loop, we indicate what the server should do when receiving each connection:

```
while True:
    data = connection.recv(1024)
    print ("Received data from the client: [%s]" %data.decode())
    if data.decode() == "exit":
        connection.send(bytes("exit".encode('utf-8')))
        break
    connection.send(data)
    print ("Sent data echoed back to the client: [%s]" %data.decode())
```

The core of our program is in this loop, and it's where we indicate the way to act when receiving the client's frames.

Finally, when the connection is closed, we indicate with a message that it has been closed and we close the socket with the `socket.close()` method:

```
connection.close()
```

You can find the full code in the `echo_server_ipv6.py` file:

```python
#!/usr/bin/env python3

import argparse
import socket

IPV6_ADDRESS = '::1'
# Up to 5 clients can connect
maxConnections = 5

def echo_server_ipv6(port, host=IPV6_ADDRESS):
    # Creating the server with ipv6 support
    # socket.AF_INET6 to indicate that we will use Ipv6
    # socket.SOCK_STREAM to use TCP/IP
    try:
        server_socket = socket.socket(socket.AF_INET6,socket.SOCK_STREAM)
        dataConection = (host,port)
        server_socket.bind(dataConection)
        # We assign the maximum number of connections
        server_socket.listen(maxConnections)
    except socket.error as err:
        print ("Socket error: %s" %err)
        server_socket.close()

    print("Waiting connections in %s:%s" %(host, port))
    connection, address = server_socket.accept()
    print ('Connected to', address)
```

In the previous code block, we established a socket connection with IPv6 support, assigning the maximum number of connections the server can accept. Later, with the `accept()` method, the server will listen to requests waiting for connections from a client:

```python
    while True:
        data = connection.recv(1024)
        print ("Received data from the client: [%s]" %data.decode())
        if data.decode() == "exit":
            connection.send(bytes("exit".encode('utf-8')))
            break
```

```
            connection.send(data)
            print ("Sent data echoed back to the client: [%s]" %data.decode())

        print("------- CLOSE CONNECTION ---------")
        connection.close()

if __name__ == '__main__':
    parser = argparse.ArgumentParser(description='IPv6 Socket Server')
    parser.add_argument('--port', action="store", dest="port", type=int,
required=True)
    given_args = parser.parse_args()
    port = given_args.port
    echo_server_ipv6(port)
```

The most important part of the server is the infinite loop simulated with the `while True:` instruction. In this part, we implement receiving the message from the client and the instruction for sending the response to the client. At the end of the script, we establish the port where the server will send the response with the `argparse` module.

The socket client

In the client part, we create a new socket that is listening in the same server host and port:

```
# Configure the data to connect to the server
# socket.AF_INET6 to indicate that we will use Ipv6
# socket.SOCK_STREAM to use TCP/IP
# These protocols must be the same as on the server

client = socket.socket (socket.AF_INET6, socket.SOCK_STREAM)
client.connect ((host, port))
print ("Connected to the server --->% s:% s"% (host, port))
```

Our socket is already created for sending data to the server:

```
#send initial data to server
message = "Hello from ipv6 client"
print ("Send data to server: %s" %message)
client.send(bytes(message.encode('utf-8')))
```

And finally we indicate what we want to do with the connection. In this case, we will also do it in a loop. Since the way of client and server interact is that the client sends a message to the server and the server will respond Received from server. When the client receives this message, they will ask for a message from the user to be able to send it back to the server. To close the connection, the user must write exit to the client and send that message to the server. When it reaches the server, it will send the exit message to the client, then it will show a message of Connection closed and it will close the connection. The client, upon receiving the exit message from the server, will do the same and the connection will end correctly on both sides. The code for this operation is the following:

```
while True:
 message = input("Write your message > ")
 client.send(bytes(message.encode('utf-8')))
 data = client.recv(1024)
 print ('Received from server:', data.decode())
 if data == "exit":
 break;
```

You can find the full code in the echo_client_ipv6.py file:

```python
#!/usr/bin/env python3

import argparse
import socket

IPV6_ADDRESS = '::1'

def echo_client_ipv6(port, host=IPV6_ADDRESS):
    # Configure the data to connect to the server
    # socket.AF_INET6 to indicate that we will use Ipv6
    # socket.SOCK_STREAM to use TCP/IP
    # These protocols must be the same as on the server
    try:
        client = socket.socket (socket.AF_INET6, socket.SOCK_STREAM)
        client.connect ((host, port))
        print ("Connected to the server --->% s:% s"% (host, port))
    except socket.error as err:
        print ("Socket error:%s" %err)
        client.close()

    # send initial data to server
    message = "Hello from ipv6 client"
    print ("Send data to server: %s" %message)
    client.send(bytes(message.encode('utf-8')))

    while True:
```

```
        message = input("Write your message > ")
        client.send(bytes(message.encode('utf-8')))
        data = client.recv(1024)
        print ('Received from server:', data.decode())
        if data.decode() == "exit":
            break;

    print("------- CLOSE CONNECTION ---------")
    client.close()

if __name__ == '__main__':
    parser = argparse.ArgumentParser(description='IPv6 socket client')
    parser.add_argument('--port', action="store", dest="port", type=int,
required=True)
    given_args = parser.parse_args()
    port = given_args.port
    echo_client_ipv6(port)
```

The most important part of the client is the infinite loop simulated with the `while`
`True`: instruction. In this part, we implement sending the message to the server and the
instruction for receiving the response from the server with the `data =`
`client.recv(1024)` code line. At the end of the script, we establish the port where the
client will send the messages with the `argparse` module.

Executing client and server

First, we start server execution with the `echo_server_ipv6.py` Python script. After
executing this script, the server it will wait for connections:

```
usage: echo_server_ipv6.py [-h] --port PORT
```

When executing the server script, we must use the port argument to establish the number
where the server is listening for connections:

```
python echo_server_ipv6.py --port 7575
  Waiting connections in ::1:7575
```

Next, we start the client with the same port parameter:

```
python echo_client_ipv6.py --port 7575
  Connected to the server --->::1:7575
  Send data to server: Hello from ipv6 client
  Write your message >
```

And we will see that the server has already identified the connection:

```
Connected to ('::1', 3210, 0, 0)
Received data from the client: [Hello from ipv6 client]
Sent data echoed back to the client: [Hello from ipv6 client]
```

Now we can write any message on the client, and in the server log we can verify that the message is sent:

```
Received data from the client: [Hello from ipv6 client]
Sent data echoed back to the client: [Hello from ipv6 client]
Received data from the client: [This is a new message]
Sent data echoed back to the client: [This is a new message]
```

In this screenshot, we can see the execution in the socket server:

```
Waiting connections in ::1:7575
Connected to ('::1', 3367, 0, 0)
Received data from the client: [Hello from ipv6 client]
Sent data echoed back to the client: [Hello from ipv6 client]
Received data from the client: [This is a new message]
Sent data echoed back to the client: [This is a new message]
Received data from the client: [I am testing sockets with IPV6]
Sent data echoed back to the client: [I am testing sockets with IPV6]
Received data from the client: [exit]
------- CLOSE CONNECTION ---------
```

In this screenshot, we can see the execution in the socket client:

```
Connected to the server --->::1:7575
Send data to server: Hello from ipv6 client
write your message > This is a new message
Received from server: Hello from ipv6 client
write your message > I am testing sockets with IPV6
Received from server: This is a new message
write your message > exit
Received from server: I am testing sockets with IPV6
write your message >
Received from server: exit
------- CLOSE CONNECTION ---------
```

Upon receiving the exit message, the server will close the connection. The client has also received an exit message and will also close the connection.

Understanding netifaces module for checking IPv6 support on your network

In this section, the reader will learn how to use the `netifaces` Python module to check IPv6 support.

Introduction to netifaces

If you want to query the network interfaces available on your computer, you can use the `netifaces` module. We can use a third-party library, `netifaces`, to find out whether there is IPv6 support on your machine. You can install it with the `pip` command:

```
pip install netifaces
```

> For more information, you can explore the netifaces documentation: https://pypi.org/project/netifaces/.

We can call the `interfaces()` function from this library to list all interfaces present in the system. This script will give a list of all interfaces, and IPv4 and IPv6 addresses available in the system.

You can find the following code in the `check_interfaces.py` file:

```python
#!/usr/bin/env python3

import itertools
from netifaces import interfaces, ifaddresses, AF_INET, AF_INET6

def all_interfaces():
    for interface in interfaces():
        print(ifaddresses(interface))

def inspect_ipv4_addresses():
    links = filter(None, (ifaddresses(x).get(AF_INET) for x in
interfaces()))
    links = itertools.chain(*links)
    ip_v4_addresses = [x['addr'] for x in links]
    return ip_v4_addresses

def inspect_ipv6_addresses():
    links = filter(None, (ifaddresses(x).get(AF_INET6) for x in
```

```
interfaces()))
    links = itertools.chain(*links)
    ip_v6_addresses = [x['addr'] for x in links]
    return ip_v6_addresses

if __name__ == '__main__':
    print(inspect_ipv4_addresses())
    print(inspect_ipv6_addresses())
    all_interfaces()
```

In the following script, we are checking whether the Python version supports IPv6 with the has_ipv6 property from the socket package. With the netifaces package, we can get more information for each interface, such as Address family, netmask, and broadcast addresses.

You can find the following code in the check_ipv6_support.py file:

```
#!/usr/bin/env python3

import socket
import netifaces

def inspect_ipv6_support():
    print ("IPV6 support built into Python: %s" %socket.has_ipv6)
    ipv6_addresses = {}
    for interface in netifaces.interfaces():
        all_addresses = netifaces.ifaddresses(interface)
        print ("Interface %s:" %interface)
        for family,addrs in all_addresses.items():
            fam_name = netifaces.address_families[family]
            print (' Address family: %s' % fam_name)
```

In the previous code block, we used the netifaces module to get interfaces and addresses related with these interfaces. Later, for each IP address we get information about the Address family. Depending the address type, we use an array called ipv6_addresses for store information related with each IP address, such as netmask and broadcast addresses. Finally, we check the ipv6_addresses array for any information about found IPv6 addresses:

```
        for addr in addrs:
            if fam_name == 'AF_INET6':
                ipv6_addresses[interface] = addr['addr']
            print (' Address : %s' % addr['addr'])
            nmask = addr.get('netmask', None)
            if nmask:
                print (' Netmask : %s' % nmask)
            bcast = addr.get('broadcast', None)
```

```
            if bcast:
                    print (' Broadcast: %s' % bcast)
        if ipv6_addresses:
            print ("Found IPv6 address: %s" %ipv6_addresses)
        else:
            print ("No IPv6 interface found!")

    if __name__ == '__main__':
        inspect_ipv6_support()
```

This is the execution of the previous script:

```
IPV6 support built into Python: True
Interface {06C67899-9BE2-49F1-AAB5-C576A234DD9A}:
  Address family: AF_LINK
    Address  : 00:ff:c0:63:12:57
  Address family: AF_INET6
    Address  : fe80::f4ca:6a17:37a3:db89%3
    Netmask  : ffff:ffff:ffff:ffff::/64
    Broadcast: fe80::ffff:ffff:ffff:ffff3
Interface {40EE5A9D-737D-40AA-BBFC-4F5833D17C0E}:
  Address family: AF_LINK
    Address  : 8c:16:45:2d:79:20
  Address family: AF_INET6
    Address  : fe80::a568:f01f:d4ae:170%6
    Netmask  : ffff:ffff:ffff:ffff::/64
    Broadcast: fe80::ffff:ffff:ffff:ffff%6
  Address family: AF_INET
    Address  : 10.80.92.211
    Netmask  : 255.255.255.0
    Broadcast: 10.80.92.255
Interface {361548CA-A87A-40B1-9E88-EAAC3B1B91B1}:
  Address family: AF_LINK
    Address  : 0a:00:27:00:00:05
  Address family: AF_INET6
    Address  : fe80::e53f:e43b:ad07:9cab%5
    Netmask  : ffff:ffff:ffff:ffff::/64
    Broadcast: fe80::ffff:ffff:ffff:ffff%5
  Address family: AF_INET
    Address  : 192.168.56.1
    Netmask  : 255.255.255.0
    Broadcast: 192.168.56.255
```

In the execution of the script, we can see that we have three address families listed. AF_LINK is the link layer interface, such as Ethernet, AF_INET is the IPv4 internet address, and AF_INET6 represents the IPv6 internet address.

Other packages for getting interfaces

There are other Python packages that are not specifically designed to obtain network interfaces in a computer, but they have some function for doing this task. For example, the `psutil` package (`https://pypi.org/project/psutil`) allows tasks related to process and system monitoring in Python.

This package provides the `net_if_addrs()` method for getting information related to network interfaces:

```
import psutil
psutil.net_if_addrs()
```

The information is returned in a dictionary structure, as follows:

```
{'Local Area Connection* 11': [snicaddr(family=<AddressFamily.AF_LINK: -1>,
address='00-FF-C0-63-12-57', netmask=None, broadcast=None, ptp=None),
snicaddr(family=<AddressFamily.AF_INET: 2>, address='169.254.219.137',
netmask='255.255.0.0', broadcast=None, ptp=None),
snicaddr(family=<AddressFamily.AF_INET6: 23>,
address='fe80::f4ca:6a17:37a3:db89', netmask=None, broadcast=None,
ptp=None)], 'Ethernet': [snicaddr(family=<AddressFamily.AF_LINK: -1>}
```

This method returns the addresses associated with each network interface card detected in the operating system. The information is returned in a dictionary data structure whose keys are the names of the NIC, and the value is a list of tuples for each address assigned to the NIC. Each named group includes five fields:

- `family`: Represents the family for Mac address.
- `address`: The primary IP address.
- `netmask`
- `ptp`: References the destination address on a point-to-point interface.
- `broadcast`

With this package, we also have the ability to get socket connections in our computer with commands such as `netstat`:

```
net_connections(kind='inet')
    Return system-wide socket connections as a list of
    (fd, family, type, laddr, raddr, status, pid) namedtuples.
    In case of limited privileges 'fd' and 'pid' may be set to -1
    and None respectively.
    The *kind* parameter filters for connections that fit the
    following criteria:

    +------------+---------------------------------------------------+
    | Kind Value | Connections using                                 |
    +------------+---------------------------------------------------+
    | inet       | IPv4 and IPv6                                      |
    | inet4      | IPv4                                               |
    | inet6      | IPv6                                               |
    | tcp        | TCP                                                |
    | tcp4       | TCP over IPv4                                      |
    | tcp6       | TCP over IPv6                                      |
    | udp        | UDP                                                |
    | udp4       | UDP over IPv4                                      |
    | udp6       | UDP over IPv6                                      |
    | unix       | UNIX socket (both UDP and TCP protocols)          |
    | all        | the sum of all the possible families and protocols|
    +------------+---------------------------------------------------+
```

We can use the `net_connections()` method to get a list of socket connections available in your local machine in the same way that we can use the `netstat` command that is available in many operating systems:

```
psutil.net_connections()
```

Here is the output from executing the `net_connections()` method:

```
[sconn(fd=115, family=<AddressFamily.AF_INET: 2>,
type=<SocketType.SOCK_STREAM: 1>, laddr=addr(ip='10.0.0.1', port=48776),
raddr=addr(ip='93.186.135.91', port=80), status='ESTABLISHED', pid=1254),
 sconn(fd=117, family=<AddressFamily.AF_INET: 2>,
type=<SocketType.SOCK_STREAM: 1>, laddr=addr(ip='10.0.0.1', port=43761),
raddr=addr(ip='72.14.234.100', port=80), status='CLOSING', pid=2987),
 sconn(fd=-1, family=<AddressFamily.AF_INET: 2>,
type=<SocketType.SOCK_STREAM: 1>, laddr=addr(ip='10.0.0.1', port=60759),
raddr=addr(ip='72.14.234.104', port=80), status='ESTABLISHED', pid=None),
 sconn(fd=-1, family=<AddressFamily.AF_INET: 2>,
type=<SocketType.SOCK_STREAM: 1>, laddr=addr(ip='10.0.0.1', port=51314),
raddr=addr(ip='72.14.234.83', port=443), status='SYN_SENT', pid=None)
 ...]
```

In the following script, we are going to obtain information about IPv4 and IPv6 interfaces with the `psutil.net_if_addrs()` method.

You can find the following code in the `check_interfaces_psutil.py` file:

```python
#!/usr/bin/env python3

import socket
import psutil

def get_ip_addresses(family):
    for interface, snics in psutil.net_if_addrs().items():
        for snic in snics:
            if snic.family == family:
                yield (interface, snic.address)

if __name__ == '__main__':
    ipv4_list = list(get_ip_addresses(socket.AF_INET))
    ipv6_list = list(get_ip_addresses(socket.AF_INET6))
    print("IPV4 Interfaces",ipv4_list)
    print("IPV6 Interfaces",ipv6_list)
```

This could be the output of the previous script:

```
IPV4 Interfaces [('Local Area Connection* 11', '169.254.219.137'),
('Ethernet', '10.80.92.211'), ('VirtualBox Host-Only Network',
'192.168.56.1'), ('Npcap Loopback Adapter', '169.254.204.194'), ('Wi-Fi',
'169.254.52.200'), ('Local Area Connection* 2', '169.254.234.2'),
('Loopback Pseudo-Interface 1', '127.0.0.1')]

IPV6 Interfaces [('Local Area Connection* 11',
'fe80::f4ca:6a17:37a3:db89'), ('Ethernet', 'fe80::a568:f01f:d4ae:170'),
('VirtualBox Host-Only Network', 'fe80::e53f:e43b:ad07:9cab'), ('Npcap
Loopback Adapter', 'fe80::8cd:714b:4e02:ccc2'), ('Wi-Fi',
'fe80::644d:7369:e8ca:34c8'), ('Local Area Connection* 2',
'fe80::856f:c54b:1d7e:ea02'), ('Teredo Tunneling Pseudo-Interface',
'fe80::ffff:ffff:fffe'), ('Loopback Pseudo-Interface 1', '::1')]
```

Using the netaddr module as a network-address manipulation library for Python

In this section, you will learn how to work with `netaddr` for network-address manipulation and interoperability between IPv4 and IPv6.

Operating with IPv6

The next module that we are going to study allows us to manipulate the network address and the interoperability between IPv4 and IPv6. For example, given a certain IP address, we can obtain it in the v4 and v6 formats. The easiest way to install `netaddr` is to use `pip`. Download and install the latest version from the Python repository (`http://pypi.python.org/pypi/pip`) and run the following command:

```
pip install netaddr
```

Also, you can see the official source code repository here: `https://github.com/drkjam/netaddr`.

The following `IPAddress` object represents a single IP address v6:

```
>>> from netaddr import *
>>> ipv6 = IPAddress('::1')
>>> ipv6.version
6
```

We can check whether we have full support for the IPv6 protocol:

```
>>> ip = IPNetwork('fe80::beef:beef/64')
>>> str(ip), ip.prefixlen, ip.version
('fe80::beef:beef/64', 64, 6)
>>> ip.network, ip.broadcast, ip.netmask, ip.hostmask
(IPAddress('fe80::'), IPAddress('fe80::ffff:ffff:ffff:ffff'),
IPAddress('ffff:ffff:ffff:ffff::'), IPAddress('::ffff:ffff:ffff:ffff'))
>>>
```

Also, we can interoperate between IPv4 and IPv6 with the `ipv6()` and `ipv4()` methods:

```
>>> ip = IPAddress('127.0.0.1').ipv6()
>>> ip
IPAddress('::ffff:127.0.0.1')
>>> ip.ipv4()
IPAddress('127.0.0.1')
>>> ip.ipv6()
IPAddress('::ffff:127.0.0.1')
```

If we are working with IPv6, it can be interesting that addresses could be compatible also with IPv4:

```
>>> ip = IPAddress('127.0.0.1').ipv6(ipv4_compatible=True)
>>> ip
IPAddress('::127.0.0.1')
>>> IPAddress('127.0.0.1').ipv6(ipv4_compatible=True).is_ipv4_compat()
```

```
True
>>> IPNetwork('::1').ipv6(ipv4_compatible=True)
IPNetwork('::1/128')
>>> IPNetwork('::1').ipv6(ipv4_compatible=True).ipv4()
IPNetwork('0.0.0.1/32')
```

With this script, we can extract IPv6 information from network interfaces, and with the netaddr package we get information about IP version, IP prefix length, network address, and broadcast address.

You can find the following code in the extract_ipv6_info.py file:

```python
#!/usr/bin/env python3

import socket
import netifaces
import netaddr

def extract_ipv6_info():
    print ("IPv6 support built into Python: %s" %socket.has_ipv6)
    for interface in netifaces.interfaces():
        all_addresses = netifaces.ifaddresses(interface)
        print ("Interface %s:" %interface)
        for family,addrs in all_addresses.items():
            fam_name = netifaces.address_families[family]
            for addr in addrs:
                if fam_name == 'AF_INET6':
                    addr = addr['addr']
                    has_eth_string = addr.split("%eth")
                    if has_eth_string:
                        addr = addr.split("%eth")[0]
                    try:
                        print (" IP Address: %s" %netaddr.IPNetwork(addr))
                        print (" IP Version: %s"
%netaddr.IPNetwork(addr).version)
                        print (" IP Prefix length: %s"
%netaddr.IPNetwork(addr).prefixlen)
                        print (" Network: %s"
%netaddr.IPNetwork(addr).network)
                        print (" Broadcast: %s"
%netaddr.IPNetwork(addr).broadcast)

                    except Exception as e:
                        print ("Skip Non-IPv6 Interface")

if __name__ == '__main__':
    extract_ipv6_info()
```

Understand ipaddress module as IPv4 and IPv6 manipulation library

In this section, you will learn to work with IP addresses for IPv4/v6 address manipulation. Here, we will focus on IPv6 address manipulation.

The Python ipaddress module

The ipaddress module simplifies working with IPv4 and IPv6 addresses in python. In this section, we will focus on the IPv6 protocol and work primarily with the following three class types:

- IPv6Address: Represents a single IPv6 address
- IPv6Network: Represents an IPv6 network
- IPv6Interface: Represents an IPv6 interface

You can get more information about this module with the help command from the Python interpreter:

```
class IPv6Address(_BaseV6, _BaseAddress)
 |   Represent and manipulate single IPv6 Addresses.
 |
 |   Method resolution order:
 |       IPv6Address
 |       _BaseV6
 |       _BaseAddress
 |       _IPAddressBase
 |       builtins.object
 |
 |   Methods defined here:
 |
 |   __init__(self, address)
 |       Instantiate a new IPv6 address object.
 |
 |       Args:
 |           address: A string or integer representing the IP
 |
 |           Additionally, an integer can be passed, so
 |           IPv6Address('2001:db8::') ==
 |               IPv6Address(42540766411282592856903984951653826560)
 |           or, more generally
 |           IPv6Address(int(IPv6Address('2001:db8::'))) ==
 |               IPv6Address('2001:db8::')
 |
 |       Raises:
 |           AddressValueError: If address isn't a valid IPv6 address.
 |
```

The `IPv6Address` class represents an IPv6 address or network. To create these objects in Python, the module provides some basic factory functions to create such objects:

```
import ipaddress
from ipaddress import IPv6Address, IPv6Network, IPv6Interface
```

After you create an IPv6 object, you can get a lot of information out of the class, for example, whether it is a global or private address, the prefix length, and `netmask`.

In this screenshot, we can see the methods you can employ to check these use cases:

```
ipv4_mapped
    Return the IPv4 mapped address.

    Returns:
        If the IPv6 address is a v4 mapped address, return the
        IPv4 mapped address. Return None otherwise.

is_global
    Test if this address is allocated for public networks.

    Returns:
        A boolean, true if the address is not reserved per
        iana-ipv6-special-registry.

is_link_local
    Test if the address is reserved for link-local.

    Returns:
        A boolean, True if the address is reserved per RFC 4291.

is_loopback
    Test if the address is a loopback address.

    Returns:
        A boolean, True if the address is a loopback address as defined in
        RFC 2373 2.5.3.

is_multicast
    Test if the address is reserved for multicast use.
```

IP network objects

When working with an IP address that represents a network, we could work with an `IPv4Network` or `IPv6Network` object depending on the IP address passed as the argument. For this task, we can use the `ip_network()` method from the `ipaddress` module using as parameter a string or integer representing the IP network.

Let's import the `ipaddress` module and define a `net6` network:

```
>>> import ipaddress
>>> net6 = ipaddress.ip_network('2001:db8::/48')
```

Now, we get some useful information, such as version, `netmask`, and the network/broadcast address:

```
>>> net6.version
6
>>> net6.netmask
IPv6Address('ffff:ffff:ffff::')
```

Similarly, you can find the network and the broadcast addresses of `net6` by doing the following:

```
>>> net6.network_address
IPv6Address('2001:db8::')
>>> net6.broadcast_address
IPv6Address('2001:db8:0:ffff:ffff:ffff:ffff:ffff')
```

Also, we can get the number of addresses `net6` can hold:

```
>>> net6.num_addresses
1208925819614629174706176
```

Subnetting in Python with IPv6

We can also find the subnet information from the `IPv6Network` objects, as follows:

```
>>> subnets = list(net6.subnets())
>>> subnets
[IPv6Network('2001:db8::/49'), IPv6Network('2001:db8:0:8000::/49')]
```

The `ipaddress` module includes various functions to create `subnets` and `supernets`, so we can check whether a network overlaps:

```
>>> ipnet = ipaddress.IPv6Network("2001:db8::/48")
>>> list(ipnet.subnets())
[IPv6Network('2001:db8::/49'), IPv6Network('2001:db8:0:8000::/49')]
```

We can use the `subnets` method to expand the network mask and obtain new networks:

```
>>> list(ipnet.subnets(prefixlen_diff=4))
[IPv6Network('2001:db8::/52'), IPv6Network('2001:db8:0:1000::/52'),
IPv6Network('2001:db8:0:2000::/52'), IPv6Network('2001:db8:0:3000::/52'),
```

```
    IPv6Network('2001:db8:0:4000::/52'), IPv6Network('2001:db8:0:5000::/52'),
    IPv6Network('2001:db8:0:6000::/52'), IPv6Network('2001:db8:0:7000::/52'),
    IPv6Network('2001:db8:0:8000::/52'), IPv6Network('2001:db8:0:9000::/52'),
    IPv6Network('2001:db8:0:a000::/52'), IPv6Network('2001:db8:0:b000::/52'),
    IPv6Network('2001:db8:0:c000::/52'), IPv6Network('2001:db8:0:d000::/52'),
    IPv6Network('2001:db8:0:e000::/52'), IPv6Network('2001:db8:0:f000::/52')]
```

Network interface objects

In the `ipaddress` module, a convenient class is used to represent an interface's IP configuration in detail. The IPv6 interface class lets you extract the `IPv6Address` and `IPv6Network` objects from a single instance:

```
>>> eth0 = ipaddress.IPv6Interface('2001:db8::/48')
>>> eth0.ip
IPv6Address('2001:db8::')
>>> eth0.with_prefixlen
'2001:db8::/48'
>>> eth0.with_netmask
'2001:db8::/ffff:ffff:ffff::'
>>> eth0.network
IPv6Network('2001:db8::/48')
>>> eth0.is_private
True
>>> eth0.is_reserved
False
>>> eth0.is_multicast
False
>>> eth0.is_link_local
False
>>> eth0.is_global
False
```

As you can see, a network interface, `eth0`, with the `IPv6Address` class has been defined. It has some interesting properties, such as IP and network address. In the same way as with the network objects, you can check whether the address is `private`, `reserved`, `multicast`, `link_local`, or `global`.

Also, we can work with the `ip_interface` method to extract the IP address and network:

```
>>> intf = ipaddress.ip_interface("2001:db8::/48")
>>> intf.ip
IPv6Address('2001:db8::')
>>> intf.network
IPv6Network('2001:db8::/48')
```

The IP address objects

In the same way as with the network objects, you can check whether the address is private, reserved, or multicast.

In this example, the loopback interface is defined with the `::1` IP address. As you can see, the is_loopback property returns true:

```
>>> loopback = ipaddress.IPv6Interface('::1')
>>> loopback.is_private
True
>>> loopback.is_reserved
True
>>> loopback.is_multicast
False
>>> loopback.is_loopback
True
```

The IP address classes have many more interesting properties. You can perform some arithmetic and logical operations on those objects. For example, we can check if an IP address is part of a network.

In this example, we check whether an IP is a part of a specific network. Here, a network net has been defined by the network address, which is `2001:db8:0:1::/64`, and the membership of eth0 and eth1 has been checked for whether these interfaces are part of the network:

```
>>> net6 = ipaddress.ip_network('2001:db8:0:1::/64')
>>> eth0 = ipaddress.IPv6Interface('2001:db8:0:1::beef')
>>> eth1 = ipaddress.IPv6Interface('2001:db7::/48')

>>> eth0 in net6
True
>>> eth1 in net6
False
>>>
```

Planning IP addresses for your local area network

Suppose you have a CIDR network address such as
`12:3456:78:90ab:cd:ef01:23:30/125`, and you want to generate a range of all the IP
addresses that it represents (`12:3456:78:90ab:cd:ef01:23:30` to
`12:3456:78:90ab:cd:ef01:23:37`). The `ipaddress` module can be easily used to
perform such calculations:

```
>>> import ipaddress
>>> net6 = ipaddress.ip_network('12:3456:78:90ab:cd:ef01:23:30/125')
>>> net6
IPv6Network('12:3456:78:90ab:cd:ef01:23:30/125')
>>> for ip in net:
... print(ip)
12:3456:78:90ab:cd:ef01:23:30
12:3456:78:90ab:cd:ef01:23:31
12:3456:78:90ab:cd:ef01:23:32
12:3456:78:90ab:cd:ef01:23:33
12:3456:78:90ab:cd:ef01:23:34
12:3456:78:90ab:cd:ef01:23:35
12:3456:78:90ab:cd:ef01:23:36
12:3456:78:90ab:cd:ef01:23:37
```

In this example, we are using the `ip_network` method from the `ipaddress` module to
generate a range of all the IP addresses that represents the network.

You can find the following code in the `net_planner_ipv6.py` file:

```python
#!/usr/bin/env python3

import ipaddress as ip

IPV6_ADDR = '2001:db8:0:1::'

mask = input("Enter the mask length: ")
mask = int(mask)
net_addr = IPV6_ADDR + '/' + str(mask)

print("Using network address:%s " %net_addr)
try:
    network = ip.ip_network(net_addr)
except:
    raise Exception("Failed to create network object")

print("This mask will give %s IP addresses" %(network.num_addresses))
```

```
print("The network configuration will be:")
print("\t network address: %s" %str(network.network_address))
print("\t netmask: %s" %str(network.netmask))
print("\t broadcast address: %s" %str(network.broadcast_address))
```

Now we are going to execute the previous script with different mask lengths.

Here's an execution with a mask length of 64:

```
Enter the mask length: 64
Using network address:2001:db8:0:1::/64
This mask will give 18446744073709551616 IP addresses
The network configuration will be:
network address: 2001:db8:0:1::
netmask: ffff:ffff:ffff:ffff::
broadcast address: 2001:db8:0:1:ffff:ffff:ffff:ffff
```

Here's an execution with a mask length of 68:

```
Enter the mask length: 68
Using network address:2001:db8:0:1::/68
This mask will give 1152921504606846976 IP addresses
The network configuration will be:
network address: 2001:db8:0:1::
netmask: ffff:ffff:ffff:ffff:f000::
broadcast address: 2001:db8:0:1:fff:ffff:ffff:ffff
```

Summary

In this chapter, we reviewed the IPv6 protocol and the standard Python libraries for IPv6 address manipulation. Three third-party libraries, ipaddress, netifaces, and netaddr, were presented for working with IPv6 and address manipulation with Python. Also, we reviewed the socket module for implementing client-server applications for sending and receiving messages.

In the next chapter, we will introduce Ansible and then explore some Python modules for working with Ansible and automating networking tasks.

Questions

1. Which types of IPv6 addresses are created automatically, are exclusively used in local subnets, and are not routable?
2. Which IPv6 address represents the loopback address, such as `127.0.0.1` in IPv4?
3. What is the method from the socket library that we can use to get information related to the IPv4 and IPv6 protocols from a specific domain?
4. How do we create a server with IPv6 support with the socket module?
5. What method from the `netifaces` module can we use to list all interfaces, and IPv4 and IPv6 addresses present in the system?
6. What are the address families available when we are working with the netifaces module?
7. What is the alternative module to `netifaces` that allows us to get socket connections and interfaces in our computer with commands such as `netstat`?
8. How do we use the `netaddr` module to interoperate between IPv4 and IPv6 addresses?
9. Which classes in the `ipaddress` module can we use to work with IPv6 addresses?
10. Which functions in the `ipaddress` module can we use to work with subnets and supernets?

Further reading

Check out the following links for more information about the tools we talked about in this chapter. The official Python documentation is also a great resource for some of the topics we covered:

- Presentations about the IPv6 protocol: `https://insinuator.net/2019/01/ipv6-talks-publications/`
- The official Python 3.7 documentation: `https://docs.python.org/3.7/howto/ipaddress.html#ipaddress-howto`
- A few useful functions and objects for manipulating IPv4 and IPv6 addresses in Python: `https://github.com/bd808/python-iptools`

- The `iptools` package is a collection of utilities for working with IP addresses: `http://python-iptools.readthedocs.org`
- Some examples and the official documentation for the `netaddr` package: `https://netaddr.readthedocs.io/en/latest/tutorial_01.htm`

Performing Network Automation with Python and Ansible

9

Ansible is an open source, general-purpose automation tool written in Python. It can be used to automate servers, network devices, load balancers, and more. In this chapter, you will learn about the principles of Ansible and how we can interact with it from Python. Ansible is used to bring structure and consistency to system deployments, implementations, and changes. In this chapter, we will explore Ansible and learn how to write a Python script to do a networking-automation task with Ansible and how to write an Ansible module with Python.

The following topics will be covered in this chapter:

- Basics of Ansible
- Ansible's components and architecture
- Automating network Python tasks with Ansible
- Writing Ansible modules with Python

Technical requirements

The examples and source code for this chapter are available in the GitHub repository in the `Chapter09` folder: `https://github.com/PacktPublishing/Learning-Python-Networking-Second-Edition`.

You will need to install the Python distribution in your local machine with the Unix operating system and have some basic knowledge of network protocols. Also, we need to install Ansible following the official documentation, depending our operating system: `https://docs.ansible.com/ansible/2.4/intro_installation.html`.

In this chapter we are assuming we have configured a network with three IP addresses: `192.168.1.160`, `192.168.1.161`, and `192.168.1.162`

Basics of Ansible

In this section, you will learn about the basics of Ansible for network automation, including how to install and configure Ansible.

Ansible introduction

Ansible (`https://docs.ansible.com`) is a software that automates software provisioning, configuration management, and application deployment. It is categorized as an orchestration tool. In other words, Ansible allows DevOps to manage their servers, configurations, and applications in a simple, robust, and parallel way.

Ansible is a deployment-automation tool, similar to Puppet and Chef, but its main characteristic is that it is agentless; that is, it does not need to install an agent on managed hosts.

This tool manages its different nodes through SSH for the provisioning of services based on Python and YAML to describe the actions to be carried out and the configurations that should be propagated to the different nodes.

One of the keys to the success of Ansible is the design of its API, which has resulted in the community being able to provide new modules that continuously incorporate the interaction with new software.

Ansible performs a deployment of configurations, installations, and actions on multiple machines, thus enabling an effective, fast, and resource-saving automated management capacity. It does not require a database to store the options or capabilities, nor the tasks to be performed. Ansible is based on flat text files written in the YAML language that will be used to define the machines, the variables, and the tasks to be performed. To perform the tasks, Ansible has a series of modules that are capable of interacting with tools within managed systems.

The Ansible configuration is defined in the YAML format. Basically, Ansible translates declarative YAML files into shell commands and runs them on remote hosts using the SSH protocol:

```
- hosts: all
  tasks:
    - name: add user into the system
      user: name=username state=present shell=/bin/bash
    - name: install ngnix into the system
      apt: pkg=nginx state=present
```

Installing Ansible

Ansible is distributed in the Fedora, Red Hat Enterprise Linux, and CentOS operating systems in package form. In addition, it is available for different Linux distributions, apart from those mentioned previously, and we can find it available in package search engine service: https://pkgs.org/download/ansible.

 For instructions on installing Ansible on other operating systems, check out the installation document: http://docs.ansible.com/ansible/intro_installation.html.

You can install Ansible on Ubuntu-and Debian-based distributions using the official package with the apt command. Here we see the steps to install the software packages; open up a Terminal:

1. Execute the following command:

   ```
   $ sudo apt-add-repository ppa:ansible/ansible
   ```

   In this screenshot, you can see the execution of the previous command:

```
You are about to add the following PPA to your system:
 Ansible is a radically simple IT automation platform that makes your applications and systems easier to deploy. Avc
id writing scripts or custom code to deploy and update your applications- automate in a language that approaches pla
in English, using SSH, with no agents to install on remote systems.

http://ansible.com/
 More info: https://launchpad.net/~ansible/+archive/ubuntu/ansible
Executing: gpg --ignore-time-conflict --no-options --no-default-keyring --homedir /tmp/tmp.PGRv4HRmuI --no-auto-chec
k-trustdb --trust-model always --keyring /etc/apt/trusted.gpg --primary-keyring /etc/apt/trusted.gpg --keyserver hkp
://keyserver.ubuntu.com:80 --recv-keys 7BB9C367
gpg: requesting key 7BB9C367 from hkp server keyserver.ubuntu.com
gpg: key 7BB9C367: "Launchpad PPA for Ansible, Inc." not changed
gpg: Total number processed: 1
gpg:              unchanged: 1
```

2. Execute these commands:

   ```
   $ sudo apt-get install python-software-properties
   $ sudo apt-get update
   $ sudo apt-get install ansible
   ```

3. It's possible to install Ansible on Fedora systems using the official package in the yum repository:

   ```
   $ sudo yum -y install ansible
   ```

4. Once Ansible is installed, you can check the Ansible version and files configuration with the following command:

```
$ ansible --version
ansible 2.7.5
 config file = /etc/ansible/ansible.cfg
 configured module search path = Default w/o overrides
ansible python module location = usr/lib/python3.7/site-
packages/ansible
executable location = /usr/bin/ansible
```

The main advantage of Ansible is that it allows us to configure many nodes in a parallel and synchronized way. There are different ways to tell Ansible which servers you are going to manage. The easy way is to add our machines to the inventory that Ansible has in our own system, which is located in `/etc/ansible/hosts`. In the host file, we can add the IP addresses of the machines we want to configure.

Run the `ansible --help` command to see the available options for executing Ansible:

```
$ ansible --help
Usage: ansible <host-pattern> [options]

Options:
  -a MODULE_ARGS, --args=MODULE_ARGS
                          module arguments
  --ask-become-pass       ask for privilege escalation password
  -k, --ask-pass          ask for SSH password
  --ask-su-pass           ask for su password (deprecated, use become)
  -K, --ask-sudo-pass     ask for sudo password (deprecated, use become)
  --ask-vault-pass        ask for vault password
  -B SECONDS, --background=SECONDS
                          run asynchronously, failing after X seconds
                          (default=N/A)
  -b, --become            run operations with become (nopasswd implied)
  --become-method=BECOME_METHOD
                          privilege escalation method to use (default=sudo),
```

Configuring Ansible

Ansible has its default configuration file in `/etc/ansible/ansible.cfg`. There are many options grouped in blocks. These are the blocks and the most-used options:

- [defaults]: The default configuration options for the execution of Ansible:
  - inventory: Defines the location of the inventory file, which by default is `/etc/ansible/hosts`

- `sudo_user`: The user with whom `sudo` will log in; by default it is root
- `forks`: The number of Ansible parallel processes; by default it is 5
- `timeout`: The timeout for an SSH connection; the default is 10 seconds
- `log_path`: The location of the log file; by default `/var/log/ansible.log`
- `nocows`: If its value is 0 and we have cowsay installed, we will see one of the animals reporting the playbooks; by default it is 1

- `[privilege_escalation]`: The options regarding privilege escalation
  - `become`: If `True`, the user that we connect with will try to scale privileges; by default `False`
  - `become_method`: The method to use to scale privileges; by default `sudo`
  - `become_user`: The user it will be scaled to; by default `root`

- `[ssh_connection]`: Options related to the SSH connection
  - `ssh_args`: The options that Ansible will use in executing SSH
  - `control_path`: Ansible makes use of multiplex to reduce the number of connections, this option defines the socket file to create
  - `scp_if_ssh`: The mechanism we use to transfer files; by default it will try to use `sftp`, and if it fails, it will try with `scp`

- `[colors]`: Define the colors of the different Ansible messages

Using Ansible

Once you have Ansible set up, there are two ways to use it:

- **Ad-hoc commands**: You can execute a command on the remote host using Ansible's command-line tool.
- **Using playbooks**: You can write your own file configuration for all or specific hosts or host groups. For this task, you can use YAML configuration specification language.

YAML (`https://yaml.org/`) is the syntax used for Ansible playbooks and other files. The YAML documentation (`https://docs.ansible.com/ansible/latest/reference_appendices/YAMLSyntax.html`) contains the full specifications of the syntax.

YAML is a format for saving data objects within a tree structure. Normally, it is used to define configuration files, although it is also possible to serialize objects, that is, to write the structure of an object in text string mode so that later it can be recovered.

This could be the syntax with YAML format:

```
development:
    database: mysql
    host: localhost
    username: root
    password: passwd
```

Ansible's components and architecture

In this section, you will learn about Ansible's components, such as the inventory file, and architecture.

Ansible's architecture

Ansible is a free software tool for automated deployments in IT environments. With this tool, we get to distribute applications or configuration files, among other things, for the different nodes of our environment. This is known as an orchestration tool, such as Puppet, Chef, or Salt. The advantage of using Ansible is that we do not need to install agents since it performs these tasks through SSH; it uses YAML as a serialization format to describe the reusable configurations of the systems.

There are two types of servers:

- **Controller or Ansible manager**: The machine from which the orchestration begins
- **Managed nodes**: The machines handled by the controller through SSH

Ansible manages its different nodes through SSH and only requires Python on the remote server where it will run.

In this diagram, we can see the components of the Ansible architecture:

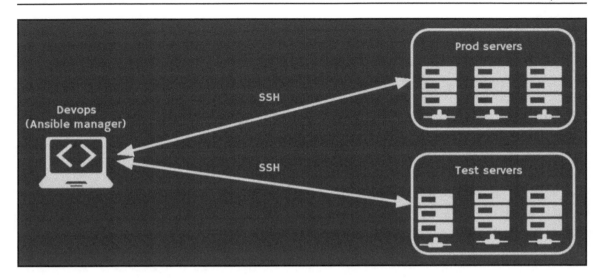

The Ansible architecture is agentless in the sense that there is no software or agent to be installed on the client that communicates back to the server. Instead of relying on remote host agents, Ansible uses SSH to push its changes to the remote host.

The idea is to have one or more control machines from where you can issue ad-hoc commands to remote machines (through Ansible tool) or execute a set of instructions in sequence through the playbooks (through the `ansible-playbook` tool).

Basically, we use the Ansible control manager machine, which will normally be your desktop, laptop, or server. From there, the control manager uses Ansible to distribute the configuration changes through SSH.

Another feature of Ansible is that it is idempotent, which means that if a task has already been done and the playbook is re-launched, it will not change anything since the task has already been executed.

The host inventory file determines the destination machines where these plays will be executed. The Ansible configuration file can be customized to reflect the configuration of your environment.

Ansible's inventory file

We use Ansible manage and automate some tasks on a remote host. All the hosts to be managed by the Ansible controller are listed in the inventory file. The file is located by default in the following path `/etc/ansible/hosts`.

Basically, this contains a lists of all the hosts that Ansible may manage. The machines can be identified by their IP address or by their hostname. You can also create groups with similar machines. The independent hosts must be at the beginning of the file, before any group.

Here is an example inventory file:

```
192.168.1.160

[test-servers]
192.168.1.161

[production-servers]
192.168.1.162
```

This configuration file specifies three hosts. The first node is specified by its IP address and the latter two hosts are specified in two groups: `test-servers` and `production-servers`.

By default, Ansible will look for the inventory file in `/etc/ansible/hosts`. You can also specify an alternative path for an inventory file with the `-i` flag:

```
A good description about the configuration of our hosts file can be found
at: https://docs.ansible.com/ansible/latest/user_guide/intro_inventory.html
```

One of the main features of Ansible is the capacity to manage machines remotely through SSH. For this task, make sure that your public SSH key is in the `authorized_keys` file on the remote machines. There are other authentication mechanisms that Ansible supports, such as providing plain-text passwords (which is not recommended) and Vault (`https://docs.ansible.com/ansible/2.4/vault.html`).

Ansible has to be able to connect to these machines over SSH, so you will likely need to have these entries in your `.ssh/config` file. Now, we can use the `ssh-keygen` command for generating our own SSH key. For this, we open a console in the central machine and execute the following command:

```
$ ssh-keygen
Generating public/private rsa key pair.
 Enter file in which to save the key (/home/user/.ssh/id_rsa):
 Enter passphrase (empty for no passphrase):
 Enter same passphrase again:
 Your identification has been saved in /home/user/.ssh/id_rsa.
 Your public key has been saved in /home/user/.ssh/id_rsa.pub.
```

Once the generation process is finished, we have two files: `~/.ssh/id_rsa` and `~/.ssh/id_rsa.pub`.

With the `ssh-copy-id` command we can copy the public key in the machine we want the controller in:

```
$ ssh-copy-id -i ~/.ssh/id_rsa.pub root@192.168.1.161
```

This is the output of the preceding command:

```
The authenticity of host '192.168.1.161' can't be established.
 ECDSA key fingerprint is b5:47:7b:dd:d7:16:07:0e:97:5a:bd:6b:21:e9:b9:e6.
 Are you sure you want to continue connecting (yes/no)? yes
 /usr/bin/ssh-copy-id: INFO: attempting to log in with the new key(s), to
filter out any that are already installed
 /usr/bin/ssh-copy-id: INFO: 1 key(s) remain to be installed -- if you are
prompted now it is to install the new keys
 Number of key(s) added: 1
 Now try logging into the machine, with: "ssh '192.168.1.161'"
 and check to make sure that only the key(s) you wanted were added.
```

Now we can start an SSH session with the root user without using a password.

Once we have defined our inventory file, we will perform our first execution, as follows:

```
$ ansible -i <path/to/custom/inventory> <group|host> -m <module> -a
"<module arguments>"
```

In the inventory file, the names of the host or their IP addresses are assigned. You can also make groupings of machines based on their role (such as database or web server). Once we have the inventory, we can start using Ansible, for example, by pinging all the machines or installing a certain package, as follows:

```
$ ansible test-servers -i hosts -m ping
```

Automating network Python tasks with Ansible

In this section, you will learn how to automate network Python tasks with Ansible and how to run playbooks.

Ansible tasks

Basically, a task is a single unit of provisioning. Each play must define the hosts on which the tasks will be executed. For example, here's the syntax to `install apache` using the `yum` command:

```
tasks:
- name: Install Apache Webserver
yum: pkg=httpd state=latest
```

Ad-hoc commands

We can check the `hostname` of IP addresses available in the hosts file:

```
$ ansible all -a "hostname"
 192.168.1.160 | SUCCESS | rc=0 >>
 node-ansible1
 192.168.1.161 | SUCCESS | rc=0 >>
 node-ansible2
```

The preceding command is equivalent to the following:

```
$ ansible 192.168.1.160,192.168.1.161 -a "hostname"
```

By default, Ansible executes the commands in parallel so that they end sooner. If we have two servers, we are practically not going to notice the difference, but as soon as we add several servers, we can verify that it goes faster if we parallelize the execution of commands.

Using playbooks

Playbooks basically allow us to manage the configuration of the deployment that we are going to make in the nodes. In them, we describe the configuration, but they also allow us to orchestrate a series of steps or tasks to follow.

In the playbook definition, we can use tasks, groups of machines, and variables; group variables; assign values to variables, conditional, loops, facts (information obtained by Ansible); get notifications and execution of actions based on them, apply labels to tasks; do includes; use templates (for the configuration files of the services, for example, of Apache or MySQL), wait for conditions, encrypt files that contain sensitive information, and include those files in a version control tool without risk of compromising the information; and we can use roles that apply all these things according to the function that we want a machine to have.

This is the basic structure of a playbook:

```
- name: Configure webserver with git
  hosts: webserver
  become: true
  vars:
    package: git
  tasks:
    - name: install git
      apt: name={{ package }} state=present
```

Each playbook must contain the following elements:

- A set of hosts to configure
- A list of tasks to execute on those hosts

You can think of a playbook as the way to connect hosts with tasks. In addition to specifying hosts and tasks, the playbook also supports a number of optional configurations. Here are two common ones:

- name: A comment that describes what the work is about. Ansible will print this when the work begins to run.
- vars: A list of variables and values.

A playbook specifies a set of tasks to be run and which hosts to run them on. To demonstrate Ansible playbook execution, we'll automate the installation of the Apache server. Following is the file configuration used for this use case.

You can find the following code in the `apache_server_playbook.yml` file:

```
- hosts: test-servers
  remote_user: username
  become: true
  vars:
    project_root: /var/www/html
  tasks:
  - name: Install Apache Server
    yum: pkg=httpd state=latest
  - name: Place the index file at project root
    copy: src=index.html dest={{ project_root }}/index.html owner=apache
group=apache mode=0644
  - name: Enable Apache on system reboot
    service: name=httpd enabled=yes
    notify: restart apache
  handlers:
  - name: restart apache
    service: name=httpd state=restarted
```

For each task, you can specify the group of target nodes and the remote user that will execute each operation. The tasks are executed in order, one at a time, against the nodes described in the hosts section. It is important to note that if any node fails to execute the task, it will be removed from the list.

The objective of each task is to execute a module. The modules will only be executed when they have something to modify. If we run the playbook again and again, we can guarantee that the module will only be executed when there is something to modify.

If there are actions that need be executed at the end of each task in the playbook, we can use the `notify` keyword. This action will only be executed once, even when they are called by different tasks. In the previous playbook, we are using `notify: restart apache` to restart the Apache service.

In this playbook, we can see the use of variables set by the `vars` key. This key takes a key-value format, where the key is the variable name and the value is the actual value of the variable. This variable will overwrite other variables that are set by a global variable file or from an inventory file.

To run a playbook, we use the `ansible-playbook` command. To execute the previous playbook, simply run the following command:

```
$ ansible-playbook apache_server_playbook.yml -f 2
```

We can also make use of options when running the playbook. For example, the -syntax-check option checks the syntax before running the playbook. This is the output of the previous command:

```
PLAY [test-servers]
*********************************************************************
*********************************************
TASK [setup]
*********************************************************************
*********************************************
ok: [192.168.1.161]

TASK [Install Apache Server]
*********************************************************************
*********************************************
changed: [192.168.1.161]

TASK [Place the index file at project root]
*********************************************************************
*********************************************
changed: [192.168.1.161]

TASK [Enable Apache on system root]
*********************************************************************
*********************************************
changed: [192.168.1.161]

RUNNING HANDLER[restart apache]
*********************************************************************
*********************************************
changed: [192.168.1.161]

PLAY RECAP
*********************************************************************
****************
192.168.1.161 : ok=5 changed=4 unreachable=0 failed=0
```

The next playbook will just execute the ping module (https://docs.ansible.com/ansible/latest/modules/ping_module.html#ping-module) on all our hosts.

You can find the following code in the ping_playbook.yml file:

```
- hosts: all
  tasks:
  - name: ping all hosts
    ping:
```

In this playbook, we are going to install Python 3 and NGINX in all machines defined in the inventory file.

You can find the following code in the `install_python_ngnix.yml` file:

```
- hosts: all
  tasks:
   - name: Install Nginx
      apt: pkg=nginx state=installed update_cache=true
     notify: Start Nginx
   - name: Install Python 3
     apt: pkg=python3-minimal state=installed
  handlers:
   - name: Start Nginx
      service: name=nginx state=started
```

The playbook has a hosts section where the hosts of the inventory file are specified. In this case, we are processing all (`hosts: all`) machines introduced in the inventory file. Then there is a task section with two tasks that install NGINX and Python 3. Finally, there is a handlers section where NGINX starts after its installation. In this example, we are passing the static inventory to `ansible-playbook` with the `ansible-playbook -i path/to/static-inventory-file myplaybook.yml` command:

```
$ ansible-playbook -i hosts install_python_ngnix.yml --sudo
```

This is the output of the previous command:

```
PLAY
*********************************************************************************

TASK [setup]
****************************************************************************

ok: [192.168.1.160]
ok: [192.168.1.161]
ok: [192.168.1.162]

TASK [Install Nginx]
***********************************************************************
changed: [192.168.1.160]
changed: [192.168.1.161]
changed: [192.168.1.162]

TASK [Install Python 3]
*********************************************************************
changed: [192.168.1.160]
changed: [192.168.1.161]
```

```
changed: [192.168.1.162]

RUNNING HANDLER [Start Nginx]
**************************************************
changed: [192.168.1.160]
changed: [192.168.1.161]
changed: [192.168.1.162]

PLAY RECAP
**********************************************************************
192.168.1.160                    : ok=4 changed=3 unreachable=0
failed=0
192.168.1.161                    : ok=4 changed=3 unreachable=0
failed=0
192.168.1.162                    : ok=4 changed=3 unreachable=0
failed=0
```

We can also install multiple packages in a single task, as follows:

```
- name: Installing Nginx and python
  apt: pkg={{ item }}
  with_items:
    - ngnix
    - python3-minimal
```

Ansible also provides a Python API for running an Ansible playbook programmatically.

In this example, we are using `VariableManager` from the `ansible.vars.manager` package and `InventoryManager` from the `ansible.inventory.manager` package. `VariableManager` takes care of merging all the different sources to give you a unified view of the variables available in each context. `InventoryManager` uses the path of the hosts configuration file as a source. We use `PlaybookExecutor` from `ansible.executor.playbook_executor` to execute the playbook defined in the `playbook_path` variable.

You can find the following code in the `execute_playbook.py` file:

```
!/usr/bin/env python3

from collections import namedtuple
from ansible.parsing.dataloader import DataLoader
from ansible.vars.manager import VariableManager
from ansible.inventory.manager import InventoryManager
from ansible.playbook.play import Play
from ansible.executor.playbook_executor import PlaybookExecutor

def execute_playbook():
```

```
    playbook_path = "playbook_template.yml"
    inventory_path = "hosts"

    Options = namedtuple('Options', ['connection', 'module_path', 'forks',
'become', 'become_method', 'become_user', 'check', 'diff', 'listhosts',
'listtasks', 'listtags', 'syntax'])
    loader = DataLoader()
    options = Options(connection='local', module_path='', forks=100,
become=None, become_method=None, become_user=None, check=False,
                    diff=False, listhosts=False, listtasks=False,
listtags=False, syntax=False)
    passwords = dict(vault_pass='secret')
```

After importing the required modules, we define the `execute_playbook` method to initialize options, where we initialize our inventory using the inventory path. To execute the playbook, we use the `PlaybookExecutor` class and pass the playbook path, inventory, loader, and options objects as parameters. Finally, we use the `run()` method to execute the playbook:

```
    inventory = InventoryManager(loader=loader, sources=['inventory'])
    variable_manager = VariableManager(loader=loader, inventory=inventory)
    executor = PlaybookExecutor(
                playbooks=[playbook_path], inventory=inventory,
    variable_manager=variable_manager, loader=loader,
                options=options, passwords=passwords)
    results = executor.run()
    print(results)

if __name__ == "__main__":
    execute_playbook()
```

With the Python API, we have the ability to run tasks in the same way we execute playbooks.

In this example, we create an inventory using the path of the hosts configuration file as a source and the variable manager takes care of merging all the different sources to give you a unified view of the variables available in each context.

Then we create a data structure dictionary that represents our play, including tasks, which is basically what our YAML loader does internally. In this case, the tasks include executing `ping` module for all hosts defined in the inventory.

We create a `play` object and execute the `load()` method from playbook object. This method will also automatically create the `task` objects from the information provided in the `play_source` variable.

To execute tasks, we need to instantiate `TaskQueueManager` from the `ansible.executor.task_queue_manager` package, which configures all objects to iterate over the host list and execute the `ping` module. For `stdout_callback`, we use the default `callback` plugin, which prints to `stdout`.

You can find the following code in the `run_tasks_playbook.py` file:

```python
#!/usr/bin/env python3

from collections import namedtuple
from ansible.parsing.dataloader import DataLoader
from ansible.vars.manager import VariableManager
from ansible.inventory.manager import InventoryManager
from ansible.playbook.play import Play
from ansible.executor.task_queue_manager import TaskQueueManager
from ansible.plugins.callback import CallbackBase

Options = namedtuple('Options', ['connection', 'module_path', 'forks',
'become', 'become_method', 'become_user', 'check', 'diff'])

# initialize objects
loader = DataLoader()
options = Options(connection='local', module_path='', forks=100,
become=None, become_method=None, become_user=None, check=False,
 diff=False)
passwords = dict(vault_pass='secret')

# create inventory
inventory = InventoryManager(loader=loader, sources=['/etc/ansible/hosts'])
variable_manager = VariableManager(loader=loader, inventory=inventory)

# create play with tasks
play_source = dict(name = "myplaybook",hosts = 'all',gather_facts = 'no',
    tasks = [dict(action=dict(module='ping')),])
play = Play().load(play_source, variable_manager=variable_manager,
loader=loader)
```

After objects initialization, we create the inventory and create a playbook with tasks in a programmatic way. We can now execute the playbook using the `TaskQueueManager` class, passing as parameters the variables created in the previous block of code:

```python
# execution
task = None
try:
    task =
TaskQueueManager(inventory=inventory,variable_manager=variable_manager,
loader=loader,options=options,passwords=passwords,stdout_callback='default'
```

```
    )
        result = task.run(play)
    finally:
        if task is not None:
            task.cleanup()
```

Writing Ansible modules with Python

In this section, you will learn about Ansible modules and writing an Ansible module with Python.

Introduction to Ansible modules

Ansible has an extensible and modular architecture in functionalities which are organized by modules. You can use modules directly with playbooks or through ad-hoc commands.

Ansible modules are small pieces of code that perform one function (copying a file, or starting or stopping a daemon, for instance). Ansible comes packaged with about 1,000 modules for all sorts of use cases. You can also extend it with your own modules and roles. Check out the modules list: `https://docs.ansible.com/ansible/latest/modules/list_of_all_modules.html`.

For example, the `ping` module (`http://docs.ansible.com/ansible/ping_module.html`) is a test module that connects to the remote host, verifies a usable Python installation, and returns the output pong if the connection with the host is successful.

Using the Ansible command-line tool, we can use the `ping` module over the two remote nodes. We can use the `-m` flag to specify the Ansible module we need, and the `-all` flag for all the hosts/groups in the inventory.

The simplest way to use Ansible is to execute ad-hoc commands. The format of using ad-hoc commands is as follows:

```
$ ansible <host group> -i <inventory file> -m <module> [-a <argument 1>,
... <argument N>]
```

For example, if you want to check whether all hosts in your inventory are active, you can use the `ping` module without using arguments. To verify that all machines available in out inventory are active, we can perform a ping. The `-m` parameter indicates the Ansible module we are using:

```
$ ansible all -m ping
```

We can now use the command-line option to test a specific host:

```
$ ansible -i hosts 192.168.1.160 -m ping
 192.168.1.160 | SUCCESS >> {
 "changed": false,
 "ping": "pong"
 }
```

If you have no connection with the host, it returns the following error message:

```
192.168.1.160| UNREACHABLE! => {
    "changed": false,
    "msg": "Failed to connect to the host via ssh.",
    "unreachable": true
}
```

The previous command reads that we will use the host file as the inventory file, and execute the `ping` module on the `192.168.1.160` host.

We can use Ansible's `shell` module (http://docs.ansible.com/ansible/shell_module.html) to test a specific group defined in the inventory file:

```
$ ansible -m shell -a "hostname" test-servers
192.168.1.161 | SUCCESS | rc=0 >>
 ansible-node1
```

For example, if we want to execute a command in all our nodes, we can do the following:

```
$ ansible all -a "/etc/init.d/apache2 start"
```

In this way, we have managed to start the Apache service of all the nodes we have previously configured.

Ansible has many modules for all common system administration tasks, such as file management, user administration, and package management. The following command extracts the internal and external IP addresses of all network hosts:

```
$ ansible all -i hosts -m shell -a '/sbin/ifconfig | grep inet.*Bcast'"
192.168.1.161 | SUCCESS | rc=0 >>
        inet addr:10.0.1.10  Bcast:10.0.1.255 Mask:255.255.255.0
        inet addr:192.168.1.161  Bcast:192.168.1.255 Mask:255.255.255.0
```

Implementing Ansible modules with Python

Ansible comes packed with a lot of built-in modules (for almost all tasks), but for some custom tasks, you can write custom modules with Python.

For example, we can use the common Ansible Boilerplate module as we can see in the documentation: http://docs.ansible.com/ansible/dev_guide/developing_modules_general.html or https://docs.ansible.com/ansible/2.3/dev_guide/developing_modules_general.html.

We can develop our own module to automate input from a playbook. Ansible also provides a Python library to parse user arguments and handle errors and returns. First, we will import the AnsibleModule class from the ansible.module_utils.basic package:

```
from ansible.module_utils.basic import AnsibleModule
if __name__ == '__main__':
    main()
```

The AnsibleModule class provides lots of common code for handling returns and parsing arguments. In the following example, we will parse three arguments for the host, username, and password, and make them required fields:

```
def main():
    data = {"host": {"default": "localhost", "type": "str"},
    "username": {"default": "username", "type": "str"},
    "password": {"default": "password", "type": "str"},
    "url": {"default": "url", "type": "str"}
    }

    module = AnsibleModule(argument_spec = data)
```

All variables need to be declared with dictionary format and the fields are passed in as argument_spec to AnsibleModule. You can then access the value of the arguments through the module.params dictionary by calling the get method on module.params:

```
host = module.params.get('host')
username = module.params.get('username')
password = module.params.get('password')
url='http://' + host + '/authentication'
module.params.update({"url": url})
```

Finally, we return the module.params value with all data values, using the exit_json method. Ansible uses this method to handle success providing a response in JSON format with the processing data:

```
module.exit_json(changed=True, meta=module.params)
```

Our `user_authenticate.yml` playbook will pass four variables to the `user_authenticate` module (`host`, `username`, `password`, and `url`) in the `user_authenticate.py` file:

```
- name: My Custom Module
  hosts: localhost
  tasks:
  - name: authenticating user service
    user_authenticate:
      host: "localhost"
      username: "username"
      password: "password"
  url :"url"
    register: result
  - debug: var=result
```

Ansible allows us to register the values returned by a task in a variable. That way, we can work with them from another task. Depending on the Ansible module used, the variable will keep different values. The keyword used in this case is `register`.

This is the output obtained when you execute `$ ansible-playbook user_authenticate.yml`:

```
PLAY [My Custom Module]
*************************************************

TASK [authenticating user service]
*********************************************************
ok: [localhost]


TASK [debug]
*****************************************************************
ok: [localhost] => {
"output": {
"changed": false,
"host": "localhost",
"username":"username",
"password": "password",
"url": "http://localhost/authentication'",
}
}

PLAY RECAP
******************************************************************
localhost : ok=2 changed=0 unreachable=0 failed=0
```

Summary

In this chapter, we reviewed Ansible as an open source project implemented in Python. It has an architecture with modules that can handle virtually any operating system, cloud environment, tool, and system-management framework. With Ansible, we can minimize the effort and time it takes to manage remote hosts.

In the next chapter, we will look at sockets and explore the Python modules that work with sockets for the TCP and UDP protocols.

Questions

1. What is the format for an Ansible configuration file?
2. What is the name and the path of the main Ansible configuration file?
3. Where is the inventory file located by default and what is the format of that file?
4. What are the two ways to execute commands with Ansible?
5. What does being agentless mean?
6. What is the Ansible command to check the hostname of the IP addresses available in the inventory file?
7. How can we use one Ansible task to install multiple packages in the hosts defined in the inventory file?
8. What is the main class that the Ansible Python API provides for executing a playbook?
9. Which Ansible module can verify a Python installation connecting to the remote host and returns the response if the connection is successful with the host?
10. What Python package and class provide lots of common code for handling returns and parsing arguments?

Further reading

Check out the following links for more information about the topics covered in this chapter:

- Ansible examples in the GitHub
  repository: https://github.com/ansible/ansible-examples
- The latest information on Ansible Python 3
  support: https://docs.ansible.com/ansible/latest/reference_appendices/python_3_support.html

- Ansible best practices: https://docs.ansible.com/ansible/latest/user_guide/playbooks_best_practices.html
- Other repositories: https://github.com/austincunningham/python-ansible
- Ansible Galaxy is a helpful tool that allows users to share their modules and roles: https://galaxy.ansible.com
- Practice with Ansible: https://www.katacoda.com/jonatanblue/scenarios/1
- Automating Python with Ansible is an interactive tutorial about how to use the Ansible configuration-management tool to run Python processes on a remote machine: https://github.com/tdhopper/automating_python

Section 4: Sockets and Server Programming

4

In this section, you will learn about the principles of socket programming, designing a multiprocessing-based TCP server, asynchronous programming, and dynamic web programming in Python with the Flask micro-framework.

This section contains the following chapters:

- `Chapter 10`, *Programming with Sockets*
- `Chapter 11`, *Designing Servers and Asynchronous Programming*
- `Chapter 12`, *Designing Applications on the Web*

10
Programming with Sockets

This chapter will introduce you to the basics of sockets and the principles of UDP and TCP through examples of socket programming with the socket module. Along the way, we'll build clients, servers with TCP and UDP protocols with the IPv4 and IPv6 protocols. We will also cover non-blocking and asynchronous programming and HTTPS and TLS for secure data transport.

The following topics will be covered in this chapter:

- Basics of sockets
- Working with UDP and TCP sockets in Python 3.7
- Working with IPv6 sockets in Python 3.7
- Non-blocking and asynchronous socket I/O
- HTTPS and securing sockets with TLS

Technical requirements

The examples and the source code for this chapter are available in the GitHub repository in the `Chapter10` folder: `https://github.com/PacktPublishing/Learning-Python-Networking-Second-Edition`.

You will need to install a Python distribution on your local machine with the Unix operating system and have some basic knowledge of network protocols to be able to work through this chapter.

Basics of sockets

In this section, you will learn about sockets, which are the main component that allows us to take advantage of the operating system's capabilities to interact with the network. You can think of sockets as a point-to-point communication channel between a client and a server.

Sockets introduction

Sockets are the basis of IP, but we can also use them to take advantage of it, that is, through sockets, we can make two applications communicate with each other. A socket in programming is a communication tunnel that helps two applications to communicate and are the basis of the internet and its protocols, such as HTTP, FTP, and SMTP.

This mechanism emerged in the early 80s with the Unix system at Berkeley, to provide a communication channel between processes and have the same functionality as communication by mail or telephone—that is, they allow a process to speak with another, even when they are in different machines. This interconnect feature makes the socket concept very useful.

For two applications to communicate, we need the following:

- **Server (the listener)**: The server always listens for communications in a specific port.
- **Client**: Normally, the client connects to the server through the port and starts sending requests and waiting for answers.
- **Transmission channel**: This can be a port of entry for the server and an exit port for the client.
- **Protocol**: This is the topic of conversation. For two applications to communicate, they must be programmed to answer each other.

These are the main applications for using sockets:

- **Server**: Application that is waiting for the client to connect
- **Client**: Application that connects to the server
- **Client/server**: Application that is a client and server at the same time, for example, a chat application, that can send messages to other applications and, at the same time, wait for other applications to send messages to it

There are two types of communication between applications:

- **Local**: When the applications are on the same computer, the `127.0.0.1` IP address or localhost is used
- **Remote**: When the applications are on different computers, the client application connects the IP address and server port

The sockets allow us to implement a client-server or peer-to-peer architecture. The communication must be initiated by one of the programs, which is called the client program. The second program waits for another to initiate the communication. For this reason, it is called the server program.

A socket is a process or thread that exists in the client machine and in the server machine, with the objective that the server and the client read and write the information. This information will be transmitted by the different network layers.

When a client connects with the server, a new socket is created. The server can continue to wait for a connections in the main socket and communicate with the connected client, in the same way a socket is established in a specific port of the client.

A server application usually listens for a specific port that is waiting for a connection request from a client; once it is received, the client and the server are connected so that they can communicate. During this process, the client is assigned to a port number, through which they send requests to the server and receive the responses from it.

Similarly, the server obtains a new local port number that will continue listening to each connection request of the original port.

Sockets are a universal feature in any programming language, and also without limits; an application made in PHP can communicate with another made in Java and vice versa, or an application made in Python can communicate with another made in C.

Thanks to this feature, we have browsers, mail clients, and FTP clients that work and communicate with the servers, regardless of the operating system, technology, or programming language.

Socket types

Currently, there are several types of sockets, and each one is usually associated with a type of protocol, for example:

- SOCK_STREAM: It is associated with the TCP protocol and provides security in the transmission of data and security in the data reception.
- SOCK_DGRAM: It is associated with the UDP protocol and indicates that packets will travel in the datagram type, which has an asynchronous communication style.

Sockets can also be classified according to their family. We have Unix sockets, socket.AF_UNIX, which were created before the concept of networks and are based on files, socket.AF_INET for the IPv4 protocol, and socket.AF_INET6 for working with IPv6.

Getting information about ports, protocols, and domains

The socket module provides the socket.getservbyport(port[, protocol_name]) method, which allows us to get the port name from the port number. For example:

```
>>> import socket
>>> socket.getservbyport(80)
'http'
>>> socket.getservbyport(23)
'telnet'
```

We can also get information about the service name at the application level if we pass the protocol name as a second parameter.

You can find the following code in the socket_finding_service_name.py file:

```
#!/usr/bin/env python3
import socket

def find_service_name():
    protocolname = 'tcp'
    for port in [80, 25]:
        print ("Port: %s => service name: %s" %(port,
socket.getservbyport(port, protocolname)))
    print ("Port: %s => service name: %s" %(53, socket.getservbyport(53,
'udp')))
```

```
if __name__ == '__main__':
    find_service_name()
```

This is the output of the previous script, where we can see the service name at the application level for each port:

```
Port: 80 => service name: http
Port: 25 => service name: smtp
Port: 53 => service name: domain
```

With the `getaddrinfo()` method, we can get information about the service that is working behind a domain. In this example, we are using this method to get the server behind the `www.packtpub.com` domain.

You can find the following code in the `socket_getaddrinfo.py` file:

```python
#!/usr/bin/env python3

import socket

try:
    infolist = socket.getaddrinfo('www.packtpub.com', 'www', 0,
socket.SOCK_STREAM, 0, socket.AI_ADDRCONFIG | socket.AI_V4MAPPED |
socket.AI_CANONNAME,)
except socket.gaierror as e:
    print('Name service failure:', e.args[1])
    sys.exit(1)

info = infolist[0]
print(infolist)
socket_args = info[0:3]
address = info[4]
s = socket.socket(*socket_args)
try:
    s.connect(address)
except socket.error as e:
    print('Network failure:', e.args[1])
else:
    print('Success: host', info[3], 'is listening on port 80')
```

This is the output of the previous script, where we can see that the `varnish.packtpub.com` service is listening on `port 80`:

```
[(<AddressFamily.AF_INET: 2>, <SocketKind.SOCK_STREAM: 1>, 0,
'varnish.packtpub.com', ('83.166.169.231', 80))]          Success: host
varnish.packtpub.com is listening on port 80
```

We can use the `socket.gethostbyname(hostname)` method to convert a domain name into the IPv4 address format. This method is equivalent to the `nslookup` command we can find in many operating systems:

```
>> import socket
> socket.gethostbyname('packtpub.com')
'83.166.169.231'
>> socket.gethostbyname('google.com')
'216.58.210.142'
```

The following example will use this method to obtain an IP address from a domain. You can find the following code in the `socket_remote_info.py` file:

```python
#!/usr/bin/env python3

import socket

def get_remote_info():
    remote_host = 'www.packtpub.com'
        try:
            print ("IP address of %s: %s" %(remote_host,
socket.gethostbyname(remote_host)))
        except socket.error as err_msg:
            print ("%s: %s" %(remote_host, err_msg))

if __name__ == '__main__':
    get_remote_info()
```

Creating a TCP client

The following code is an example of a simple TCP client. If you look carefully, you can see that the following code will create a raw HTTP client that fetches a web page from a web server. It sends an HTTP GET request to pull the home page.

To create our connection, we need to import the socket module and use the `connect` method to pass the `(HOST, PORT)` tuple as a parameter. With the `send` method from the socket client object, we send the data for the request and get the response in the data object using the `recv` method.

You can find the following code in the `socket_tcp_client.py` file:

```python
import socket

HOST = 'www.yahoo.com'
PORT = 80
```

```
BUFSIZ = 4096
ADDR = (HOST, PORT)

if __name__ == '__main__':
    client_sock = socket.socket(socket.AF_INET,socket.SOCK_STREAM)
    client_sock.connect(ADDR)
    while True:
        data = 'GET / HTTP/1.0\r\n\r\n'
        if not data:
            break
        client_sock.send(data.encode('utf-8'))
        data = client_sock.recv(BUFSIZ)
        if not data:
            break
        print(data.decode('utf-8'))
    client_sock.close()
```

This is the output of the `socket_tcp_client.py` script over the `yahoo.com` domain for getting information about the server:

```
HTTP/1.0 200 OK
Date: Mon, 18 Feb 2019 16:20:04 GMT
P3P: policyref="https://policies.yahoo.com/w3c/p3p.xml", CP="CAO DSP COR CUR ADM DEV TAI PSA PSD IVAi IVDi CONi TELo OTP
i OUR DELi SAMi OTRi UNRi PUBi IND PHY ONL UNI PUR FIN COM NAV INT DEM CNT STA POL HEA PRE LOC GOV"
Referrer-Policy: strict-origin-when-cross-origin
Cache-Control: max-age=3600, public
Vary: Accept-Encoding
Content-Length: 3388
Content-Type: text/html; charset=UTF-8
Age: 711
Connection: keep-alive
Server: ATS
X-Frame-Options: DENY
X-Content-Type-Options: nosniff
X-XSS-Protection: 1; mode=block

<!doctype html public "-//W3C//DTD HTML 4.01//EN" "http://www.w3.org/TR/html4/strict.dtd">
<html><head><title>Yahoo!</title><meta name="ROBOTS" content="NOINDEX" /><style>
/* nn4 hide */
/*/*/
```

In the next section, we are going to study a specific use case with the socket module to obtain information about a server that is running in a specific domain.

Banner grabbing with the socket module

Banners expose information related to the name of the web server and the version that is running on the server. Some expose the backend technology (PHP, Java, Python) that's used and its version. With the socket module, we can get information related to the version server for a specific domain.

The simplest way to obtain the banner of a server is by using the socket module. We can send a get request and get the response through the `recvfrom()` method, which would return a tuple with the result.

You can find the following code in the `socket_BannerGrabbing.py` file:

```python
#!/usr/bin/python3

import socket
import re

sock = socket.socket(socket.AF_INET, socket.SOCK_STREAM)
sock.connect(("www.packtpub.com", 80))

http_get = b"GET / HTTP/1.1\nHost: www.packtpub.com\n\n"
data = ''
try:
    sock.sendall(http_get)
    data = sock.recvfrom(1024)
    strdata = data[0]
    headers = strdata.splitlines()
    for header in headers:
        print(header.decode())
except socket.error:
    print ("Socket error", socket.errno)
finally:
    print("closing connection")
    sock.close()
```

This is the output of the `socket_BannerGrabbing.py` script over the `packtpub.com` domain for getting information about the server:

```
HTTP/1.1 301 https://www.packtpub.com/                    Location:
https://www.packtpub.com/
Accept-Ranges: bytes
Date: Fri, 15 Feb 2019 14:17:02 GMT
Age: 0
Via: 1.1 varnish
Connection: close
X-Country-Code: NL
Server: packt
```

In the next section, we are going to study a specific use case for port scanning in a specific IP address or domain.

Port scanning with sockets

Sockets are the fundamental building blocks for network communications, and we can easily check whether a specific port is open, closed, or filtered by calling the `connect_ex()` method. For example, we could have a script that reads the IP address and a list of ports and return information about each port regarding whether it is open or closed.

You can find the following code in the `socket_port_scan.py` file:

```python
#!/usr/bin/env python3

import socket

ipaddress =input("Enter ip address or domain for port scanning:")

port_init= input("Enter first port: ")
port_end = input("Enter last port: ")

for port in range(int(port_init), int(port_end)+1):
    sock= socket.socket(socket.AF_INET,socket.SOCK_STREAM)
    sock.settimeout(5)
    result = sock.connect_ex((ipaddress,port))
    if result == 0:
        print(port, "--> Open")
    else:
        print(port, "--> Closed")
    sock.close()
```

This is the output of the previous script over the `packtpub.com` domain for getting information about the port states between `80` and `85`:

```
Enter ip address or domain for port scanning:www.packtpub.com
Enter first port: 80
Enter last port:   85
80 --> Open
81 --> Closed
82 --> Closed
83 --> Closed
84 --> Closed
85 --> Closed
```

Inspecting the client and server communication

The interaction between the client and server through the exchange of network packets can be analyzed using any network-packet-capturing tool, such as Wireshark. You can configure Wireshark to filter packets by port or host. In this case, we can filter by `port 80`. You can get the options under the **Capture** | **Options** menu and type `port 80` in the input box next to the **Capture Filter** option, as shown in the following screenshot:

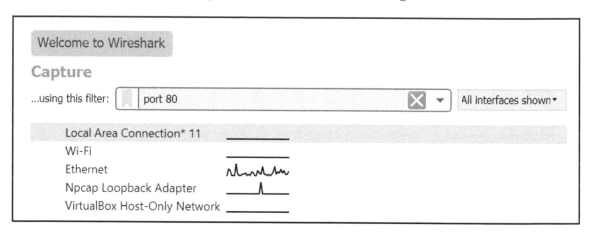

In the Interface option, we choose to capture packets that are passing through any interface. Now, run the preceding TCP client to connect to `www.yahoo.com`. The first three packets establish the TCP connection by a three-way handshake between the client and server. You can see the sequence of packets being exchanged in Wireshark:

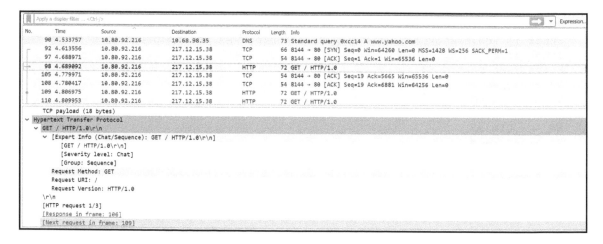

As you can see, the HTTP GET request has other components, such as **Request URI** and **Request Version**. Now, you can check the **HTTP response** from the web server to your client. It comes after the TCP acknowledgment packet, that is, the sixth packet. Here, the server typically sends an HTTP response code (in this case, the response is 200 ok), content length, and the data or web page content. The structure of this packet is shown in the following screenshot:

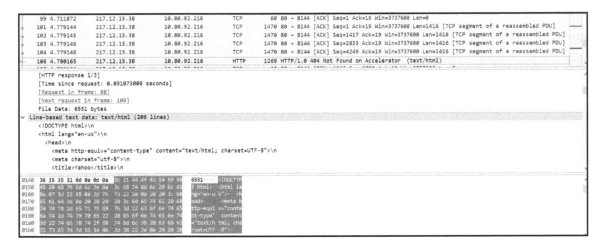

From the preceding analysis of the interaction between the client and server, you can now understand, at a basic level, what happens behind the scenes when you visit a web page using your web browser. In the next section, you will be shown how to create your own TCP server and examine the interactions between your personal TCP client and server.

In this section, we introduced socket concepts and reviewed practical use cases with the Python socket module, such as creating a TCP client, banner grabbing, and port scanning. We also reviewed how to inspect the client and server's communication with Wireshark.

Working with UDP and TCP sockets in Python 3.7

In this section, you will learn about basic TCP/IP socket programming using Python sockets in Python 3.7 with the TCP and UDP protocols.

Introduction to the TCP and UDP protocols

The properties of a socket depend on the characteristics of the protocol in which they are implemented. Generally, communication with sockets is done through a protocol of the TCP/IP family. The two most common are TCP and UDP.

When implemented with the TCP protocol, the sockets have the following properties:

- Connection-oriented.
- The transmission of all packets is guaranteed without errors or omissions.
- It is guaranteed that every packet will reach its destination in the same order in which it was transmitted. These properties are very important to guarantee the correctness of the programs that deal with this information.

The UDP protocol has the following properties:

- Is a non-connection-oriented protocol
- It only guarantees that if a message arrives, it arrives in a reliable way
- In no case is it guaranteed that all messages will arrive, or arrive in the same order in which they were sent

Sockets can be implemented through a different number of channels: Unix domain sockets, TCP, and UDP. The Python `socket` library provides specific classes to handle common transport, as well as a generic interface to control everything else.

Starting network programming with Python

The Python socket module provides an interface to the Berkeley sockets API (another name for internet sockets). Programming networks in Python depends on the socket objects. To create an object of this type in Python, we must use the `socket.socket()` function that's available in the socket module, with the `socket_0 = socket.socket(socket_family, socket_type, protocol=0)` syntax.

Let's see a detailed description of the parameters:

- `socket_family`: This is the family of protocols that is used as a transport mechanism. These values are constants, such as `AF_INET`, `PF_INET`, `PF_UNIX`, and `PF_X25`.
- `socket_type`: The type of communication between the two ends of the connection. `SOCK_STREAM` is usually used for connection-oriented protocols and `SOCK_DGRAM` for protocols without connections.

- `protocol`: Normally 0, this parameter is used to identify the variant of a protocol within a family and socket type.

These are the methods of socket objects:

- `socket.bind()`: This method binds an address (hostname, port number) to a socket
- `socket.listen()`: This method configures and starts a TCP listener
- `socket.accept()`: This function passively accepts a TCP client connection, waiting until the connection arrives

For more detailed information regarding the methods in the socket module, you can check out the documentation at `https://docs.python.org/3/library/socket.html`.

TCP sockets

As you will see in a moment, we will create socket objects using the `socket.socket()` function and specify the socket type as `socket.SOCK_STREAM`. When we do this, the default protocol that it uses is the TCP.

For network programming in Python, we need to create a `socket` object and then use this to call other functions of the module. The following code will start a web server using the sockets library. The script waits for a connection to be made; if it is received, it will show the received bytes.

You can find the following code in the `tcp_server.py` file:

```python3
#!/usr/bin/env python3

import socket

host = '127.0.0.1'
port = 12345
BUFFER_SIZE = 1024

#The socket objects support the context manager type
#so we can use it with a with statement, there's no need to call
socket_close ()
#We create a TCP type socket object
with socket.socket(socket.AF_INET,socket.SOCK_STREAM) as socket_tcp:
    socket_tcp.bind((host, port))
    # We wait for the client connection
    socket_tcp.listen(5)
```

```
        # We establish the connection with the client
        connection, addr = socket_tcp.accept()
        with connection:
            print('[*] Established connection')
                while True:
                    # We receive bytes, we convert into str
                    data = connection.recv(BUFFER_SIZE)
                    # We verify that we have received data
                    if not data:
                        break
                    else:
                        print('[*] Data received:
{}'.format(data.decode('utf-8')))
                    connection.send(data)
```

Let's see what this script does in detail:

- We define the host, the port, and the size of the data buffer that will receive the connection
- We link these variables to our socket object with the `socket.bind()` method
- We establish the connection, we accept the data, and we visualize the sent data

Starting a client

We are going to write a program that defines a client that opens the connection in a given port and host. This is very simple to do with the `socket.connect (hostname, port)` function, which opens a TCP connection to the hostname on the port. Once we have opened an object socket, we can read and write this in as any other object of **input** and **output** (**I/O**), always remembering to close it as we close files after working with them.

You can find the following code in the `tcp_client.py` file:

```python
#!/usr/bin/env python3

import socket

# The client must have the same server specifications
host = '127.0.0.1'
port = 12345
BUFFER_SIZE = 1024

MESSAGE = 'Hello world,this is my first message'

with socket.socket(socket.AF_INET, socket.SOCK_STREAM) as socket_tcp:
    socket_tcp.connect((host, port))
```

```
# We convert str to bytes
socket_tcp.send(MESSAGE.encode('utf-8'))
data = socket_tcp.recv(BUFFER_SIZE)
```

This script is similar to the previous one, only this time, we define a `MESSAGE` variable that simulates the data packets, we make the connection like we did before, and call the `socket.send(data)` method after converting our string into bytes to ensure the integrity of our data.

To execute this pair of sample scripts, we must first execute the server with the following command:

```
$ python tcp_server.py &
```

We append the ampersand, `&`, so that this line is executed and the process is open and waiting for another command (when pressing *Enter*, the server will be executed until we execute the client), and then we initiate the client:

```
$ python tcp_client.py
```

The result in the server part is as follows:

```
$ python tcp_server.py
 [*] Established connection
 [*] Data received: Hello world,this is my first message
```

Capturing packets in a loopback interface

You can configure Wireshark to capture packets in localhost. Visit `https://wiki.wireshark.org/CaptureSetup/Loopback` to see how you can configure the loopback interface to capture packets in the `127.0.0.1` localhost interface.

> If you are working with the Unix operating system, you can capture traffic directly with Wireshark. For more information, check out `https://wiki.wireshark.org/CaptureSetup/Loopback`.

If you are working with the Windows operating system, you may have problems capturing packets on localhost with Wireshark. At this point, the recommendation is to use a raw socket sniffer, such as RawCap (`http://www.netresec.com/?page=RawCap`), to capture localhost network traffic in Windows. You can read more about this at `http://www.netresec.com/?page=Blogmonth=2011-04post=RawCap-sniffer-for-Windows-released`.

The following is the execution of `RawCap.exe` on a windows system for capturing packets on the loopback interface. By default, it creates a `dumpfile.pcap` file with sniffed packets.

In the following screenshot, we can see the execution of `RawCap.exe` for getting machine interfaces:

```
Interfaces:
    0.      169.254.219.137 Local Area Connection* 11        Ethernet
    1.      10.80.92.216    Ethernet        Ethernet
    2.      192.168.56.1    VirtualBox Host-Only Network     Ethernet
    3.      169.254.204.194 Npcap Loopback Adapter  Ethernet
    4.      169.254.52.200  Wi-Fi   Wireless80211
    5.      169.254.234.2   Local Area Connection* 2         Wireless80211
    6.      127.0.0.1       Loopback Pseudo-Interface 1      Loopback
Select interface to sniff [default '0']: 6
Output path or filename [default 'dumpfile.pcap']:
```

Inspecting the client and server interaction

In the following example, we are capturing packets on localhost with the execution of the TCP client and server on port `12345`. When the client sends a message to the server, we can capture the packets that are being exchanged in the communication.

We can perform packet filtering by using `ip.dst == 127.0.0.1`, as shown in the following screenshot:

As we are capturing packets on a non-standard port, Wireshark doesn't decode data packets in the data section (as shown in the middle pane of the preceding screenshot). However, you can see the decoded text on the bottom pane, where the server's timestamp is shown on the right-hand side.

Code limitations

If we execute these scripts and try to connect to that same server from another Terminal, it will simply reject the connection.

The BUFFER_SIZE variable of the 1024 value is the maximum amount of data that can be received at one time. But this does not mean that the function will return 1024 bytes. The send() function also has this behavior. send() returns the number of bytes sent, which may be less than the size of the data that is sent.

Normally in network programming, to make a server handle multiple connections at the same time, concurrency or parallelism is implemented. The problem with concurrency is that it is complicated to make it work. Of course, if an application needs scalability, it is almost an obligation to apply concurrency for the use of more than one processor or kernel. Concurrency aspects will be reviewed in the following chapters. In the next section, we will use something simpler than parallelism that is much easier to use: the selectors library.

Creating a simple UDP client and UDP server

In this section, we will review how you can set up your own UDP client-server application with Python's Socket module. The application will be a server that listens for all connections and messages over a specific port and prints out any messages to the console.

UDP is a protocol that is on the same level as TCP, that is, above the IP layer. It offers a service in disconnected mode for applications that use it. This protocol is suitable for applications that require efficient communication that doesn't have to worry about packet loss. The typical applications of UDP are internet telephony and video streaming.

In this example, we'll create a synchronous UDP server, which means each request must wait until the end of the process of the previous request. The bind() method will be used to associate the port with the IP address.

For the reception of the message, we use the recvfrom() method and for sending the message, we use sendto() method.

Implementing the UDP server

When working with UDP, the only difference if we compare this to working with TCP in Python is that when creating the socket, you have to use SOCK_DGRAM instead of SOCK_STREAM. Use the following code to create the UDP server.

You can find the following code in the udp_server.py file inside the udp folder:

```python
#!/usr/bin/env python3

import socket,sys

UDP_IP_ADDRESS = "127.0.0.1"
UDP_PORT = 12345
buffer=4096

socket_server=socket.socket(socket.AF_INET,socket.SOCK_DGRAM) #UDP
socket_server.bind((UDP_IP_ADDRESS,UDP_PORT))

while True:
    print("Waiting for client...")
    data,address = socket_server.recvfrom(buffer)
    data = data.strip()
    print("Data Received from address: ",address)
    print("message: ", data)
    try:
        response = "Hi %s" % sys.platform
    except Exception as e:
        response = "%s" % sys.exc_info()[0]
    print("Response",response)
    socket_server.sendto(response.encode(),address)
socket_server.close()
```

In the preceding code for implementing the UDP server, we see that socket.SOCK_DGRAM creates a UDP socket, and data, addr = s.recvfrom(buffer), returns the data and the source's address.

Now that we have finished our server, we need to implement our client program. The server will be continuously listening on our defined IP address and port number for any received UDP message. It is essential that this server is run prior to the execution of the Python client script, or the client script will fail.

Implementing the UDP client

To begin implementing the client, we will need to declare the IP address that we will be trying to send our UDP messages to, as well as the port number. This port number is arbitrary, but you must ensure you aren't using a socket that has already been taken:

```
UDP_IP_ADDRESS = "127.0.0.1"
UDP_PORT = 6789
message = "Hello, Server"
```

Now, it's time to create the socket through which we will be sending our UDP message to the server: `clientSocket = socket.socket(socket.AF_INET, socket.SOCK_DGRAM)`.

Once we've constructed our new socket, it's time to write the code that will send our UDP message: `clientSocket.sendto(Message, (UDP_IP_ADDRESS, UDP_PORT))`.

You can find the following code in the `udp_client.py` file inside the `udp` folder:

```python
#!/usr/bin/env python3

import socket

UDP_IP_ADDRESS = "127.0.0.1"
UDP_PORT = 12345
buffer=4096

address = (UDP_IP_ADDRESS ,UDP_PORT)
socket_client=socket.socket(socket.AF_INET,socket.SOCK_DGRAM)

while True:
    message = input('Enter your message > ')
    if message=="exit":
        break
    socket_client.sendto(message.encode(),address)
    response,addr = socket_client.recvfrom(buffer)
    print("Server response => %s" % response)

socket_client.close()
```

In the preceding code snippet, the UDP client sends a single line of text, **Hello UDP server**, and receives the response from the server. The following screenshot shows the request that's sent from the client to the server:

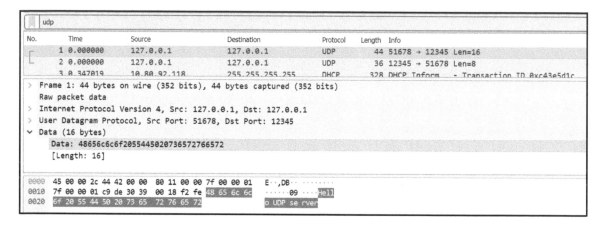

After inspecting the UDP client and server packets, we can easily see that UDP is much simpler than TCP. It's often termed as a connectionless protocol as there is no acknowledgment or error-checking involved.

The following screenshot shows the server's response, which was sent to the client:

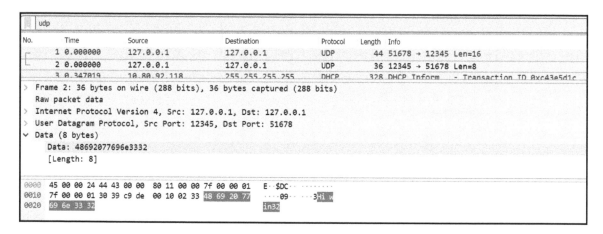

In this section, we introduced the UDP and TCP protocols and the implementation of applications with the socket module, analyzing use cases such as creating a TCP client/server, and UDP client and server applications. We also reviewed how to inspect the client and server communication for TCP and UDP protocols with Wireshark.

Working with IPv6 sockets in Python 3.7

In this section, you will learn how we can implement IPv6 with sockets in Python 3.7.

Implementing the IPv6 server

We will start with the server implementation in a script called `echo_server_ipv6.py`. The first lines will be the libraries that we will use, which are `socket` (network and connection utilities) and `subprocess` (which will allow us to execute commands on the server):

```
import socket
import subprocess
```

Then, we will create the variables: `ip`, `port`, `max_connections`, and `server`. The `ip` variable will have the `string ::1` value, which will be the IPv6 address of the localhost server; the port through which it will accept connections will be passed as an argument to the script; and `max_connections` will have a numerical value of 5, which indicates the maximum number of simultaneous connections. Finally, with the socket method, we tell Python to wait for connection with the following parameters:

- `socket.AF_INET6`: Indicates that we are using the IPv6 protocol
- `socket.SOCK_STREAM`: Indicates the type of socket that we are creating, which uses the TCP protocol as a basis and ensures that messages that are sent to the destination arrive in the same order in which they were sent

For example: `server_socket = socket.socket(socket.AF_INET6, socket.SOCK_STREAM)`.

Assign to `server.bind` the values of IP and port, and to `server.listen` the number of maximum connections, shown as follows:

```
dataConection = (host,port)
server_socket.bind(dataConection)
# We assign the maximum number of connections
server_socket.listen(maxConnections)
```

Finally, we use the `server_socket.accept()` method to wait for connections from the client:

```
print("Waiting connections in %s:%s" %(host, port))
connection, address = server_socket.accept()
print ('Connected to', address)
```

If any data that's received from the client is a command, the logic could be executing that command with the `subprocess` package and run method. You can find the full documentation about the `subprocess` module at https://docs.python.org/3.7/library/subprocess.html. For this example, we need the command to execute in a string and the `stdout` parameter to save the command output in the response variable:

```python
if "command" in data.decode():
 s,command = data.decode().split("/")
 print("Command:"+command)
 response = subprocess.run([command], stdout=subprocess.PIPE)
 print(response.stdout)
 connection.send(response.stdout)
 print ("Sent data command back to the client: [%s]"
%response.stdout.decode())
```

You can find the full server implementation that's given in the following code in the `echo_server_ipv6.py` file:

```python
#!/usr/bin/env python3

import argparse
import socket
import subprocess

IPV6_ADDRESS = '::1'
# Up to 5 clients can connect
maxConnections = 5

def echo_server_ipv6(port, host=IPV6_ADDRESS):
    # Creating the server with ipv6 support
    # socket.AF_INET6 to indicate that we will use Ipv6
    # socket.SOCK_STREAM to use TCP/IP
    try:
        server_socket = socket.socket(socket.AF_INET6,socket.SOCK_STREAM)
        dataConection = (host,port)
        server_socket.bind(dataConection)
        # We assign the maximum number of connections
        server_socket.listen(maxConnections)
    except socket.error as err:
        print ("Socket error: %s" %err)
        server_socket.close()

    print("Waiting connections in %s:%s" %(host, port))
    connection, address = server_socket.accept()
    print ('Connected to', address)
```

If we continue analyzing the code, we can see how our infinite loop is listening for client connections. For each message it receives, it will transform it into a command for execution with the `subprocess` module:

```python
    while True:
        data = connection.recv(4096)
        print ("Received data from the client: [%s]" %data.decode())
        if "command" in data.decode():
            s,command = data.decode().split("/")
            print("Command:"+command)
            response = subprocess.run([command], stdout=subprocess.PIPE)
            print(response.stdout)
            connection.send(response.stdout)
            print ("Sent data command back to the client: [%s]"
%response.stdout.decode())
        if data.decode() == "exit":
            connection.send(bytes("exit".encode('utf-8')))
            break
        if "command" not in data.decode():
            connection.send(data)
            print ("Sent data echoed back to the client: [%s]"
%data.decode())

    print("------- CLOSE CONNECTION ---------")
    connection.close()

if __name__ == '__main__':
    parser = argparse.ArgumentParser(description='IPv6 Socket Server')
    parser.add_argument('--port', action="store", dest="port", type=int,
required=True)
    given_args = parser.parse_args()
    port = given_args.port
    echo_server_ipv6(port)
```

After implementing the server, we started to implement our client, which will send the messages to the socket that was opened by the server.

Implementing the IPv6 client

First, we need to configure the data to connect to the server and send initial data to the server:

```python
client = socket.socket (socket.AF_INET6, socket.SOCK_STREAM)
client.connect ((host, port))

message = "Hello from ipv6 client"
```

```
print ("Send data to server: %s" %message)
client.send(bytes(message.encode('utf-8')))
data = client.recv(4096)
print ('Received initial message from server:', data.decode())
```

Then, we will create a loop and use the `send` and `recv` methods from the socket client to transmit information from the client to the server. We use the exit message to close the connection between the client and server.

You can find the following code in the `echo_client_ipv6.py` file:

```python
#!/usr/bin/env python3

import argparse
import socket

IPV6_ADDRESS = '::1'

def echo_client_ipv6(port, host=IPV6_ADDRESS):
    # Configure the data to connect to the server
    # socket.AF_INET6 to indicate that we will use Ipv6
    # socket.SOCK_STREAM to use TCP/IP
    # These protocols must be the same as on the server
    try:
        client = socket.socket (socket.AF_INET6, socket.SOCK_STREAM)
        client.connect ((host, port))
        print ("Connected to the server --->% s:% s"% (host, port))
    except socket.error as err:
        print ("Socket error:%s" %err)
        client.close()
    # send initial data to server
    message = "Hello from ipv6 client"
    print ("Send data to server: %s" %message)
    client.send(bytes(message.encode('utf-8')))
    data = client.recv(4096)
    print ('Received initial message from server:', data.decode())
```

If we continue analyzing the code, we can see how our infinite loop requests the introduction of messages and commands that are entered by the user to send them to the server:

```python
    while True:
        message = input("Write your message > ")
        client.send(bytes(message.encode('utf-8')))
        data = client.recv(4096)
        print ('Received from server:', data.decode())
        if data.decode() == "exit":
```

```
          break;
       command = input("Write your command > ")
       command = "command/"+command
       client.send(bytes(command.encode('utf-8')))
       data = client.recv(4096)
       print ('Received command server:', data.decode())

    print("------- CLOSE CONNECTION ---------")
    client.close()

if __name__ == '__main__':
    parser = argparse.ArgumentParser(description='IPv6 socket client')
    parser.add_argument('--port', action="store", dest="port", type=int,
required=True)
    given_args = parser.parse_args()
    port = given_args.port
    echo_client_ipv6(port)
```

Executing client and server

We start the server with the `echo_server_ipv6.py` Python command and wait for a connection:

```
usage: echo_server_ipv6.py [-h] --port PORT
```

We must pass the port for listening connections as an argument:

```
$ python echo_server_ipv6.py --port 7575
Waiting connections in ::1:7575
```

Next, we start the client with the same port parameter:

```
$ python echo_client_ipv6.py --port 7575
 Connected to the server --->::1:7575
 Send data to server: Hello from ipv6 client
Received initial message from server: Hello from ipv6 client
```

We will see that the server has already found the connection:

```
Connected to ('::1', 5223, 0, 0)
 Received data from the client: [Hello from ipv6 client]
 Sent data echoed back to the client: [Hello from ipv6 client]
```

Now we can write any message and command on the client, and in the server log we can verify that the message was sent and that the command was executed.

In the following screenshot, we can see the execution in the socket server:

```
Waiting connections in ::1:7575
Connected to ('::1', 5223, 0, 0)
Received data from the client: [Hello from ipv6 client]
Sent data echoed back to the client: [Hello from ipv6 client]
Received data from the client: [hi can i get list files]
Sent data echoed back to the client: [hi can i get list files]
Received data from the client: [command/ls]
Command:ls
b'echo_client_ipv6.py\necho_server_ipv6.py\n'
Sent data command back to the client: [echo_client_ipv6.py
echo_server_ipv6.py
]
Received data from the client: [thank you]
Sent data echoed back to the client: [thank you]
Received data from the client: [command/dir]
Command:dir
b'echo_client_ipv6.py  echo_server_ipv6.py\n'
Sent data command back to the client: [echo_client_ipv6.py  echo_server_ipv6.py
]
Received data from the client: [exit]
------- CLOSE CONNECTION ---------
```

In the following screenshot, we can see the execution in the socket client and the output when sending messages and commands:

```
Connected to the server --->::1:7575
Send data to server: Hello from ipv6 client
Received initial message from server: Hello from ipv6 client
Write your message > hi can i get list files
Received from server: hi can i get list files
Write your command > ls
Received command server: echo_client_ipv6.py
echo_server_ipv6.py

Write your message > thank you
Received from server: thank you
Write your command > dir
Received command server: echo_client_ipv6.py  echo_server_ipv6.py

Write your message > exit
Received from server: exit
------- CLOSE CONNECTION ---------
```

We analyzed the implementation of a client-server application with an IPv6 protocol for sending messages and commands and the execution of them on the server.

Non-blocking and asynchronous socket I/O

In this section, you will learn about socket programming with non-blocking socket I/O.

Introducing non-blocking I/O

First, we are going to review a simple example of non-blocking I/O for the socket server. This script will run a socket server and listen in a non-blocking style. This means that you can connect more clients who won't be necessarily blocked for I/O.

You can find the following code in the server_socket_async.py file:

```
#!/usr/bin/env python3

import socket

if __name__ == '__main__':
    sock = socket.socket(socket.AF_INET, socket.SOCK_STREAM)
    #unset blocking
    sock.setblocking(0)
    sock.settimeout(0.5)
    sock.bind(("127.0.0.1", 12345))
    socket_address =sock.getsockname()
    print("Asynchronous socket server launched on socket: %s"
%str(socket_address))
    while(1):
        sock.listen(1)
```

From a client point of view, when we make a socket non-blocking by calling setblocking(0), it will never wait for the operation to complete. So, when we call the send() method, it will put as much data in the buffer as possible and return.

You can find the following code in the client_socket_async.py file:

```
#!/usr/bin/env python3

import socket

if __name__ == '__main__':
    sock = socket.socket()
    sock.connect(("127.0.0.1", 12345))
    #setting to non-blocking mode
    sock.setblocking(0)
    data = "Hello Python"
    sock.send(data.encode())
```

The client-server model with multiple connections

If we are working with Python version 3.4+, there is a module called selectors, which provides an API for quickly building an object-oriented server based on the I/O primitives. The documentation and an example of this is available at https://docs.python.org/3.7/library/selectors.html.

In this example, we are going to implement a server that controls several connections using the selectors package.

You can find the following code in the tcp_server_selectors.py file:

```python
#!/usr/bin/env python3

import selectors
import types
import socket

selector = selectors.DefaultSelector()

def accept_connection(sock):
    connection, address = sock.accept()
    print('Connection accepted in {}'.format(address))
    # We put the socket in non-blocking mode
    connection.setblocking(False)
    data = types.SimpleNamespace(addr=address, inb=b'', outb=b'')
    events = selectors.EVENT_READ | selectors.EVENT_WRITE
    selector.register(connection, events, data=data)
```

In the previous code block, we defined the accept_connection() method for accepting connections from the clients, put the socket in non-blocking mode, and registered a selector for capturing read and write events. In the following code block, we are defining the service_connection() method for differentiating messages marked as event read selector and messages marked as event write selector:

```python
def service_connection(key, mask):
    sock = key.fileobj
    data = key.data
    if mask & selectors.EVENT_READ:
        recv_data = sock.recv(BUFFER_SIZE)
    if recv_data:
        data.outb += recv_data
    else:
        print('Closing connection in {}'.format(data.addr))
```

```
        selector.unregister(sock)
        sock.close()
    if mask & selectors.EVENT_WRITE:
        if data.outb:
            print('Echo from {} to {}'.format(repr(data.outb), data.addr))
            sent = sock.send(data.outb)
            data.outb = data.outb[sent:]
```

In the following block of code, we can see our main program for establishing the host, port, and BUFFER_SIZE constants, and configuring our socket in non-blocking mode. We will also register the socket to be monitored by the selector functions:

```
if __name__ == '__main__':
    host = 'localhost'
    port = 12345
    BUFFER_SIZE = 1024
    # We create a TCP socket
    socket_tcp = socket.socket(socket.AF_INET, socket.SOCK_STREAM)
    # We configure the socket in non-blocking mode
    socket_tcp.setblocking(False)
    socket_tcp.bind((host, port))
    socket_tcp.listen()
    print('Openned socket for listening connections on {} {}'.format(host,
port))
    socket_tcp.setblocking(False)
    # We register the socket to be monitored by the selector functions
    selector.register(socket_tcp, selectors.EVENT_READ, data=None)
    while socket_tcp:
        events = selector.select(timeout=None)
        for key, mask in events:
            if key.data is None:
                accept_connection(key.fileobj)
            else:
                service_connection(key, mask)
    socket_tcp.close()
    print('Connection finished.')
```

Let's explore our implementation a bit more:

- Like before, we defined the variables that are necessary to link with the socket: host, port, BUFFER_SIZE, and MESSAGE.

- We configured the socket for non-blocking mode with `socket_tcp.setblocking(False)`. Socket module functions return a value immediately, they have to wait for a system call to complete to return a value. When we configure the socket in non-blocking, we make sure our application does not stop waiting for a response from the system.

- We start a while loop in which the first line is `events = sel.select (timeout = None)`. This function blocks until there are sockets ready to be written/read. Then it returns a list of pairs (key, event), one for each socket. The key is a `SelectorKey` that contains a `fileobj` attribute. `Key.fileobj` is the `socket` object, and mask is an event mask for operations that are ready.

- If `key.data` is `None`, we know that it comes from the socket that is open and we need to accept the connection. We call the `accept_connection()` function that we defined to handle this situation.

- If `key.data` is not `None`, it is a client socket that is ready to be accepted and we need to address it. So we call the `service_connection()` function with key and mask as arguments, which contain everything we need to operate the socket.

Now, let's look at an implementation of a client. It is quite similar to the implementation of the server but instead of waiting for connections, the client starts to initiate connections with the `start_connections()` function.

You can find the following code in the `tcp_client_selectors.py` file:

```python
#!/usr/bin/env python3

import socket
import selectors
import types

selector = selectors.DefaultSelector()
messages = ['This is the first message', 'This is the second message']
BUFFER_SIZE = 1024

def start_connections(host, port, num_conns):
    server_address = (host, port)
    for i in range(0, num_conns):
        connid = i + 1
        print('Starting connection {} towards {}'.format(connid,
server_address))
        socket_tcp = socket.socket(socket.AF_INET, socket.SOCK_STREAM)
        # We connect using connect_ex () instead of connect
        socket_tcp.connect_ex(server_address)
        events = selectors.EVENT_READ | selectors.EVENT_WRITE
        data = types.SimpleNamespace(connid=connid,
```

```
            msg_total=sum(len(m) for m in messages), recv_total=0,
            messages=list(messages),outb=b'')
    selector.register(socket_tcp, events, data=data)
events = selector.select()
    for key, mask in events:
        service_connection(key, mask)
```

In the previous code block, we defined the `start_connections()` method to connect with the server and register a selector for capturing read and write events. In the following code block, we define the `service_connection()` method for differentiating messages marked as event read selector and event write selector:

```
def service_connection(key, mask):
    sock = key.fileobj
    data = key.data
    if mask & selectors.EVENT_READ:
        recv_data = sock.recv(BUFFER_SIZE)
        if recv_data:
            print('Received {} from connection {}'.format(repr(recv_data),
data.connid))
            data.recv_total += len(recv_data)
        if not recv_data or data.recv_total == data.msg_total:
            print('Closing connection', data.connid)
            selector.unregister(sock)
            sock.close()
    if mask & selectors.EVENT_WRITE:
        if not data.outb and data.messages:
            data.outb = data.messages.pop(0).encode()
        if data.outb:
            print('Sending {} to connection {}'.format(repr(data.outb),
data.connid))
            sent = sock.send(data.outb)
            sock.shutdown(socket.SHUT_WR)
            data.outb = data.outb[sent:]

if __name__ == '__main__':
    host = 'localhost'
    port = 12345
    BUFFER_SIZE = 1024
    start_connections(host, port, 2)
```

Now, we execute our new server and client implementation for multiple connections:

```
$ python tcp_server_selectors.py &
 Openned socket for listening connections on localhost 12345

$ python tcp_server_selectors.py &
 $ python tcp_client_selectors.py
```

```
Starting connection 1 towards ('localhost', 12345)
Starting connection 2 towards ('localhost', 12345)
Connection accepted in ('127.0.0.1', 7107)
Connection accepted in ('127.0.0.1', 7109)
Sending 'This is the first message' to connection 1
Sending 'This is the first message' to connection 2
Closing connection in  ('127.0.0.1', 7107)
Closing connection in  ('127.0.0.1', 7109)
```

As we can see, our clients communicate with our server and it echoes to verify that the messages were received.

In this section, we looked at non-blocking I/O with the `socket` and `selectors` modules to build an object-oriented server based on the I/O primitives.

HTTPS and securing sockets with TLS

In this section, you will learn how we can implement secure sockets with TLS and the SSL module. We will demonstrate how simple TCP sockets can be wrapped with TLS and used to carry encrypted data.

Implementing the SSL client

You have probably come across the discussion around secure web communication using SSL, or more precisely TLS, which is adopted by many other high-level protocols. Let's see how we can wrap a plain sockets connection with SSL. Python has a built-in SSL module that serves this purpose.

In the following example, we would like to create a plain TCP socket and connect to an HTTPS-enabled web server. We can establish that connection using the SSL module and check the various properties of the connection. For example, to check the identity of the remote web server, we can see whether the hostname is the same in the SSL certificate, as we expect it to be. The following is an example of a secure socket-based client.

You can find the following code in the `ssl_client.py` file:

```
#!/usr/bin/python3

import socket
import ssl

from ssl import wrap_socket, CERT_NONE, PROTOCOL_TLSv1, SSLError
```

```
from ssl import SSLContext
from ssl import HAS_SNI
from pprint import pprint

TARGET_HOST = 'www.google.com'
SSL_PORT = 443

# Use the path of CA certificate file in your system
CA_CERT_PATH = 'certfiles.crt'

def ssl_wrap_socket(sock, keyfile=None, certfile=None,cert_reqs=None,
ca_certs=None, server_hostname=None,ssl_version=None):
    context = SSLContext(ssl_version)
    context.verify_mode = cert_reqs
    if ca_certs:
        try:
            context.load_verify_locations(ca_certs)
        except Exception as e:
            raise SSLError(e)
    if certfile:
        context.load_cert_chain(certfile, keyfile)
    if HAS_SNI: # OpenSSL enabled SNI
        return context.wrap_socket(sock,server_hostname=server_hostname)
    return context.wrap_socket(sock)
```

In the preceding code, we have declared our `ssl_wrap_socket()` method, which accepts the socket as a parameter and information about the certificate. This method internally checks the certificate and loads the information in the context object to return the `SSLContext` object. The following code is our main program, which asks the user for the destination host and calls the previous method for extracting remote host certificate details with the `getpeercert()` method from the `SSLContext` object:

```
if __name__ == '__main__':
    hostname = input("Enter target host:") or TARGET_HOST
    client_sock = socket.socket(socket.AF_INET,socket.SOCK_STREAM)
    client_sock.connect((hostname, 443))
    ssl_socket = ssl_wrap_socket(client_sock,ssl_version=PROTOCOL_TLSv1,
    cert_reqs=ssl.CERT_REQUIRED,
    ca_certs=CA_CERT_PATH,server_hostname=hostname)
    print(ssl_socket.cipher())
    print("Extracting remote host certificate details:")
    cert = ssl_socket.getpeercert()
    pprint(cert)
    if not cert or ('commonName', TARGET_HOST) not in cert['subject'][4]:
        raise Exception("Invalid SSL cert for host %s. Check if this is a
man-in-the-middle attack!" )
    ssl_socket.write('GET / \n'.encode('utf-8')
```

```
    pprint(ssl_socket.recv(1024).split(b"\r\n"))
    ssl_socket.close()
    client_sock.close()
```

If you run the preceding example, you will see the details of the SSL certificate of a remote web server, such as `www.google.com`. Here, we have created a TCP socket and connected it to HTTPS `port 443`. Then, that socket connection is wrapped into SSL packets using our `ssl_wrap_socket()` function. This function takes the following parameters as arguments:

- `sock`: TCP socket
- `keyfile`: SSL private key file path
- `certfile`: SSL public certificate path
- `cert_reqs`: Confirmation of whether certificate is required from the other side to make a connection and whether a validation test is required
- `ca_certs`: Public certificate authority certificate path
- `server_hostname`: The target's remote server's hostname
- `ssl_version`: The intended SSL version to be used by the client

At the beginning of the SSL socket-wrapping process, we created an SSL context using the `SSLContext()` class. This is necessary to set up the SSL connection-specific properties. Instead of using a custom context, we could also use a default context, which is supplied by default with the SSL module, using the `create_default_context()` function. You can specify whether you'd like to create client- or server-side sockets using a constant. The following is an example for creating a client-side socket: `context = ssl.create_default_context(Purpose.SERVER_AUTH)`.

The `SSLContext` object takes the SSL version argument, which in our example is set to `PROTOCOL_TLSv1`, or you should use the latest version. Note that SSLv2 and SSLv3 are broken and they should not be used in any production server because it could cause serious security problems.

In the preceding example, `CERT_REQUIRED` indicates that the server certificate is necessary for the connection to continue, and that this certificate will be validated later.

If the CA certificate parameter has been presented with a certificate path, the `load_verify_locations()` method is used to load the CA certificate files.

This will be used to verify the peer server certificates. If you'd like to use the default certificate path on your system, you'd probably call another context method: `load_default_certs(purpose=Purpose.SERVER_AUTH)`.

When we operate on the server side, the load_cert_chain() method is usually used to load the key and certificate file so that clients can verify the server's authenticity.

Finally, the wrap_socket() method is called to return an SSL-wrapped socket. Note that if the OpenSSL library comes with **Server Name Indication** (SNI) support enabled, you can pass the remote server's host name while wrapping the socket. This is useful when the remote server uses different SSL certificates for different secure services using a single IP address, for example, name-based virtual hosting.

If you run the preceding SSL client code, you will see the cipher type by calling the cipher() method and the properties of the SSL certificate of the remote server, as shown in the following screenshot. This is used to verify the authenticity of the remote server by calling the getpeercert() method and comparing it with the returned hostname.

In the following screenshot, we can see the execution of the previous script for getting information about the certificate that is using a specific domain:

```
Enter target host:www.google.com
('ECDHE-ECDSA-AES128-SHA', 'TLSv1/SSLv3', 128)
Extracting remote host certificate details:
{'OCSP': ('http://ocsp.pki.goog/GTSGIAG3',),
 'caIssuers': ('http://pki.goog/gsr2/GTSGIAG3.crt',),
 'crlDistributionPoints': ('http://crl.pki.goog/GTSGIAG3.crl',),
 'issuer': ((('countryName', 'US'),),
            (('organizationName', 'Google Trust Services'),),
            (('commonName', 'Google Internet Authority G3'),)),
 'notAfter': 'Apr 23 14:58:00 2019 GMT',
 'notBefore': 'Jan 29 14:58:00 2019 GMT',
 'serialNumber': '726B68C873C67FB2',
 'subject': ((('countryName', 'US'),),
             (('stateOrProvinceName', 'California'),),
             (('localityName', 'Mountain View'),),
             (('organizationName', 'Google LLC'),),
             (('commonName', 'www.google.com'),)),
 'subjectAltName': (('DNS', 'www.google.com'),),
 'version': 3}
```

Interestingly, if any other fake web server wants to pretend to be Google's web server, it simply can't do that. At this point we could verify that the SSL certificate is signed by an accredited certification authority and check if accredited CA has been compromised/subverted. This form of attack to your web browser is commonly referred to as a **man-in-the-middle** (MITM) attack.

In the following example, we are using the wrap_socket() method to get the SSL socket and we use the match_hostname() method from that socket to check the certificate.

You can find the following code in the `ssl_client_check_certificate.py` file:

```python
#!/usr/bin/env python3

import socket, ssl, sys
from pprint import pprint

TARGET_HOST = 'www.google.com'
SSL_PORT = 443

#Use the path of CA certificate file in your system
CA_CERT_PATH = 'certfiles.crt'

if __name__ == '__main__':
    hostname = input("Enter target host:") or TARGET_HOST
    client_sock = socket.socket(socket.AF_INET, socket.SOCK_STREAM)
    client_sock.connect((hostname, 443))
    # Turn the socket over to the SSL library
    ssl_socket = ssl.wrap_socket(client_sock,
    ssl_version=ssl.PROTOCOL_TLSv1, cert_reqs=ssl.CERT_REQUIRED,
ca_certs=CA_CERT_PATH)
    print(ssl_socket.cipher())
    try:
        ssl.match_hostname(ssl_socket.getpeercert(), hostname)
    except ssl.CertificateError as ce:
        print('Certificate error:', str(ce))
        sys.exit(1)
    print("Extracting remote host certificate details:")
    cert = ssl_socket.getpeercert()
    pprint(cert)
    ssl_socket.close()
    client_sock.close()
```

If the hostname doesn't match the name that appears on the certificate, the script execution will throw an exception of the `ssl.CertificateError` type:

```
Enter target host:www.google.com
('ECDHE-RSA-AES128-SHA', 'TLSv1/SSLv3', 128)
Certificate error: hostname 'other_hostname' doesn't match 'www.google.com'
```

In the previous examples, we used `CA_CERT_PATH = 'certfiles.crt'`, which contains the path of the CA certificate file in your system. You can also generate your own certificate using specific tools, such as OpenSSL (`https://www.openssl.org`). There are other methods we can use to generate a certificate for a specific domain, such as the web service (`http://www.selfsignedcertificate.com/`).

Inspecting standard SSL client and server communication

Now, we are going to capture packets with Wireshark when executing the script showed in the previous section to see the communication between the client and the domain server.

The following screenshot shows the interaction between the SSL client and the remote server:

No.	Time	Source	Destination	Protocol	Length	Info
346	14.000573	10.80.92.1	255.255.255.255	DHCP	342	DHCP ACK - Transaction ID 0x77b0de07
347	14.174945	10.80.92.216	172.217.168.196	TLSv1	234	Client Hello
348	14.196753	172.217.168.196	10.80.92.216	TCP	60	443 → 20365 [ACK] Seq=1 Ack=181 Win=15744 Len=0
349	14.256451	172.217.168.196	10.80.92.216	TLSv1	1482	Server Hello
350	14.256744	172.217.168.196	10.80.92.216	TLSv1	958	Certificate, Server Key Exchange, Server Hello Done
351	14.256855	10.80.92.216	172.217.168.196	TCP	54	20365 → 443 [ACK] Seq=181 Ack=2333 Win=65536 Len=0
352	14.261750	10.80.92.216	172.217.168.196	TLSv1	188	Client Key Exchange, Change Cipher Spec, Encrypted Handshake Message
353	14.283431	172.217.168.196	10.80.92.216	TCP	60	443 → 20365 [ACK] Seq=2333 Ack=315 Win=16768 Len=0
354	14.338848	172.217.168.196	10.80.92.216	TLSv1	341	New Session Ticket, Change Cipher Spec, Encrypted Handshake Message
355	14.341408	10.80.92.216	172.217.168.196	TLSv1	128	Application Data, Application Data
356	14.364007	172.217.168.196	10.80.92.216	TCP	60	443 → 20365 [ACK] Seq=2620 Ack=389 Win=16768 Len=0
357	14.409954	10.80.92.216	216.58.211.106	TCP	55	20088 → 443 [ACK] Seq=1 Ack=1 Win=256 Len=1 [TCP segment of a reassembled PDU]
358	14.431593	216.58.211.106	10.80.92.216	TCP	66	443 → 20088 [ACK] Seq=1 Ack=2 Win=153 Len=0 SLE=1 SRE=2
359	14.454253	172.217.168.196	10.80.92.216	TLSv1	1467	Application Data
360	14.456540	172.217.168.196	10.80.92.216	TLSv1	1467	Application Data

```
> Frame 351: 54 bytes on wire (432 bits), 54 bytes captured (432 bits) on interface 0
> Ethernet II, Src: LcfcHefe_2d:79:20 (8c:16:45:2d:79:20), Dst: HewlettP_79:fd:89 (78:48:59:79:fd:89)
> Internet Protocol Version 4, Src: 10.80.92.216, Dst: 172.217.168.196
> Transmission Control Protocol, Src Port: 20365, Dst Port: 443, Seq: 181, Ack: 2333, Len: 0
```

```
0000  78 48 59 79 fd 89 8c 16  45 2d 79 20 08 00 45 00   xHYy···· E-y ··E·
0010  00 28 78 0e 40 00 80 06  c5 fb 0a 50 5c d8 ac d9   ·(x·@··· ···P\···
0020  a8 c4 4f 8d 01 bb 95 68  eb f1 62 da 3f b8 50 10   ··O····h ··b·?·P·
0030  01 00 7c d9 00 00                                  ··|···
```

Let's examine the SSL handshake process between the client and the server:

- In the first step of an SSL handshake, the client sends a `Hello` message to the remote server, saying what it is capable of in terms handling key files, encrypting messages, doing message integrity checks, and so on.
- Then, it sends the TLS version 1.0 and a random number to generate a master secret to encrypt the subsequent message exchanges. This is helpful for preventing any third-party from looking inside the packets.
- Finally, the random numbers that are seen in the hello messages are used to generate the pre-master secret, which both ends will process further to arrive at the master secret, and then use that to generate the symmetric key.

In the following screenshot, you can see that the client is presenting a set of 29 cipher suites to the server to choose relevant algorithms:

```
347 14.174945    10.80.92.216       172.217.168.196   TLSv1   234 Client Hello
348 14.196753    172.217.168.196    10.80.92.216      TCP      60 443 → 20365 [ACK] Seq=1 Ack=181 Win=15744 Len=0
349 14.256451    172.217.168.196    10.80.92.216      TLSv1  1482 Server Hello
350 14.256744    172.217.168.196    10.80.92.216      TLSv1   958 Certificate, Server Key Exchange, Server Hello Done
351 14.256855    10.80.92.216       172.217.168.196   TCP      54 20365 → 443 [ACK] Seq=181 Ack=2333 Win=65536 Len=0
352 14.261750    10.80.92.216       172.217.168.196   TLSv1   188 Client Key Exchange, Change Cipher Spec, Encrypted Handshake Message
353 14.283431    172.217.168.196    10.80.92.216      TCP      60 443 → 20365 [ACK] Seq=2333 Ack=315 Win=16768 Len=0
```
```
  ⌄ Handshake Protocol: Client Hello
      Handshake Type: Client Hello (1)
      Length: 171
      Version: TLS 1.0 (0x0301)
    > Random: c7b278216e2018f293a9c8d1b0725d50c5c4606db7e5b9a1...
      Session ID Length: 0
      Cipher Suites Length: 58
  ⌄ Cipher Suites (29 suites)
        Cipher Suite: TLS_ECDHE_RSA_WITH_AES_256_CBC_SHA (0xc014)
        Cipher Suite: TLS_ECDHE_ECDSA_WITH_AES_256_CBC_SHA (0xc00a)
        Cipher Suite: TLS_ECDH_RSA_WITH_AES_256_CBC_SHA (0xc00f)
        Cipher Suite: TLS_ECDH_ECDSA_WITH_AES_256_CBC_SHA (0xc005)
```

- In the second packet that's sent from server to client, the server selects the `TLS_ECDHE_RSA_WITH_RC4_128_SHA` cipher suite for the purpose of connecting to the client. This means that the server wants to use the RSA algorithm for key handling, RC4 for encryption, and SHA for integrity checking (hashing). This is shown in the following screenshot:

```
347 14.174945    10.80.92.216       172.217.168.196   TLSv1   234 Client Hello
348 14.196753    172.217.168.196    10.80.92.216      TCP      60 443 → 20365 [ACK] Seq=1 Ack=181 Win=15744 Len=0
349 14.256451    172.217.168.196    10.80.92.216      TLSv1  1482 Server Hello
350 14.256744    172.217.168.196    10.80.92.216      TLSv1   958 Certificate, Server Key Exchange, Server Hello Done
351 14.256855    10.80.92.216       172.217.168.196   TCP      54 20365 → 443 [ACK] Seq=181 Ack=2333 Win=65536 Len=0
352 14.261750    10.80.92.216       172.217.168.196   TLSv1   188 Client Key Exchange, Change Cipher Spec, Encrypted Handshake Message
353 14.283431    172.217.168.196    10.80.92.216      TCP      60 443 → 20365 [ACK] Seq=2333 Ack=315 Win=16768 Len=0
```
```
      Version: TLS 1.0 (0x0301)
      Length: 59
  ⌄ Handshake Protocol: Server Hello
      Handshake Type: Server Hello (2)
      Length: 55
      Version: TLS 1.0 (0x0301)
    > Random: 5c6d326d6e24ddf286d34d4ba9a98dcba0d5582a615a5077...
      Session ID Length: 0
      Cipher Suite: TLS_ECDHE_ECDSA_WITH_AES_128_CBC_SHA (0xc009)
      Compression Method: null (0)
      Extensions Length: 15
  ⌄ Extension: renegotiation_info (len=1)
```

- In the second phase of the SSL handshake, the server sends an SSL certificate to the client. This certificate is issued by a CA, as mentioned in the *Implementing the SSL client* section. It contains a serial number, public key, validity period, and the details of the subject and the issuer.

The following screenshot show the remote server certificate, where we can see the server's public key inside the packet:

```
347 14.174945     10.80.92.216       172.217.168.196    TLSv1    234 Client Hello
348 14.196753     172.217.168.196    10.80.92.216       TCP       60 443 → 20365 [ACK] Seq=1 Ack=181 Win=15744 Len=0
349 14.256451     172.217.168.196    10.80.92.216       TLSv1   1482 Server Hello
350 14.256744     172.217.168.196    10.80.92.216       TLSv1    958 Certificate, Server Key Exchange, Server Hello Done
351 14.256855     10.80.92.216       172.217.168.196    TCP       54 20365 → 443 [ACK] Seq=181 Ack=2333 Win=65536 Len=0
352 14.261750     10.80.92.216       172.217.168.196    TLSv1    188 Client Key Exchange, Change Cipher Spec, Encrypted Handshake Message
353 14.283431     172.217.168.196    10.80.92.216       TCP       60 443 → 20365 [ACK] Seq=2333 Ack=315 Win=16768 Len=0
     Length: 145
   ∨ Handshake Protocol: Server Key Exchange
       Handshake Type: Server Key Exchange (12)
       Length: 141
     ∨ EC Diffie-Hellman Server Params
         Curve Type: named_curve (0x03)
         Named Curve: secp256r1 (0x0017)
         Pubkey Length: 65
         Pubkey: 04ef0da73a37825475309a957d8dc24dd04ca6a0ca27b28f...
         Signature Length: 70
         Signature: 304402205b301f3586210bfc6da21e1093e614775beaaa59...
 ∨ TLSv1 Record Layer: Handshake Protocol: Server Hello Done
```

- In the third phase of the handshake, the client exchanges a key and calculates a master secret to encrypt the messages and continue further communications. The client also sends the request to change the cipher specification that was agreed on the previous phase. From that moment, the encryption of the message begins. The following screenshot shows this process:

```
347 14.174945     10.80.92.216       172.217.168.196    TLSv1    234 Client Hello
348 14.196753     172.217.168.196    10.80.92.216       TCP       60 443 → 20365 [ACK] Seq=1 Ack=181 Win=15744 Len=0
349 14.256451     172.217.168.196    10.80.92.216       TLSv1   1482 Server Hello
350 14.256744     172.217.168.196    10.80.92.216       TLSv1    958 Certificate, Server Key Exchange, Server Hello Done
351 14.256855     10.80.92.216       172.217.168.196    TCP       54 20365 → 443 [ACK] Seq=181 Ack=2333 Win=65536 Len=0
352 14.261750     10.80.92.216       172.217.168.196    TLSv1    188 Client Key Exchange, Change Cipher Spec, Encrypted Handshake Message
353 14.283431     172.217.168.196    10.80.92.216       TCP       60 443 → 20365 [ACK] Seq=2333 Ack=315 Win=16768 Len=0
Transmission Control Protocol, Src Port: 20365, Dst Port: 443, Seq: 181, Ack: 2333, Len: 134
Secure Sockets Layer
  ∨ TLSv1 Record Layer: Handshake Protocol: Client Key Exchange
      Content Type: Handshake (22)
      Version: TLS 1.0 (0x0301)
      Length: 70
    ∨ Handshake Protocol: Client Key Exchange
        Handshake Type: Client Key Exchange (16)
        Length: 66
      ∨ EC Diffie-Hellman Client Params
          Pubkey Length: 65
          Pubkey: 04b485085bc07d2cb4fd164ce2c9422d8ca416cab978d4d9...
  ∨ TLSv1 Record Layer: Change Cipher Spec Protocol: Change Cipher Spec
      Content Type: Change Cipher Spec (20)
      Version: TLS 1.0 (0x0301)
      Length: 1
      Change Cipher Spec Message
  ∨ TLSv1 Record Layer: Handshake Protocol: Encrypted Handshake Message
      Content Type: Handshake (22)
      Version: TLS 1.0 (0x0301)
```

- In the final part of the SSL handshake process, a new session ticket is generated by the server for the client's particular session. This happens due to a TLS extension where the client advertises its support by sending an empty session ticket extension in the `Hello` client message. The server answers with an empty session ticket extension in its Hello server message. This session ticket mechanism enables the client to remember the whole session state, and the server becomes less engaged in maintaining a server-side session cache.

The following screenshot shows an example for presenting an SSL session ticket, where we can see the **Session Ticket Lifetime**:

```
350 14.256744    172.217.168.196    10.80.92.216      TLSv1   958 Certificate, Server Key Exchange, Server Hello Done
351 14.256855    10.80.92.216       172.217.168.196   TCP     54 20365 → 443 [ACK] Seq=181 Ack=2333 Win=65536 Len=0
352 14.261750    10.80.92.216       172.217.168.196   TLSv1   188 Client Key Exchange, Change Cipher Spec, Encrypted Handshake Message
353 14.283431    172.217.168.196    10.80.92.216      TCP     60 443 → 20365 [ACK] Seq=2333 Ack=315 Win=16768 Len=0
354 14.338848    172.217.168.196    10.80.92.216      TLSv1   341 New Session Ticket, Change Cipher Spec, Encrypted Handshake Message
355 14.341408    10.80.92.216       172.217.168.196   TLSv1   128 Application Data, Application Data
356 14.364007    172.217.168.196    10.80.92.216      TCP     60 443 → 20365 [ACK] Seq=2620 Ack=389 Win=16768 Len=0

Transmission Control Protocol, Src Port: 443, Dst Port: 20365, Seq: 2333, Ack: 315, Len: 287
Secure Sockets Layer
  ∨ TLSv1 Record Layer: Handshake Protocol: New Session Ticket
      Content Type: Handshake (22)
      Version: TLS 1.0 (0x0301)
      Length: 223
    ∨ Handshake Protocol: New Session Ticket
        Handshake Type: New Session Ticket (4)
        Length: 219
      ∨ TLS Session Ticket
          Session Ticket Lifetime Hint: 100799 seconds (1 day, 3 hours, 59 minutes, 59 seconds)
          Session Ticket Length: 213
          Session Ticket: 00c7df9abc456b89e6e2c8e7a453e5f1e2c63d47766a5799...
  ∨ TLSv1 Record Layer: Change Cipher Spec Protocol: Change Cipher Spec
      Content Type: Change Cipher Spec (20)
      Version: TLS 1.0 (0x0301)
      Length: 1
      Change Cipher Spec Message
  ∨ TLSv1 Record Layer: Handshake Protocol: Encrypted Handshake Message
      Content Type: Handshake (22)
```

Summary

In this chapter, we reviewed the socket module for implementing client-server architectures in Python with the TCP and UDP protocols. We also discussed basic TCP/IP socket programming using Python's socket and the SSL module. We demonstrated how simple TCP sockets can be wrapped with TLS and used to carry encrypted data. We also talked about the ways to validate the authenticity of a remote server using SSL certificates. Some other minor issues regarding socket programming, such as non-blocking socket I/O, were also presented. The detailed packet analysis with Wireshark in each section helps us to understand what happens under the hood in our socket programming scripts.

In the next chapter, you will learn about the principles of socket-based server design and how to build asynchronous network applications with the asyncio, aiohttp, Tornado, Twisted, and Celery frameworks.

Questions

1. Which method of the socket module allows a server socket to accept requests from a client socket from another host?
2. Which method of the socket module allows you to send data to a given address?
3. Which method of the socket module allows you to associate a host and a port with a specific socket?
4. What is the difference between the TCP and UDP protocols, and how do you implement them in Python with the socket module?
5. Which method of the socket module allows you to implement port scanning with sockets and to check the port state?
6. What is the alternative tool on the windows system for capturing packets on a loopback interface?
7. What is the socket configuration for the client-and-server IPv6 protocol?
8. What Python module can we use from version 3.4+ that provides an API to quickly build an object-oriented server based on the I/O primitives?
9. What method and parameters from the SSL module can we use to establish an SSL socket connection?
10. What method from the SSL module can we use to extract remote host certificate details and verify the authenticity of the remote server?

Further reading

Check out the following links for more information about the tools mentioned in this chapter. The official
Python documentation is also a great resource:

- Wireshark documentation: `https://wiki.wireshark.org`
- Sockets in Python 3: `https://docs.python.org/3/library/socket.html`
- *Sockets programming in Python*: `https://www.geeksforgeeks.org/socket-programming-python/`
- `https://realpython.com/python-sockets/`
- *What's New in Sockets for Python 3.7*: `https://www.agnosticdev.com/blog-entry/python/whats-new-sockets-python-37`

11
Designing Servers and Asynchronous Programming

In this chapter, you will learn about the principles of socket-based server design, and learn how to build small servers based on multiprocessing approaches. We will continue using `asyncio` and `aiohttp` for asynchronous operations. Finally, we will review Tornado, Twisted, and Celery for building asynchronous network applications.

The following topics will be covered in this chapter:

- Building a multiprocessing-based TCP server
- Building asynchronous applications with asyncio and aiohttp
- Building asynchronous network applications with Tornado
- Building asynchronous network applications with Twisted
- Building asynchronous network applications with Celery

Technical requirements

The examples and source code for this chapter are available in the GitHub repository in the `Chapter11` folder: https://github.com/PacktPublishing/Learning-Python-Networking-Second-Edition.

You will need to install a Python distribution in your local machine with a Unix-like operating system and have some basic knowledge of network protocols. The examples in this chapter are compatible with Windows as well.

Building a multiprocessing-based TCP server

In this section, we will learn how to build a multiprocessing-based server with the `concurrent.futures` package.

When working with multiprocessing in Python 3, we have many alternatives, among which we can highlight the `concurrent.futures` and `multiprocessing` modules.

Introducing the concurrent.futures module

In this section, we are going to explain the `concurrent.futures` module, whose objective is to introduce a layer of simplification on the modules that are threading and multiprocessing.

`concurrent.futures` is a module that is part of the standard Python library and provides a high-level abstraction layer where the threads are modeled as asynchronous tasks.

The term *futures* is synonymous with promises, delay, or deferred when working with asynchronous tasks. In general, regardless of what you call it, you can see it as a pending result. Futures are a replacement for a result that is not yet available, usually because their computation has not yet ended, or their transfer over the network has not been completed.

The module has an abstract base class called an *executor*, which is used for the `ThreadPoolExecutor` (used for multithreading) and `ProcessPoolExecutor` (used for multiprocessing) subclasses. The `max_workers` parameter identifies the max number of workers that execute the call asynchronously, and are as follows:

- `concurrent.futures.ThreadPoolExecutor` (max_workers)
- `concurrent.futures.ProcessPoolExecutor` (max_workers)

The approach we are adopting here involves using a `ThreadPoolExecutor`. We will deliver the tasks that have been assigned to the pool and return them later, which are results that we will return to when they are available in the future. Of course, we can wait for the `future` to become real results. Let's look at an example of the first subclass, `ThreadPoolExecutor`, with a practical case that allows you to download files asynchronously from `https://docs.python.org/3/download.html`.

You can find the following code in the `download_async_files.py` file:

```python
#!/usr/bin/python3

from concurrent.futures import ThreadPoolExecutor

import requests
import itertools
import time

docs =
['https://docs.python.org/3/archives/python-3.7.2-docs-pdf-letter.zip',
 'https://docs.python.org/3/archives/python-3.7.2-docs-pdf-a4.zip',
 'https://docs.python.org/3/archives/python-3.7.2-docs-html.zip',
 'https://docs.python.org/3/archives/python-3.7.2-docs-text.zip',
 'https://docs.python.org/3/archives/python-3.7.2-docs.epub'
]

def download_documents(documents, workers=4):
    def get_document(url):
        response = requests.get(url)
        filename = url.split("/")[5]
        print('Downloading '+ filename)
        open(filename, 'wb').write(response.content)
        return url
```

In the previous code block, we define the document list we are downloading and the `download_documents()` method, which accepts the document list and worker's number that's used by `ThreadPoolExecutor` as parameters. In the following code block, we are defining our executor, which we will use for downloading documents in a concurrent way:

```python
    message = 'Downloading docs from https://docs.python.org/3/archives'
    symbol = itertools.cycle('\|/-')
    executor = ThreadPoolExecutor(max_workers=workers)
    mydocs = [executor.submit(get_document, url) for url in documents]
    while not all([doc.done() for doc in mydocs]):
        print(message + next(symbol), end='\r')
        time.sleep(0.1)
    return mydocs

if __name__ == '__main__':
    t1 = time.time()
    print(download_documents(docs, workers=4))
    print(time.time() - t1, 'seconds passed')
```

This is the output of the previous script. We can see information about futures that are complete when we download certain files:

```
Downloading python-3.7.2-docs-text.ziphon.org/3/archives-
Downloading python-3.7.2-docs-pdf-a4.zipn.org/3/archives/
Downloading python-3.7.2-docs-pdf-letter.zipg/3/archives\
Downloading python-3.7.2-docs.epub.python.org/3/archives\
Downloading python-3.7.2-docs-html.ziphon.org/3/archives/

[<Future at 0x3cc8970 state=finished returned str>, <Future at 0x3ce0430
state=finished returned str>, <Future at 0x3ce07f0 state=finished returned
str>, <Future at 0x3ce0bb0 state=finished returned str>, <Future at
0x3ce0f90 state=finished returned str>]
```

We will study each of the actions that are carried out in detail, as follows:

- Inside the download_documents function, another call has been defined—get_document (URL). This function makes the requests to the file and downloads it to the local filesystem.
- Later, we instantiated ThreadPoolExecutor and created a list, mydocs, which is where we will save the futures. Instanced objects of the Future class (each of the elements in the mydocs list) encapsulate the asynchronous execution of the callable. Each of these objects come from Executor.submit().
- Within the whole block, we ask each of the downloads whether they have finished by using the Future.done() method. If it has finished, it will return True, otherwise it will return False.
- Finally, we return the mydocs list with the calculated futures.

Application for checking websites

Now, we will build an application that checks the running time of websites. The purpose of this application is to notify when a site or domain is not available. The application visits a list of URLs and checks whether these sites are operational. If, when making an HTTP request, the returned status is in the range of 400-500, this means that the site is not available and it would be a good idea to notify the owner.

We need to adopt a concurrent approach to solve this problem because, since we have more addresses to check in the list of websites, nothing guarantees that each site is reviewed every five minutes or less.

In the following example, we are going to use the `concurrent.futures` package for processing domains in a concurrent way to check whether each website is available. The `requests` module will help us to obtain the status of each domain.

You can find the following code in the `demo_concurrent_futures.py` file:

```python
#!/usr/bin/python3
import concurrent.futures
import requests

URLS = ['http://www.foxnews.com/','http://www.cnn.com/',
 'http://www.bbc.co.uk/',
 'http://some-made-up-domain.com/']

# Retrieve a single page with requests module
def load_requests(domain):
 with requests.get(domain, timeout=60) as connection:
 return connection.text
```

In the previous code block, we define our URL list for checking the website and the `load_requests()` method that accepts as parameters a domain and tries to establish a connection with the `requests` package.

In the following code block, we define our executor that we use for checking the state for each domain in a concurrent way:

```python
with concurrent.futures.ThreadPoolExecutor(max_workers=5) as executor:
future_executor = {executor.submit(load_requests, domain): domain for
domain in DOMAINS}
 for domain_future in concurrent.futures.as_completed(future_executor):
 domain = future_executor[domain_future]
 try:
 data = domain_future.result()
 print('%r page is %d bytes' % (domain, len(data)))
 except Exception as exception:
 print('%r generated an exception: %s' % (domain, exception))
```

The following is the output of the previous script, where we can see information about the sizes for download pages for domains that are available:

```
'http://www.foxnews.com/' page is 221581 bytes
 'http://www.bbc.co.uk/' page is 303120 bytes
 'http://www.cnn.com/' page is 1899465 bytes
 'http://some-made-up-domain.com/' generated an exception:
HTTPConnectionPool(host='ww1.some-made-up-domain.com', port=80): Max
retries exceeded with url: / (Caused by
NewConnectionError('<urllib3.connection.HTTPConnection object at
0x00000295B3E0BEF0>: Failed to establish a new connection: [WinError 10060]
A connection attempt failed because the connected party did not properly
respond after a period of time, or established connection failed because
connected host has failed to respond'))
```

The executor is the one who manages threads (`ThreadPoolExecutor`) or processes (`ProcessPoolExecutor`). Also, when we define the `ThreadPoolExecutor` constructor for getting the executor object, you can put the number of workers that you want to use, depending on the number of cores in our CPU.

In the previous example, we used the `as_completed` method to obtain the results as they were obtained. This method returns an iterator over the future instances that are given by the `future_executor` variable, which yields futures as they finish. You can check the full documentation and other examples about this function at `https://docs.python.org/dev/library/concurrent.futures.html#threadpoolexecutor-example`.

The multiprocessing approach

The `multiprocessing` module is an alternative to using the `threading` module. It is a module that's similar to the `threading` module, which offers a very similar interface, but at a low level. It works with processes instead of threads. In this case, we will take a similar approach to `concurrent.futures`. We are establishing a multiprocessing pool and presentation of tasks by assigning a function to the address list.

You can find the following code in the `demo_multiprocessing.py` file:

```
#!/usr/bin/python3

import time
import multiprocessing
import logging
import requests

from utils import check_website
```

```
from utils import WEBSITE_LIST
NUM_WORKERS = 3

if __name__ == '__main__':
    start_time = time.time()
    with multiprocessing.Pool(processes=NUM_WORKERS) as pool:
        results = pool.map_async(check_website, WEBSITE_LIST)
        results.wait()
        print(results)
    end_time = time.time()
    print("Time for multiprocessing: %s secs" % (end_time - start_time))
```

This script uses `check_website()`, which is available in the `utils.py` file of the same directory:

```
#!/usr/bin/python3

import requests

WEBSITE_LIST = ['http://www.foxnews.com/',
 'http://www.cnn.com/',
 'http://www.bbc.co.uk/',
 'http://some-other-domain.com/']

class WebsiteException(Exception):
 pass

def ping_website(address, timeout=6000):
    try:
        response = requests.get(address)
        print("Website %s returned status_code=%s" % (address,
response.status_code))
        if response.status_code >= 400:
            print("Website %s returned status_code=%s" % (address,
response.status_code))
            raise WebsiteException()
    except requests.exceptions.RequestException:
        print("Timeout expired for website %s" % address)
        raise WebsiteException()

def check_website(address):
    try:
        ping_website(address)
    except WebsiteException:
        pass
```

The following is the output of the execution of `demo_multiprocessing.py`. For each URL defined in `WEBSITE_LIST`, check the status code of the domain and show information about it:

```
Website http://www.bbc.co.uk/ returned status_code=200
 Website http://www.foxnews.com/ returned status_code=200
 Timeout expired for website http://some-other-domain.com/
 Website http://www.cnn.com/ returned status_code=200
 <multiprocessing.pool.MapResult object at 0x00000204C59A8B70>
 Time for multiprocessing: 2.0654103755950928 sec
```

In this section, you have learned about the `concurrent.futures` package for processing tasks in an asynchronous way with the `ThreadPoolExecutor` class. We also reviewed the `multiprocessing` package as an alternative to the `threading` module for creating a pool of processes for assigning tasks.

Building asynchronous applications with asyncio and aiohttp

In this section, you will learn about asyncio and aiohttp for developing asynchronous applications, which can greatly simplify the process of writing servers when using an event-driven approach.

Introducing asyncio

asyncio is a Python module that is part of its standard library. It allows you to write single-threaded asynchronous code and implement concurrency in Python. This module is available from Python 3.4 and its documentation is available at `https://docs.python.org/3/library/asyncio.html`.

Basically, asyncio provides an `event` loop for asynchronous programming. For example, if we need to make requests without blocking the main thread, we can use the `asyncio` library. Python 3.4 provides an `asyncio` module that has event loops and coroutines for I/O operations and networking, futures, and tasks. In the next section, we will review these elements.

Using asyncio

The `asyncio` module allows for the implementation of asynchronous programming using a combination of the following elements:

- **Event loop**: The `asyncio` module allows an event loop per process.
- **Coroutines**: A coroutine is a generator that follows certain conventions. Its most interesting feature is that it can be suspended during execution to wait for external processing (the some routine in I/O) and return from the point it had stopped when the external processing was done.
- **Futures**: Futures represent a process that has still not finished.
- **Tasks**: This is a subclass of `asyncio.Future` that encapsulates and manages coroutines. We can use the `asyncio.Task` object to encapsulate a coroutine.

Introducing event loops

The most important concept within asyncio is the event loop. An event loop allow you to write asynchronous code using either callbacks or coroutines.

The keys to understanding asyncio are the terms of coroutines and the event loop. Coroutines are stateful functions whose execution can be stopped while another I/O operation is being executed. An event loop is used to orchestrate the execution of the coroutines.

To run any `coroutine` function, we need to get an `event` loop. We can do this with `loop = asyncio.get_event_loop()`.

This gives us a `BaseEventLoop` object. This has a `run_until_complete` method that takes in a coroutine and runs it until completion. Then, the coroutine returns a result. At a low level, an `event` loop executes the `BaseEventLoop.rununtilcomplete(future)` method.

Futures

One of the most important elements in asyncio are futures, which represent a process that has not yet finished. A future is an object that is supposed to have a result in the future and represents uncompleted tasks.

A good example for starting with asyncio is collecting all of the responses from its URL list and performing post-processing on them. In the following example, we are using an asyncio future object and passing whole lists of future objects as tasks to be executed in the loop. Each future is a task that is going to be executed in the loop.

 For more information on asyncio futures, check out the following documentation: `https://docs.python.org/3/library/asyncio-task. html#future`.

You can find the following code in the `future_example.py` file:

```
#!/usr/local/bin/python3

import asyncio
from aiohttp import ClientSession
import time

async def fetch(url, session):
    async with session.get(url) as response:
        # async operation must be preceded by await
        return await response.read()
```

In the following code block, we are defining our `execute` method, which uses the `ClientSession()` class from the `aiohttp` package for resolving requests and getting responses with the `async-await` pattern:

```
async def execute(loop):
    url = "http://httpbin.org/{}"
    tasks = []
    sites = ['headers','ip','user-agent']
    # Fetch all responses within one Client session,
    # keep connection alive for all requests.
    async with ClientSession() as session:
        for site in sites:
            task = asyncio.ensure_future(fetch(url.format(site), session))
            tasks.append(task)
        # async operation must be preceded by await
        responses = await asyncio.gather(*tasks)
        # you now have all response bodies in this variable
        for response in responses:
            print(response.decode())
```

This is our main program, which initializes the `event` loop and calls the `execute` method inside the context created by the `asyncio.ensure_future()` method. This is shown as follows:

```
if __name__ == '__main__':
    t1 = time.time()
    loop = asyncio.get_event_loop()
    future = asyncio.ensure_future(execute(loop))
    loop.run_until_complete(future)
    print(time.time() - t1, 'seconds passed')
```

Among the main methods we are using, we can highlight the following:

- `loop.run_until_complete()` is the `event` loop that runs until a particular coroutine completes.
- `asyncio.gather()` collects future objects in one place and waits for all of them to finish.
- `response.read()` is an async operation. This means that it does not return a result immediately—it just returns a generator. This generator still needs to be called and executed, but this does not happen by default; we need to use `await`.

The following is the output of the previous script, where we can see headers for request and response:

```
{
 "headers": {
 "Accept": "*/*",
 "Accept-Encoding": "gzip, deflate",
 "Host": "httpbin.org",
 "User-Agent": "Python/3.7 aiohttp/3.5.4"
 }
 }


{
 "origin": "192.113.65.10, 192.113.65.10"
 }


{
 "user-agent": "Python/3.7 aiohttp/3.5.4"
 }

0.4722881317138672 seconds passed
```

In this script, we were introduced to the `await` keyword, which is one of the fundamental building blocks of asynchronous programs in Python. The `await` keyword tells the Python interpreter that the succeeding expression is going to take some time to evaluate so that it can spend that time on other tasks.

Task manipulation with asyncio

The `asyncio` module provides the `asyncio.Task()` method to handle coroutines with tasks. The `asyncio.Task` class is a subclass of asyncio. Future and aims are used to manage coroutines. A task is responsible for the execution of a `coroutine` object in an `event` loop. When a coroutine is wrapped in a task, it connects the task to the `event` loop and then runs automatically when the loop is started, thus providing a mechanism to automatically drive the coroutine.

 For more information on task manipulation with asyncio, check out the following documentation: `https://docs.python.org/3.7/library/asyncio-task.html`.

You can find the following code in the `asyncio_task.py` file:

```python
#!/usr/bin/python3
import asyncio
import time

@asyncio.coroutine
def task_sleep(name, loop, seconds=1):
 future = loop.run_in_executor(None, time.sleep, seconds)
 print("[%s] coroutine will sleep for %d second(s)..." % (name, seconds))
 yield from future
 print("[%s] done!" % name)
```

In the previous code block, we defined the `task_sleep()` method annotated with `@asyncio.coroutine`, this method will execute the task with a specific time sleep, when execution is finished this time it will return the future.

In the next code block, we define our main program, where we define the event loop and our task list using `asyncio.task`.

We execute the tasks until complete with `run_until_complete()` method:

```python
if __name__ == '__main__':
 loop = asyncio.get_event_loop()
```

```
  tasks = [asyncio.Task(task_sleep('Task-A', loop, 10)),
asyncio.Task(task_sleep('Task-B', loop,5)),asyncio.Task(task_sleep('Task-
C', loop))]
  loop.run_until_complete(asyncio.gather(*tasks))
```

The following is the output of this script's execution:

```
[Task-A] coroutine will sleep for 10 second(s)...
[Task-B] coroutine will sleep for 5 second(s)...
[Task-C] coroutine will sleep for 1 second(s)...
[Task-C] done!
[Task-B] done!
[Task-A] done!
```

We can see how the first task ends with C, then B, and finally A, depending on the defined sleep times.

Downloading files with asyncio

In the following example, we will import the modules that we need and then create our first coroutine using the async syntax. This coroutine is called download_file, and it uses Python's requests module to download whatever file is passed to it. When it is done, it will return a message that's related to the file that is being downloaded.

You can find the following code in the download_files_asyncio.py file:

```
#!/usr/bin/python3

import asyncio
import os
import requests
import time

files =
['https://docs.python.org/3/archives/python-3.7.2-docs-pdf-letter.zip',
'https://docs.python.org/3/archives/python-3.7.2-docs-pdf-a4.zip']

async def download_file(url):
    response = requests.get(url)
    filename = os.path.basename(url)
    print('Downloading {filename}'.format(filename=filename))
    open(filename, 'wb').write(response.content)
    msg = 'Finished downloading {filename}'.format(filename=filename)
    return msg
```

In the previous code block, we defined our file list for downloading and the `download_file()` method, which accepts the URL that contains the file as a parameter. In the following code block, we are defining the main function that we are going to use for downloading files in an asynchronous way. We will do this by using coroutines with the `async-await` mechanism:

```python
async def main(files):
    coroutines = [download_file(file) for file in files]
    completed, pending = await asyncio.wait(coroutines)
    for item in completed:
        print(item.result())


if __name__ == '__main__':
    t1 = time.time()
    event_loop = asyncio.get_event_loop()
    try:
        event_loop.run_until_complete(main(files))
    finally:
        event_loop.close()
print(time.time() - t1, 'seconds passed')
```

This is the output of this script's execution:

```
Downloading python-3.7.2-docs-pdf-a4.zip
 Downloading python-3.7.2-docs-pdf-letter.zip
 Finished downloading python-3.7.2-docs-pdf-letter.zip
 Finished downloading python-3.7.2-docs-pdf-a4.zip
 11.149724960327148 seconds passed
```

In this execution, we can see the files to be downloaded, as well as the execution time for downloading these files.

Introducing aiohttp

The next module we are going to review is frequently used in conjunction with asyncio. This is because it provides a framework for working with asynchronous requests. It is an excellent solution for complementing the server part of a web application with Python 3.5+ as well.

The main tool for making requests is the `requests` module. The main problem with requests is that the thread is blocked until we obtain a response. By default, request operations are blocking. When the thread calls a method such as `get` or `post`, it pauses until the operation completes.

To download multiple resources at once, we need many threads. At this point, `aiohttp` allows us to make requests asynchronously. You can install aiohttp by using the `pip install aiohttp` command:

```
Collecting aiohttp
  Downloading https://files.pythonhosted.org/packages/bc/bd/08f0900d62b4ea1ca10bb2e2a1596ac3b04024c7daf7350debee0bd022fb
/aiohttp-3.5.4-cp37-cp37m-win_amd64.whl (611kB)
    100% |████████████████████████████████| 614kB 1.0MB/s
Collecting async-timeout<4.0,>=3.0 (from aiohttp)
  Using cached https://files.pythonhosted.org/packages/e1/1e/5a4441be21b0726c4464f3f23c8b19628372f606755a9d2e46c187e65ec
4/async_timeout-3.0.1-py3-none-any.whl
Collecting multidict<5.0,>=4.0 (from aiohttp)
  Downloading https://files.pythonhosted.org/packages/38/c7/07d8d88c3c16fe65d8596da429d104229dd7433b07432694a3ab45a72eaa
/multidict-4.5.2-cp37-cp37m-win_amd64.whl (138kB)
    100% |████████████████████████████████| 143kB 999kB/s
Collecting yarl<2.0,>=1.0 (from aiohttp)
  Downloading https://files.pythonhosted.org/packages/7d/dc/fb3617b3de980566b54b1ae59eb72fc72810350d7ed9164b26f155fa682d
/yarl-1.3.0-cp37-cp37m-win_amd64.whl (121kB)
    100% |████████████████████████████████| 122kB 885kB/s
Collecting chardet<4.0,>=2.0 (from aiohttp)
  Using cached https://files.pythonhosted.org/packages/bc/a9/01ffebfb562e4274b6487b4bb1ddec7ca55ec7510b22e4c51f14098443b
8/chardet-3.0.4-py2.py3-none-any.whl
Collecting attrs>=17.3.0 (from aiohttp)
  Downloading https://files.pythonhosted.org/packages/3a/e1/5f9023cc983f1a628a8c2fd051ad19e76ff7b142a0faf329336f9a62a514
/attrs-18.2.0-py2.py3-none-any.whl
Collecting idna>=2.0 (from yarl<2.0,>=1.0->aiohttp)
  Downloading https://files.pythonhosted.org/packages/14/2c/cd551d81dbe15200be1cf41cd03869a46fe7226e7450af7a6545bfc474c9
/idna-2.8-py2.py3-none-any.whl (58kB)
    100% |████████████████████████████████| 61kB 613kB/s
Installing collected packages: async-timeout, multidict, idna, yarl, chardet, attrs, aiohttp
Successfully installed aiohttp-3.5.4 async-timeout-3.0.1 attrs-18.2.0 chardet-3.0.4 idna-2.8 multidict-4.5.2 yarl-1.3.0
```

The documentation for aiohttp is available at `http://aiohttp.`
`readthedocs.io/en/stable`, and the source code is available at `https://`
`github.com/aio-libs/aiohttp`.

`ClientSession` is the recommended primary interface for `aiohttp` to make requests.
`ClientSession` allows you to store cookies between requests and keeps objects that are common for all requests (event loop, connection, and access resources).

After you open a client session, you can use it to make requests. At this point, we will execute the request where another asynchronous operation starts. The context manager's with statement ensures it will be closed properly in all cases.

To start the execution, you need to run it in an event loop, so you need to create an instance of the `asyncio` loop and add a task to it.

You can find the following code in the `aiohttp_request.py` file:

```
#!/usr/local/bin/python3

import asyncio
from aiohttp import ClientSession
import time

async def request():
    async with ClientSession() as session:
        async with session.get("http://httpbin.org/headers") as response:
            response = await response.read()
            print(response.decode())

if __name__ == '__main__':
    t1 = time.time()
    loop = asyncio.get_event_loop()
    loop.run_until_complete(request())
    print(time.time() - t1, 'seconds passed')
```

This is the output of the preceding script:

```
{
"headers": {
"Accept": "*/*",
"Accept-Encoding": "gzip, deflate",
"Host": "httpbin.org",
 "User-Agent": "Python/3.6 aiohttp/3.5.4"
}
}
```

In a similar way, we can use the `aiohttp` module to request a URL. We can do this with `aiohttp.ClientSession().get(url)`. In this example, we are using the `yield` keyword to await the response.

You can find the following code in the `aiohttp_single_request.py` file:

```
#!/usr/bin/python3

import asyncio
import aiohttp
url = 'http://httpbin.org/headers'

@asyncio.coroutine
def get_page():
    resp = yield from aiohttp.ClientSession().get(url)
    text = yield from resp.read()
    return text
```

```
if __name__ == '__main__':
    loop = asyncio.get_event_loop()
    content = loop.run_until_complete(get_page())
    print(content)
    loop.close()
```

This is the output of the preceding script:

```
Unclosed client session
client_session: <aiohttp.client.ClientSession object at
0x000001BFE94117F0>
Unclosed connector
connections: ['[(<aiohttp.client_proto.ResponseHandler object at
0x000001BFE954F708>, 789153.843)]']
connector: <aiohttp.connector.TCPConnector object at 0x000001BFE9411EB8>
b'{\n  "headers": {\n    "Accept": "*/*", \n    "Accept-Encoding": "gzip,
deflate", \n    "Host": "httpbin.org", \n "User-Agent": "Python/3.7
aiohttp/3.5.4"\n  }\n}\n'
```

Downloading files with aiohttp

First, we must import the modules we need to make our HTTP requests asynchronous. All asynchronous functions will need to have the `async` keyword in the function definition.

We will start by defining our `download_file` function, which will take two parameters: the first parameter is the URL for downloading the image, and the second parameter is called parts, which is the number of parallel requests we want to make to the server.

To make our asynchronous program faster, this is how our script is going to work:

1. We are going to make a head request to the file URL with the `aiohttp.ClientSession().head(url)` method.
2. We are going to get the value of the `Content-Length` header for getting the file size with the `size = int(resp.headers["Content-Length"])` instruction.
3. With the `get_partial_content` method, we are sending multiple `GET` requests to the file URL using the range header to specify the range of bytes that we want.
4. We are going assimilate all the responses using the `final_result = sorted(task.result() for task in response)` instruction.

You can find the following code in the `download_file_aiohttp.py` file:

```python
#!/usr/bin/python3

import asyncio
import itertools
import aiohttp
import time
import os

async def download_file(url, parts):
    async def get_partial_content(u, i, start, end):
        async with aiohttp.ClientSession().get(u, headers={"Range":
"bytes={}-{}".format(start, end - 1 if end else "")}) as _resp:
            return i, await _resp.read()

    async with aiohttp.ClientSession().head(url) as resp:
        size = int(resp.headers["Content-Length"])

    ranges = list(range(0, size, size // parts))

    response, _ = await asyncio.wait([get_partial_content(url, i, start,
end) for i, (start, end) in enumerate(itertools.zip_longest(ranges,
ranges[1:], fillvalue=""))])

    final_result = sorted(task.result() for task in response)
    return b"".join(data for _, data in final_result)
```

In the previous code block, we defined our `download_file()` method, which accepts the `url` and the `parts` number that divides requests as parameters. In the following code block, we are defining our main function, which we will use to download a file in an asynchronous way. We are going to use the `asyncio` event loop and the `run_until_complete()` method:

```python
if __name__ == '__main__':
    file_url =
'https://docs.python.org/3/archives/python-3.7.2-docs-pdf-letter.zip'
    loop = asyncio.get_event_loop()
    t1 = time.time()
    bs = loop.run_until_complete(download_file(file_url, 10))
    filename = os.path.basename(file_url)
    with open(filename, 'wb') as file_handle:
        file_handle.write(bs)
    print('Finished downloading {filename}'.format(filename=filename))
    print(time.time() - t1, 'seconds passed')
```

This is the output we get when we execute the `download_file_aiohttp.py` script:

```
client_session: <aiohttp.client.ClientSession object at 0x000001FABBB42DD8>
Unclosed connector
connections: ['[(<aiohttp.client_proto.ResponseHandler object at
0x000001FABBCEED08>, 715247.328)]']
connector: <aiohttp.connector.TCPConnector object at 0x000001FABBCE6C88>
Finished downloading python-3.7.2-docs-pdf-letter.zip
2.9168717861175537 seconds passed
```

When you execute the script, you will see information about the objects that were created internally by `aiohttp`, among which we can highlight `aiohttp.client.ClientSession` for managing the client session, `aiohttp.client_proto.ResponseHandler` for managing the response, and `aiohttp.connector.TCPConnector` for managing the connection.

Other event loop solutions

We can define event loops as abstractions that ease up by using polling functions to monitor events. Internally, event loops make use of `poller` objects, taking away the responsibility of the programmer to control the tasks of addition, removal, and control of events. Some examples of applications that implement event loops in Python are as follows:

- **Tornado web server** (http://www.tornadoweb.org/en/stable): Tornado uses epoll as the polling function if the environment is Linux and has kqueue support in the case of BSD or Mac OS X
- **Twisted** (https://twistedmatrix.com): This is a popular framework that offers an implementation of the event loop and is used by the Scrapy framework
- **Gevent** (http://www.gevent.org): This provides an event loop based on `libev`
- **Eventlet** (https://pypi.python.org/pypi/eventlet): This implements an event loop based on `libevent`

In this section, you have learned about the `asyncio` and `aiohttp` packages, which simplify the process of writing servers when using an event-driven approach, and we explained some uses cases related to file downloading in an asynchronous way. In the next section, we are going to introduce the Tornado framework for building asynchronous network applications.

Building asynchronous network applications with Tornado

In this section, you will learn about building asynchronous network applications with the Tornado framework.

Introducing Tornado

The traditional model for creating applications such as web servers that support several clients concurrently is based on a multithread system in which a new thread is created for each client that connects to the service. This results in a fairly high consumption of system resources and performance problems, which can be quite serious.

Tornado is a module written in Python that allows you to create asynchronous and non-blocking systems for network operations, where each request executed by a client can be asynchronous. The way in which the library is implemented allows you to scale to several thousand open connections, something that is ideal for applications that require connections with a long lifetime.

You can install it with the `pip install tornado` command or download the latest version that's available from our the GitHub repository (`https://github.com/tornadoweb/tornado`) and install it manually using the `setup.py` script.

Tornado can be considered an alternative to Twisted and is suitable for handling a large number of connections since it can respond to an incoming client, send a request to the controller, and not return a control to the client until the result of the call is obtained. Asynchronous processing facilitates functional decoupling and access to shared data. This works very well with a stateless design such as REST, or other service-oriented architectures.

You can get more information about the framework and the source code in the GitHub repository: `https://github.com/tornadoweb/tornado`.

Implementing the Tornado web server

Tornado has several classes and functions that allow you to create different types of network elements, both synchronous and asynchronous. In this particular case, we will focus on the module that allows for the creation of servers and web applications with Tornado. This will be useful to perform proof of concept and understand the operation of certain features in web environments.

The following script will allow for the creation of a basic web server using Tornado, which will accept normal HTTP connections if the user requests the '/' resource.

You can find the following code in the `tornado_web_server.py` file:

```python
#!/usr/bin/python3

import tornado.ioloop
import tornado.web
from tornado.options import define, options

class MyHandler(tornado.web.RequestHandler):
    def get(self):
        self.render("index.html")

if __name__ == '__main__':
    define("port", default=8080, help="run on the given port", type=int)
    app = tornado.web.Application([('/', MyHandler)])
    app.listen(options.port)
    print("Tornado web server listening on port 8080");
    tornado.ioloop.IOLoop.instance().start()
```

The `tornado.web.Application` object is responsible for defining the URIs that are available to the web server. In this specific case, it has been defined that the user will be able to access the path '/'. If the user requests the resource '/', the server will be responsible for executing the `MyHandler` handler.

The `MyHandler` class inherits from the `tornado.web.RequestHandler` class, which is responsible for processing HTTP requests that are made by clients that use the GET method. In this case, the class is simply responsible for responding to the client with the `index.html` page.

Finally, the actual definition of the web server is given by an instance of the `tornado.ioloop.IOLoop` class which is responsible for creating a thread that will run indefinitely and use the options per line of commands that have been defined by means of the `tornado.options.define` function.

With all of the preceding information under our belt, it is now possible to run the web server with the following command:

```
$ python tornado_web_server.py
```

When you execute the preceding command, you will see the following message on your console:

```
Tornado web server listening on port 8080
```

If the user requests the resource '/', the server will respond with the index.html page, as shown in the following screenshot:

In this section, we have analyzed how to create our own server with Tornado using the event loop that's provided by the tornado.ioloop package.

Implementing an asynchronous client with AsyncHTTPClient

Tornado includes a class called AsyncHTTPClient, which performs HTTP requests asynchronously. The first thing is to create our application, which will inherit from application. Then, we will run an HTTP server that supports our application. Next, we will indicate in which port we want the server to listen. Finally, we will launch the event loop, which will listen to requests with the IOLoop.current().start() instruction.

In the following example, we are using the `fetch` method of `AsyncHTTPClient`, which specifies the method or function that will be called when the HTTP request is complete as a `callback` parameter. In this example, we specified the `on_response` method as the `callback`. Also note the use of the `@tornado.web.asynchronous` decorator and the call to `self.finish()` at the end of the `callback` response method.

You can find the following code in the `tornado_request_async.py` file:

```python3
#!/usr/bin/python3

import tornado.ioloop
import tornado.web
import tornado.httpclient

class Handler(tornado.web.RequestHandler):
 @tornado.web.asynchronous
 def get(self):
 http_client = tornado.httpclient.AsyncHTTPClient()
 http_client.fetch("https://www.google.com/search?q=python",
callback=self.on_response)

 def on_response(self, response):
 self.write(response.body)
 self.finish()
```

In the previous code block, we define our Handler class that extends from `tornado.web.RequestHandler`. This class contains the asynchronous `get()` method and `on_response()` method, which is called when getting a response from the `http_client` object.

In the following code block we define our main program, where we define the event loop and our application managed by the `Handler` class:

```python
if __name__ == '__main__':
 app = tornado.web.Application([ tornado.web.url(r"/", Handler)])
 app.listen(8080)
 tornado.ioloop.IOLoop.current().start()
```

If we execute this script and go to (`http://localhost:8080`), we will see the response related to the Python search in the Google domain.

Another way to implement an asynchronous client is to create a `TornadoAsyncClient()` class with a method that handle requests. In this example, we can see this implementation where the URL is requested as a parameter in the script.

You can find the following code in the `tornado_async_client.py` file:

```python
#!/usr/bin/python3

import argparse
import tornado.ioloop
import tornado.httpclient

class TornadoAsyncClient():
 def handle_request(self,response):
 if response.error:
 print ("Error:", response.error)
 else:
 print(response.body)
 tornado.ioloop.IOLoop.instance().stop()
```

In the previous code block, we define our `TornadoAsyncClient` class that manages the request and the `event` loop.

In the next code block we define our `run_server()` method and main program , where we instantiate the `TornadoAsyncClient` class, starting the `event` loop, and set the `url` parameter to do the request:

```python
def run_server(url):
 tornadoAsync = TornadoAsyncClient()
 http_client = tornado.httpclient.AsyncHTTPClient()
 http_client.fetch(url, tornadoAsync.handle_request)
 tornado.ioloop.IOLoop.instance().start()

if __name__ == '__main__':
 parser = argparse.ArgumentParser(description='Tornado async client')
 parser.add_argument('--url', action="store", dest="url", type=str,
required=True)
 given_args = parser.parse_args()
 url = given_args.url
 run_server(url)
```

The previous execution script will create a Tornado server that will execute requests asynchronously. To execute it, it is necessary to pass the URL that we want to obtain the response from as a parameter:

```
usage: tornado_async_client.py [-h] --url URL
tornado_async_client.py: error: the following arguments are required: --url
```

When you run the preceding command, you will see the response body of the URL that is passed as a parameter.

Asynchronous generators

Another way to write asynchronous code in Tornado is by using coroutines. Instead of using a `callback` function for processing the response, we can use the `yield` keyword to resume and suspend the execution. Tornado 2.1 introduced the `tornado.gen.coroutine` module, which provides a pattern for performing asynchronous requests.

You can find the following code in the `tornado_request_async_coroutine.py` file:

```python
#!/usr/bin/python3

import tornado.ioloop
import tornado.web
import tornado.httpclient

class Handler(tornado.web.RequestHandler):
 @tornado.web.asynchronous
 @tornado.gen.coroutine
 def get(self):
 http_client = tornado.httpclient.AsyncHTTPClient()
 response = yield tornado.gen.Task(http_client.fetch,
"https://www.google.com/search?q=python")
 self.write(response.body)
```

In the previous code block, we define our Handler class that extends from `tornado.web.RequestHandler`. This class contains the asynchronous `get()` method and write body response when getting a response from the `http_client` object.

In the next code block, we define our main program, where we define the event loop and our application managed by the `Handler` class:

```python
if __name__ == '__main__':
 app = tornado.web.Application([tornado.web.url(r"/", Handler)])
 app.listen(8080)
 tornado.ioloop.IOLoop.current().start()
```

As you can see, this code is identical to the previous version of the code. The main difference is in how we call the `fetch` method of the `AsyncHTTPClient` object.

In the example in the *Asynchronous generators* section, we will be using Python's yield keyword, which returns control of the program to Tornado, allowing it to execute other tasks while the HTTP request is in progress. When the task is completed, this instruction returns the HTTP response in the request handler and the code is easier to understand.

Note the use of the `@tornado.gen.coroutine` decorator just before the definition of the `get` method. This decorator allows Tornado to use internally the `tornado.gen.Task` class. For more details, you can look over the module documentation, which can be found at `http://www.tornadoweb.org/en/stable/gen.html`.

Utilities in Tornado for asynchronous network operations

The `tornado.netutil` module includes several functions that are quite useful for both clients and servers. The use of some of these functions are commented as follows:

```
>>> from tornado import netutil

>>> sockets = netutil.bind_sockets(8080)

>>> sockets

[<socket.socket fd=1108, family=AddressFamily.AF_INET6,
type=SocketKind.SOCK_STREAM, proto=0, laddr=('::', 8080, 0, 0)>,
<socket.socket fd=1112, family=AddressFamily.AF_INET,
type=SocketKind.SOCK_STREAM, proto=0, laddr=('0.0.0.0', 8080)>]

>>> netutil.is_valid_ip('127.0.0.1')
True

>>> netutil.is_valid_ip('::1')
True

>>> netutil.is_valid_ip('::11111')
False

>>> dnsResolver = netutil.Resolver()

>>> dnsResolver
<tornado.netutil.DefaultExecutorResolver object at 0x0341FD10>

>>> dnsResolver.resolve('www.packtpub.com',80)

<Future pending
cb=[_make_coroutine_wrapper.<locals>.wrapper.<locals>.<lambda>()>
```

The `bind_sockets` function is responsible for creating the sockets in all of the available network interfaces and returns a list with each of the references that were created.

The `is_valid_ip` function validates whether an IPv4 or IPv6 address is valid or not.

Finally, the `Resolver` class allows you to configure several types of resolvers for blocking and non-blocking DNS requests. The default resolver is `tornado.netutil.DefaultExecutorResolver`.

For more information about the utilities that are available in Tornado, it is recommended to review the documentation, which can be found at `http://tornado.readthedocs.org/en/latest/netutil.html`.

In this section, we have reviewed the Tornado framework for creating asynchronous and non-blocking systems. In the following section, we are going to review the Twisted framework for developing asynchronous applications using an event-driven network engine.

Building asynchronous network applications with Twisted

In this section, you will learn about building asynchronous network applications with the Twisted framework.

Introduction to Twisted

Twisted is an event-driven network engine that can be used to develop asynchronous and publish/subscribe-based applications.

Twisted can be obtained from the PyPI repository at `https://pypi.org/project/Twisted`. You may need to install some additional packages on Windows and Linux hosts. The installation procedure is documented at `https://twistedmatrix.com/trac`. You can use the `pip install twisted` command to install Twisted and its dependencies.

If you are under an Debian/Ubuntu operating system, another way to download and install Twisted is to use the following command:

```
sudo apt-get install python-twisted
```

For other platforms, the latest versions of Twisted and its dependencies can be found at `https://twistedmatrix.com/trac/wiki/Downloads`.

Twisted is based on the paradigm of event-driven programming, meaning that Twisted users can write small predefined callbacks in the framework to perform complex tasks.

The Twisted design is based on the complete separation between logical protocols (which usually depend on the semantic connection based on streams or flows, such as HTTP or POP3) and transport in physical layers that are supported as semantics in streams (such as files, sockets libraries, or SSL).

Protocols

Twisted is a network framework that implements a large number of protocols. It uses the paradigm known as event-driven programming, where the flow of a program is determined by the events that occur during its execution. The main objective of this framework is to provide a solution to the problems that are established by the use of sockets at a low level, mediating with threads and with the problems that this also presents (for example, access to shared data).

Twisted implements a multitude of protocols that we can use in our applications in a simple and asynchronous way—it contains a web server, instant messaging clients, chat servers, mail servers and clients, servers and SSH clients, and much more.

Twisted is designed to separate the logical protocols (SMTP, HTTP, and SSH) and transport in physical layers (sockets or SSL). The connection between protocols and layers takes place at the last moment just before the data is delivered to the logical protocol instance. It is at that moment when the protocol layer can make use of the transport layer, that is, as long as they are semantically compatible.

Twisted is responsible for reading data through the protocol that it integrates with the `protocol.Protocol` class, which is from the `twisted.internet` package.

The most common use of Twisted is for the definition of the type protocol, which is used from a Twisted factory. It is responsible for managing connections. Finally, we use a `reactor` object to establish the endpoint of the factory.

Objects of the protocol type are non-persistent, which means that they are created and destroyed after each connection, while a factory is an object with a state where the information is kept between several connections.

Building a basic Twisted server

At the time of making a server using the Python socket libraries, a loop was implemented that is in charge of verifying the new connections. We will manage the event handlers with Twisted.

We can manage events for many situations, such as a new connection by a client, the reception of data, or whether a client has been disconnected. These event handlers are defined in a protocol, and this protocol needs a `Factory` that can build the objects of the events. This may sound confusing, but the code will make everything clearer.

In the following example, we are going to write a basic server using the Twisted framework. You can find the following code in the `twisted_basic_server.py` file:

```python
#!/usr/bin/python3

from twisted.internet import reactor
from twisted.internet.protocol import Protocol, Factory

class MessageLogger(Protocol):
    def connectionMade(self):
        print('Client connection from:', self.transport.client)

    def connectionLost(self, reason):
        print('Client disconnected from:', self.transport.client)

    def dataReceived(self, data):
        self.transport.write(data)
        print("Message sent by the client: ", data.decode("utf-8"))
```

In the previous code block, we defined our `MessageLogger` class, which functions as a protocol. In the following code block, we are defining the `MessageFactory` class for managing the connection. Finally, our main program connects the protocol to a server running on port `8080` using the `MessageFactory` class:

```python
class MessageFactory(Factory):
    def buildProtocol(self, addr):
        return MessageLogger()

    def clientConnectionFailed(self, connector, reason):
        print ("Connection failed")
        reactor.stop()

    def clientConnectionLost(self, connector, reason):
        print ("Connection lost")
        reactor.stop()
```

```
#this connects the protocol to a server running on port 8080
if __name__ == '__main__':
    #factory = Factory()
    #factory.protocol = MessageLogger
    reactor.listenTCP(8080, MessageFactory())
    reactor.run()
```

We will start by creating a server that forwards everything it receives. Then, we will use a basic client using the standard `socket` module to test the code.

The first thing we need to do is import the necessary libraries and components, which in this case, are the reactor, protocol, and factory. Then, we will handle the events within a class, such as when we have a new connection, `connectionMade`, a lost connection, `connectionLost`, and if we receive data, `dataReceived`.

This is a simple server program that forwards everything it receives. To achieve this, a protocol must be established. It is for that reason that a new class is created, `MessageLogger`, of which there will be one instance per connection. The `dataReceived` method is an event that will be called for each portion of data that has been received. This data is passed to the event in a data argument, which is then used to send what has been received to the client:

```
class MessageLogger(Protocol):
    def dataReceived(self, data):
        self.transport.write(data)
        print("Message sent by the client: ", data.decode("utf-8"))
```

`self.transport` is an instance of `twisted.internet.tcp.Server`, through which we send data to the client.

Factory

The class that's responsible for creating a `MessageLogger` instance for each client that connects to our server is the `MessageFactory` class, which is an instance of `twisted.internet.protocol.Factory`. It is responsible for making protocols for each incoming connection.

`buildProtocol` is an event that will be called every time an incoming connection is found. It will assign a protocol to it. In this way, each connection will be tied to a protocol that's specified by the developer in this method. In this case, all connections will be handled through the same `MessageLogger` protocol, which forwards everything that's received.

We will make an instance of `Factory` that will be in charge of building the necessary objects. We will also specify that its protocol will be the class that we have made. Finally, we will make our program listen in a specific port with a reactor.

The following is the class we used for defining our `Factory` class. This will be instantiated every time an incoming connection is received:

```
class MessageFactory(Factory):
    def buildProtocol(self, addr):
        return MessageLogger()
```

The argument that `buildProtocol` receives is an instance of `IPv4Address` or `IPv6Address`, as appropriate. It contains information about the client, and the incoming connection, such as the IP address and port, among other things. This data can also be accessed in the protocol through the `self.transport.getPeer` function.

Reactor

Twisted implements the reactor design pattern, which describes how to obtain and redirect events from multiple sources to their respective handlers in a single thread.

The Twisted core is the reactor event loop. The event loop waits for these events and then processes them, abstracting specific behavior of a platform and presenting interfaces to facilitate the response.

The reactor is the main `Twisted` loop, and is responsible for calling the events at the appropriate time and alternating between the different connections to achieve (rather than simulate) concurrency.

For creating a reactor that's listening in a specific port, we can use the `listenTCP()` method. We will pass in the port and the `Factory` class that was created in the *Factory* section as parameters:

```
reactor.listenTCP(8080, MessageFactory())
reactor.run()
```

In this case, it is used to listen to TCP connections through port `8080`. As a second parameter, an instance of our factory is passed, which, as we indicated previously, is responsible for assigning a protocol to each incoming connection.

Finally, we execute the main loop by calling the `reactor.run()` function.

Building a socket client

For simplicity, our client will be a socket that connects to our server that was developed with Twisted.

You can find the following code in the `socket_client.py` file:

```python
#!/usr/bin/env python3
from socket import socket

s = socket()
s.connect(("127.0.0.1", 8080))
while True:
    output_data = input("Enter message> ")
    if output_data:
        s.send(output_data.encode())
        input_data = s.recv(1024)
        if input_data:
            print(input_data.decode("utf-8"))
```

In this section, we have analyzed how to create our own socket client for communicating with the Twisted server on port 8080.

Executing the client and server

First, we need to run the server with the following command:

```
$ python twisted_basic_server.py
```

At this moment, the server is waiting for connections from the client. If we run the client, we can write any message in the console and you will see how the server responds with what it has received. The following could be the messages that the server receives from two connected clients:

```
Client connection from: ('127.0.0.1', 8229)
 Message sent by the client: hi this is my message
 Message sent by the client: Message from client 1
 Client connection from: ('127.0.0.1', 8282)
 Message sent by the client: Message from client 2
 Client disconnected from: ('127.0.0.1', 8282)
 Client disconnected from: ('127.0.0.1', 8229)
```

The `twisted_basic_server.py` script starts a TCP server listening for connections on port 8080.

This script sends the information through the transport channel using the `MessageLoggerprotocol` class. The client socket establishes a TCP connection to the server, resending the server response, terminating the connection, and stopping the reactor. The `MessageFactory` class is used to connect both client and server, creating instances of the `MessageLogger` class.

Communication is asynchronous on both sides; `connectTCP` is in charge of registering the callbacks in the reactor so that we're notified when the information is available to be read from the socket.

Building a Twisted client

For creating a Twisted client, we can follow the same programming model we used for creating a server with Twisted. Basically, we need to define a protocol type, a factory, and a reactor.

To create clients with Twisted, we can use the `TCP4ClientEndpoint` class to establish a connection with the server. We will use the `connectProtocol` method and pass through the host and the port as parameters.

There are multiple classes and utilities to make connections to remote servers using Twisted. The use of such classes depends on the protocol that's used for communication with the server.

You can find the following code in the `twisted_basic_client.py` file:

```python
#!/usr/bin/python3

from twisted.internet import reactor
from twisted.internet.protocol import Protocol
from twisted.internet.protocol import ClientFactory

class MyTwistedClient(Protocol):
 def connectionMade(self):
 self.transport.write('Connection established'.encode())

 def connectionLost(self, reason):
 print('Connection Lost %s ' %(reason))

 def dataReceived(self, data):
 print('Server data: ', data)
 self.transport.loseConnection()
```

In the previous code block, we defined our `MyTwistedClient` class that functions as protocol. In the following code block, we define the `MyTwistedClientFactory` class for managing the connection.

Finally, our main program that connects the protocol to a server running on port 8080 using the `MyTwistedClientFactory())` class is as follows:

```python
class MyTwistedClientFactory(ClientFactory):
 protocol = MyTwistedClient

 def clientConnectionFailed(self, connector, reason):
 print('Connection Failed')
 reactor.stop()

 def clientConnectionLost(self, connector, reason):
 print('Connection Lost')
 reactor.stop()

reactor.connectTCP('localhost', 8080, MyTwistedClientFactory())
reactor.run()
```

In this section, we have built our own Twisted client for communicating with a Twisted server on port 8080. In this case, we are creating a class called `MyTwistedClient` that acts as protocol, as well as a class called `MyTwistedClientFactory`, which manages connections between the client and server.

Building a Twisted web server

Twisted contains a series of classes and utilities to create various types of servers and clients. It is possible to create configurations for web servers and configurations to use the SSL protocol between clients and servers. In this example, we are developing a server that receives HTTP requests.

You can find the following code in the `twisted_web_server.py` file:

```python
#!/usr/bin/env python3

from twisted.internet import reactor
from twisted.web import server, resource

class TwistedResource(resource.Resource):
    def render_GET(self, request):
        return b"<html><center><h1>Twisted server is running on port
8080</h1></center></html>"
```

```
root = resource.Resource()
root.putChild(b"twisted", TwistedResource())
site = server.Site(root)
reactor.listenTCP(8080, site)
reactor.run()
```

The following is the output of the web server after executing this script:

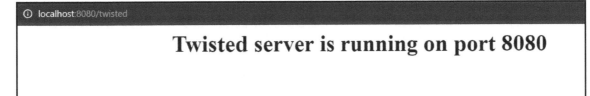

In this section, we have analyzed how to create our own server with Twisted by using the `event` loop that was provided by the `twisted.internet` package.

Building asynchronous network applications with Celery

In this section, you will learn about building asynchronous network applications with the Celery framework.

Celery architecture

Celery is an efficient and scalable way to execute tasks asynchronously and acts as a distributor of high-level tasks where tasks are queued and run concurrently using various paradigms such as `multiprocessing` or `gevent`.

An efficient and scalable way to perform tasks asynchronously is to use a queue library as Celery. With this library, you define workers that are processes for executing the heavy tasks. An interesting aspect of this solution is that there can be many workers (even in different servers) executing the tasks.

The architecture of the solution is as follows:

- **Consumer**: This is the application that users use. If it is a web application, it can be a Django or Flask application.

- **Producer**: This is the worker who does the heavy work.
- **Broker**: This is the mechanism that the consumer uses to store the pending work.
- **Backend**: This is the mechanism that's used by the producer to store the results of the task.

At this point, we can see how the elements interact with each other in the Celery architecture:

- The consumer application is responsible for generating tasks that will receive a message broker like RabbitMQ or Redis. In this chapter, we will work with the Redis message broker.
- The message broker allows you to send and receive messages, and it generates tasks to be executed in Celery workers.
- When the tasks are finished, Celery stores this information in the form of events.

Installing Celery

Celery is a set of tools that allows us to easily work with multiple services, with some syntactic sugar and annotations in the code. It is a way of launching services that see them as tasks. First, we will need to install Celery with the following command:

```
pip install celery
```

The most important concept that Celery handles are tasks. Celery offers the ability to execute them in real time, or to be scheduled synchronously or asynchronously through the use of processes or system events.

The broker is the channel that's used to transport messages from one service to another. In this case, we are going to use a message queue. Celery can use other services to send and receive messages. These messages are usually the tasks or the results of the tasks. In this case, we will use Redis since it is very easy to install and configure for related tasks such as caching and publisher/subscriber models.

Installing Redis

You can install Redis by following the instructions on the *Redis Quick Start* page (`https://redis.io/topics/quickstart`). It is also necessary to install the Redis Python library, `pip install redis`, since this package is required for using Redis and Celery:

```
pip install celery [redis]
```

To install Redis for the Windows operating system, you can choose either of these sources:

- https://github.com/MSOpenTech/redis/releases
- https://github.com/rgl/redis/downloads

If you are working in a Windows operating syatem, you can download `Redis-x64-2.8.2104.zip` and extract the ZIP to the prepared directory and execute the `redis-server.exe` file.

In the following screenshot, we can see the execution of the Redis server on port `6379`:

In you are on a Unix operating system, you can start the Redis server with the following command:

```
$ redis-server
```

Introduction to Redis

Basically, Redis is a tool for data structures in memory and is used as a database cache. With it, most of the data is in memory, making the request for information that's required through queries much faster.

We can create a connection to Redis from Python by using the `redis-py` package, where `port=6379` and `db=0` are default values:

```
>>> import redis
>>> redis_client = redis.Redis(host='localhost', port=6379, db=0)
>>> print(redis_client)
Redis<ConnectionPool<Connection<host=localhost,port=6379,db=0>>>
```

Now that we are connected to Redis, we can start reading and writing data. The following instruction writes the my_value to the Redis my_key key, reads it back, and prints it:

```
>>> redis_client.set('my_key','my_value')
True
>>> redis_client.get('my_key')
b'my_value'
```

With Redis, we can also manage lists in an easy way. These are the methods we can use for managing this list:

- rpush: Allows you to insert elements at the end of the list
- llen: Returns the list's length
- lindex: Returns the element passing a specific index as a parameter, where the first element is index 0
- lrange: Returns elements from a list, passing the name of the list and indexes for the start and end elements as parameters:

```
>>> redis_client.rpush('my_list', 'http')
1
>>> redis_client.rpush('my_list', 'ftp')
2
>>> redis_client.rpush('my_list', 'smtp')
3
>>> redis_client.rpush('my_list', 'tcp')
4
>>> redis_client.rpush('my_list', 'udp')
5
>>> redis_client.llen('my_list')
5
>>> redis_client.lindex('my_list',2)
B'smtp'

>>> redis_client.lrange('my_list',0,4)
[b'http', b'ftp', b'smtp', b'tcp', b'udp']
```

In the previous script execution, we can see how we can add elements in the redis_client list, get the list's length, get an element from a specific index, and get elements from the start and end indexes of the list.

Distributing Python with Celery and Redis

The following is a simple application that uses Redis as a broker, where `consumer.py` sends messages to `producer.py`. Both the consumer and the producer require this configuration, where you can use the database with number 0 of your local Redis installation:

```
app = Celery
('celery_tasks',broker='redis://localhost:6379/0',backend='redis://localhost
:6379/0')
```

To establish a connection with Celery, we need to set broker and `backend` parameters. The `broker` parameter allows specification of the server address, where the tasks are stored and the `backend` parameter is the address where Celery puts the results so that we can use them in our application. In this case, both addresses are the same, executing in localhost in the same port.

To start building things with Celery, we will first need to create a Celery application with the following command:

```
$ celery -A producer worker --loglevel=debug --concurrency=4 --pool=solo
```

The different options that can be used when starting a worker are detailed in the Celery documentation, which can be found at `http://docs.celeryproject.org/en/latest/reference/celery.bin.worker.html#module-celery.bin.worker`.

In the following screenshot, we can see the execution of the previous command:

```
[2019-02-25 14:40:19,150: DEBUG/MainProcess] | worker: Preparing bootsteps.
[2019-02-25 14:40:19,150: DEBUG/MainProcess] | worker: Building graph...
[2019-02-25 14:40:19,150: DEBUG/MainProcess] | worker: New boot order: {Beat, StateDB, Timer, Hub, Pool, Autoscaler, Consumer}
[2019-02-25 14:40:19,181: DEBUG/MainProcess] | Consumer: Preparing bootsteps.
[2019-02-25 14:40:19,181: DEBUG/MainProcess] | Consumer: Building graph...
[2019-02-25 14:40:19,219: DEBUG/MainProcess] | Consumer: New boot order: {Connection, Events, Heart, Agent, Mingle, Tasks, Control,
sip, event loop}

 -------------- celery@LES005256 v4.2.1 (windowlicker)
---- **** -----
--- * ***  * -- Windows-10-10.0.15063-SP0 2019-02-25 14:40:19
-- * - **** ---
- ** ---------- [config]
- ** ---------- .> app:         celery_tasks:0x4954b10
- ** ---------- .> transport:   redis://localhost:6379/0
- ** ---------- .> results:     redis://localhost:6379/0
- *** --- * --- .> concurrency: 4 (prefork)
-- ******* ---- .> task events: OFF (enable -E to monitor tasks in this worker)
--- ***** -----
 -------------- [queues]
                .> celery           exchange=celery(direct) key=celery


[tasks]
  . celery.accumulate
  . celery.backend_cleanup
  . celery.chain
  . celery.chord
  . celery.chord_unlock
  . celery.chunks
  . celery.group
  . celery.map
  . celery.starmap
  . producer.task_execution
```

After that, Celery needs to know what kind of tasks it can execute. For this, we have to register the tasks for the Celery application. This is the content of `producer.py`, which exposes a task called `task_execution` that takes five seconds before printing the result. We will do this with the `@app.task` decorator.

You can find the following code in the `producer.py` file:

```
!/usr/bin/python3

from celery import Celery
from time import sleep

app = Celery('celery_tasks',broker='redis://localhost:6379/0',
backend='redis://localhost:6379/0')

@app.task
def task_execution(message):
    sleep(5)
    print('Message received: %s' % message)
```

The following is the `consumer.py` code. All it does is receive a message from the console and send it to the producer:

```
#!/usr/bin/python3
from producer import task_execution

while True:
    message = input('Enter Message> ')
    task_execution.delay(message)
```

The consumer runs with the following command:

```
$ python consumer.py
Enter Message> This is my message
```

When writing a message to the consumer, you can see that the producer receives it and, after 5 seconds, prints it. The interesting thing is that the consumer does not need to wait 5 seconds—it is instantly available to process another message. If the producer receives many messages, then they are added to the message queue.

Also, keep in mind that the records are now in the standard output of the Celery processes, so check them out at the appropriate Terminal.

In the following screenshot, you can see the output when you send a message from the consumer Terminal in debug mode:

```
[2019-03-14 17:05:48,496: INFO/MainProcess] Received task: producer.task_execution[69b6d8b6-5389-4f
a1-931d-ea7f53a1b5b2]
[2019-03-14 17:05:48,497: DEBUG/MainProcess] TaskPool: Apply <function _fast_trace_task at 0x0481E2
70> (args:('producer.task_execution', '69b6d8b6-5389-4fa1-931d-ea7f53a1b5b2', {'lang': 'py', 'task'
: 'producer.task_execution', 'id': '69b6d8b6-5389-4fa1-931d-ea7f53a1b5b2', 'shadow': None, 'eta': N
one, 'expires': None, 'group': None, 'retries': 0, 'timelimit': [None, None], 'root_id': '69b6d8b6-
5389-4fa1-931d-ea7f53a1b5b2', 'parent_id': None, 'argsrepr': "('This is the message',)", 'kwargsrep
r': '{}', 'origin': 'gen36412@LES005256', 'reply_to': 'f40843f4-6ad3-3c34-9e04-cadcf13977a2', 'corr
elation_id': '69b6d8b6-5389-4fa1-931d-ea7f53a1b5b2', 'delivery_info': {'exchange': '', 'routing_key
': 'celery', 'priority': 0, 'redelivered': None}}, b'[["This is the message"], {}, {"callbacks": nu
ll, "errbacks": null, "chain": null, "chord": null}]', 'application/json', 'utf-8') kwargs:{})
[2019-03-14 17:05:48,499: DEBUG/MainProcess] Task accepted: producer.task_execution[69b6d8b6-5389-4
fa1-931d-ea7f53a1b5b2] pid:41300
```

In the following screenshot, you can see the output when you send a message from the consumer Terminal with info mode, `--loglevel=info`:

```
[2019-03-14 17:31:10,666: INFO/MainProcess] Connected to redis://localhost:6379/0
[2019-03-14 17:31:10,678: INFO/MainProcess] mingle: searching for neighbors
[2019-03-14 17:31:11,704: INFO/MainProcess] mingle: all alone
[2019-03-14 17:31:11,724: INFO/MainProcess] celery@LES005256 ready.
[2019-03-14 17:31:19,928: INFO/MainProcess] Received task: producer.task_execution[901aef18-f
2ba-471b-a0dd-e7f596102e42]
[2019-03-14 17:31:24,929: WARNING/MainProcess] Message received: This is the message
[2019-03-14 17:31:24,934: INFO/MainProcess] Task producer.task_execution[901aef18-f2ba-471b-a
0dd-e7f596102e42] succeeded in 5.0s: None
```

There is the option to put the consumer and producer in the script.

You can find the following code in the `demo_celery.py` file:

```python
#!/usr/bin/python3

# Celery full example: publisher/subscriber
from celery import Celery

# Redis
app = Celery('demo_celery', broker='redis://localhost:6379/0',
backend='redis://localhost:6379/0')

@app.task
def task_execution(message,count):
 array=[]
 print('Message received: %s' % message)
 for index in range(0,int(count)):
 array.append(message)
 return (array)
```

In the previous code block, we defined our Celery application using `redis` as a message broker. The `task_execution()` method is annotated with `@app.task`. This method will add the message in array that will return.

In the next code block, we define infinite loop to request user message. For each message, it generates a task calling the `task_execution()` method:

```
def main():
 while True:
 message = input('Enter Message> ')
 count = input('Enter times appears the message> ')
 promise = task_execution.delay(message,count)

if __name__ == '__main__':
 main()
```

In this example, we are using the `eventlet` event manager. You can install it with the `pip install eventlet` command. With the `-P gevent` command parameter, we can execute Celery with the following manager event:

```
$ celery -A demo_celery worker --loglevel=debug --concurrency=4 -P gevent
```

This is the output when you enter the number of message and times you want it to appear in the message.

In the following screenshot, we can see how its execution returns an array with the message repeated as many times as you have entered:

```
[2019-03-14 17:38:46,676: INFO/MainProcess] Received task: demo_celery.task_execution[9
3533208-285b-4b6f-97ab-0b147139f092]
[2019-03-14 17:38:46,678: DEBUG/MainProcess] TaskPool: Apply <function _fast_trace_task
 at 0x03569BB8> (args:('demo_celery.task_execution', '93533208-285b-4b6f-97ab-0b147139f
092', {'lang': 'py', 'task': 'demo_celery.task_execution', 'id': '93533208-285b-4b6f-97
ab-0b147139f092', 'shadow': None, 'eta': None, 'expires': None, 'group': None, 'retries
': 0, 'timelimit': [None, None], 'root_id': '93533208-285b-4b6f-97ab-0b147139f092', 'pa
rent_id': None, 'argsrepr': "('This is the message', '4')", 'kwargsrepr': '{}', 'origin
': 'gen45476@LES005256', 'reply_to': '3585f47a-bfed-3708-82fb-0ef67d37c111', 'correlati
on_id': '93533208-285b-4b6f-97ab-0b147139f092', 'delivery_info': {'exchange': '', 'rout
ing_key': 'celery', 'priority': 0, 'redelivered': None}}, b'[["This is the message", "4
"], {}, {"callbacks": null, "errbacks": null, "chain": null, "chord": null}]', 'applica
tion/json', 'utf-8') kwargs:{})
[2019-03-14 17:38:46,683: DEBUG/MainProcess] Task accepted: demo_celery.task_execution[
93533208-285b-4b6f-97ab-0b147139f092] pid:47872
[2019-03-14 17:38:46,684: WARNING/MainProcess] Message received: This is the message
[2019-03-14 17:38:46,694: INFO/MainProcess] Task demo_celery.task_execution[93533208-28
5b-4b6f-97ab-0b147139f092] succeeded in 0.015999999945051968s: ['This is the message',
'This is the message', 'This is the message', 'This is the message']
```

In this section, you have learned about the Celery and Redis projects for building applications. They allow you to send messages between a consumer and a producer with the help of a broker as a mechanism, which allows a consumer to store pending tasks.

Summary

In this chapter, we reviewed some frameworks and libraries that try to solve the problem of sequential programming by using event-driven programming, in which a single main loop is executed. This is responsible for calling the functions that are defined by the programmer, known as events. In this way, in a server that serves information to several clients, it is possible to share this information among all the connections without having to worry about blocking or allowing access to it. We reviewed asyncio, aiohttp, Tornado, Twisted, and Celery for building asynchronous network applications.

In the next chapter, you will learn about the basics of Python web frameworks and developing web applications with the Flask framework and SQLAlchemy.

Questions

1. What is the main advantage of using aiohttp regarding the requests module for HTTP requests?
2. What are the classes from the `concurrent.futures` package that use the executor abstract base class?
3. What is the most important concept within asyncio that allows us to write asynchronous code using either callbacks or coroutines?
4. Which class from asyncio is a subclass of `asyncio.Future` and allows you to encapsulate and manage coroutines?
5. Which keyword from asyncio tells the Python interpreter that the succeeding expression is going to take some time to evaluate so that it can spend that time on other tasks?
6. Which Tornado class is responsible for defining the URIs that are available for the web server?
7. Which Tornado class can perform HTTP requests asynchronously?
8. Which method, when creating a protocol with Twisted, will be called for each portion of data that has been received?
9. What is the event, when working with Twisted, that will be called every time an incoming connection is found, so that you can assign a protocol to it?
10. What Twisted class can we use to create clients to establish a connection with the server?

Further reading

In the following links, you will find more information about the tools mentioned and the official Python documentation for some of the modules that we talked about in this chapter:

- *Python ThreadPoolExecutor Tutorial*: `https://tutorialedge.net/python/concurrency/python-threadpoolexecutor-tutorial`
- Concurrent futures documentation: `https://docs.python.org/3/library/concurrent.futures.html`
- asyncio documentation: `https://docs.python.org/3/library/asyncio.html`
- Tornado web demos: `https://github.com/tornadoweb/tornado/tree/stable/demos`
- Other solutions based on Tornado: `http://cyclone.io`
- Alternatives to aiohttp. Sanic as an async Python 3.5+ web server: `https://sanicframework.org`
- Celery project: `http://www.celeryproject.org`
- Twisted project: `https://twistedmatrix.com/trac`
- *Writing Servers*: `https://twistedmatrix.com/documents/current/core/howto/servers.html`
- *Writing Clients*: `https://twistedmatrix.com/documents/current/core/howto/clients.html`
- Twisted code style guide: `https://twistedmatrix.com/documents/current/core/development/policy/coding-standard.html`

12
Designing Applications on the Web

In this chapter, you will learn how to implement a web application using the **Web Server Gateway Interface** (**WSGI**). You will be introduced to existing web application frameworks and how to start working with dynamic web programming. We will introduce the Flask microframework that's written in Python, which is designed to facilitate the development of web applications under the **Model-View-Controller** (**MVC**) pattern. Finally, we will review how to work with HTTP requests in Flask and how to interact with databases through SQLAlchemy.

The following topics will be covered in this chapter:

- Writing a web application with WSGI
- A discussion of existing web application frameworks (Django, Flask, Plone)
- The MVC pattern and dynamic web programming with Python
- Creating RESTful web applications and working with Flask and HTTP requests
- Interacting with Flask with the SQLAlchemy database

Technical requirements

The examples and source code for this chapter are available in the GitHub repository in the `Chapter12` folder, at `https://github.com/PacktPublishing/Learning-Python-Networking-Second-Edition`.

You will need to install the Python distribution on your local machine with a Unix operating system and have some basic knowledge of network protocols. The examples in this chapter also are compatible with the Windows operating system.

Writing a web application with WSGI

In this section, we are going to introduce the necessary concepts to create a web page that's been developed with Python without using any framework. For this, it is necessary to know about the concept of WSGI, which is a specification of a simple and universal interface between web servers and web applications or frameworks that are developed with Python.

Introducing WSGI

Python web applications were originally written against these CGI and FastCGI protocols, and a now mostly defunct `mod_python` Apache module. This proved troublesome, though, since Python web applications were tied to the protocol or server they had been written for. Moving them to a different server or protocol required some reworking of the application code.

This problem was solved with PEP 333, which defined the WSGI protocol. This established a common calling convention for web servers to invoke web application code, similar to CGI. When web servers and web applications both support WSGI, servers and applications can be exchanged with ease. WSGI support has been added to many modern web servers and is nowadays the main method of hosting Python applications on the web. It was updated for Python 3 in PEP 3333.

Many of the web frameworks we discussed earlier support WSGI behind the scenes to communicate with their hosting web servers, Flask and Django included. This is another big benefit to using such a framework – you get full WSGI compatibility for free.

There are two ways a web server can use WSGI to host a web application. First, it can directly support hosting WSGI applications. Pure Python servers such as Gunicorn follow this approach, and they make serving Python web applications very easy. This is becoming a very popular way to host Python web applications.

The second approach is for a non-Python server to use an adapter plugin, such as Apache's `mod_wsgi`, or the `mod_wsgi` plugin for Nginx.

The exception to the WSGI revolution is event-driven servers. WSGI doesn't include a mechanism to allow a web application to pass control back to the calling process, and so there is no benefit to using an event-driven server with a blocking-IO style WSGI web application because as soon as the application blocks for database access, for example, it will block the whole web server process.

Hence, most event-driven frameworks include a production-ready web server. Making the web application itself event-driven and embedding it in the web server process is really the only way to host it. To host web applications with these frameworks, check out the framework's documentation. In this chapter, we will review specific frameworks such as Django and Flask.

Creating a WSGI application

All the requests that we make to our server will be handled by the WSGI application, which will be a single file. This application will be responsible for handling the requests and returning the appropriate response according to the requested URL. In this application, we will have to define a function that acts with each user's request. This function must be a valid application WSGI function. This means that it should be called application and it should receive two parameters: environ, from the os module, which provides a dictionary of standard HTTP requests and other environment variables, and the start_response function, from WSGI, which is responsible for delivering the HTTP response to the user.

In the following example, we will create a web server that responds to the localhost on port 8080.

You can find the following code in the wsgi_example.py file:

```python
#!/usr/bin/env python3

from wsgiref.simple_server import make_server

def page(content, *args):
    yield b'<html><head><title>wsgi_example.py</title></head><body>'
    yield (content % args).encode('utf-8')
    yield b'</body></html>'

def application(environ, start_response):
    # I keep the output that I will return in response
    response = "<p>This is my web page built with python wsgi</p>"
    # A response to the browser is generated
    start_response('200 OK', [('Content-Type', 'text/html;
charset=utf-8')])
    return page(response)

if __name__ == '__main__':
    print('Listening on localhost:8080')
    srv = make_server('localhost', 8080, application)
    srv.serve_forever()
```

The controller that we used previously does not take into account the URL that we accessed the server with, and will always generate the same response. Using the information about the request that we have stored in the `environ` dictionary, we can build different answers according to the request by taking into account the access URL, for example.

The `environ` dictionary that is received with each HTTP request contains the standard variables of the CGI specification, including the following:

- `REQUEST_METHOD`: `GET` and `POST` methods
- `SCRIPT_NAME`: The initial part of the route, which corresponds to the application
- `PATH_INFO`: The second part of the route determines the virtual location within the application
- `QUERY_STRING`: The portion of the URL that follows the ?
- `CONTENT_TYPE`, `CONTENT_LENGTH` of the HTTP request
- `SERVER_NAME`, `SERVER_PORT`, that, combined with `SCRIPT_NAME` and `PATH_INFO`, give the URL
- `SERVER_PROTOCOL`: The protocol version (HTTP/1.0 or HTTP/1.1)

In this way, we can develop a controller to check the access URL and work with the parameters that were sent by the `GET` method. In this example, we are using the `QUERY_STRING` environment variable to perform a basic operation by parameters in the URL. For example, if we want to multiply two numbers, we can use these parameters in the URL query string, like so: `operation?operator1=2&operator2=10&operation=*`.

You can find the following code in the `wsgi_example2.py` file:

```python
#!/usr/bin/env python3
from wsgiref.simple_server import make_server

def page(content, *args):
    yield b'<html><head><title>wsgi_example.py</title></head><body>'
    yield (content % args).encode('utf-8')
    yield b'</body></html>'
```

In the first code block, we imported the module for creating our server and defined the function that will generate the HTML page. In the following code block, we are defining the application method for processing the query string and parameters:

```
def application(environ, start_response):
    if environ['PATH_INFO'] == '/':
        response = "<p>This is my web page built with python wsgi</p>"
        start_response('200 OK', [('Content-Type', 'text/html;
charset=utf-8')])
        return page(response)
    elif environ['PATH_INFO'] == '/operation':
        print('environ["QUERY_STRING"]:',environ["QUERY_STRING"])
        params = environ["QUERY_STRING"].split("&")
        print('Parameters ',params)
        operator1 = params[0].split("=")[1]
        print('Operator 1:',operator1)
        operator2 = params[1].split("=")[1]
        print('Operator 2:',operator2)
        operation = params[2].split("=")[1]
        print('Operation:',operation)
        result = str(eval(operator1+operation+operator2))
        print('Result:',result)
        response = "<p>The operation result is %s</p>" %result
        start_response('200 OK', [('Content-Type', 'text/html;
charset=utf-8')])
        return page(response)
    else:
        response = "<p>This URL is not valid</p>"
        start_response('404 Not Found', [('Content-Type', 'text/html;
charset=utf-8')])
        return page(response)
```

Finally, we have our main program for creating the server in localhost 8080, which we provide by using the application method defined in the previous code block:

```
if __name__ == '__main__':
    print('Listening on localhost:8080')
    server = make_server('localhost', 8080, application)
    server.serve_forever()
```

In the following screenshot, we can see the execution of the `wsgi_example2.py` script, where we can see the server running in `localhost:8080`. When we invoke the `operator url endpoint`, it shows information about the operation and the result:

```
Listening on localhost:8080
environ["QUERY_STRING"]: operator1=200&operator2=5&operation=/
Parameters ['operator1=200', 'operator2=5', 'operation=/']
Operator 1: 200
Operator 2: 5
Operation: /
Result: 40.0
127.0.0.1 - - [12/Mar/2019 13:33:10] "GET /operation?operator1=200&operator2=5&operation=/ HTTP/1.1" 200 104
environ["QUERY_STRING"]: operator1=10&operator2=5&operation=*
Parameters ['operator1=10', 'operator2=5', 'operation=*']
Operator 1: 10
Operator 2: 5
Operation: *
Result: 50
127.0.0.1 - - [12/Mar/2019 13:33:23] "GET /operation?operator1=10&operator2=5&operation=* HTTP/1.1" 200 102
environ["QUERY_STRING"]: operator1=10&operator2=5&operation=+
Parameters ['operator1=10', 'operator2=5', 'operation=+']
Operator 1: 10
Operator 2: 5
Operation: +
Result: 15
127.0.0.1 - - [12/Mar/2019 13:33:30] "GET /operation?operator1=10&operator2=5&operation=+ HTTP/1.1" 200 102
```

In this section, we have introduced the `wsgiref.simple_server` package to create a web page that's been developed with Python using the WSGI standard, which is a specification of a universal interface between web servers and web applications.

Existing web application frameworks (Django, Flask, and Plone)

In this section, you will learn about the web frameworks that are available in the Python ecosystem.

Web frameworks

In the modern development of web applications, different frameworks are used, which are tools that give us a working scheme and a series of utilities and functions that facilitate and abstract us away from the construction of dynamic web pages.

In general, frameworks are associated with programming languages (Ruby on Rails (Ruby), Symphony (PHP)) in the Python world. The most well-known one is Django, but Flask is an interesting option that may not have such a high learning curve. It allows us to create web applications that are just as complex as those that can be created in Django.

A **web framework** is a layer that sits between the web server and our Python code, which provides abstractions and streamlined APIs to perform many of the common operations of interpreting HTTP requests and generating responses. Ideally, it is also structured so that it guides us into employing well-tested patterns for good web development. Frameworks for Python web applications are usually written in Python, and can be considered part of the web application.

The basic services a framework provides are as follows:

- Abstraction of HTTP requests and responses
- Management of the URL space (routing)
- Separation of Python code and markup (templating)

There are many Python web frameworks in use today, and here's a non-exhaustive list of some popular ones:

- **Django:** www.djangoproject.com
- **Pyramid:** www.pylonsproject.org
- **Flask:** www.flask.pocoo.org
- **Web2py:** www.web2py.com
- **CherryPy:** www.cherrypy.org
- **Tornado:** www.tornadoweb.org
- **TurboGears:** www.turbogears.org
- **Plone:** https://plone.org

An up-to-date list of frameworks is maintained at http://wiki.python.org/moin/WebFrameworks and http://docs.python-guide.org/en/latest/scenarios/web/#frameworks.

Some frameworks provide the minimum to quickly build a simple web application. These are often called micro frameworks, and one of the most popular is Flask. Although they may not include the functionality of some of the heavyweight frameworks, they provide hooks to allow for the easy extension of more complex tasks. This allows a fully customizable approach to web application development.

Other frameworks take a much more batteries-included stance, providing all the common needs of modern web applications. The major contender here is Django, which includes everything from templating to form management and database abstraction, and even a complete out-of-the-box web-based database admin interface. **TurboGears** provides similar functionality by integrating a core micro framework, with several established packages for the other features.

However, other frameworks provide features such as supporting web applications with an event-driven architecture, including Tornado and CherryPy. Both of these also feature their own built-in production-quality web servers.

Here, we have provided a small description for some of these frameworks:

- **Django**: This is perhaps the most well-known web framework of Python that brings more features to its core. The main feature offered by Django is the possibility of having an interface for the administration of its applications, from which you can work with the database models and forms. At the database level, an ORM system (**Object Relational Mapper**) is used to relate the models declared in Django with tables in databases.
- **Pyramid**: This was one of the first web frameworks that was compatible with Python 3. It is considered the best option if your target is to have a quick prototype of the website or to develop large web applications, such as a **content management system** (**CMS**).
- **Web2py**: Architecturally, Web2py follows the MVC. It incorporates generated forms with validation of fields, and the sessions are stored on the server side. Database support includes built-in SQL generation for the most popular databases. Once you have defined your models, you will get a full administrative interface automatically.
- **Flask**: Flask is a micro framework based on the **Web Server Gateway Interface** (**WSGI**), which is responsible for handling requests between the client and the server. It supports Jinja2 templates; a friendly, modern, safe, and popular template language that's also used by Django.
- **Plone**: Plone is a framework that acts as a CMS, with functionalities that make it especially suitable for the business world. It is built on top of the Zope platform (http://www.zope.org), a well-known framework based on the Python language. Zope serves as an application server and is very popular within the Python community.

The MVC pattern and dynamic web programming with Python

In this section, you will learn how use the MVC paradigm in the construction of dynamic web applications in Python. We will also review the Django framework for introducing web programming with Python.

The MVC pattern

The **MVC pattern** is a way of working that makes it possible to differentiate and separate what the data model is (the data that the app will have that is normally stored in DB), the view (an HTML page), and the controller (where the requests of the web app are managed).

The MVC is a pattern for software development that is based on separating the data, the user interface, and the logic of the application. It is mostly used in web applications, where the view is the HTML page, the model is the database manager system and the internal logic, and the controller is responsible for receiving the events and solving them. Let's explore each element in more detail:

- **Model**: This is the representation of the information in the system. It works with the view to show the information to the user and is accessed by the controller to add, delete, consult, or update data.
- **View**: This is presented to the model in a suitable format so that the user can interact with it. In most cases, it is the graphical user interface.
- **Controller**: This is the most abstract element. It can receive, process, and respond to events that are sent by the user or by the application itself. It interacts with both the model and the view.

For a detailed understanding for the use of the MVC model, let's look at its control flow:

1. The user activates an event in the interface (for example clicking on button, link)
2. The controller receives the event and manages it
3. The controller consults or modifies the model
4. The controller sends the response to the interface and it reacts depending on it (changes the screen, opens a link, and so on)
5. The interface waits for a new user action

In the following diagram, we can see the steps we just described:

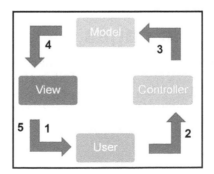

Among the advantages that this pattern provides us, we can highlight the following:

- **It is focused on separating responsibilities**: Let's think about how current applications and websites are created; that is, HTML is used for the visual components, CSS is used for the style, and Javascript is used for the logic, each with its own approach and its own responsibility. The concept is the same for MCV including the components that we mentioned before.
- **It reuses code**: Any framework that's created from MVC allows you to reuse code and return total or partial views, avoiding duplicating styles or content in the views. All of the data handling is done in the models, so if you modify your database, it is only necessary to modify the corresponding model so that it can handle the updated data, without the need to update each place where it was used.
- **We avoid spaghetti code**: With this design pattern, we can reduce and even eliminate the use of server and presentation code in one place.
- **Perfect for multidisciplinary teams**: With this design pattern, we can have teams where each person deals with a certain layer. For example, we can have someone in charge of designing the application and someone else in charge of creating the business rules and other activities. Each person can work independently of the other without suffering affectations.

Dynamic web pages

Dynamic web pages are those where the information that's presented is generated from a request that's been made on the page. Contrary to what happens with static pages, in which their content is predetermined, in dynamic pages, the information appears immediately after a request is made by the user. The result of the page that's obtained in the answer will depend on several aspects, such as the information that's stored in the database, the content of a cookie or session, and the parameters in the HTTP request.

Processing dynamic pages

When the web server receives a request to display a dynamic page, it transfers the page to a special piece of software that's in charge of finalizing the page. This special software is called an application server.

In the following diagram, we can see a schema for processing a request in a web server:

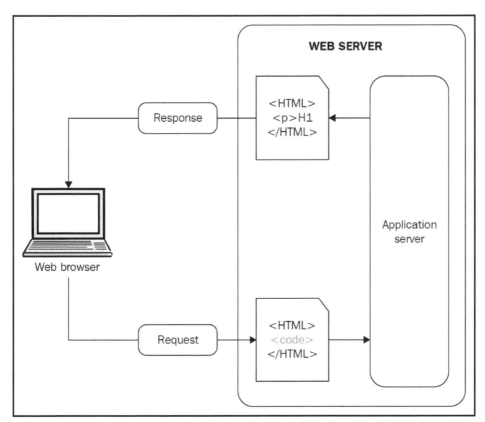

The application server, according to the request that has been made, executes a program in a certain programming language and returns an HTTP response, whose content is usually an HTML page.

Accessing a database

When working with databases, today's application servers have the ability to connect in a simple way by configuring data sources. For example, our application could use an application server to serve pages dynamically by querying a database to obtain or modify data, and display them later in an HTML page using asynchronous server queries.

The use of a database to store content allows you to separate the design of the website from the content that you want to show to the users of the site. Instead of writing individual HTML files for each page, you only need to write a page or template so that you can present the data in the database to the user. You can also dynamically submit HTML forms that add or modify information in the database.

In the following diagram, we can see a schema for processing a request in a web and database server:

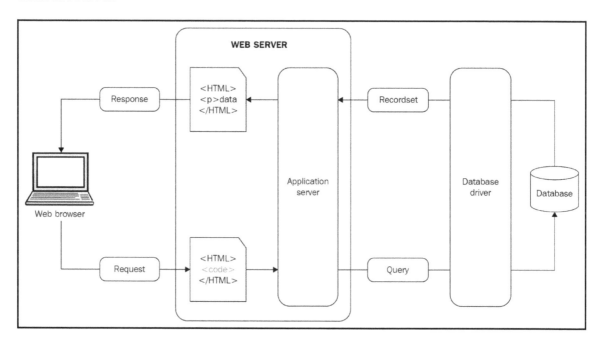

In the previous diagram, we can see how the client makes a request to the application server, connects to the database to perform the query through database driver, and when the query result returns to the application server, the response object is returned to the client browser.

In next section, we are going to review Django and study some commands to introduce this framework and its powerful administration panel.

Django introduction

In this section, we are going to review how to start working with the Django framework. To install `django`, just execute the `pip install django` command.

Once installed, we can use the `django-admin.py` script to create the file structure that's necessary to create applications with the framework.

These are the self-generated files that appear when you run the `$ django-admin.py startproject djangoApplication` command:

- `__init__.py` tells Python that this folder is a Python package and allows Python to import all of the scripts into the folder as modules.
- `manage.py` is a utility script that executes from the command line. It contains some functions to manage your website.
- `settings.py` contains the settings of your website. This file is simply a number of variables that define the configuration of your site.
- `urls.py` is the file that assigns the URLs to the pages.

We can see that in the `settings.py` generated file, there is a default configuration for `sqlite3 database`:

```
DATABASES = {
'default': {
'ENGINE': 'django.db.backends.sqlite3',
'NAME': os.path.join(BASE_DIR, 'db.sqlite3'),
}
}
```

To create a database in our application, we can run the following command in the `djangoApplication` directory that contains the `manage.py` file:

```
$ python manage.py migrate
```

If the execution is correct, you should see something like this:

```
Operations to perform:
Apply all migrations: admin, auth, contenttypes, sessions
Running migrations:
Applying contenttypes.0001_initial... OK
Applying auth.0001_initial... OK
Applying admin.0001_initial... OK
Applying admin.0002_logentry_remove_auto_add... OK
Applying admin.0003_logentry_add_action_flag_choices... OK
Applying contenttypes.0002_remove_content_type_name... OK
```

```
Applying auth.0002_alter_permission_name_max_length... OK
Applying auth.0003_alter_user_email_max_length... OK
Applying auth.0004_alter_user_username_opts... OK
Applying auth.0005_alter_user_last_login_null... OK
Applying auth.0006_require_contenttypes_0002... OK
Applying auth.0007_alter_validators_add_error_messages... OK
Applying auth.0008_alter_user_username_max_length... OK
Applying auth.0009_alter_user_last_name_max_length... OK
Applying sessions.0001_initial... OK
```

In this way, we can start the web server by running the $ `python manage.py runserver` command, and we will have the application running on `http://localhost:8000`.

Creating a Django application

Once we have the base and file structure, we can create our application. To create an application, we need to execute the following command in the console:

```
$ python manage.py startapp djangoApp
```

With this command, a new `djangoApp` directory has been created with the following structure:

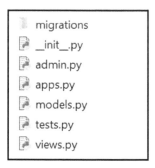

After creating an application, we also need to tell Django to use it. This is done in the `djangoApplication/settings.py` file, where we have to find the `INSTALLED_APPS` array in the `Application definition` section and add a line that contains the name of our `djangoApp` application:

```
# Application definition

INSTALLED_APPS = [
  'django.contrib.admin',
```

```
    'django.contrib.auth',
    'django.contrib.contenttypes',
    'django.contrib.sessions',
    'django.contrib.messages',
    'django.contrib.staticfiles',
    'djangoApp'
]
```

We can create our model in the `djangoApp/models.py` file and define the object **Model** inside this file that represents a post from a blog. This model includes information about the author, title, content, and timestamp:

```
from django.db import models

class post(models.Model):
    author = models.CharField(max_length = 30)
    title = models.CharField(max_length = 100)
    content= models.TextField()
    timestamp = models.DateTimeField()
```

The last step is to add our new model to the database. First, we have to let Django know that we have generated a new model with the following command:

```
$ python manage.py makemigrations djangoApp.
```

This is the output we receive when we execute the previous command:

```
Migrations for 'djangoApp':
 djangoApp\migrations\0001_initial.py
  - Create model post
```

In this way, Django has prepared a migration file that we have to apply to our database with the following command:

```
$ python manage.py migrate djangoApp
Operations to perform:
Apply all migrations: djangoApp
Running migrations:
Applying djangoApp.0001_initial... OK
```

Once we have defined our models, we can use Django to manage the objects of our model. We can do this by using the administrator (admin) of Django. To do this, you must go to the `djangoApp/admin.py` file and add the following code:

```
from django.contrib import admin
from .models import post
admin.site.register(post)
```

We can use the `admin.site.register (post)` command to register our model in the application. This can also be used in the Django administrator page.

With this, we are able to execute the `python manage.py runserver` command to run the web server and access `http://127.0.0.1:8000/admin`. You'll see a sign-in page:

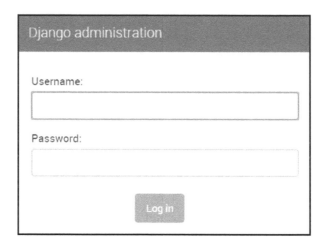

To log in, first, you must create a user in the Django database, which is a user that has control over the entire site. By executing the `$ python manage.py createsuperuser` command, we can create a user to access the administration area:

```
Username: admin
Email address: admin@admin.com
Password:
Password (again):
Superuser created successfully
```

After logging in with the user that we just created, we can see the **Django administration panel**:

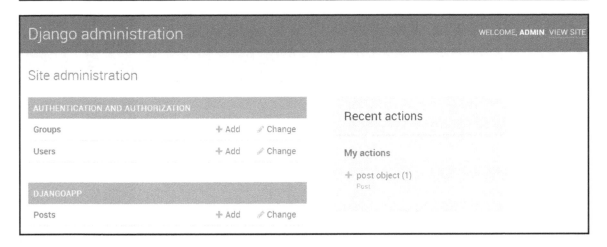

From here, we could, for example, create a post for our application with the **Add** button:

We can also see the objects that are saved in the Django database:

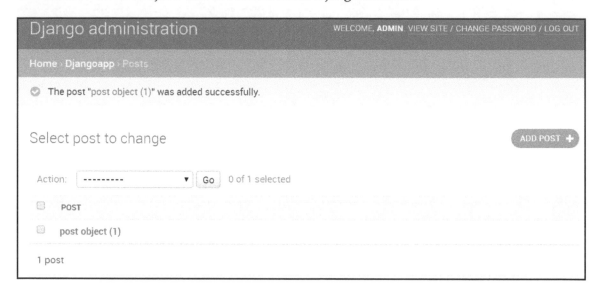

 For more information, check out the official Django documentation at https://docs.djangoproject.com/en/2.0/ref/contrib/admin.

In this section, you have learned about the MVC paradigm in the construction of dynamic web applications, and were introduced to the Django framework, its main commands, and the administration panel.

Creating RESTful web applications and working with Flask and HTTP requests

In this section, you will learn how to create RESTful web applications and work with HTTP requests with Flask. You will manage the separation of application logic and HTML with the Flask template engine.

Introducing Flask

Flask is a micro framework designed to facilitate the development of web applications under the MVC pattern and provides a simple interface. The main advantage is that it doesn't require any complex preconfiguration; all we need to do is install it with a command:

```
>>> pip install flask
 Downloading/unpacking flask
```

Flask can also be downloaded from the project's home page at `http://flask.pocoo.org`. Note that to run Flask under Python 3, you will need Python 3.3 or higher.

Among the main features of Flask, we can highlight the following:

- **Open source**: Flask is open source and is covered under a BSD license.
- **Includes web server development**: You do not need any infrastructure with a web server to test the applications, as you can simply run a web server to see the results that are obtained.
- **It has a debugger and integrated support for unit tests:** If we have an error in the code that is being built, we can debug that error and we can see the values of the variables. There is also the possibility of integrating unit tests.
- **It is compatible with WSGI**: WSGI is a protocol that uses web servers to serve web pages that are written in Python.
- **Good route management**: When you work with web apps that have been made in Python, you have the driver that receives all the requests that the clients make, and it has to determine which route the client is accessing to execute the necessary code.
- **Build web services:** It is used to build web services (such as RESTful APIs) or static content applications.

Among the main objects and methods that Flask provides for work, we can highlight the following:

- `flask`: This is the main object of the framework and is a way to agglutinate the callable WSGI with a set of routes. Our application is going to be an instance of this object.
- `request`: An object that allows us to access the data referring to the request that was made to us. It includes the GET parameters, cookies, and headers, among other things.
- `response`: An object that allows us to modify our responses; add headers, status codes, and cookies; and other concepts.

- `render_template`: This is a method that injects our context into a template and returns the answer in its complete form, ready to be returned.
- `redirect`: A helper that allows us to return a redirect to another URL in our code.
- `abort`: A helper that allows us to return an error status from our controller.

Our app is going to allow us to browse the `docstrings` for the Python built-in functions. An application that's built with Flask is basically an instance of the Flask object, which we will record routes in.

You can find the following code in the `flaskapp_demo.py` file on the GitHub repository (`https://github.com/PacktPublishing/Learning-Python-Networking-Second-Edition`):

```python
#!/usr/local/bin/python3

from flask import Flask, abort

app = Flask(__name__)
app.debug = True
objs = __builtins__.__dict__.items()

docstrings = {name.lower(): obj.__doc__ for name, obj in objs if
name[0].islower() and hasattr(obj, '__name__')}

...
```

Flask includes a development web server, so to try it out on our application, all we need to do is run the following command:

```
$ python flaskapp_demo.py

* Serving Flask app "demo" (lazy loading)
* Environment: production
WARNING: Do not use the development server in a production environment.
Use a production WSGI server instead.
* Debug mode: on
* Restarting with stat
* Debugger is active!
* Debugger PIN: 190-598-045
* Running on http://127.0.0.1:5000/ (Press CTRL+C to quit)
```

We can see that the Flask server tells us the IP address and port it's listening on. Connect to the `http://127.0.0.1:5000/` URL. It will now display in a web browser, and you should see a page with a list of Python built-in functions. Clicking on one should display a page showing the function name and its `docstring`. If you want to run the server on another interface or port, you can change this data in the `app.run()` call, for example, to `app.run(host='0.0.0.0', port=5000)`.

Let's go through our code. From the top, we created our Flask app by creating a Flask instance, in this case giving it the name of our main module. We then set the debug mode to active, which provides nice tracebacks in the browser when something goes wrong, and also sets the development server to automatically reload code changes without needing a restart. Note that the debug mode should never be left active in a production app! This is because the debugger has an interactive element, which allows code to be executed on the server. By default, debug is off, so all we need to do is delete the `app.config.debug` line when we put the app into production.

Routing in Flask

One of the biggest advantages of Flask is its ability to create routes. A route is a web entry in which we can render a page or serve an endpoint of a RESTful service.

To create routes with Flask, we must use the `@route` annotation, which will receive the route that we will respond with as a parameter. It is necessary to associate a function that carries out the processing of the request with this annotation.

We could define a route in Flask in the following way:

```
@app.route("/message/")
def message(name):
    return "Welcome "+name+"!"
```

Now, we are going to create a route that receives a name as a parameter and returns a reply message. This will help us to see how we can pass parameters in Python Flask routes. The first thing is to focus on the route, that is, `@app.route('/message/<name>',methods=['GET'])`.

Now, let's define a method that addresses this route. The peculiarity of this method will be that it must have a parameter, which will correspond to the variable of the route. Now, we can use this variable within the method. In our case, we have used it in the response as part of the greeting. Finally, the entire route will remain as follows:

```
@app.route('/message/<name>',methods=['GET'])
def message(name):
 return Welcome' + name+ '!'
```

If we return our previous `flaskapp_demo.py` script, we will have defined a set of functions, usually called **views**, that handle requests for various parts of our URL. `index()` and `show_docstring()` are such functions. You will see that both are preceded by a Flask decorator function, `app.route()`. This tells Flask which parts of our URL space the decorated function should handle. That is, when a request comes in with a URL that matches a pattern in an `app.route()` decorator, the function with the matching decorator is called to handle the request. View functions must return a response that Flask can return to the client, but we'll cover more on that in a moment.

The URL pattern for our `index()` function is just the site root, `/`, meaning that only requests for the root will be handled by `index()`.

In `index()`, we just compile our output HTML as a string – first, our list of links to the functions' pages, then a header – and then we return the string. Flask takes the string and creates a response out of it, using the string as the response body and adding a few HTTP headers. In particular, for `str` return values, it sets `Content-Type` to `text/html`.

The `show_docstrings()` view does a similar thing – it returns the name of the built-in function we're viewing in an HTML header tag, plus the `docstring` wrapped in a `<pre>` tag (to preserve new lines and whitespace).

The interesting part is the `app.route('/functions/<func_name>')` call. Here, we're declaring that our functions' pages will live in the functions directory, and we're capturing the name of the requested function using the `<func_name>` segment.

Flask captures the section of the URL in angle brackets and makes it available to our view. We pull it into the view namespace by declaring the `func_name` argument for `show_docstring()`.

In the view, we check that the name that's supplied is valid by seeing whether it appears in the docstrings dictionary. If it's okay, we build and return the corresponding HTML. If it's not okay, then we return a **404 Not Found** response to the client by calling Flask's abort() function. This function raises a Flask HTTPException, which, if not handled by our application, will cause Flask to generate an error page and return it to the client with the corresponding status code (in this case, 404). This is a good way to fail fast when we encounter bad requests.

Jinja2 templating

In this section, we are going to introduce Jinja2 as a template language that allows you to insert processed data and predetermined text within your HTML code. Basically, Jinja searches and substitutes the names, expressions, and statements that are enclosed by { } within text.

You can see from our preceding views that even when omitting the usual HTML formalities such as <DOCTYPE> and the <html> tag to save complexity, constructing HTML in Python code is clunky. It's difficult to get a feel for the overall page, and it's impossible for designers with no Python knowledge to work on the page design. The templates help to implement the separation between the logic of the backend application and the visual part related to the views.

Flask uses the Jinja2 templating engine for this task. Let's adapt our application to use templates. You can find the following files in the templates folder: base.html, index.html, docstring.html.

The base.html file will look like this:

```
<!DOCTYPE html>
<html>
<head>
<title>Python Builtins Docstrings</title>
</head>
<body>
{% block body %}{% endblock %}
</body>
</html>
```

The `index.html` file will be like this:

```
{% extends "base.html" %}
{% block body %}
<h1>Python Builtins Docstrings</h1>
<div>
{% for func in funcs %}
<div class="menuitem link">
<a href="/functions/{{ func }}">{{ func }}</a>
</div>
{% endfor %}
</table>
{% endblock %}
```

The `docstring.html` file will look like this:

```
{% extends 'base.html' %}
{% block body %}
<h1>{{ func_name }}</h1>
<pre>{{ doc }}</pre>
<p><a href="/">Home</a></p>
{% endblock %}
```

As you can see, we write a standard page in HTML, with the only difference that there are some bookmarks for the dynamic content enclosed in `{{...}}` sections.

At this point, you need to use the `render_template` method that looks in the templates folder for the file that's supplied as the first argument, reads it, runs any processing instructions in the file, then returns the processed HTML as a string. Any keyword arguments that are supplied to `render_template()` are passed to the template and become available to its processing instructions.

The `render_template` function takes the filename of the template and a variable list of template arguments to return the template armed with all the arguments replaced. At low level, the Jinja2 template engine is used, which will replace the `{{...}}` blocks with the values provided as arguments in the `render_template` function.

You can find the following code in the `flaskapp_demo_template.py` file on the GitHub repository (https://github.com/PacktPublishing/Learning-Python-Networking-Second-Edition):

```
#!/usr/local/bin/python

from flask import Flask, abort, render_template

app = Flask(__name__)
```

```
app.debug = True
objs = __builtins__.__dict__.items()

docstrings = {name.lower(): obj.__doc__ for name, obj in objs if
name[0].islower() and hasattr(obj, '__name__')}
```

...

Looking at the templates, we can see they are mostly HTML, but with some extra instructions for Flask contained in `{{ }}` and `{% %}` tags. The `{{ }}` instructions simply substitute the value of the named variable into that point of the HTML. So, for example, the `{{ func_name }}` in `docstrings.html` substitutes the value of the `func_name` value we passed to `render_template()`.

The `{% %}` instructions contain logic and flow control. For example, the `{% for func in funcs %}` instruction in `index.html` loops over values in `funcs` and repeats the contained HTML for each value.

Finally, you may have spotted that templates allow for **inheritance**. This is provided by the `{% block %}` and `{% extends %}` instructions. In `base.html`, we declare some shared boilerplate HTML, then in the `<body>` tag, we just have a `{% block body %}` instruction. In `index.html` and `docstring.html`, we don't include the boilerplate HTML; instead, we extend `base.html`, meaning that these templates will fill the block instructions that were declared in `base.html`. In both `index.html` and `docstring.html`, we declare a body block, the contents of which Flask inserts into the HTML in `base.html`, replacing the matching `{% block body %}` there. Inheritance allows for the reuse of common code, and it can cascade through as many levels as needed.

If we need to apply inheritance within our template, we need to use the extended block in such a way that the template engine allows for the inclusion of a `base.html` file inside another HTML file. The two templates have a block declaration matching the name of the content, which allows Jinja2 to know how to combine the two into one.

There is a lot more functionality available in Jinja2 template instructions; check out the template designer documentation for a full list, at `http://jinja.pocoo.org/docs/dev/templates/`.

POST parameters with Flask

The usual way to send information to the different pages of our web application is by using HTML5 forms. It is advisable to use the POST method (the information is sent in the body of the request) for sending information using forms, although if necessary we can also use the GET method (the information is sent in the URL of the request).

Creating a form in a POST application will lead us to know how to control the data we upload. Here, we will look at an example of how we can handle the POST parameters with Flask.

The first way will be to create a route that accepts a GET request that returns a form that we will render using the render_template() method:

```
@app.route('/',methods=['GET'])
def index():
    return render_template('index.html')
```

The template of the form will be very simple. The important thing is that the method is POST and the action field in the form object is pointing to the /validat. route.

You can find the following code in the index.html file inside the post_parameters folder:

```
<form action="/validate" method="post">
 <label for="user">User</label>
 <input type="text" id="user" name="user"><br/>

 <label for="password">Password</label>
 <input type="password" id="password" name="password"><br/>

 <input type="submit" value="Submit" />
</form>
```

It is very important to put the name attributes in the form, since it will be that attribute that we use to recover the value. Now, we will create the route that accepts the POST requests. If a URL receives information through the POST method and we do not want it to be accessed with a GET method, it will be defined as follows:

```
@app.route('/validate',methods=['POST'])
 def validate():
```

To access the information of the attributes of the form, we can use the `request.form` object. This object has attributes in a collection. So, we will retrieve the value of the `user` and `password` fields of the form, as you can see in the following script.

You can find the following code in the `flaskapp_post.py` file inside the `post_parameters` folder:

```
#!/usr/local/bin/python3
from flask import Flask, request, render_template
import json

app = Flask(__name__)
app.debug = True

@app.route('/',methods=['GET'])
def index():
    return render_template('index.html')

@app.route('/validate',methods=['POST'])
def validate():
    user = request.form['user']
    password = request.form['password']
    if user == 'admin' and password == 'password':
        response = {'user_validate':True,'message':'User authenticated'}
    else:
        response = {'user_validate':False,'message':'User incorrect'}
  return json.dumps(response)

if __name__ == '__main__':
    app.run()
```

Once the method has been performed and the client has sent the values, we would have an answer like this. If the user and passwords match when defined in the code, it will return `{"user_validate": true, "message": "User authenticated"}`, otherwise it will return `{'user_validate':False,'message':'User incorrect'}`.

In this way, we have already seen how to manipulate and recover POST parameters with Flask.

Other templating engines

Jinja2 is certainly not the only templating package in existence. You can find a maintained list of Python templating engines at `https://wiki.python.org/moin/Templating`.

Like frameworks, different engines exist because of differing philosophies on what makes a good engine. Some feel that logic and presentation should be absolutely separate and that flow control and expressions should never be available in templates, providing only valued substitution mechanisms. Others take the opposite approach and allow full Python expressions within template markup. Others, such as Jinja2, take a middle ground approach. Some engines also use different schemes altogether, such as XML-based templates, or declare logic via special HTML tag attributes.

Flask extensions

Flask provides a set of extensions that can help us add more functionality to our application quickly and easily. Here, we will mention the most common plugins that are used with Flask:

- **flask-script**: Allows you to have a command line to manage the application (`https://flask-script.readthedocs.io/en/latest/`)
- **flask-Bootstrap**: It helps to create link, style sheets for HTML pages (`https://pythonhosted.org/Flask-Bootstrap`)
- **flask-WTF**: Used to generate HTML forms with classes and objects (`https://flask-wtf.readthedocs.io/en/stable/`)
- **flask-login**: A plugin for user authentication and passwords (`https://flask-login.readthedocs.io/en/latest/`)
- **flask-Sqlalchemy**: Used to generate the data model (`http://flask-sqlalchemy.pocoo.org/2.3`)
- **flask-Security**: Allows you to manage the registration and authentication processes (`https://pythonhosted.org/Flask-Security`)

Working with a database in Flask with SQLAlchemy

In this section, you will learn how to work with a database in Flask with SQLAlchemy.

Introducing SQLAlchemy

SQLAlchemy is an engine developed in Python that has several components for working with databases. It follows some of the most frequently used patterns for relational object mapping, where classes can be mapped in the database in multiple ways, which allows you to develop the object model and the database schema in an uncoupled way from the very beginning.

SQLAlchemy includes various tools that are focused on interacting with relational databases, among which we can highlight the following:

- **SQLAlchemy Core**, which allows you to create a generic and independent interface of the database manager by means of an expression language based on SQL.
- **SQLAlchemy ORM**, a mapper between objects and relational transactions or ORM (object relational mapper). It includes support for SQLite, MySQL, PostgreSQL, Oracle, and MS SQL, among others.

To install SQLAlchemy, just execute the following command:

```
pip install sqlalchemy
```

This example will show us how to create a table, insert data, and select it from the database by using SQLAlchemy Core and ORM modules. For more information about SQLAlchemy ORM, the official documentation is available at https://docs.sqlalchemy.org/en/latest/orm/tutorial.html.

To illustrate the idea, the following diagram shows a data model for a system that is responsible for managing book records and authors:

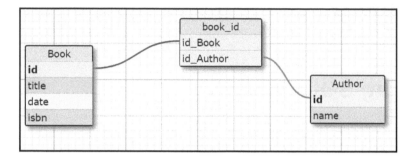

Our model consists of the **Book** and **Author** tables. The intermediate table, book_author, is used to express the many-to-many relationship among the book and author tables. First, we must map the model or schema of the database by means of SQLAlchemy.

You can find the following code in the models.py file inside the sqlalchemy folder:

```
#!/usr/local/bin/python3

from sqlalchemy import (create_engine, Column, Date, Integer, ForeignKey,
String, Table)
from sqlalchemy.ext.declarative import declarative_base
from sqlalchemy.orm import relationship

engine = create_engine('sqlite:///books_authors.db', echo=True)
Base = declarative_base()

#Relation many to many between book and author
author_book = Table('author_book', Base.metadata,
 Column('book_id', Integer, ForeignKey('book.id')),
 Column('author_id', Integer, ForeignKey('author.id'))
)
```

In the previous code block, we defined the database connection and the relationship between the book and author entities by creating a new table with two columns. Each one is the foreign key to the book and author tables. In the following code block, we will define the Book entity with the init constructor and its relation with the Author table through the author_book relation:

```
class Book(Base):
    __tablename__ = 'book'
    id = Column(Integer, primary_key=True)
    title = Column(String(120), index=True, nullable=False)
```

```
date = Column(Date)
isbn = Column(String(13))
authors = relationship("Author", secondary=author_book)

def __init__(self, title, date, isbn):
    self.title = title
    self.date = date
    self.isbn = isbn

def __repr__(self):
    return self.title
```

Finally, we create the `Author` model and initialize our database with the `create_all()` method from the `metadata` object:

```
class Author(Base):
    __tablename__ = 'author'
    id = Column(Integer, primary_key=True)
    name = Column(String(120), nullable=False)
    def __init__(self, name):
        self.name = name

Base.metadata.create_all(engine)
```

By executing the `models.py` script, we can see how the `books_authors.db` file is generated in your local filesystem.

In the following screenshot, we can see the tables that are created when you visualize this file with the SQLite browser:

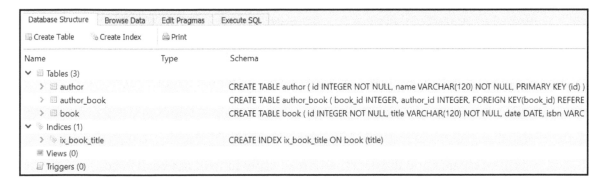

Now, let's explain the content of the `models.py` script. First, we will need to connect to our database. The `sqlalchemy.engine.base.Engine` class is responsible for instantiating objects, connecting to a database, and in turn mapping the attributes of the objects that are created by the ORM model. To instantiate an object from `sqlalchemy.engine.base.Engine`, the `sqlalchemy.create_engine()` function is used with the following syntax:

```
from sqlalchemy import create_engine
engine = create_engine('sqlite:///books_authors.db', echo=True)
```

After creating our engine, we need to create our tables. In ORM, the process of creating tables begins with defining the classes that we will use in the mapping process.

Before creating the database, it is necessary to define a model that maps to an object with at least one table in the database. The `sqlalchemy.ext.declarative.declarative_base()` function allows us to create a model from the subclasses of `sqlalchemy.ext.declarative.api.DeclarativeMeta`:

```
from sqlalchemy.ext.declarative import declarative_base
Base = declarative_base()
```

Now that our base mapper has been declared, we can make a subclass of it to build our declarative maps or models. The `Base` subclasses correspond to tables within a database. These subclasses have the attribute `__tablename__`, which corresponds to the name of the table to which you are mapping their attributes. The generic syntax is as follows:

```
from sqlalchemy import Column, Integer, String

class MyTable(Base):
    __tablename__ = 'table'
    id = Column(Integer, primary_key=True)
    message = Column(String)
```

To create the database with the defined tables, the `Base.metadata.create_all()` method is used in the database that's managed by the instantiated object of `sqlalchemy.engine.base.Engine`:

- If there is no file in the database, it will be created
- In case there are already tables defined in the database, only those that are new will be created and the data they already contain will not be deleted

Creating a session and ORM queries

The `sqlalchemy.orm.sessionmaker()` function allows you to create a `sqlalchemy.orm.session.sessionmaker` class that contains attributes and methods that allow you to interact with the database. You can use the following methods to manage session data:

- The `add()` method, which adds or replaces the record that's bound to the instantiated object of a `Base` subclass in the corresponding record within the database
- The `delete()` method, which deletes the record that's bound to the object
- The `commit()` method, which applies the changes to the database

Now that our tables have been assigned and created, we can insert data. This insertion is done by creating instances of the class, which is created with `MyTable`. At this point, all we have is an instance of the objects at the ORM abstraction level, but nothing has been saved in the database yet. To do this, we first need to **create a session**:

```
from sqlalchemy.orm import sessionmaker
Session = sessionmaker(bind=engine)
session = Session()
```

This session object is our database manager. According to the SQLAlchemy documentation, this object allows us to recover a connection from a group of connections that's maintained by the engine, and maintains it until we confirm all of the changes or close the session object. Now that we have our session, we can add a new object to it and confirm our changes in the database:

```
object = MyTable(message="Hello World!")
session.add(object)
session.commit()
```

Once we have our session defined, we can perform queries related to `Base` instantiate objects from sessions and the tables linked to them.

For performing queries, we can use the following methods:

- `query.first()` returns to the first object that's found in a search
- `query.all()` returns a list type object with all the objects resulting from a search
- `query.filter()` returns a `Query` object with the objects found when executing a search that satisfies the logical expression on the attributes of the class, which is entered as an argument

Now that we have data, we can take advantage of the ORM query language to retrieve our data:

```
query = session.query(MyTable)
instance = query.first()
print (instance.message) # Hello World!
```

The `Session` class allows you to add new objects or update existing ones in the database. To add new objects, we can use the `session.add(obj)` method. You can also add a list of objects by using the `session.add_all([obj1, obj2, obj3])` method.

When calling the `add()` method, an `INSERT` will be made in the database and a `commit()` will be performed to confirm the session data. In this example, we are using the session object for access, thus inserting or updating data in the SQLite database.

You can find the following code in the `insert_data.py` file:

```
#!/usr/local/bin/python3

from datetime import date
from sqlalchemy import create_engine
from sqlalchemy.orm import sessionmaker
from models import Author, Book

# connection with sqlite database
engine = create_engine('sqlite:///books_authors.db', echo=True)

# get sesion
Session = sessionmaker(bind=engine)
session = Session()

# inserting authors
author_1 = Author('Author1')
author_2 = Author('Author2')
author_list = (author_1, author_2)
session.add_all(author_list)
session.commit()
```

In the previous code block, we defined the connection with the SQLite database, got a session, and inserted some authors with the `add_all()` method from the `session` object. In the following code block, we're using the `Book` model to insert one book instance with the `add()` and `commit()` methods:

```
# inserting books
book1 = Book('Book1', date(2019, 1, 1), '123456789')
book1.authors.append(author_1)
```

```
session.add(book1)
session.commit()

# book query
book = session.query(Book).filter(Book.isbn=='123456789').first()
print(book)

# modifying book data
book.title = 'Learning Python Networking'
session.commit()

print(book)
```

At this point, it is important to realize how the relationship between the book and the author is established through the `append` method. We will also use `query` method from the `session` object to execute a database query by applying a specific filter. Finally, we will modify the title of the book and save its information with the `commit()` method.

After you execute the previous `insert_data.py` script, you can check the `book_authors.db` file to see whether the book information has been updated in the database. You can open this file with the SQLite browser, which is available at `https://sqlitebrowser.org`.

Using Flask with SQLAlchemy

For the most common web applications, it is generally recommended that you use a Flask extension such as `flask-sqlalchemy`. To install the package for working with SQLAlchemy from Flask, just execute the following command:

pip install flask-sqlalchemy

Once we have our Flask application created, to integrate it with `sqlalchemy`, we would have to create a configuration file with the database path, from which the SQLAlchemy object is created to manage the database.

In this example, we will use a SQLite database to simplify the configuration without having a database server.

We can add the database configuration in the `config.py` file inside the `flask_sqlalchemy` folder:

```
#!/usr/local/bin/python3
import os
DEBUG = True
```

```
SQLALCHEMY_DATABASE_URI = 'sqlite:///'+
os.path.join(os.path.dirname(__file__), 'books_database.db')
SECRET_KEY = 'SECRET_KEY'
```

`SQLALCHEMY_DATABASE_URI` is required by the Flask-SQLAlchemy extension and represents the local address to our database file. We also need to define the `SECRET_KEY` for working with Flask-forms.

You can find the following code in the `books.py` file inside the `flask_sqlalchemy` folder on the GitHub repository at `https://github.com/PacktPublishing/Learning-Python-Networking-Second-Edition`:

```
#!/usr/local/bin/python3

from flask import Flask, render_template, request
from flask_sqlalchemy import SQLAlchemy
import json

from flask_wtf import FlaskForm
from wtforms import StringField
from wtforms import TextAreaField
from wtforms.validators import DataRequired
from datetime import date

# Flask application and config
app = Flask(__name__)
app.config.from_object('config')
db = SQLAlchemy(app)

...
```

In the previous code block, we defined the Flask application and configuration from the `config.py` file. The `Book` class is our model that represents a book entity, while the `CreateBookForm` class represents our form object. In the following code block, we define our methods for threat application requests.The `index` method will show the `index.html` from the templates folder, and the `new_book` method will receive book information with the POST method using the `request.form` syntax. To save book information in the database, we will use the `session.add()` and `session.commit()` methods from the `db` object:

```
@app.route('/new_book', methods=['POST'])
def new_book():
    form = CreateBookForm()
    if request.method == 'POST':
        post = Book(request.form['title'], request.form['author'],
request.form['description'])
```

```
        db.session.add(post)
        db.session.commit()
        # validate the received values
        if request.form['title'] and request.form['author']:
            return json.dumps({'html':'<span>New book saved in
database</span>'})
    return render_template('index.html',form = form,conf = app.config)

@app.route('/', methods=['GET'])
def index():
    form = CreateBookForm()
    return render_template('index.html',form = form,conf = app.config)

if __name__ == '__main__':
    app.run()
    db.create_all()
```

Finally, the following is the content of index.html. It contains the form for sending book information:

```
<html>
<body>
 <form method="post" action="/new_book">
 <dl>
 {{ form.csrf_token }}
 {{ form.title.label }} {{ form.title(style="width:100%") }}
 {% for error in form.title.errors %} {{ error }} {% endfor %}
 <br />
 {{ form.author.label }} {{ form.author(style="width:100%") }}
 {% for error in form.author.errors %} {{ error }} {% endfor %}
 <br />
 {{ form.description.label }}
{{form.description(style="height:100px;width:100%") }}
 {% for error in form.description.errors %} {{ error }} {% endfor %}
 </dl>
 <p><input type="submit" value="submit">
 </form>
</body>
</html>
```

In the previous form object, we also added a CSRF token with the {{ form.csrf_token }} instruction to avoid some security attacks like cross-site scripting and cross-site request forgery.

In the following screenshot, we can see the HTML form for saving book information in the database:

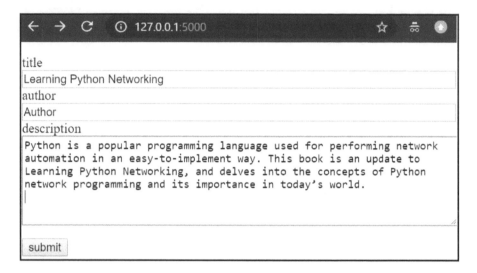

When you submit the form, you will get a message indicating that the book has been saved in the SQLite database:

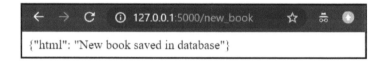

In this section, we have worked with Flask and SQLAlchemy to persist data in an SQLite database. We used the `flask-sqlalchemy` and `flask_wtf` packages for working with forms in an easy way.

Summary

In this chapter, you have learned how to implement a web application using WSGI and started working with dynamic web programming in Python. We introduced the Django and Flask micro frameworks, which are designed to facilitate the development of web applications under the MVC pattern. Finally, we reviewed how we can work with HTTP requests in Flask and interact with databases through SQLAlchemy.

Questions

1. What Python module is used for developing our own WSGI server?
2. What is the main advantage that the MVC pattern provides, from a developer's point of view?
3. What Django script can we use to create the file structure that's necessary to create applications with the framework?
4. What Django command can we use to create a database in our application?
5. What is the annotation that's used for creating routes in Flask?
6. What method is used in Flask that looks in the templates folder for the file that's supplied as the first argument?
7. If we are working in Flask with the POST method to send information to a server, what object can we use to access information on the attributes of the form?
8. What is the Flask extension for managing the registration and authentication processes in your application?
9. What class from SQLAlchemy is responsible for instantiating objects and connecting to a database?
10. What is the config keyword that's required by the Flask-SQLAlchemy extension, and that represents the local address to your database file?

Further reading

In the following links, you will find more information about the mentioned tools and the official Python documentation for some of the modules we talked about in this chapter:

- **Flask blueprints:** http://flask.pocoo.org/docs/1.0/blueprints. Blueprints are very useful for projects that need more separation between components. Basically, a blueprint is a way to organize your application into smaller, reusable pieces.
- **Comparing Django, Flask, and Pyramid:** https://www.airpair.com/python/posts/django-flask-pyramid
- **An SQLAlchemy tutorial, step by step:** http://www.rmunn.com/sqlalchemy-tutorial/tutorial.html
- **The Flask-Security extension:** https://pythonhosted.org/Flask-Security/quickstart.html#sqlalchemy-application
- **Using fastcgi with Flask:** http://flask.pocoo.org/docs/1.0/deploying/fastcgi/

Assessment

Chapter 1, Network Programming with Python

1. The application layer
2. The reason why we have to replace the IPv4 system with IPv6 is because the internet is running out of IPv4 address space, and IPv6 provides an exponentially large number of IP addresses
3. Dynamic Host Configuration Protocol (DHCP)
4. Network Address Translation (NAT)
5. Conda and `pip`
6. `virtualenv`
7. The `urllib` and `requests` packages
8. The socket module
9. `pyshark`
10. The `apply_on_packets()` method is the main way to iterate through the packets, passing in a function to apply to each packet

Chapter 2, Programming for the Web with HTTP

1. `urlopen`
2. Headers
3. User-Agent
4. `HTMLParser` and `urllib`
5. The requests module and the `whois.domaintools.com` service
6. We use the following method:

```
import requests
proxies = { "http": "http://<ip_address>:port"}
requests.get("http://example.org", proxies=proxies)
```

7. Its main purpose is to identify the user by storing their activity history on a specific website so that they can offer the most appropriate content according to their habits

8. `HTTPCookieProcessor`

9. `request.cookies.RequestsCookieJar`

10. Digest-based access authentication

Chapter 3, Application Programming Interface in Action

1. `json.dumps()`.

2. `json.loads()`.

3. OAuth.

4. `requests-oauthlib`.

5. `CONSUMER_KEY`, `CONSUMER_SECRET`, `OAUTH_TOKEN`, and `OAUTH_TOKEN_SECRET`.

6. Tweepy.

7. The `xml.etree.ElementTree` package.

8. `AmazonS3FullAccess`.

9. `requests-aws4auth` is a library for the `Requests` module that automatically handles signature generation.

10. Every bucket has its own URL of the form `http://s3.<region>.amazonaws.com/<bucketname>`. In the URL, `<bucketname>` is the name of the bucket and `<region>` is the AWS region where the bucket is present.

Chapter 4, Web Scraping with BeautifulSoup and Scrapy

1. XPath selectors

2. `code_html.xpath('//img/@src')`

3. `links = code_html.xpath('//a/@href')`

4. `bs.find_all("<html_tag_label>")`

5. `items.py`, `pipelines.py`, `settings.py`, and spiders

6. `spiders/my_sypder.py.`
7. `pipelines.py`
8. CrawlSpider
9. `process_item (item, spider)`
10. Scrapinghub

Chapter 5, Engaging with Email

1. The main difference is that IMAP allows for the connection of multiple users or mail manager programs simultaneously to the same mailbox, facilitating subsequent access to the mail messages that are available on the server via web mail. POP3, on the other hand, downloads messages by deleting them from the server, and so email messages are no longer available in the server.

2. `Sendmail` is the method of sending emails with the following syntax: `SMTP.sendmail(from_addr, to_addrs, msg[, mail_options, rcpt_options]`.

3. `from email.mime.text import MIMEText.`

4. `message = MIMEText(mail_msg, 'html', 'utf-8').`

5. You must first create a `MimeMultipart()` instance.

6. `POP3.stat()`. The result is a tuple of two integers: (message count, mailbox size).

7. The secure version of `POP3()` is its subclass, `POP3_SSL()`. It takes additional parameters, such as keyfile and certfile: `mailbox = poplib.POP3_SSL(<POP3_SERVER>, <SERVER_PORT>)`.

8. `response, headerLines, bytes = mailbox.retr(i+1).`

9. This protocol has the advantage that, when we connect to read our mail from different devices, for example, our laptop or smartphone, we know that we can always access all of our messages, and that the mailbox will be updated. It is also interesting to preserve our privacy when we read our mail from a public or shared computer, as it does not store information on the local machine.

10. The derived class, `IMAP4_SSL()`.

11. We can use the following code to open an IMAP connection:

```
from imapclient import IMAPClient
server = IMAPClient('imap_server', ssl=True)
server.login('user', 'password')
select_info = server.select_folder('INBOX',readonly=True)
```

Chapter 6, Interacting with Remote Systems

1. `sshd_config`, which is located in the `/etc/ssh` path.

2. It is recommended that you use at least a 2048-bit encryption.

3. We must set the `PermitRootLogin` variable to `no`.

4. You can implement an interactive shell using `paramiko`. That way, the channel does not close after a command is executed in the remote shell. After creating `SSHClient`, using `connect`, you can use the `invoke_shell()` method, which will open a channel that it doesn't close after you send something through it.

5. The way `paramiko` creates SFTP session for downloading files in a secure way from a SSH server is as follows:

```
import paramiko
ssh_transport = paramiko.Transport(hostname, port)
ssh_transport.connect(username='username', password='password')
sftp_session =
paramiko.SFTPClient.from_transport(ssh_transport)sftp_session.get(s
ource_file, target_file)
```

6. To retrieve the binary file from the remote host, the syntax that's shown here can be used, along with the RETR command: `ftp_client.retrbinary('RETR remote_file_name', file_handler.write)`.

7. `FTP.nlst(path)`.

8. We can use the following command:

```
from pysnmp.entity.rfc3413.oneliner
import cmdgen cmd_generator = cmdgen.CommandGenerator()
```

9. The directory service is the hierarchically organized structure of the objects in the LDAP directory.

10. We can use the following method:

```
import ldap
ldap_client = ldap.initialize("ldap://<ldap_server>:port_number/")
```

Chapter 7, Working with IP and DNS

1. `pygeoip` allows you to retrieve geographic information from an IP address. It is based on GeoIP databases, which are distributed in several files, depending on their type (city, region, country, and ISP).

2. `netifaces.interfaces()`.
3. 53 (UDP).
4. The `subnets (prefixlen_diff=1, new_prefix=None)` method has the capacity to generate subnets with additional host bits or with a specific amount of network bits.
5. `country_name_by_addr(<ip_address>)`.
6. `record_by_addr(<ip_address>)`.
7. `org_by_name(<domain_name>)`.
8. `dns.resolver.query('domain','AAAA')`.
9. `dns.resolver.query('domain','MX')`.
10. `dns.resolver.query('domain','NS')`.

Chapter 8, Implementing IPv6 and Address Manipulation

1. Link-local.
2. `:: 1/128`.
3. `socket.getaddrinfo`.
4. Use the following code to create a server with IPv6 support with a socket module:

   ```
   # socket.AF_INET6 to indicate that we will use Ipv6
   client = socket.socket (socket.AF_INET6, socket.SOCK_STREAM)
   ```

5. We can call the `interfaces()` function from this library to list all of the interfaces that are present in the system.
6. `AF_LINK` is the link layer interface (for example, Ethernet), `AF_INET` represents the IPv4 internet address, and `AF_INET6` represents the IPv6 internet address.
7. `psutil`.
8. We can interoperate between IPv4 and IPv6 with the `ipv6()` and `ipv4()` methods.
9. From `ipaddress`, we can import `IPv6Address`, `IPv6Network`, and `IPv6Interface`.

10. The `subnets(prefixlen_diff=1, new_prefix=None)` method also has the capacity to generate subnets with additional host bits or with a specific amount of network bits. Any `IPv4Network` object can find out information about its parent with the `supernet()` method, which is the opposite of the subnet.

Chapter 9, Performing Network Automation with Python and Ansible

1. YAML.
2. `/etc/ansible/ansible.cfg`.
3. `/etc/ansible/hosts`.
4. Ad hoc commands and playbooks.
5. The Ansible architecture is agentless in the sense no software or agent has to be installed on the client to communicate back to the server. Instead of relying on remote host agents, Ansible uses SSH to push its changes to the remote host.
6. The Ansible command for checking the hostname of IP addresses is as follows:

```
$ ansible all -a "hostname"
```

7. We can install by using the following code:

```
name: Installing Nginx and python
apt: pkg={{ item }}
with_items:
- ngnix
- python3-minimal
```

8. `PlaybookExecutor` from `ansible.executor.playbook_executor`.
9. The `ping` module.
10. The `AnsibleModule` class from the `ansible.module_utils.basic` package.

Chapter 10, Programming with Sockets

1. `socket.accept()` is used to accept the connection from the client. This method returns two values, `client_socket` and `client_address`, where `client_socket` is a new socket object that's used to send and receive data over the connection.
2. `socket.sendto(data, address)` is used to send data to a given address.

3. The `bind(IP,PORT)` method allows you to associate a host and a port with a specific socket, for example, `server.bind(("localhost", 9999))`.

4. The main difference between TCP and UDP is that UDP is not connection-oriented. This means that there is no guarantee that our packets will reach their destinations, and there is no error notification if a delivery fails.

5. `socket.connect_ex(address)` is used for implementing port scanning with sockets.

6. `RawCap.exe`.

7. `socket.socket (socket.AF_INET6, socket.SOCK_STREAM)`.

8. There is a module called selectors.

9. The connection is wrapped into SSL packets using our `ssl_wrap_socket()` function.

10. By calling the `getpeercert()` method and comparing it with the returned hostname.

Chapter 11, Designing Servers and Asynchronous Programming

1. aiohttp is an independent library that's developed using asyncio at a low level and facilitates our handling of HTTP connections

2. `ThreadPoolExecutor`, `ProcessPoolExecutor`

3. The event loop

4. The `asyncio.Task` class is a subclass of `asyncio.Future` and aims to manage coroutines

5. `await`

6. The `tornado.web.Application` object

7. `AsyncHTTPClient`

8. `dataReceived`

9. `buildProtocol`

10. We can use the `TCP4ClientEndpoint` class

Chapter 12, Designing Applications on the Web

1. From `wsgiref.simple_server import make_server`
2. The Model-View-Controller is a pattern for software development that is based on separating the data, the user interface, and the logic of the application
3. `django-admin.py`
4. We can run the following command in the `djangoApplication` directory that contains the `manage.py` file: `python manage.py migrate`
5. With Flask, we must use the `@route` annotation
6. `render_template`
7. `request.form`
8. Flask-Security
9. `sqlalchemy.engine.base.Engine`
10. `SQLALCHEMY_DATABASE_URI`, which has been added in your config file

Another Book You May Enjoy

If you enjoyed this book, you may be interested in another book by Packt:

Mastering Python Networking - Second Edition
Eric Chou

ISBN: 978-1-78913-599-2

- Use Python libraries to interact with your network
- Integrate Ansible 2.5 using Python to control Cisco, Juniper, and Arista eAPI network devices
- Leverage existing frameworks to construct high-level APIs
- Learn how to build virtual networks in the AWS Cloud
- Understand how Jenkins can be used to automatically deploy changes in your network
- Use PyTest and Unittest for Test-Driven Network Development

Leave a review - let other readers know what you think

Please share your thoughts on this book with others by leaving a review on the site that you bought it from. If you purchased the book from Amazon, please leave us an honest review on this book's Amazon page. This is vital so that other potential readers can see and use your unbiased opinion to make purchasing decisions, we can understand what our customers think about our products, and our authors can see your feedback on the title that they have worked with Packt to create. It will only take a few minutes of your time, but is valuable to other potential customers, our authors, and Packt. Thank you!

Index

creating 430

S

CPSIA information can be obtained
at www.ICGtesting.com
Printed in the USA
LVHW021942150122
708348LV00003B/11